Horatio Nelson

Horatio Nelson

TOM POCOCK

THE BODLEY HEAD
LONDON

British Library Cataloguing in Publication Data

Pocock, Tom
Horatio Nelson.
1. Nelson, Horatio Nelson, Viscount
2. Great Britain. Royal Navy—Biography
3. Admirals—Great Britain—Biography
359.3'31'0924   DA87.1.N4
ISBN 0 370 31124 8

Printed in Great Britain for
The Bodley Head Ltd
32 Bedford Square, London WC1B 3EL
by The Alden Press Ltd, Oxford

Dedicated to
JOHN AND LILY McCARTHY
to whom students of Nelson owe so much.

NOTE ON STYLE

Nelson and his contemporaries wrote clear and robust English prose but their spelling and punctuation could be haphazard. So, while such defects have been remedied for the sake of clarity, their words have not been changed.

CONTENTS

LIST OF ILLUSTRATIONS

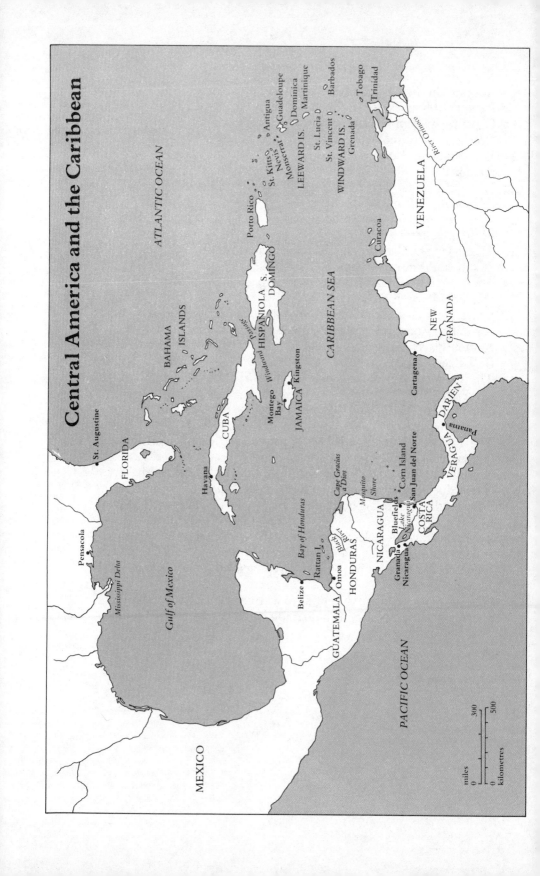

Central America and the Caribbean

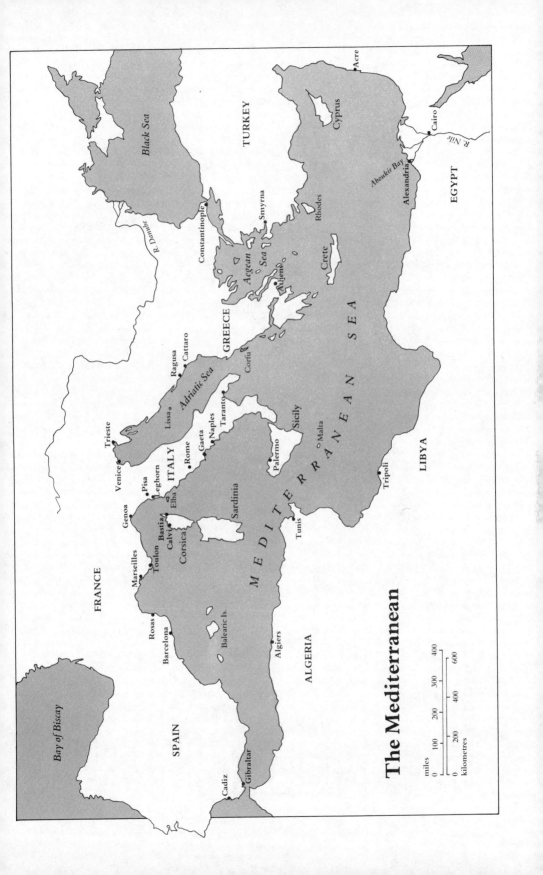

The Mediterranean

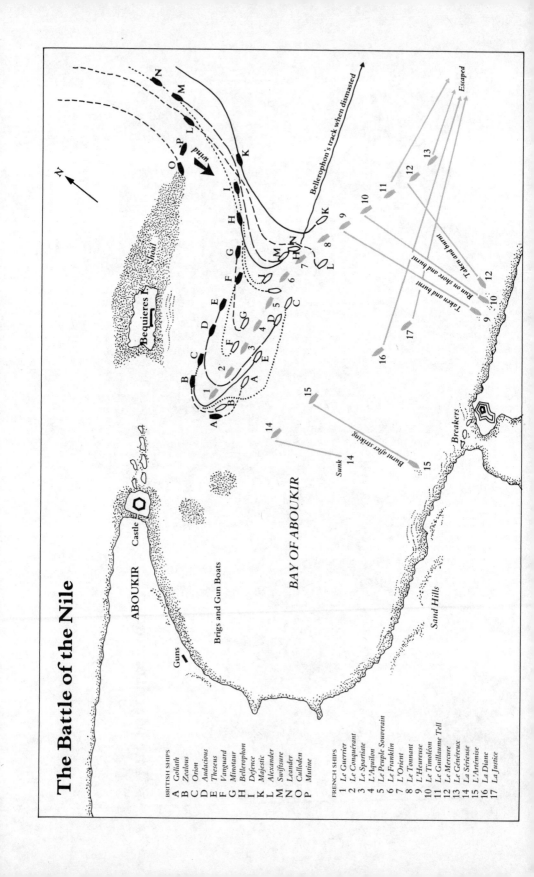

The Battle of the Nile

N

ABOUKIR

Castle

Guns

Brigs and Gun Boats

BAY OF ABOUKIR

Sand Hills

Bequieres I.

Shoal

wind

Breakers

Sunk 14

Burnt after sinking 15

Bellerophon's track when dismasted

Escaped

Taken and burnt

Run on shore and burnt

Taken and burnt

BRITISH SHIPS
A   Goliath
B   Zealous
C   Orion
D   Audacious
E   Theseus
F   Vanguard
G   Minotaur
H   Bellerophon
I   Defence
K   Majestic
L   Alexander
M   Swiftsure
N   Leander
O   Culloden
P   Mutine

FRENCH SHIPS
1   Le Guerrier
2   Le Conquérant
3   Le Spartiate
4   L'Aquilon
5   Le Peuple Souverain
6   Le Franklin
7   L'Orient
8   Le Tonnant
9   L'Heureuse
10 Le Timoléon
11 Le Guillaume Tell
12 Le Mercure
13 Le Généreux
14 La Sérieuse
15 L'Artémise
16 La Diane
17 La Justice

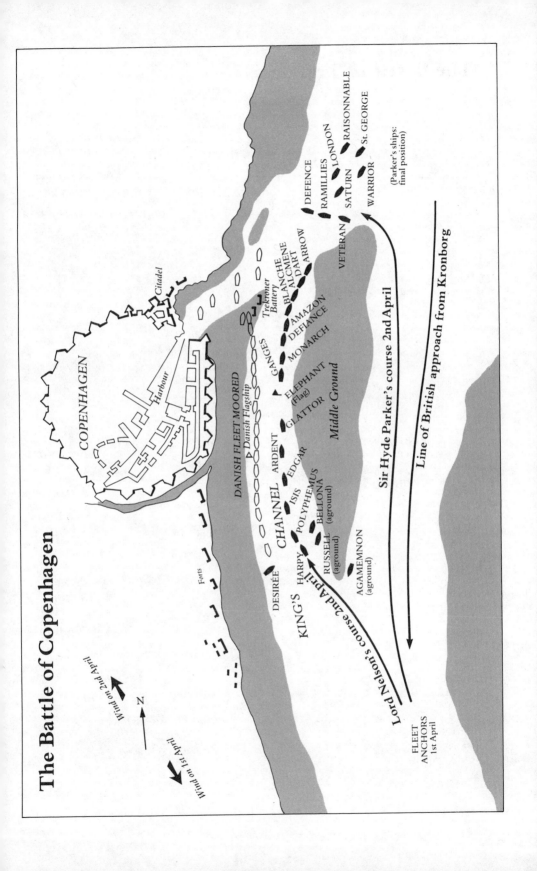

The Battle of Copenhagen

Wind on 2nd April

N

Wind on 1st April

COPENHAGEN

Citadel

Harbour

Forts

DANISH FLEET MOORED

Danish Flagship

Trekroner Battery

GANGES

BLANCHE
ALCMENE
DART
ARROW

AMAZON
DEFIANCE

MONARCH

ELEPHANT
(Flag)

GLATTON

VETERAN

DEFENCE

RAMILLIES

LONDON

RAISONNABLE

St. GEORGE

SATURN

WARRIOR

(Parker's ships:
final position)

CHANNEL

ARDENT

EDGAR

ISIS

POLYPHEMUS

BELLONA
(aground)

RUSSELL
(aground)

AGAMEMNON
(aground)

Middle Ground

DESIRÉE

HARPY

KING'S

Lord Nelson's course 2nd April

Sir Hyde Parker's course 2nd April

Line of British approach from Kronborg

FLEET
ANCHORS
1st April

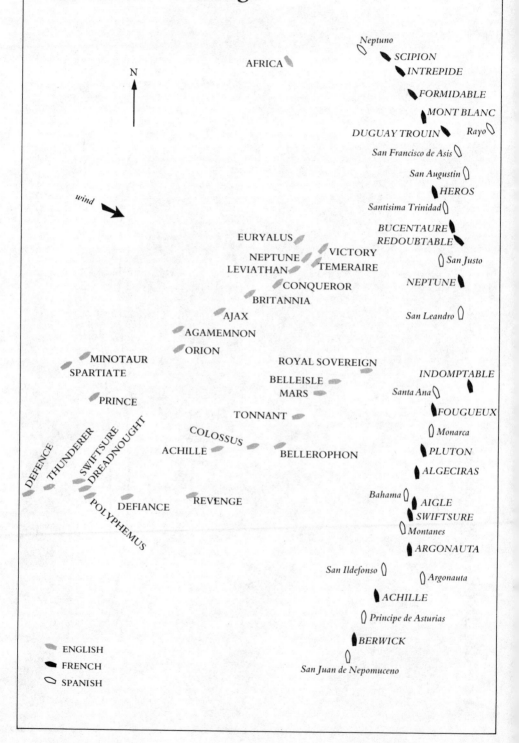

The Battle of Trafalgar

N

wind

Neptuno
SCIPION
AFRICA
INTREPIDE
FORMIDABLE
MONT BLANC
DUGUAY TROUIN   Rayo
San Francisco de Asis
San Augustin
HEROS
Santisima Trinidad
BUCENTAURE
EURYALUS   REDOUBTABLE
NEPTUNE   VICTORY   San Justo
LEVIATHAN   TEMERAIRE
NEPTUNE
CONQUEROR
BRITANNIA
San Leandro
AJAX
AGAMEMNON
ORION
MINOTAUR   ROYAL SOVEREIGN   INDOMPTABLE
SPARTIATE
BELLEISLE   Santa Ana
MARS   FOUGUEUX
PRINCE
Monarca
TONNANT
PLUTON
DEFENCE THUNDERER SWIFTSURE DREADNOUGHT   COLOSSUS   ALGECIRAS
ACHILLE   BELLEROPHON
Bahama
AIGLE
POLYPHEMUS   DEFIANCE   REVENGE   SWIFTSURE
Montanes
ARGONAUTA
San Ildefonso   Argonauta
ACHILLE
Principe de Asturias
BERWICK
ENGLISH   San Juan de Nepomuceno
FRENCH
SPANISH

INTRODUCTION

"I have both day and night accompanied your Lordship," wrote Hercules Ross, a retired sugar-planter from Jamaica to his friend Lord Nelson in the summer of 1805, "and imagination has often carried me aloft to look for the flying enemy."

Nelson was killed in action a few weeks later but, ever since then, those who can think of him as a friend, or, at least, as a familiar acquaintance, have followed him in imagination. He has not only been the national hero who secured a century of maritime supremacy for his country but also the focus of British identity and aspirations. Yet he has remained a human being in memory and tradition: vivid, generous and brave; sometimes vain; occasionally weak: somebody with whom everybody can, in some way, identify. As another of his friends, Lord Minto, said of his contradictions: "He is in many points a great man; in others, a baby."

Valiant yet vulnerable, Nelson has fascinated for two centuries. He continues to be the subject of books, paintings, plays and, even now, commemorative knick-knacks. The anniversary of his death is still marked with memorial services and his final victory by celebratory dinners. Now as then, he is the butt of half-admiring jokes; bawdy, when his name is coupled with that of Emma Hamilton. He can seem a contemporary and it requires no great leap of the imagination to think of him being interviewed on television. There may also be a deeper reason for his abiding appeal: perhaps, as the saviour of his people, sacrificed for their sake, he is an echo of the Christian tradition.

I offer another biography of Nelson with confidence that it will not waste the time of those who already know his story well. Over the twenty years since I wrote the first of four books about him and his time, new material has come to light and I have found many hitherto unpublished letters which illuminate him with shafts of light from fresh angles. In that time, other students of Nelson have made similar discoveries, which have been published as papers or in historical journals but not, until now, in a full biography.

My own interest in him has its roots both in Norfolk and the Navy.

Exactly a century after the death of his father Edmund Nelson, the rector of Burnham Thorpe, my maternal grandfather became rector of the adjoining parish of North Creake. I have spent much time thereabouts and stories told by my mother suggested that social life in the county had not changed greatly over that century. I have walked the paths that Nelson walked, seen the views he saw, visited most of the houses he had, and enjoyed much talk about him in the parlour of the inn at Burnham Thorpe, which he knew as The Plough and has, since his last visit, been re-named the Lord Nelson. My father, born of a family with naval connections, taught history at the Royal Naval College, Dartmouth, for a decade and he explained to me that Nelson's achievement was as much in the setting of standards as in winning battles.

My own encounters with my subject – such as the laws of time and mortality will allow – began in 1944 when, during the invasion of Normandy, my ship passed the battleship *Nelson* at Spithead to berth in Portsmouth harbour within pistol-shot of his former flagship, the *Victory*. She was still wearing the flag of a commander-in-chief and came under fire again that June as VI flying-bombs, fired from France, flew overhead; their bearing right but their range wrong.

On the 150th anniversary of Nelson's death at Trafalgar, I was at sea in the aircraft carrier *Triumph*, named after one of his ships. We were on passage from the Baltic to the Nore and were out in the North Sea when a gale blew as the Trafalgar Night dinner was about to be served in the wardroom. The officers attended in their mess kit, the silver was fixed to the tables with wooden frames and a Royal Marines "band of music" played nautical airs that Nelson would have known as the ship lurched, creaked and groaned in the storm. My friend and colleague David Woodward, naval historian and former war correspondent, was also on board – we were returning from the first post-war visit of the Home Fleet to Leningrad; he representing the BBC; myself, *The Times* – and he had been invited to propose the toast to "The Immortal Memory" and to speak of Nelson. As he rose, bracing himself against the roll of the deck, he said that he had felt diffident, as a civilian, when asked to address naval officers on this subject. But, on reflection, he said, he had decided otherwise. It was appropriate for anybody to talk of Nelson because he belonged to us all.

Later, as a travelling journalist, I was able to visit almost all the places of significance in his life and I believe I am the only one of his biographers to have done so. This involved some strange journeys, notably through the jungle of Nicaragua and down the Rio San Juan to El Castillo de la Inmaculada Concepción, which he had besieged in 1780 and where he nearly died. I twice visited the shores of Aboukir Bay and became involved in a British attempt to dive upon the wreckage of the French flagship *l'Orient* in the hope of discovering evidence of the Battle of the Nile if not the looted treasure of the Knights of Malta, which may have been on board. This ended prematurely with a twist that would have amused the men of 1798. Our consortium had sought permission from the Egyptian Government to dive on the wreckage in their territorial waters but, while we awaited their reply, a French warship anchored on the site and sent down its own divers. The French had, apparently, offered the Egyptians any treasure they found; themselves only wanting to retrieve whatever relics might be found and, of course, *la gloire*. Such experiences as these have enabled me to describe places which remain much as Nelson himself would have seen them.

I am grateful to those with whom I have enjoyed stimulating conversation about Nelson and in the past these have included my father, Guy Pocock, David Woodward, Oliver Warner and Christopher Lloyd. My thanks are also due to those naval historians who dine together each year during the anniversary of the Trafalgar campaign. These include, particularly, Richard Hough, who urged me to write this book; Lt. Cdr. Peter Kemp, who kindly read and commented upon the typescript; Admiral Sir Horace Law, of the Nelson family; Roger Knight and Roger Morriss, both of the National Maritime Museum; Richard Walker, the authority on Nelson's portraits; Colin White of the Royal Naval Museum; and Lt. Cdr. Peter Whitlock, who commanded the *Victory* for two commissions.

To many others I am grateful for help with research and in finding illustrations. In the United Kingdom, these include Lt. Cdr. Charles Addis, who also commanded HMS *Victory*; Sir Nicholas Bonsor, Bt., MP, also of Nelson's family; Viscount Bridport; Mr. Ben Burgess, Mr. Ronald Fiske and Mr. Michael Nash of the Nelson Society; Viscount Coke and Mr. F. C. Jolly, the administrator of Holkham Hall, Norfolk; Mr. Leslie Cousins of Deal; Miss Audrey Earle and Col. Charles Earle; Mr. John Ehrman; Miss Bridget Everitt; Mrs. June Jeffreys of Newhouse, the Matchams' former home; Mrs. Gillian Ford; Mr. Bryan Hall; Mrs. Suzanne Hunter; Mrs. Lily McCarthy; Mrs. Judy Mair; Mr. Douglas Matthews; Mr. John May; Major Malcolm Munthe, descended from Nelson's neighbours of Merton days, the Penningtons; Mr. M. A. K. Murray; Mr. R. O. Ramsay: Mr. Clive Richards; Miss Venetia Turner; Mr. Rupert Willoughby; and Mr. Leslie Winter, landlord of The Lord Nelson at Burnham Thorpe. In assessing Nelson's medical condition after the Battle of the Nile, Dr. Geoffrey Bolt, Dr. William Dorrell and Dr. Gordon Ostlere (Richard Gordon) were particularly helpful.

My thanks are also due to the Directors and staff of the National Maritime Museum, Greenwich; the Royal Naval Museum, Portsmouth; the Nelson Collection at the Monmouth Museum, Gwent; the Public Record Office at Kew; and to the Librarians and staff at the British Library, the London Library, the Royal United Service Institution, the Central Library at Portsmouth, the Central Library at Norwich; the National Portrait Gallery, the Courtauld Institute of Art and Messrs. Christie's, Sotheby's and Phillips', the London salerooms through which Nelsoniana continues to pass. My gratitude is due to the present Earl Nelson for granting me permission to quote from his family's papers.

For help abroad, I would like to thank Mr. E. C. Stevens of English Harbour, Antigua; Mr. Clinton V. Black of Spanish Town, Jamaica; Mr. Spencer Byron of Nevis; Mr. Kenneth Matheson of Managua, Nicaragua; Dr. Carlo Knight of Naples; M. Pierre Vieillefosse of Toulon; M. Pierre-André Wimet of Boulogne; Mr. C. E. Thomas of Halifax, Nova Scotia, and Professor Gerald Jordan of York University, Ontario, Canada.

My wife, Penny, suggested many improvements to the text and compiled the index and to her and to our daughters, Laura and Hannah, I am grateful for the home from which I so often and for so long followed Lord Nelson in imagination.

Tom Pocock,
Chelsea, 1987

CHAPTER I

Outward Bound
(1759–77)

"The thought of former days brings all my mother into my heart, which shows itself in my eyes."
– Vice-Admiral Viscount Nelson, H.M.S. *Victory*, 14 May, 1804

Before the gale blew, the wind dropped and only the sound of surf on sand could be heard along the Norfolk shore. Then that, too, was stilled and only distant voices and sometimes hoofbeats broke the silence. "All is hush at high noon as at midnight," wrote Edmund Nelson of winter there. "Darkness and light to me are alike." The Christmas of 1767 was drowned in melancholy at the parsonage in Burnham Thorpe, a remote village near this coast, for it was occupied with grief and mourning. On Boxing Day, Catherine Nelson, the rector's wife, had died at the age of forty-two, leaving her husband, Edmund, with the care of their eight children.

"It has fallen to my lot to take upon me the care and affection of a double parent," was his stoic response to the loss of the generous, forthright Catherine. He alone would have to bring up and see to the education of their five boys and three girls, helping to launch the former in appropriate careers and find suitable husbands for the latter. The two eldest boys, Maurice and William – the first, dutiful but earnest; the other, timid but greedy – did not seem marked for success; the two youngest, Edmund and Suckling, might show some promise once they went to boarding-school. Only the middle son, Horace – the name he preferred to Horatio, as he had been christened after a rich godfather and distant cousin – showed, at the age of nine, spirit and originality.

Edmund Nelson cut a sad figure with his long, lugubrious face and pendulous lower lip; prematurely grey hair hanging to his collar, giving looks that suggested more than his forty-six years. The prospect of raising his family alone – for his mother-in-law was old and ill and was to die five days after his wife – sharpened his sense of inadequacy.

"As to the society in me," he mused, "I never mixed with the word eno' at the proper period of life to make it entertaining or valuable on any account, except a willingness to make my family comfortable when near me and not unmindful of me when at a distance." He was a cultured but unsophisticated man, who had not had his father's introduction to worldliness at Eton College and only ventured beyond family and village life to Cambridge for his education at Caius College before ordination. He had then returned to the confines of a village and, after his marriage to Catherine Suckling, to that of his own family.

The little parsonage where Edmund Nelson and his children grieved was symbolic of the family's own situation. It was remote from centres of activity – the journey from Burnham Thorpe to London lasting two tiring days by stage-coach – and from the village itself, the church being a half-mile distant. The little house was built like that of any yeoman farmer with a high-pitched roof but a gentlemanly touch had been introduced by the addition of a wing standing at right-angles to the façade with elegant three-sashed Venetian windows in both of its dormers. Its modest barns and stables served the thirty acres of glebeland, riverside meadow and low chalk downs. From the high ground above the village could be seen the sea, sometimes flecked with white, storm-blown spume, or sails hinting at voyages to excitements far from the sheltered valley where the parsonage lay.

To the robust and unassuming stock of the Nelsons, which bred country parsons, farmers and East Anglian merchants, Edmund's marriage to Cathering Suckling in 1749, had added some social distinction. The Nelsons had been able to exert a little influence themselves; even Edmund's father-in-law, John Bland, a prosperous baker in Cambridge, had been able to help his son-in-law, who had courted his daughter when an undergraduate at the university, to find a suitable parish when he became a priest. But this stood no comparison with the splendour reflected upon the Sucklings by their relations: Catherine's grandmother had been the sister of Sir Robert Walpole, who had, in the second quarter of the century, became the first prime minister of England. Walpole had been created Earl of Orford and established a powerful political and social dynasty with its seat at Houghton Hall, some twenty miles from Burnham Thorpe, and ties of blood and influence with many of the great landowners of East Anglia.

It was to the Walpole connection that the Nelsons owed their present social position, such as that was. The living of Hilborough, another Norfolk parish, where Edmund had followed his father and grandfather as rector, where the present incumbent was his brother-in-law and might perhaps be granted to one of his own sons, was in the gift of the Earls of Orford, as was that of Burnham Thorpe. The Nelsons were not regarded as relations of sufficient standing to warrant an invitation to

Houghton but they were accorded an annual invitation to Wolterton Hall near Aylsham, the seat of Lord Walpole, whose father, the first baron, had been Catherine's great-uncle. His name, Horatio, had been chosen by the Nelsons for their third son, and, when he died in infancy, to the next, the godson of the second Lord Walpole. His sister's marriage to a successful naval officer, Captain Maurice Suckling – Catherine Nelson's elder brother – formed another link with the family at Burnham Thorpe. The Sucklings had had the advantage of a father who had been an affluent parson, able to combine the pastoral pleasures of a country living with some influence in the capital as a Prebendary of Westminster. He had been able to place his sons in government service – a younger son, William, was now a Commissioner in the Customs Office – leaving Maurice a handsome house at Woodton in South Norfolk, while the younger could afford another at Kentish Town in the northern suburbs of London.

It was Captain Suckling whose exploits dominated the imaginations of the Nelson children. Three weeks after little Horatio's first birthday had been celebrated on 29th September, 1759, he had fought in a victorious engagement with the French in the Caribbean and the anniversary of this battle, 21st October, coinciding with the fair following the harvest at Burnham Thorpe, became an annual celebration for the Nelson family. To the boys of the family, Uncle Maurice became hero and *beau idéal*: brave, handsome and urbane; somebody who might, perhaps, be emulated, unlike the lordly Walpoles who belonged to a higher form of creation altogether.

It was not so much the details of the action, in which their uncle's ship, the *Dreadnought*, had fought a superior French squadron, that they remembered but a particular story he liked to tell about it. When his ship had been cleared for action a pet monkey, belonging to one of the officers, escaped, shinned up the mizzen shrouds and watched the battle from the masthead. When it was over and the smoke had cleared, it had descended to seek its master.

The deeds of Maurice Suckling made tangible the news that reached the Nelsons through the *Norwich Mercury* each week. This news was never more dramatic than in this particular year, which came to be called "The Year of Victories", when news of Hawke's success at sea vied with that of Wolfe's in Canada. In Norfolk there was particular interest in the latter because Brigadier George Townshend, the heir to Raynham Hall, was Wolfe's second-in-command and took his place when he was killed at the head of his army before Quebec. It was this same officer who had brought home to Norfolk the realities of the international crisis by helping to raise the county militia – the first in England – to meet the threat of invasion by France. This call to arms struck a responsive chord in the county, where place-names and legends recalled the raids and, finally, the occupation by the Danes, who had appeared off their long, low coastline a millennium before.

A reminder of that time came in the week following Catherine Nelson's death and perhaps helped to distract the thoughts of the Nelson boys from the loss of their mother and grandmother. On Saturday, 2nd January, 1768, the *Norwich Mercury* was preoccupied with political news and comment because an election was imminent and one of the Norfolk candidates in the Whig interest was the former Brigadier – now Marquess – Townshend. In the course of the Quebec campaign his conduct had been subject to criticism and a letter from a subordinate officer, writing in his defence, was published. Townshend, an exotic and remote figure living a dozen miles to the south of Raynham, was described attractively: "Whenever his brigade was ordered upon any kind of duty he marched at its head; was beloved of the troops as a brave and humane officer, was ever easy of access, facetious and in high spirits ..." He had been a worthy successor to the supreme command on "General Wolfe being mortally wounded in the very grasp of victory". Such words could strike a spark in a boy's imagination and, perhaps, his ambition.

Other reminders of the world beyond Norfolk came soon after their mother's death with the arrival at the parsonage of her brother Captain Suckling. Edmund Nelson was well aware that the prospects of his sons would depend largely upon the interest shown by their two Suckling uncles. To show due respect to their family, he was arranging that his wife's grave should be marked in aristocratic style, the black marble slab in the chancel of the parish church being carved with the Suckling coat of arms with his own; her epitaph in Latin with the instructions in English beneath, "Let these alone. Let no man move these bones." This sepulchral splendour looked particularly grand in contrast to the dilapidated church and the visitor would learn that the other two churches for which the rector was responsible, at Burnham Ulph and Burnham Sutton, were so derelict that they could not be used.

Captain Suckling was a kindly man, comforting his brother-in-law with the assurance that he would help with finding suitable employment for the boys. He would take one of them to sea with him in due course, rated as captain's servant, or able seaman, before he could be classed as midshipman and begin the career of a professional naval officer. This was the most exciting of the two principal options open to boys of their social class: the Church of England, or the Royal Navy. The former offered modest security and a genteel occupation; the latter, certainly hardship and possibly a violent death but also the chance of making a fortune from prize money after taking enemy ships and cargoes; many a retired naval officer now lived in a handsome house surrounded by its park to prove that this was possible.

The eldest boy, named Maurice after his uncle, probably did not strike the captain as suitable material for a naval officer. He was now aged twelve, solemn and bookish, so perhaps a place might be found for him as a clerk in the Navy Office in a few years' time. There would have been little difficulty in deciding between the suitability of the next two boys, William and Horace: the former big and something of a bully; the latter small and said to be delicate but full of fire. He had doubtless heard how his sister had been asked to stop the two brothers fighting since William was the bigger and stronger. "Let them alone," she had replied. "Little Horace will beat him."

Then there was the story often told by his grandmother, old Mrs Nelson, of the time Horace had been staying with them at Hilborough when he and an older boy – possibly William again – had set out on a birds-nesting expedition into the woods. Losing their way, they had found themselves on the far side of the narrow, but deep and fast-flowing little river Wissey. The elder boy had managed to return, leaving Horace to find his own way home. As dinner-time was past, searchers were sent from the rectory and found the boy alone but unperturbed on the riverside. Later, scolding him for causing such worry, his grandmother had declared, "I wonder that fear did not drive you home." "I never saw fear," Horace was said to have replied. "What is it?"

The small boy was showing as much spirit at school. He had followed his brothers to the Royal Grammar School at Norwich, a fourteenth-century foundation within the cathedral close, where the boys lived in term-time sometimes visiting a great-aunt and a cousin living in the city. Now, following the death of their mother and the visit of their uncle, they were to be moved to the Paston School at North Walsham, which was nearer to Burnham Thorpe and was gaining a reputation as the best school in the county. A handsome new schoolhouse had just been built in red brick, its big, airy rooms and wide sash windows seeming healthier than the medieval stone halls at Norwich. Within the past year a new headmaster had been appointed, a Welsh clergyman and classicist named John Price Jones, a disciplinarian whose methods were soon being compared with those of a headmaster of Westminster School in London, as being "as keen a flogger as merciless Busby of birch-loving memory". The combination of modern buildings, a brisk headmaster and the promise of a firm grounding in Latin and Greek, which was essential for advancement, was prompting the rural gentry, clergymen, farmers and prosperous tradesmen all over the county to move their sons to North Walsham. The school could take about sixty "young gentlemen boarders" as well as day-boys from the town and surrounding villages. Here Horace and his brothers were sent in 1768.

Again the stories told about Horace suggest a lively, audacious boy, in contrast to his brother William. Once when the two left Burnham Thorpe for the beginning of the January term – probably making for Burnham Market to take the coach to North Walsham – they were turned back by deep snow. Back at the parsonage, their father urged them to try again, putting them on their honour to make the journey if it were possible. Resuming their struggle through deepening drifts, William wanted to turn back again but Horace persisted, reminding his brother that it had become a question of honour. Then, at school one summer, the boys in his dormitory had been planning to steal some of the headmaster's pears but dare not risk the birch by being caught in the orchard. So it was Horace who made the night raid on the trees but refused to eat the stolen fruit, giving it to the more cautious boys, who, next day, resisted threats and bribes to protect the culprit.

At home in Burnham Thorpe, the place of Catherine Nelson's strong character (patriotic and devout; hating the French as almost personal enemies) could not be taken by her scholarly, whimsical widower. When Horace and William returned for the Christmas holidays of 1770, even his gentle presence was absent. He had begun to feel the need of escape from what he described as "the pomp and parade of Winter, wind and storm and rattling hail" and the ague, a recurrent fever common in such marshy countryside, so he had departed for several weeks' holiday in the mild climate and comfortable lodgings of Bath. As Maurice had left home, having now been found work as a clerk in the Excise Office by William Suckling, Horace and William were left in the company of their two younger brothers, Edmund and Suckling, and their sisters, Susannah, Anne and their favourite, Kitty. William was destined for Cambridge University, ordination and, in due course, a country rectory but Horace needed activity. He could ride his pony over the low hills to Burnham Overy Staithe to watch the coasters being warped up the creek to load their cargoes of grain and malt, or a few miles further to the bigger port of Wells, where Dutch herring-boats might be landing boxes of blue and white pottery from Delft.

Now the newspapers were reporting news of ships and the sea and remote islands that fired the imagination. These were the Falkland Islands, which had been formally declared to be British possessions six years earlier but were also claimed by the traditional maritime enemy, Spain. They did not seem worth the trouble of defending since a visiting naval officer had described them as "a mass of islands on which the soil is nothing but a bog and with no better prospect than that of barren mountains beaten by storms almost perpetual", but when the Spanish had the temerity to land upon them and lower the British flag, national pride was outraged and war threatened. The *Norfolk Chronicle* might forecast that the government was "determined to give up the Falkland Islands after the present dispute is settled" but also reported preparations for war. "Five sail of battleships, fully manned and equipped are now waiting at St. Helen's for a wind. Their destination is secret," it announced, adding that, in the week before Christmas, the Navy's press gang had rounded up sixteen thousand men in coastal towns to help man the ships being made ready for active service. Amongst unemployed naval officers living in the county, now being recalled to duty, was Captain Suckling, who had been enjoying the life of a country gentleman at Woodton since the end of the Seven Years War. He, so Horace read, had been appointed to command the sixty-four-gun ship of the line *Raisonn- able*, which had been captured from the French in the year of his birth, and was now at Chatham preparing for sea.

The opportunity was obvious and Horace asked, "Do, brother William, write to my father at Bath and tell him I should like to go with my Uncle Maurice to sea." Relieved that his own future would be more comfortable, if less exciting, William wrote as elder brother and senior member of the family at Burnham Thorpe. His letter to Bath, his father's reply and letter to Captain Suckling and the latter's favourable answer were exchanged by the mail-coaches in little more than a week. Then all the family knew Maurice Suckling's jocular acceptance of Horace into his ship's company. "What has poor Horace done, who is so weak, that he, above all the rest, should be sent to rough it out at sea?" he had written to his brother-in-law. "But let him come and the first time we go into action a cannon-ball may knock off his head and provide for him at once."

So, on 1st January, 1771, Captain Suckling entered his nephew's name in the muster-book of his ship as a midshipman – rather than the more usual "captain's servant", or "able seaman", for boys aspiring to be officer – so that his seniority could date from that time. But there was no point in Horace – the name Horace now began to be dropped in favour of a name with classical and family origins more suited to a future naval officer – joining the ship immediately. She was still a newly manned hulk, damp and cold, and no place for a supposedly delicate child of twelve in mid-winter so the boy was told to join the ship at Chatham in a few weeks' time when she would be more habitable.

Horatio returned to North Walsham for the new term to await instructions from his uncle. These arrived one morning at the beginning of March and were that he should take the coach to King's Lynn, where his father would meet him and they would travel together to London, staying with his other Suckling uncle in Kentish Town. This proved a reassuring interlude because it was a comfortable house with fine furniture and silver, family portraits on the walls and a black butler in attendance. If one brother lived in such style, surely the other, for all his talk about roughing it out at sea, must also live in some state, albeit afloat?

Father and son parted in the yard of the inn from which the coaches left for Chatham and the six or so hours of jolting out of London and along Kentish roads gave Horatio time to reflect on the career which he had now embarked upon. If he had expected a welcome from his jolly seafaring uncle to equal that of the brother, he was disappointed. At the staging-inn where the coach stopped at Chatham, nobody had heard of the captain or his ship, and the boy, wandering down the dirty, cobbled streets towards the dockyard, had to ask sailors if they knew where the *Raisonnable* lay.

Eventually one did and pointed across the grey, wind-whipped water of the Medway to a big ship lying at her moorings. There were no boats to take him out to her, nor, at that distance, could he attract the attention of anybody on board. Finally a passing officer noticed the forlorn child, took pity on him and arranged for a boat to ferry him across the river.

Climbing aboard a warship for the first time, his mounting dread was confirmed. Captain Suckling was not on board, nor was he expected for some days and nobody had heard of the new midshipman, or seemed to be interested in him. The ship's upper deck was swept by "fresh gales with squally weather and snow", as her log-book recorded, and the new arrival waited miserably for somebody to tell him what to do, or where to go. Eventually, he was ordered to carry his baggage down two steep ladders to the midshipmen's berth on the orlop deck: dark, low-beamed and smelling of damp hemp and tar. For the rest of that day he walked the decks, ignored by all, realising that to sit would appear idle. Somebody must have given him a hammock and showed him how to sling it from ring-bolts but it was not until next morning that an officer questioned him and explained something of the discipline and working of the ship.

When Captain Suckling eventually returned – to much saluting and squealing of boatswains' calls – Horatio was summoned to his great cabin, which was in striking contrast to the cramped quarters elsewhere. The width of the ship with its wide, gently curved rows of windows, this was furnished in elegant but masculine style like a gentleman's drawing-room. In his blue, white-faced, gold-trimmed uniform he looked far more imposing than the familiar, avuncular figure dressed as a squire. It would have been on one such visit to the cabin that he explained to his nephew the complexities of a naval career. A midshipman was not a commissioned officer any more than were the captain's servants, able seamen and even the few boys from the Naval Academy at Portsmouth, with whom he would share the discomforts of the orlop deck. A royal commission would follow the passing of the examination for lieutenant, which should not be taken before the age of twenty and without six years' service at sea. These regulations were not always strictly obeyed, the degree of latitude depending upon the influence – known in the Navy as "interest" – that the candidate could bring to bear upon the authorities. The only interest that midshipman Nelson could depend upon was that of his uncle and captain.

Meanwhile there was discipline to be followed and seamanship to be learned. When Horatio had joined his ship she had not looked like a warship because her armament had not been embarked and her gun-decks were clear from the bow to the partitions separating the officers from the rest of the ship's company; clear, that is, except for the colonnades of stanchions – the turned, wooden pillars supporting the deck above – and the three great trunks of the masts passing through the decks to rest upon the keel. After he had helped load the ship's storerooms with salt beef, cheese, biscuit, butter and beer, came three days of heavy work in embarking the guns. These were brought out from the ordnance depot by lighter and swung aboard by tackle rigged to the main-yard from which the mainsail was spread at sea. The twenty-six heavy guns, firing twenty-four-pound shot, were taken aboard first, to be mounted on their wooden carriages at the gun-ports down either side of the lower gun-deck, followed by a similar number of eighteen-pounders for the deck above and twelve nine-pounders.

During those first weeks in the Medway, the whole ship's company would be mustered on the upper-deck to witness punishment. Twice a sailor was tied to a grating, rigged vertically, and given a dozen lashes with a cat-o'-nine-tails whip by a boatswain's mate; one for theft, the other for brawling. This was the standard punishment for the usual run of offences: drunkenness, pilfering, insolence to an officer and minor disobedience. To watch it inflicted, when aged twelve, and be told that the spectacle of a lacerated back streaming with blood was part of a warship's routine, might lead to its acceptance as such.

The tension and the expectation of active service that gave purpose to such tight discipline did not last. The *Raisonnable* had dropped down the Medway to the little dockyard at Sheerness to await orders for sea but, no sooner had her guns been harnessed to their rope tackle, than the prospect of war evaporated: the Falklands dispute was settled by diplomacy. The ship was likely to be left at her moorings until the

Admiralty could decide whether or not to undo the work of the past weeks and return her to reserve. Meanwhile her captain was appointed to command another, bigger ship, the *Triumph* of seventy-four guns, which lay at the Nore, the sandbank sheltering the anchorage off the mouth of the river. She was guardship at the Medway and Thames estuaries and was kept busy, although she, too, was likely to spend the coming months at anchor. On 15th May, 1771, Suckling wrote in his log, "Discharged myself into the *Triumph*" and was rowed out to his new command followed by his baggage, furniture, pictures and silver and by his nephew Horatio.

Life in a guardship was not suitable for a boy, Suckling decided. He would gain experience running boats between ship and shore but he would also be exposed to the moral dangers of the little seaport towns, where drink and trollops were the principal diversions. It was then the captain heard that one of his old shipmates, John Rathbone, who had been master's mate of the ship he had commanded in his celebrated action with the French and was now commanding a fine West Indiaman belonging to the reputable firm of Hibbert, Purrier and Horton, was soon to sail from the Thames for the Caribbean. Such a voyage would teach a boy more seamanship than he could learn from instruction in an anchored guardship, so early that summer Horatio Nelson was put aboard this ship and sailed for the tropics.

Now, for the first time, he felt the movement of a ship at sea, heard the creak and groan of her hemp and timber and the wail of wind in her rigging. He could taste the salt spray on his lips and suffer the first queasy chill of sea-sickness. As remarkable as the play of the elements on his senses was the contrast in life in a merchantman with that in a warship. Here no marine sentry, stiff in red coat and pipe-clayed cross-belts, guarded the doors to the officers' quarters; no boatswain's mate hurried men about their work with a cut from a rope's end and they were no longer mustered to witness punishment by flogging. Here there was an easy comradeship and relations between the sailors on their wet and draughty mess-decks forward and the officers in their wardroom and cabins aft were relaxed and based upon shared skills and the hope of profit from successful trading. Horatio's shipmates were rough and kindly and he soon found himself understanding their loathing and fear of the Navy and its press-gangs. He heard stories of merchant ships being stopped by warships flying their own country's flag to abduct seamen for their own ships' companies, sometimes at the end of a long voyage and in sight of a home-port. "If I did not improve my education, I returned a practical seaman," he later wrote of this voyage, "with a horror of the Royal Navy and with a saying then constant with the seamen, 'Aft the more honour, forward the better man!'"

On his return to the *Triumph* after nearly a year's absence, Captain Suckling noted the changes in his nephew and the self-confidence gained on two crossings of the Atlantic and cruises among tropical perils: sudden storms, unexpected shoals and the dangers of endemic, often lethal, disease. He may also have noticed that the boy was not so ready to jump at orders and seemed as resentful of them as a merchant seaman for, as he himself later admitted, "It was many weeks before I got in the least reconciled to a man-of-war." In any case, the boy was now given his first taste of independence in command. He had already taken charge of ships' boats but a guardship's duties required not only her own cutter but a decked longboat to work as her tender and despatch-boat, her crew sleeping aboard if necessary. Captain Suckling gave command of such craft to midshipmen as reward for success in studying navigation, and he now chose his nephew.

The Medway and the Swin channel, leading to Chatham from Sheerness, were already familiar but the sandbanks of the Thames estuary, and the strong tides of the river itself, were not. Yet it would not have seemed wholly strange and daunting because often he, as a child, had watched boats working up the estuary of the little river Burn a mile or so from his home at Burnham Thorpe. Here, although the river ran between counties rather than salt-marshes and sand-dunes, the problems were the same. So it was that Midshipman Nelson took his command up the Thames past the naval dockyards at Woolwich and Deptford and the Navy's Royal Hospital at Greenwich, where blue-coated pensioners who had sailed with Hawke and Boscawen watched him pass from the terrace of the palace Sir Christopher Wren had designed for them, to the Pool of London where the noble bulk of St. Paul's Cathedral stood above the thickets of masts in the greatest trading-port in the world. "Thus by degrees I became a good pilot for vessels of that description," ran his own account of this time, "from Chatham to the Tower of London, down the Swin, and the North Foreland and confident of myself amongst rocks and sands."

He was now to experience another change of scene as dramatic as the contrast between the mud-flats of the Thames estuary and the white sands of Caribbean beaches. This began when, on passage between the *Triumph* and London, sailors pointed out two ships under refit: one, the *Carcass*, at Sheerness; the other, the *Racehorse*, at Deptford. They were bomb-ketches, sturdy, broad-beamed and strengthened to mount and fire heavy mortars for shore bombardment and to withstand their recoil; ketch-rigged to keep masts and rigging clear of the steep trajectory of their great shells. But, he heard, they were not being prepared for war – indeed six of the eight broadside guns were being put ashore from each –

although they were bound for an extraordinary mission and, when they were manned, would offer exciting employment.

In wartime, conversation amongst naval officers in their wardrooms harped on the chances of promotion and prize-money; in peacetime, upon hopes of future employment and voyages of exploration. This had been particularly so since Captain James Cook had returned from Botany Bay two years before with his reports of an unexplored southern continent; he had been away on another expedition for several months past and was now assumed to be back in the South Sea. Ships bound for exploration were small, crowded with various scientists and appointments for seamen-officers were few and, for them, there was no prospect of prize-money but much glory. An officer who had sailed with Cook could hold the attention of any wardroom in the fleet, any drawing-room in London and, indeed, of the Board Room at the Admiralty.

The two bomb-ketches were being fitted out, it was said, for an "expedition towards the North Pole". There had long been speculation about a sea-way between the Atlantic and the Pacific existing to the far north of Asia or America and this had recently been the subject of lively debate in the capitals of Europe. In Paris, Louis-Antoine Bougainville, the circumnavigator and explorer of the Pacific – or South Sea – had been talking of a *passage par le nord* and the Swiss geographer Samuel Engel had written a book about the possibility. His theory that ice was only formed of fresh water discharged into the sea by rivers and so would be encountered only near land, leaving "*une mer vaste et libre*" to the far north, had stimulated imaginations. Dr. Samuel Johnson speculated that "our former navigators have kept too near land and so have found the sea frozen far north because the land hinders the free motion of the tide; but in the wide ocean, where the waves tumble at their full convenience, it is imagined that the frost does not take effect."

The idea was taken up by the Royal Society in London and, in January, 1773, its vice-president, Daines Barrington, a lawyer, antiquarian and naturalist, discussed it with Lord Sandwich, the First Lord of the Admiralty. This was followed by an official request for the Royal Navy to mount such an expedition for there seemed to be "room to hope that a passage by, or near, the North Pole to the East Indies may be thereby found". By the beginning of February, the scheme had been approved by King George III and, in the second week of the month, the Admiralty had chosen the two bomb-ketches to be fitted out and strengthened to face the rigours of the Arctic. When Nelson saw them in dock, shipwrights were doubling the thickness of their hulls and buttressing their bows with baulks of timber. Replacement stocks of spars, sails and rigging, cables and anchors were doubled. Each ship was to carry enough boats to embark the crews of both in an emergency and bricks and mortar with which to build shelter ashore in case of shipwreck. The two hundred men manning the ships were each to be issued with two sets of warm clothing, including thick, lined jackets, waistcoats, trousers and mittens. The best quality cured beef and pork were ordered, together with jars of warming mustard. There were to be double stocks of wine and spirits and a hundred butts of strong, dark beer "to fortify themselves against the rigours of the climate".

The leader of the expedition, who was also to command the *Racehorse*, was to be Captain the Honourable Constantine Phipps, the future Lord Mulgrave. Not yet aged thirty, he was what his contemporaries described as "a man of bottom"; when at home in Yorkshire he was as likely to be found walking the dales as reading in his library of rare nautical books. He had a lively interest in politics and was a fellow of both the Royal Society and the Society of Antiquaries. He had seen action in the Seven Years War, been present at the capture of Havana and was liked by the sailors for his humanity and sense of humour. The *Carcass* was to be commanded by Captain Skeffington Lutwidge, whom Nelson had met and whose eye he had caught – perhaps by his handling of the *Triumph*'s tender off Sheerness – because, although boys were not supposed to accompany the polar expedition, his request to join the ship as a coxswain was approved and Captain Suckling agreed to let him go.

At the end of May then, Midshipman Nelson shifted his sea-chest across to the *Carcass*, where he found much more than the activity of a warship preparing for sea to engage his interest. This voyage was to be far more than a survey: the brilliant Jewish astronomer Israel Lyons was to sail in the *Carcass*; new equipment, including apparatus for distilling drinking-water from the sea and a new type of log for measuring the speed of a ship, was to undergo trials. Before they sailed, Captain Phipps was asked by his friend Joseph Banks, the naturalist who had accompanied Cook to Australia, to make notes on the habits of "white bears", seals and whales and, indeed, all forms of Arctic life down to lichens, and on the migration of birds and shoals of herring. On 4th June, 1773, the two ships made sail and steered north past the low shores of Essex, Suffolk and Norfolk until they lost sight of land somewhere to the east of Burnham Thorpe, their mission giving substance to the saying of villagers in the Burnhams on a cold winter's day that there was nothing between them and the North Pole but sea and ice.

Between the familiar grey waters of the North Sea and the heaving, hostile wastes of the North Atlantic, a thick bank of fog spread out from the Shetland Islands so that it was impossible to see more than the length of the ship. With little wind in their sails, they drifted through this limbo, keeping in touch, when close, with the tapping of drums and, when distant, by the firing of signal-guns. When the fog thinned and blew away, they seemed to be on a different ocean, where whales spouted and flipped their forked tails. It was much colder and the captains ordered extra mustard and pepper to be served with the rations.

Before the end of June, they saw the pale sun shine on the glaciers – the "ice hills" – of Spitzbergen and marvelled at their forms and colours. A shipmate of Nelson's in the *Carcass* – possibly the surgeon, William Wallis – wrote in his journal, "By looking at these hills a stranger may fancy a thousand different shapes of trees, castles, churches, ruins, ships, whales, monsters and all the various forms that fill the universe ... When the air is clear and the sun shines full upon these mountains the prospect is inconceivably brilliant. They sometimes put on the light glow of the evening rays of the setting sun when reflected upon glass at his going down; sometimes they appear of a light blue, like sapphire, and sometimes like the variable colours of a prism, exceeding in lustre the richest gems in the world."

The land itself appeared barren and forlorn but the air was sharp and alive with "myriads of shining particles that sparkle like diamonds and when the sun shines hot, as it sometimes does, so as to melt the tar in the seams of the ships when they lie sheltered from the wind, these shining atoms seem to melt away and descend like dew". At this latitude, the sun did not set and Captain Phipps noted that "the smooth water, bright sunshine and constant daylight" gave "a cheerfulness and novelty to the whole of this smiling and romantic scene". The sailors, who had no need for the thick flannel clothing that had been issued to them joked that they were off to the North Pole to "cut a piece of it to make a walking-stick for the Prince of Wales".

Such delights gave way to more fog as they sailed up the west coast of Spitzbergen, taking soundings, noting the lie of the land and whales "spouting their fountains towards the skies". Early in July, the strange light in the sky reflected from ice-fields was seen and, soon after, the floes themselves; sometimes like drifting islands; sometimes a smooth, white plain stretching for miles. Nudging through pack-ice north-east of the island they sighted strange creatures such as they had heard about in the far-fetched yarns old sailors had spun in dockside taverns. A boat pulled away from the *Carcass* for a closer look, her crew firing muskets at a monster with a dripping moustache and long ivory tusks, only to be attacked by other walrus. The creatures slithered off the ice to crash against the sides of the boat and would have stove it in had not another boat, commanded by Midshipman Nelson, driven them away.

It was soon after this, somewhere north of Spitzbergen, where the outlying islands of black rock give way to the world of ice, that the boy, still not yet fifteen, gave his companions reason to remember him. Captain Lutwidge particularly liked to tell the story and it was later recorded in his words. Young Nelson, he would say, had "a daring shipmate, to whom he had become attached. One night, during the mid-watch, it was concerted between them that they should steal together from the ship and endeavour to obtain a bear's skin. The clearness of the nights in those high latitudes rendered the accomplishment of this object extremely difficult: they, however, seem to have taken advantage of the haze of an approaching fog and thus to have escaped unnoticed. Nelson, in high spirits, led the way over the frightful chasms in the ice, armed with a rusty musket.

It was not long, however, before the adventurers were missed by those on board, and, as the fog had come on very thick, the anxiety . . . was very great. Between three and four in the morning, the mist somewhat dispersed and the hunters were discovered at a considerable distance, attacking a large bear. The signal was instantly made for their return; but it was in vain that Nelson's companion urged him to obey it. He was at this time divided by a chasm in the ice from his shaggy antagonist, which probably saved his life; for the musket had flashed in the pan and their ammunition was expended. 'Never mind,' exclaimed Horatio, 'do but let me get a blow at this devil with the butt end of my musket and we shall have him.' His companion, finding that entreaty was in vain, regained the ship.

Captain Lutwidge therefore ordered a blank charge to be fired from one of the guns, the startled bear loped away and the lone hunter returned to his ship. The boy was summoned by his captain who "reprimanded him rather sternly for such rashness, and for conduct so unworthy of the situation he occupied, and desired to know what motive he could have for hunting a bear?" The midshipman, "pouting his lip, as he was wont to do when agitated, replied, 'Sir, I wished to kill the bear, that I might carry its skin to my father.'"

His resilience, as well as his courage, was about to be tested. By the end of July, the short Arctic summer was ending and the ice was beginning its annual spread south. The way ahead for the two ships appeared to be blocked and, as Captain Lutwidge wrote in his log, "There now appeared no farther open water or passage for the ships, the main body of ice seems to be firmly joined from one island to another. I went in the boat to one of these islands, about five or six miles to the north-eastward of the ships, through narrow channels, being obliged to haul the boat over the ice in several places. Here I had an extensive view of the sea to the eastward, which was entirely frozen over, not like the ice we had hitherto coasted, but a flat, even surface as far as the eye could reach."

The weather was fine and clear with the snowy mountains of Spitzbergen on the southern horizon "sparkling like gems at a vast distance". As the ships lay anchored to the edge of the ice-field, the sailors were allowed to skylark on it and play leap-frog. But the Greenland pilots they had with them had begun to worry, for the ice had not only closed ahead of them but was beginning to cut off their escape. By the end of the first week of August, this was seen to be so with the ships trapped in an "ice-dock" while all around "nothing was to be seen but a vast continent of ice, to which there was no end".

Phipps and Lutwidge conferred with their pilots and found the choice as bleak as their surroundings. The ships were trapped in the ice and would probably be crushed. They could try cutting their way to clear water and, if that failed, either dragging the ships' boats over the ice to the open sea and sailing south to Spitzbergen in the hope of taking passage to Europe, or building shelters on the nearest island and spending the winter there. Before trying the first, forlorn hope, the ships' companies were ordered to get a good night's rest and "they rose in the morning with as much alacrity and unconcern as if they had been sailing with a fine breeze in the British Channel". But it was to no avail. They hacked and sawed at the ice but even at the edge it was eight feet thick, then fifteen and soon became too deep to measure; after the day's work the ships had been moved three hundred yards through the ice to the south-west while, together with the surrounding ice, they had drifted more than that distance to the north-east.

So a reconnaissance party was sent across the ice to an island about twelve miles distant and, on their return, they reported sighting open water some way to the west of that. So it was decided to try reaching this with the boats "by skating them over the ice", but not yet abandoning the two ships. After another long night's sleep, their crews put on their thickest clothing, the boats were swung on to the ice and loaded with provisions; one of them, the four-oared cutter manned by twelve seamen commanded by Midshipman Nelson for, as he put it, "I prided myself in fancying I could navigate her better than any other boat in the ship." The boats' crews then began hauling on the ropes with much jollity for "it was inconceivably laughable to see these motley bands yoked in their new harness; and to say the truth there was not one solemn face among the two companies." But after six hours of effort, the boats had only been dragged a mile.

Next day, they managed three miles and then, the day after, those remaining in the two ships saw that the ice was shifting, cracking and drifting in other directions. As the diarist on board the *Carcass* put it, "The Omnipotent, in the very moment when every hope of deliverance from their own united endeavours had relinquished them, interposed in their favour and caused the wind to blow and the ice to part in an astonishing manner, rending and cracking with a tremendous noise surpassing that of the loudest thunder. At this very instant, the whole continent of ice, which before was extended beyond the reach of sight ... moved together in various directions, splitting and dividing into vast bodies and forming hills and plains of various figures and dimensions. All hearts were now revived and the prospect of being released from the frozen chains of the north inspired the men with fresh vigour. Every officer and every idler on board laboured now for life. The sails were all spread that the ships might have the full advantage of the breeze to force them through the channels that had already opened and to help them, like wedges, to rend the cliffs that were but just cracking."

It was blowing from the east, opening the ice "as fast as it had closed when the wind blew westerly"; the ships recovered their boats and pressed through the floes until a mast-head look-out shouted that he could see open water; "Then festivity and jollity took the place of ... gloomy apprehensions and before they arrived at Spitzbergen there was not a sailor on board with a serious face." Running before the wind over the open sea, they looked back at the beautiful, terrible spectacle astern. "The ice ... they now had time to admire," wrote the diarist, giving his descriptive writing free rein. "The various shapes were indeed very curious and amusing. One remarkable piece described a magnificent arch so large and completely formed that a sloop of considerable burden might have sailed through without lowering her mast; another represented a church with windows and pillars; and a third, a table with icicles hanging round it like the fringes of a damask cloth."

No matter that a violent storm slowed their homeward passage and separated the two ships, for on 19th September it was noted on board the *Carcass*: "At seven in the evening to our great joy saw Yarmouth church, bearing south-west" and beyond stretched familiar Norfolk to Burnham Thorpe. Progress was slow and it was more than a week before Captain Lutwidge exchanged signals with the guardship at the Nore and took his ship up the Thames to dock at Deptford.

Although the expedition had penetrated no farther north than other ships, it was not seen as a total failure. Daines Barrington read a paper to the Royal Society expressing guarded optimism that "the polar seas are at least sometimes navigable". On board the *Carcass* there was more specific satisfaction, owing more to enthusiasm than evidence, that "we have shown incontestibly that the North Sea communicates with the Eastern

Sea and that the passage to China and Japan may be performed with difficulty by a north-easterly course by watching the opportunity when, a few days in the year, the North Sea is open". This claim was not, however, followed by any call to repeat the exploration because "who would think of exposing a ship's company to the hazard of being frozen to death in a tedious, uncertain and dangerous passage when a safe, certain and, one may say, speedy passage at all times lies open?"

The *Carcass* was paid off soon after Horatio Nelson's fifteenth birthday. Few midshipmen of his age would have experienced voyages both to the tropics and the Arctic but he was yet to sail in a fighting-ship on active service. This was to be the next stage of his training and his uncle had arranged for him to join a frigate, the *Seahorse*, now bound for the East Indies. She was a small ship of only twenty guns, commanded by Captain George Farmer, a high-mettled disciplinarian, who now lived up to his reputation by having two of his men flogged, on average, each week. The *Seahorse* was to join Rear-Admiral Sir Edward Hughes's squadron in Indian waters and, although these were almost as fever-ridden as the Caribbean, there, too, fortunes could be won from prize-money, loot or trade and, even if this remained a mirage for almost all who sailed east of the Cape of Good Hope, it added spice to their expectations.

Having sailed west and north, Nelson now went south and east, his ship calling at Madeira and the Cape, on passage for Madras. Stories of Clive's victories at the time of Nelson's birth had merged with others of vaster fortunes than those of naval officers' dreams amassed by the nabobs, such as Warren Hastings, the present Governor-General of Bengal, to give India an aura of infinite promise. Once the ship's boats had ridden the rollers and burst through the surf to beach beneath the battlements, pediments and spires of British-built Fort St. George at Madras the horizons of ambition seemed limitless.

Nelson served in the *Seahorse* for two years, learning the necessity for strict naval discipline that he had so despised when in a merchantman. He sailed north-east to Calcutta and south to Ceylon, where he thought Trincomalee the finest harbour in the world, and north-west to Bombay and across the Indian Ocean to Basrah on the Persian Gulf. He made one life-long friend in another midshipman, Thomas Troubridge; heard his first gun fired in anger when the frigate encountered a ship flying the colours of Hyder Ali, the Indian prince allied with the French, and exchanged a few shots with her; and won £300 at cards, which led him to reflect on the consequences had he lost.

Despite childhood delicacy, the substantial meals provided on the Arctic expedition had filled out his slight body and heightened the colour of his lively face. He was, noted a naval surgeon, William Perry, "All manliness and mind". Had he not been so, he would not have survived the onset of malaria that followed a mosquito-bite but was, of course, thought to have been caused by the chilling land-winds off the Malabar Coast where the ship had lain at anchor. When the *Seahorse* returned to Bombay at the end of 1775, he was so ill that he was not expected to survive and Sir Edward Hughes was told that he was likely to lose a promising young officer. The admiral sent his own surgeon across from the flagship and his conclusion was that the boy's one chance of survival was his immediate return to the cool of England. The only ship due to sail for home was another frigate, the *Dolphin*, which was completing a refit at Bombay and Admiral Hughes arranged that Nelson should return with her, if he survived long enough.

The *Dolphin* was a comfortable ship since she had been adapted for recent voyages of exploration, which had taken her twice round the world, and was commanded by Captain James Pigot, a kindly man. So, before the *Seahorse* sailed from Bombay early in March, the invalid was hoisted aboad the *Dolphin* – then reeking of the pitch for her decks were being caulked – and on the 23rd March, 1775, she put to sea for the long voyage home. The first few days were soothing, as a light breeze filled the sails and, as the sick boy's cot swayed to the movement of the ship, the shadows of her masts and rigging swung to and fro across her deck and her hull groaned softly to the gentle heaving of the sea. But across the horizon lay a black band of cloud and at night distant lightning flickered. Early in April, the first storm struck the ship. Squalls, thunder and lightning, rain that flooded decks when the scuppers choked, suddenly struck. Sails split, topsail yards and booms carried away, heavier yards were sprung from the slings. When the gale eased, the misery continued, as Captain Pigot wrote in his log, on "a confus'd sea, the ship rolled very much". Other squalls followed, throwing men about the ship or prostrating them with sea-sickness. The boatswain died and young Nelson, sick, sleepless and exhausted, nearly followed him.

Then out of the wild water rose Table Mountain and, once again, the Cape of Good Hope showed sailors why it had been so named. Two months after leaving Bombay, the *Dolphin* anchored in Simon's Bay, and her crew set about repairing the storm-damage: mending the sails and re-rigging; lowering the sprung yards and hoisting them back firmly into the slings; again caulking the decks. It was the month spent lying off Simon's Town that saved Nelson's life: the air was warm and fresh after the stifling humidity of the Indian coast and the food fresh and wholesome; indeed Captain Pigot had planned to victual his ship here rather than load her with the tainted food often sold at Bombay. When they sailed for home on 20th June, health, if not strength, was returning.

There were two more months under sail before the ship would anchor at Spithead and as she rippled across a calm, hazy sea, or swooped with the big, blue rollers of the South Atlantic, Nelson had time to brood. Extreme weakness – the fever, sea-sickness and difficulty in eating and sleeping – had reduced him to a skeletal caricature of the sturdy boy who had left England two and a half years before, and it brought on bouts of depression.

Amongst the ship's officers, whose company he was now beginning to keep, the perennial subject of conversation was, as so often, the prospects of promotion and command. There being no casualties amongst more senior officers to be replaced, only death from disease, or shipwreck and "interest" could help careers forward. True, there had been recent reports of rebellion in the American colonies but that would provide opportunities for soldiers. To Nelson, his own prospects seemed bleak to the point of hopelessness, relying solely on the interest of an uncle commanding a guardship, who was unlikely to be able to offer more than the occasional introduction to the captain of a sea-going ship. Other than the two Suckling uncles, neither he nor his brothers and sisters could hope for any practical help, so, as there was no family money, they would have to earn their livings as country parsons, clerks or shopkeepers. As for himself, even if he passed the coming examination for promotion to lieutenant and the King's commission, would there be employment for him? It seemed unlikely.

Depression deepened into despair. "I felt impressed with a feeling that I should never rise in my profession," he recalled later. "My mind was staggered with a view of the difficulties I had to surmount and the little interest I possessed. I could discover no means of reaching the object of my ambition." But he was rested, health was returning and his uneasy imagination soothed by the gentle rocking of the sea. It was then that he was inspired by the sudden surge of a spiritual experience, unsought and unexpected.[1] Had he followed his father and brother into the church, it might have been religious; in the secular context of the Royal Navy, it was patriotic and professional, but just as powerful and strengthening.

There was a visitation of "a radiant orb" and an infusion of joy and confidence. In his own words, "After a long and gloomy reverie, in which I almost wished myself overboard, a sudden glow of patriotism was kindled within me and presented my King and Country as my patron. 'Well, then,' I exclaimed, 'I will be a hero and, confiding in Providence, I will brave every danger.'"

---

[1] For studies of such experiences, see the works of Professor Sir Alister Hardy (*The Spiritual Nature of Man*, 1979, etc.) and, subsequently, of the Alister Hardy Research Unit at Manchester College, Oxford.

Although the experience was not overtly religious, it drew upon deep-laid beliefs and influences. His father was a priest as were at least a dozen of his family and immediate forebears, believing themselves to be in communion with God. Although a clergyman might not be placed much above the social standing of the doctor, who was little higher than a tradesman, unless he was related closely to the aristocracy, or could afford to hunt and fish with the squires; yet, in the final accounting, they were the most privileged of all. Eventually, everybody upon whom they depended for earthly comfort – the rich and the powerful, the peerage and royalty, even admirals – must ask for their intercession with the deity. Consciously, or unconsciously, they were aware of this final power and this clergyman's son had, on board a ship somewhere in the South Atlantic, been touched by the same inspired omnipotence. He was never to forget it and never to lose the confidence and drive that it gave.

The *Dolphin* passed the island of St. Helena, weathered a gale in the Bay of Biscay and anchored off the Isle of Wight at the end of August. She was to continue along the south coast to the Thames and to the dockyard at Woolwich, where she would be paid off. All at once, Nelson's newfound optimism was confirmed for, in his absence, his uncle had been promoted beyond all expectation from the command of the guardship to Comptroller of the Navy and the senior member of the Navy Board, and was now able to offer all the patronage a young officer could require. Moreover, there was now no lack of employment since the rebellion in North America had led to conflict with France, which supported the insurgents, albeit without a formal declaration of war. Attacks on British merchant ships in the Atlantic had necessitated the introduction of a convoy system and this required escorting warships. But it was Captain Suckling's influence that ensured his nephew's immediate promotion to acting-lieutenant and that, two days after the end of the *Dolphin*'s commission, he should receive orders to join another ship. This was to be his first sea-time in a ship of the line, designed to fight as part of a fleet or squadron, rather than cruise or scout; she was the *Worcester*, classed as a third-rate since her sixty-four guns gave her only about half the fire-power of the great three-decked, first-rate battleships.

Another sign of the new influence of his patronage came on joining the ship at Portsmouth. As her commanding officer prepared her for sea to escort a convoy to Gibraltar, Captain Mark Robinson found time to give a small dinner party for the Mayor of Portsmouth to meet probationary Lieutenant Nelson. The reason was that Captain Suckling was to stand for election as Member of Parliament for the town so that, when the invitation was returned, his nephew was invited to dine ashore with his captain. When the convoy reached Gibraltar, it was young Nelson, and not a more senior, commissioned lieutenant, who was sent ashore with despatches for forwarding to the British Consul at Cadiz. A captain could benefit from a kindly word from the Comptroller of the Navy as much as an aspiring young officer and such favouring could be put down to the latter's capabilities. As Nelson himself put it: "Although my age might have been a sufficient cause for not entrusting me with the charge of a watch, yet Captain Robinson used to say, 'He felt as easy when I was upon deck as any officer in the ship.'"

The *Worcester* weathered a rough winter in the Atlantic and Channel and the experience of watch-keeping on stormy nights, when the safety of the ship depended upon his immediate judgement, put the final touches to the young man's education. So it was with confidence that, in the second week of April, 1777, Nelson travelled to London to take his examination for a commission as a lieutenant, which would involve an interview with three captains at the Admiralty. Under naval regulations he should not have been considered before the age of twenty, and he was not yet nineteen, but such obstacles could often be avoided; particularly when the candidate was related to the Comptroller of the Navy.

So it was that on 9th April he reported to the Admiralty with his journal and the certificates signed by his former commanding officers testifying to his ability during six years' service. Ushered into the interview-room, he was startled to see that one of the captains seated in their blue, white and gold uniforms behind the polished table was his uncle. Yet Captain Suckling gave no flicker of recognition and the questioning began. It was quickly clear that the candidate was more than satisfactory, the captains exchanged nods of assent and only then did the Comptroller introduce his nephew, saying, "I did not wish the younker to be favoured. I felt convinced that he would pass a good examination and you see, gentlemen, I have not been disappointed."

Next day the newly commissioned lieutenant was given his next appointment: to the frigate *Lowestoft*, commanded by a Captain Locker, which lay at Sheerness, preparing to sail for Jamaica. Now there was a happy reunion with his father who arrived from Norfolk, two sisters who were staying with William Suckling at Kentish Town, and his brother Maurice, now in his ninth year behind a desk, where he had earned promotion to Clerk for Foreign Accounts at the Navy Office.

His elder brother William remained at Cambridge, where he was studying for ordination at Christ's College, and Horatio wrote to tell him his news with a touch of the whimsical humour he shared with his father: "I passed my Degree as Master of Arts on the 9th Instant." He did not mention their influential uncle but added with a curious mixture of self-pity and self-confidence, "So I am now left in the world to shift for myself, which I hope I shall do so as to bring credit to myself and friends."

Now he established a firm, adult friendship with Maurice Suckling, admiring his sophistication and humour. Here was much to envy and perhaps emulate: the smart, modern house in Park Street, close to Hyde Park; his portrait as an elegant and relaxed young captain painted by Thomas Bardwell; even the talk of combining politics with his career in the Navy. Suckling had set social as well as professional standards for his nephew, who quickly warmed towards his seniors who showed themselves to be amiable gentlemen as well as efficient officers. Captain Phipps had been one such, as had been one of his officers, John Baird, the first lieutenant of the *Carcass*, who, whatever the difficulties or dangers, "never was heard . . . to enforce his commands with oath, or to call a sailor by any other than his usual name." In his new commanding officer, Captain William Locker, he was to meet another.

At forty-six, Locker still limped from a leg-wound suffered twenty years before when boarding an enemy privateer in the Mediterranean and could remember chasing the French fleet amongst the shoals of Quiberon Bay, despite a gale, and fighting them there until dark. He could tell how Admiral Hawke, when warned of the dangers, just told his pilot, "You have done your duty in pointing out to me the danger; now lay me alongside the enemy's flagship." Memories of the greatest sea-battle of the Seven Years War had left Locker with confidence in the aggressive spirit with which he tried to inspire his young officers. Nelson, having graduated as a lieutenant, now continued his education and was later to tell Locker, "I have been your scholar; it is you who taught me to board a Frenchman . . . It is you who always told me 'Lay a Frenchman close and you will beat him'; and my only merit in my profession is being a good scholar." But Locker was also a man of the world, well-read and with some knowledge of the arts; a good conversationalist, his character suggested by a humorous mouth and reflected in perceptive, wide-set eyes.

In one talk with Captain Locker, probably prompted by Lieutenant Nelson's account of his uncle's house in Mayfair, the subject of portrait-painting came up. Locker's own had been painted by Gilbert Stuart, an American pupil of the celebrated Benjamin West, and he remarked encouragingly that there was no reason why an officer should not have his portrait painted while still a lieutenant. Indeed, a suitable artist was suggested: John Rigaud, a Swiss who had worked in Italy and was beginning to attract attention as a portrait-painter in London. As it happened, the captain was about to send the lieutenant up the Thames to the capital on duty and, since it was unpleasant duty, interludes in an artist's studio might prove agreeable. Nelson was to command the

Lowestoft's press-gang, seizing seamen, whether employed or unemployed, and any watermen, who could not produce certificates of exemption, to make up the numbers of the ship's company; if enough could not be captured, then any likely lad without such exemption or influence would be taken. The lieutenant himself need not raid the taverns with his gang; he would remain at an inn in the hope of receiving volunteers, who had seen the posters announcing that he would be recruiting for Captain Locker's frigate and tempting with hints of prize-money. He would also have to accept prisoners sent by the magistrates for service in the Navy instead of prison and send them down-river in the ship's tender.

But he could also make his way from the inn near the Tower of London to Great Titchfield Street, a turning off the north side of Oxford Street, where Mr Rigaud worked. It was probable that his portrait would not be finished before his ship sailed for the Caribbean but it could wait until his return and, presumably, so could payment. They discussed poses and a three-quarter-length standing figure was chosen instead of one seated, which seemed more appropriate to a captain with time for relaxation, and, because the subject stood barely five and a half feet tall, the sword, upon the hilt of which his hands would rest, would be painted as smaller than it was. As expected, progress with the portrait was cut short but not by orders for sea. One night when on recruiting and impressment duty, Nelson was taken ill, collapsed and became delirious. It was a recurrence of the malaria that had come close to killing him the year before.

Back on board the *Lowestoft*, Captain Locker recognised a passing bout of fever and that there was no need to send him ashore and apply for another second lieutenant. Soon after, they sailed for Jamaica, leaving the portrait in the artist's studio, as striking and promising as its subject but, like him, still incomplete.

CHAPTER II

To the Americas
(1777–81)

"I know myself to be so steady in my friendships that I can't bear the
least coolness or inattention in others."
– Captain Horatio Nelson, to Fanny Nisbet, from H.M.S. *Boreas*,
9th March, 1786

"My most worthy friend," wrote Lieutenant Nelson, aged eighteen,
beginning a letter to his middle-aged commanding officer. Captain
Locker had been sent ashore with a bad bout of malaria when the
Lowestoft arrived at Port Royal, Jamaica, on 19th July, 1777, and there
were fears for his life. "Should anything happen to you (which I sincerely
pray God, may not)," he continued, "you may be assured that nothing
shall be wanting on my part for the taking care of your effects and
delivering them safe to Mrs. Locker." If something did happen, he would
have the consolation of having "served faithfully the best of friends and
the most amiable of women".

Horatio Nelson was beginning to exercise his remarkable aptitude for
making friends. This emotional letter was not a lieutenant trying to
ingratiate himself with his captain; it was the expression of friendship
founded on weeks of conversation during an Atlantic crossing. Locker
was a man of wide experience but young Nelson, too, had tales to tell with
a new self-confidence and was a receptive listener to the older man's
stories. His combination of enthusiasm and tact won him friends among
the frigate's other officers, too. This was demonstrated when, after the
captain's recovery, the ship was again at sea, searching for American
ships trying to trade illegally with British colonies (see map, page xii).

That November, the *Lowestoft* had chased and caught an American
merchantman in heavy seas. It was the duty of the first lieutenant to board
the prize and a boat was brought alongside to take him across but he
flinched at the prospect of trying to scramble aboard the lurching ship
from a tossing boat and disappeared below with the excuse that he must
collect his sword. At this moment, Captain Locker came on deck, saw the
Lowestoft's boat plunging alongside and in danger of being stove in, and

shouted, "Have I no officer in this ship who can board the prize?"
Nelson, eager to go, did not like to usurp the senior lieutenant's
responsibility, but as the master – the frigate's non-commissioned
navigator – ran to board the boat, Nelson reached it first calling, "It's my
turn now! If I come back it's yours!" Boarding the prize was as dangerous
as it looked and sometimes Locker, watching from his pitching quarterdeck saw her disappear in the trough between huge waves. But Nelson
succeeded not only in bringing the prize to port but in cutting a dash
without being responsible for the humiliation of his timid superior. "This
little incident has often occurred to my mind," he mused long afterwards.
"I know it is in my disposition that difficulties and dangers do but
increase my desire for attempting them."

It was not only his brother-officers who took a liking to him. On their
third cruise out of Port Royal, they captured a schooner in the waters
between Hispaniola and the Bahamas and Locker, deciding that she
would make a useful consort for his frigate, renamed her after his
daughter, the *Little Lucy*, and manned her with his own seamen under
Lieutenant Nelson. This was his first independent command and, on his
first cruise, he sighted an American schooner and captured her after a
chase of eight hours. She proved to be the *Abigail*, bound for Nantucket
and commanded by a Captain Ellis. Nelson put a prize crew aboard to
take her into Port Royal but, instead of giving his report to the
commander of the British prize-crew, he courteously handed it to the
captured American, for passing to Locker on arrival. He began it, "I am
happy of having an opportunity of writing by Mr. Ellis ..." The
American skipper was unlikely to forget the courteous British lieutenant.

Patrols in search of American traders and privateers suddenly seemed
trivial when news reached Jamaica that, on 6th February, 1778, the
British government had declared war on France. This came as no
surprise, such had been the scale of French support of the insurgent
Americans, but it meant that henceforth a descent upon the Caribbean by
the French fleet, or even an expeditionary force, could be expected. Port
Royal was therefore to become an operational base with a new and
experienced admiral in command. This was Rear-Admiral Sir Peter
Parker, who had spent the past two years in American waters and arrived
off Kingston in March in a flagship, the fifty-gun *Bristol*, still scarred from
her disastrous attempt to force the defences of Charleston harbour in
South Carolina, when she had lost two hundred men. He was a tough,
opinionated member of an established naval family and was quick to note
that a nephew of Captain Suckling had come under his command, and
with an eye to future favours, appointed him to his own flagship as third
lieutenant.

Since Locker had again retired ashore, feverish with malaria, and as, in war with France, a ship of the line offered most chance of action, Nelson was delighted. He joined the *Bristol* in June and so quickly impressed the admiral with his efficiency that he had been promoted to first lieutenant by September. On one offensive sweep, Parker's squadron took seventeen prizes but on their return to Port Royal at the end of October, Nelson's euphoria was doused by the news that in July, shortly before they had sailed across the stretch of sea where his uncle had fought his celebrated action with the French nearly twenty years before, Captain Suckling had died.

Although he had left his estate to his brother, there were legacies of £500 to each of his nephews and twice as much for his nieces, which would release Susannah from servitude in the milliner's shop in Bath, where she worked behind the counter. Shortly before his death he had told Edmund Nelson that he expected Horatio to become an admiral and, to add emphasis, asked that he be given the sword he inherited from his great-uncle, Captain Galfridus Walpole, and had himself worn in battle. Even before hearing this, Nelson had written to his surviving uncle, in a mood reflecting his moment of patriotic inspiration, "Had I been near him when he was removed, he would have said, 'My boy, I leave you to my country; serve her well and she'll never desert but will ultimately reward you.'"

Suckling had done his work well, both in the education of his nephew and in beginning the chain of friendships which would continue to support him. One such had been Admiral Parker, who in turn was responsible for another. Before the end of the year, he realised that his first lieutenant was restive for higher command and so gave him the brig *Badger* with the rank of commander. His replacement in the *Lowestoft* was to be a Lieutenant Cuthbert Collingwood, whom he had met some years earlier when both had been midshipmen and who, although now junior in rank, was his senior by a decade. Zeal and his uncle's influence had taken Nelson ahead of the solemn Northumbrian, who had been sent to sea at the age of eleven, having to make his way without favouritism and winning his commission in action when running supplies ashore to the soldiers fighting the American rebels at what came to be called the Battle of Bunker Hill. Although a big-built man, Collingwood lacked self-confidence but beneath his diffidence seemed to lurk an originality, charm and even wit.

In all but professional competence, the two men seemed opposites but, complementing one another, founded a friendship that was to be established by a sequence of chances when, for the first time, Collingwood followed closely in Nelson's footsteps; the next occasion was to follow in a few months. The task of the *Badger* was to patrol the eastern seaboard of Central America "to protect the Mosquito Shore and the Bay of Honduras", as he was told, "from the depredations of the American privateers". It was a strange, wild coast of mangrove swamp, savannah and jungle, made rich by its hardwood forests and populated by a mixture of freebooting loggers, escaped slaves and Mosquito Indians; although the British had established settlements on the shores of Honduras, most was nominally the Spanish colonial provinces of Guatemala, Nicaragua and Costa Rica.

Nelson visited the British lumber-camps where the settlers stressed their vulnerability to Spanish attack in the hope of acquiring a British garrison and, with it, colonial status. There were few excitements. The *Badger* took one small prize, which Nelson identified as being French only after searching for her papers and finding them after two days, hidden in an old shoe. Then there was the burning of the *Glasgow*, a British frigate which caught fire on anchoring in Montego Bay on the north coast of Jamaica. "It was a most shocking sight," Nelson remarked later, but he took his boats across not only to rescue her crew but to shout orders that before abandoning ship they should elevate their loaded guns to the maximum so that when the flames fired their charges they would be less likely to damage other ships in the bay. The *Glasgow*, hopelessly engulfed in the blaze, was towed out to sea where she blew up.

Nelson thereupon sailed his ship round the island to join the dozen ships of Parker's squadron off Port Royal. There he heard the news upon which every naval officer's career depended: that, on 11th June, 1779, he had been promoted to post-captain; "made post", as it was said, so that henceforth his promotion would be by seniority and automatic. Only breaches of conduct, illness or death could now prevent him becoming an admiral as his uncle had forecast. He was to command the frigate *Hinchinbroke* – so named after the estate of the First Lord of the Admiralty, the Earl of Sandwich – when she returned from a cruise. To await her return he was to move into an officers' mess ashore and hand over command of the brig. On 20th June, he made his final entry in her log: "At noon Cuthbert Collingwood Esq. superseded me in command. Horatio Nelson."

The *Hinchinbroke* became overdue and was presumed lost as a French fleet was ranging the Caribbean. The Comte d'Estaing, having escaped Lord Howe's ships in American waters, had steered south and, in mid-June, taken the British islands of St. Vincent and Grenada. On the 16th, Spain had declared war on Britain, which now had to face her two most formidable rivals together with the American rebels. Jamaica, the richest of all British colonies, was now at risk and all naval officers

1 The aspirant. Horatio Nelson painted by John Rigaud, who began the portrait in 1777, when his sitter was a nineteen-year-old lieutenant, and completed it three years later when he was a post-captain home from war.

2 *Above*: The family home. The Parsonage at Burnham Thorpe, Norfolk, where the Nelson family lived from 1755 to 1802, painted by Francis Pocock.

3 *Below*: The church where Horatio Nelson was baptised and where he expected to be buried. All Saints', Burnham Thorpe, built in the fourteenth century and restored for the centenary of Trafalgar; as it was in 1987.

4 *Above*: The grand cousins lived at Wolterton Hall, Norfolk. Horatio Nelson's maternal grandmother had been a Walpole and his cousin Lord Walpole would occasionally invite the impecunious Nelsons to stay.

5 *Below*: The feckless brother failed to become a successful shopkeeper at North Elmham, Norfolk. Suckling Nelson's general store as it appeared in the 1970s. The shop was later named Nelson House.

6 *Above left*: The lost mother. Catherine Nelson, generous and strong-willed, who died in 1767, when her son Horatio was aged nine.

7 *Above right*: The faithful father. The Reverend Edmund Nelson, whimsical and scholarly, who found himself a "double parent" to eight children.

8 *Below left*: The socially-successful grandmother. Mary Bland, daughter of a prosperous Cambridge baker, who married Horatio Nelson's paternal grandfather, the rector of Hilborough.

9 *Below right*: The inspiring uncle. Captain Maurice Suckling, Royal Navy, the brave and urbane brother of Catherine Nelson, who first took Horatio to sea.

without sea-appointments would be expected to take part in the defence of the island. Hitherto, Nelson had usually lived on board ship but his frequent visits to Admiral's Pen, Parker's residence in Kingston, where Lady Parker, a busy hostess, had introduced him to life ashore. There, too, he exercised his talent for making friends.

Jamaica, a hilly, wooded island, about one hundred and fifty miles long by fifty miles wide, had a population of nearly a quarter of a million of whom some 13,000 were of European stock. These ranged from prosperous planters owning great sugar estates and living in handsome, stone-built country houses, merchants and ship-owners, a middle class of shopkeepers, clerks and estate-managers and "poor whites", who included the descendants of prisoners transported from England, Irish contract-labourers and sailors. Reflecting this stratified society, and parallel with it, were the regiments and ships' companies of the Army and Navy defending this fount of British wealth. Beneath the ruling minority lived the bulk of the population, mostly of African descent: slaves, some freed slaves and mulattoes, creoles and quadroons of mixed racial ancestry. In the face of the threat from France, most were united for even the slaves had little interest in exchanging one master for another.

Hitherto, Nelson had had little opportunity to enjoy life ashore. Now, as a captain of the Royal Navy he became a sought-after guest at the plantation houses, of the homes of the Kingston merchants and the official residences at the political capital, Spanish Town, fourteen miles across the rich, rolling country from the port. There was a hectic pace to social life in Jamaica, spurred by the constant reminders of mortality; amidst the comforts, the tending by black servants and the luxuriant climate and landscape, were sudden disease and death. Perversely it seemed that it was the young and hopeful, those just arrived from the British Isles to make a fortune in trade or a reputation in uniform, who were most at risk. Life seemed as cheap as the Jamaica rum, which cheered the life and often hastened its end.

Some who lived in the island had the resilience to withstand its dangers and temptations and one of these, with whom Captain Nelson became friends, was Hercules Ross. They had been introduced by Locker, before repeated malarial infection made his return to England imperative, and the state of emergency brought about more meetings. Ross was a man of parts: a prosperous sugar-planter and ship-owner, a gregarious host and a tropical version of the hard-riding Scottish laird; he was also a practical patriot and as soon as the French threat became acute helped to raise and train a local militia, armed several of his ships and sent them to sea as privateers in search of enemies and prizes.

Nelson, too, became directly involved when he was appointed to command Fort Charles, the keystone of the capital's defences. The anchorage off Kingston, which could have held the entire British fleet, was sheltered by the long sandy spit of the Palisadoes; at the landward end of this stood two forts, Castile and Rock Fort, and at its tip, near the site of the buccaneers' capital of Port Royal, which had sunk under the sea in an earthquake a century before, lay Fort Charles. It was a powerful shore battery rather than a conventional castle, mounting more than a hundred heavy guns in two tiers which, together with those of Fort Augustus across the harbour and Apostles' Battery on the opposite side of its entrance, could close it to an attacking fleet. Fort Charles had been named after the second king of that name and strengthened by the old buccaneer Sir Henry Morgan when appointed Deputy Governor of the island, and had survived the earthquake. It lay like a battleship at the edge of the sea, an illusion increased when Nelson paced the wooden deck of its upper storey and looked through the gun-ports pierced in the thick walls of whitewashed brick to the hard line of the horizon.

Nelson had five hundred men in his garrison and more than six thousand soldiers – most of them militia, since there were only two regular battalions on the island – were camped around Kingston and manning the other forts; Admiral Parker mooring his ships before the city. Against this, it was feared, d'Estaing might be able to attack with more than a hundred ships, including nearly thirty sail of the line, and put ashore an army of twenty-five thousand, most of them trained regular troops. "I leave you in England to judge what stand we shall make," wrote Nelson to Locker. "I think you must not be surprised to hear of my learning to speak French."

He had been given his important command by the Governor of Jamaica, Major-General John Dalling, at the admiral's recommendation, and here again friendship was struck up. Dalling too was an enthusiast, although this was not balanced by cool judgement. He was a regular soldier of forty-eight, who had fought under the command of Nelson's hero Wolfe at Quebec; a handsome man but, due to gout and consequent lack of exercise, running to fat. His particular bond with the young captain was that both were East Anglians and from the same set of social circumstances; Dalling was also related to the aristocracy through his mother, who had been a Windham but had married a Suffolk tradesman. His maternal grandfather had been comptroller of the household to the Duke of Cumberland, who had become Commander-in-Chief of the Army, so launching the young Dalling on a military career. During the Scottish rebellion of 1745, he had been aide-de-camp to the Duke in the war against the clans and thereafter a staunch "Williamite", as his patron's admirers were known. Nelson liked to tell a story about Dalling's response to a Jacobite toast he had heard proposed at a dinner-party: "He was in company and a gentleman gave sentiments, as was the fashion: 'May the seed of the thistle extirpate the seed of the turnip.' It was drunk and Dalling begged to give a sentiment: 'May there never want a Williamite to kick the arse of a Jacobite' – and put his sentiment instantly into execution."

At the end of August, the *Hinchinbroke* arrived off Port Royal and her safe return was followed by the news that the French were not coming after all, having heeded an appeal from the American rebels' leader, General George Washington, for urgent reinforcement. "It seems strange," mused the relieved Admiral Parker, "that the Comte d'Estaing should let slip so favourable an opportunity of attacking this island." So Nelson could now leave his fortress and, after more than three months, return to sea, this time in command of a frigate. On 1st September, he wrote in her log, "Moderate breezes and clear weather. Took command of the ship and read my commission to the ship's company." A month later he took her out of Kingston Bay for another cruise to the Mosquito Shore.

That long coast of the isthmus linking the two American continents was also attracting the attention of Governor Dalling. At his residence, the King's House in Spanish Town, he was poring over a huge volume of Thomas Jefferys' *West India Atlas*, published four years earlier. On page seven this displayed an exquisitely engraved map of the Nicaragua and Costa Rica provinces of New Spain, the eastern seaboard of which was the Mosquito Shore and to the west of which lay the great ocean that was then called the South Sea. Over the page were maps of other Spanish territories, including Cuba and most of Central and South America, within striking distance of Jamaica. He studied these intently because secret letters from Lord George Germain, the Colonial Secretary in London, had been warning that war with Spain might be imminent and on 16th June, 1779, it was formally declared. In September the Spanish raided a British settlement on the coast of Honduras: Dalling countered with his own raid on the Spanish settlement of Omoa, where Guatemalan gold was stored for shipment to Havana, seizing a fortune in bullion and cargoes. So delighted was he with his success that he was planning another raid since Germain had suggested that this would pin down Spanish and French garrisons and prevent reinforcements being sent to the American rebels.

And so when Nelson returned in December from a cruise that had taken him along the Mosquito Shore to the mouth of the San Juan river, which marked the boundary between Nicaragua and Costa Rica, he found that the mood had changed; the apprehension of the summer had

given way to confidence and an aggressive spirit that radiated from the
gouty soldier at the King's House. Here Nelson was made privy to some
ambitious plans and told that he himself might be involved. Prompted by
Germain's urging to harrass the Spanish colonies and pondering over the
atlas, Governor Dalling's imagination had been inspired by a memorandum that had reached him from a Scottish adventurer named James
Lawrie, who had recently been given the semi-official title of Superintendent-General of the Mosquito Shore as the representative of the
British settlers there. Dalling had invited his opinion on various military
options.

Hoping to inspire military adventures on the mainland – and subsequent occupation leading to colonial status and a governorship for
himself – Lawrie described the Mosquito Shore in beguiling detail: rivers
full of fish, forests of valuable hardwoods that "abound in the highest
degree with game" and "excellent pasture capable of maintaining vast
herds of cattle – the beef I have killed there would not disgrace
Leadenhall Market." But when he moved south to the little town of San
Juan del Norte at the mouth of the Rio San Juan that flowed for more
than a hundred miles through the forests from Lake Nicaragua to reach
the sea, he became lyrical. "The River St. John," he wrote, "is pretty
broad and, in high floods, navigable for flat-bottomed schooners. About
thirty miles above its mouth stands the Castle of St. John's ... From the
castle to Granada, situated on the further bank of the Lake of Nicaragua
towards the South Sea, is navigated by flat-bottomed schooners."
Granada was the largest city in Nicaragua, although Leon was the capital,
and the country around it was, he wrote, "open and dry, full of towns and
villages and abounding with necessities of every kind". Then he concluded, "The river and the Lake of Nicaragua present an easy channel
for distressing them in some of their richest provinces; there is nothing to
interrupt the passage of the troops but the Castle of St. John, which
would be easily attacked and carried."

Dalling turned again to Jefferys' atlas. He could see that the Rio San
Juan, and the lake from which it flowed east, together almost cut through
the isthmus of Central America; the castle of San Juan was not marked
but the river itself was engraved so strongly that he could well understand
why the buccaneers of the past had seen it as the easiest route by which to
plunder the towns of inland Nicaragua. The text of the atlas confirmed
Lawrie's account of the riches of the region for here were pastures for
cattle, timber, grain, fruit, sugar-cane, cotton, cocoa, hemp and tar.
Moreover, Thomas Jefferys had speculated that if a canal were to be cut
through the eleven miles of land between the western shore of the lake
and the ocean beyond "it would produce a new order of things in the

government, trade and navigation of the West Indies". Suddenly the most ambitious schemes of raiding Spanish possessions were replaced by something infinitely more exciting: it would be possible to cut the Americas in two.

To ascend the Rio San Juan and command the lake and the strip of land beyond would divide New Spain with a British army between Mexico and Peru; perhaps a British squadron on both oceans eventually able to sail between the two by river, lake and a canal. Even if the North American rebels could not be suppressed and the thirteen colonies were lost, they could be replaced by these Spanish territories, which were weakly defended and, by all accounts, ripe for conquest. In high excitement Dalling wrote to Lord George Germain proposing such an expedition into the interior of Nicaragua and adding, "I see hardly a possibility of not succeeding in whole or in part".

This bold proposal was well received in London for Germain had recently received a similar suggestion from a former Superintendent-General of the Mosquito Shore, who had returned to England and sent "a paper containing a digested view of the manner to obtain a South Sea port by way of Lake Nicaragua". So the British Government approved the scheme and Governor Dalling was authorised to mount his "secret expedition". His own enthusiasm was not, however, widely shared: the Assembly of Jamaica was far more interested in peaceful trade than in financing expeditionary forces and feared that the despatch of the few troops in the island to Central America would leave them open to French or Spanish attack. Admiral Parker was appalled, as his ships were fully occupied and he wrote to the Governor that "the intended Expedition . . . may be a detriment to this Island and cannot, in my opinion, promise much to the adventurers".

Dalling went ahead with his plans, first appointing Hercules Ross as his Agent-General, responsible for the logistics of the expedition. There were some fifteen hundred regular soldiers in Jamaica – mostly in the 60th Regiment of Foot, known as the Royal American Regiment and recruited from loyal colonists, which was seasoned in the tropics, and the newly raised 79th Regiment, nicknamed "The Liverpool Blues" from its town of origin and the colour of its uniform, which was not. But reinforcement of about three thousand more regulars was expected from England during the next few months, so that the attack could be made in two waves. The first would consist of the 60th and the 79th supported by irregulars raised in Jamaica and along the Mosquito Shore. This would ascend the river to the lake, capturing the castle on their way, thus leaving the way open for the main force which would follow some months later to occupy the towns of Nicaragua and establish itself on the brink of the South Sea.

To command the first wave of the attack, Dalling chose Captain John Polson, "a steady and good officer" of the 60th, to whom he gave the temporary rank of lieutenant-colonel. In time he would be superseded by more senior officers and, he imagined, he himself would eventually take command of the conquering army so that he could return to England a hero and reap his rewards.

Although it was to be essentially a military operation, the Navy would be involved at the beginning and the end. Troopships would have to be escorted to the mouth of the San Juan river, a flotilla of small ships would have to be launched on Lake Nicaragua and finally there would have to be a squadron to cruise the South Sea off the west coast of the isthmus. For these tasks, Dalling recommended the efficient young Captain Nelson, who had had the most recent experience of the Mosquito Shore. Both Dalling and Parker knew his worth but others were surprised by his youth and Colonel Polson later remembered their first meeting thus: "A light-haired boy came to me in a little frigate, of whom I at first made little account."

For his part, Nelson saw his task as no more than a spell of escort duty which would end once the convoy had reached its destination. Indeed, he only mentioned it in passing in a long letter to Locker in January, 1780, much given over to news of mutual friends, mostly naval officers but including a Jamaican woman, Cuba Cornwallis, who had taken her surname after their friend Captain the Honourable William ("Billy Blue") Cornwallis; he had freed her from slavery and when he shared quarters ashore with Nelson, she had become their housekeeper. Of the coming expedition, he only remarked, "How it will turn out, God knows. I do not expect to return before the beginning of June ..." It would be a tiresome interlude that would delay his hopes of a return home for, he wrote: "You must not be surprised to see me in England after this trip; for if my health is not much better than it is at present, I shall certainly come home as all the doctors are against my staying so long in this country. You know my old complaint in my breast: it is turned out to be the gout got there."

Amongst the doctors responsible for this diagnosis for what was probably stress combined with recurrent malarial symptoms, was another strong character to whom Nelson took an immediate liking. This was Dr. Benjamin Moseley, the Surgeon-General of the colony, who had just been appointed chief medical officer of the expedition. Now aged thirty-seven and having had his medical training in London, Paris and Leyden, he was regarded as a foremost authority on tropical diseases but was less highly regarded as a surgeon as many of his patients had died of tetanus. He was fascinating company and his intelligent, heavy-lidded eyes seemed to have been witness to the most curious phenomena, which he would recall in bizarre detail. He had made a study of black magic as practised by negro slaves, superstition and the pathological effects of phases of the moon; of shark-bites and hydrophobia; and the effects of coffee and sugar in the diet, each of which became the subject of a scholarly treatise. His treatment of the prevalent tropical illnesses was sometimes unconventional for he had less confidence than most doctors in the use of quinine for malaria, or "intermittent fever", unless it was combined with much cinnamon, sweat-inducing diaphoretics and draughts of beer for, he maintained, "nothing was so grateful as London bottled porter". He was also prudent in avoiding unnecessary risks and so decided that he could best supervise the medical services of the coming expedition from Jamaica, while the practicalities on the spot could be attended to by the much younger Dr. Thomas Dancer, whose interest in tropical botany was a good reason for sending him into the Nicaraguan jungle. In any case, no medical problems – other than a little of the usual dysentery from infected drinking-water – were expected as Nicaragua was said to be healthy.

Amongst the other specialists appointed to Colonel Polson's staff was an engineer officer to site the camps and batteries, whatever siege-work might prove necessary and make use of twenty-five civilian artificers who would accompany the force. This was to be Captain Edward Despard, who had been promoted from lieutenant for his efficiency in designing and building fortifications during the recent fear of invasion. He was a well-built man of twenty-eight; not handsome but his high-bridged nose and alert eyes combined with a nervous energy to attract attention. Of Irish and French Huguenot descent he was one of six brothers of whom five had joined the Army when the eldest had inherited the family estate at Donore near Mountrath to the south-west of Dublin. Edward Despard had served in Jamaica as a youth then, when back in England, had been appointed, together with his younger brother Thomas, to the newly raised Liverpool Blues, with whom he had returned to the Caribbean. A quick and enquiring mind had suited him for more than drilling foot-soldiers and an aptitude for mathematics led him to military engineering. Like Dr. Moseley, his was a strong, original character that met another in Captain Nelson and a friendship was formed.

As the expeditionary force collected in the camps around Kingston, it appeared increasingly grotesque. Only about 250 men from the two regular battalions were to accompany the vanguard – the rest following with the second wave – but numbers were to be made up by some 800 irregulars. These would include some volunteers but were mostly waterfront drifters, "straggling seamen", released prisoners and freed slaves prompted to enlist by hope of booty. Officers of some ability were given command and each formation granted a name with a martial ring to it: the Royal Jamaica Volunteers, the Loyal Irish, the Jamaica Legion and, for boatmen, the Royal Batteaux Corps; for freed slaves, the Black Regiment. As well as Despard's artificers, shipwrights were to accompany the expedition to assemble a prefabricated gun-boat on the San Juan river and, once the lake had been reached, start building small ships from local timber.

The expedition was to embark at the beginning of February, 1780, and General Dalling sent his Lieutenant-Governor, Brigadier Archibald Campbell – another veteran of the Quebec campaign – to take the salute at a final parade on the dockside. The regular troops were smart enough but Campbell later described the irregulars as being drawn up "in a ragged line, half-clothed and half-drunk, they seemed to possess the true complexion of buccaneers and it would be illiberal to suppose their principles were not in harmony with their faces. A hundred of them were only collected together and seemed so volatile and frolicsome, I thought it good policy to order ten guineas for them to be drunk in grog on board their transports and embarked them with three cheers to the great satisfaction of the town of Kingston."

Finally as many as could be collected embarked in the seven transports, the senior officers and headquarters staff joining Captain Nelson in the *Hinchinbroke*, which was to escort the convoy. On 3rd February, they sailed in fine weather and during the first two days of the voyage the frigate's routine was only broken for the flogging of a sailor and a marine for "neglect of duty and insolence" and for Nelson to read the burial service at the first funeral; that of a sergeant of the 79th who had died of malaria.

The convoy sailed for a week to the first of a series of calls at islands and settlements along the Mosquito Shore, where they would collect pilots familiar with the San Juan river and more European volunteers. Lawrie had gone ahead to recruit Indians as boatmen and porters and the first of these were expected to appear when they reached Cape Gracias a Dios, the southern extremity of the Bay of Honduras. There were none to be seen and no news of Lawrie so Polson and Nelson, worried by the effects on the health of the soldiers of nearly two weeks in overcrowded ships, took the opportunity to send them ashore. A camp was established on a swampy savannah a mile from the sea. Here they waited for three weeks, tormented each evening by mosquitoes, but reassured by medical opinion that they were no more than a nuisance which could be lessened by wearing "loose linen buskins", rigging mosquito-nets and lighting bonfires.

Eventually Lawrie arrived, followed by a few volunteers and Indians; the prospect of looting having overcome the former's apprehension that the expedition would disrupt their trading with Spanish settlements and the latter's fear that, once on board ship, they might be taken to Jamaica and sold as slaves. So the convoy slowly continued southwards, the newly recruited pilot showing his inadequacy by running it on to a reef which would have destroyed it had there been a strong wind. At the settlements and villages, where they sent boats ashore, few recruits were found, sometimes none. Only when Nelson himself accompanied Polson ashore and convinced the Indians that there was no risk of enslavement, did some volunteer. After a month of delays, with the expected onset of the rainy season in six weeks' time, there was no time to wait in the hope of attracting more.

On 24th March, 1780, forty-nine days after they had left Kingston, the convoy anchored within the sand-bar at the mouth of the San Juan river. Nelson's task officially ended here, although the *Hinchinbroke* was to remain off the estuary as guardship until relieved, and further decisions were to be Polson's alone. Already a month of the dry, campaigning season had been lost by delays and the first summer storms could be expected soon, so there was a sense of urgency. Leaving Lawrie to recruit more volunteers and then try to catch up, the colonel ordered that the invasion of Nicaragua begin immediately. Captain Despard was sent ashore to survey the beach of dark, volcanic sand for the landing and choose sites for the base camp and a shore battery.

Two days later, a dozen European volunteers, sixty of their slaves and 220 Indians had arrived from the Mosquito Shore and Polson decided that any others would have to follow him up the river. Meanwhile, the transports discharged their cargoes on to the beach and essential stores, arms and ammunition were loaded into smaller craft for the voyage into the interior. In addition to the prefabricated gunboat *Lord George Germain*, the tender *Royal George* and a Spanish coaster called the *Chichito*, the flotilla was composed of two types of large canoe carved from the solid hardwood of giant forest trees by the Indians. The panga was about forty feet long, its sides heightened with planking and was propelled by as many as twenty-two oars; with a beam of up to nine feet and a draught of five, it could carry about sixteen tons of cargo. The *pipante*, or pitpan, was about half the length of the panga and there were smaller craft, the dory and the ordinary canoe, which could be stacked on board the larger.

Into these went the small, four-pounder cannon and their shot, barrels of gunpowder and musket balls, tents, bedding and cooking pots together with the rations – kegs of salt beef, bags of dried peas, beans and biscuit and Dr. Dancer's medical supplies. By 27th March, all seemed ready and Polson ordered the expedition to embark. As the final boarding lasted all day and, when complete, only two hours of daylight remained, the colonel ordered that they cross the anchorage to a small island at the mouth of the river and begin the ascent from there at dawn next day.

Nelson, who had had no part in the planning or the loading, watched the departure with mounting unease as the boats were thrust out from the beach into the smooth, swirling currents where the brown water of the San Juan poured into the transparent peacock-blue of the Caribbean. Many of the boats looked overloaded and top-heavy and, as they swung in the current, soldiers stood up to steady the swaying stacks of stores. In a moment all was chaos: one boat capsized and then another; soon others were colliding and the harbour was suddenly strewn with upturned boats, sinking or floating cargoes and struggling men. Nelson's sailors and Indian boatmen saved what they could and, amazingly, only one soldier was drowned, but less than an hour after they had left the beach they were back upon it, wet, weary and disheartened.

Nelson, whose own experience of handling boats in such waters went back to his boyhood and a Norfolk creek, realised that if the expedition could not even cross the open anchorage they could never ascend an uncharted river where there were known to be shoals and cataracts. The only hope was for himself to accompany them and accordingly he volunteered his services, telling Polson that he would bring fifty sailors and marines with him in his frigate's cutter and pinnace. The colonel was overwhelmed with relief and gratitude, saying later, "I want words to express the obligations I owe that gentleman." Nelson's motives were not entirely altruistic: if expectations were fulfilled, there would be fame and fortune for the invaders of Nicaragua and this was the first time that a chance of either had come his way.

And so the expedition was reorganised with professional naval advice. It would now travel in two divisions and the loads of each boat would be drastically reduced. There was still no sign of the additional Indians Lawrie was supposed to be collecting, but, on 28th March, just as Polson was again about to order embarkation, a British sloop arrived with despatches from Jamaica, including a letter to the colonel from Governor Dalling. "From the time elapsed since your departure," he had written, "I begin to be anxious for news of you." But he assumed that the expedition had already ascended the river, taken the castle of San Juan and sailed across Lake Nicaragua to capture Granada, and apologised that, as a reinforcement of some six hundred regulars and volunteers was shortly to sail from Kingston, Polson would have to be superseded by the more senior Colonel Kemble of the Royal Americans. "I sincerely hope I may have given you time to gather the laurels about Fort San Juan and the Lake," he wrote. "Colonel Kemble is sensible that he must be equally superseded in his turn and should the King adopt the ideas I have had the honour to lay before him and still reinforce the troops on the Main, a superior officer must be sent to take command, likely it will be myself."

Dismay at the Governor's assumption that they had already conquered the country they had yet to invade was countered by the encouragement that help was on the way not only from Jamaica but from England. So it was with renewed optimism that on the morning of the 28th Polson ordered the expedition to start.

The first division was led by volunteer officers with experience of the jungle, embarked with pilots and Indian guides in canoes to find the deepest channels and scout for the enemy; then came Polson himself with Nelson, Captain Despard, Dr. Dancer and the rest of his staff in the *Hinchinbroke*'s cutter and pinnace together with thirty-four seamen and thirteen marines from the frigate; next the pangas and pitpans, carrying the troops with their equipment and rations; finally, the heavier stores, including the artillery, loaded into the three biggest craft. Some of the less important stores were left behind to follow with the second division, commanded by a major, which would set out when more of Lawrie's Indians and the reinforcements from Jamaica had arrived. Since the hinterland of Nicaragua was expected to be dry and healthy, and the troops had been remarkably free from sickness since leaving Kingston, it was thought prudent to leave behind almost all Dr. Dancer's stocks of medicines, bedding tents and light food suitable for invalids as being an unnecessary burden.

Once the flotilla had pulled away from the shore and formed into line ahead, Nelson gave the order and scores of oars and paddles plunged into the water. The boats lurched forward into the current that ran between the islands and sandbanks of the estuary and then the banks seemed to close behind them. Instead of ships and tents and the horizon, was tropical greenery and the tall grass of the riverside savannahs ruffling in the warm wind. Along the banks white egrets perched on branches and cormorants spread their black wings to dry, watching with sharp, unblinking eyes. As the column of boats pulled into the deeper, smooth water of a united channel, the young men of the Liverpool Blues, fresh to the tropics, stared in wonder at the flocks of green parrots, monkeys swinging in the trees and the turtles that sunned themselves on rocks or bobbed to the surface for a quizzical peep at the intruders. Occasionally, a slithering movement among the blue water-hyacinths and a shout of alarm might mean the presence of an alligator. Along the shores, thick, tall grass gave way to palms and these to the jungle.

It was not easy going. Sometimes a boat would grind on to a shoal and the sailors would thrust at it with their oars and, when that failed, jump over the side and push, waist-deep in water. By late afternoon, the flotillas straggled over many miles: the scouts' canoes darting ahead; the heavily-loaded craft at the rear, grounded and stuck fast. After covering six and a half miles, Nelson advised that it was time to stop, bring the column together and make camp for the night. So, while the soldiers and sailors lit fires to cook a meal and slung their hammocks between trees, he and Polson decided that the next day must be devoted to lightening the loads of the stranded transports and bringing them upstream to the camp which would become a depot for the heavier stores that could be collected later.

At about six the sun set and darkness closed in. The hot, damp air whined with mosquitoes and the darkness filled with a nightmare of jungle noise: croaks and grunts, whistles and whoops, coughs and trills. Beyond the firelight, eyes and fireflies gleamed. Then the air chilled and men who had been sweating began to shiver. After twelve hours the sky turned grey between the trees and they woke from an exhausted sleep, stiff in a heavy dew, to see thick white mist upon the river. As they tried to light the damp wood of their fires, howler-monkeys bellowed a welcome to the sunrise from the tree-tops; shafts of sunlight slanted through the leaves to burn away the mist and in an hour the sun was burning in a clear, hot, blue sky.

The second day was spent as planned and the third in pushing a few more miles upstream. More craft grounded and, as the heaviest vessels that had been stranded on the first day had still not been moved up to the camp, the column was strung along nearly a dozen miles of river. Nelson advised that more small boats were needed to spread the loads and a canoe was sent down-river to ask for these at the base camp. The fourth day proved even more difficult and not only because the groundings continued. The river was now walled by the rain forest, the columns of tree-trunks and their canopies of leaves a hundred or two hundred feet above, shutting out any cooling breeze while sand-banks reflected the sun in glare and heat. Islands appeared and the column had pushed up one reach for nearly three miles before it was realised that they had blundered up a tributary.

Nelson finally lost faith in the pilots and henceforth directed the advance himself, often leading it in a canoe, accompanied by Despard. Now the going was easier, the river running deep between higher banks so that on each of the next three days they covered about ten miles. They would start at dawn and stop in late afternoon at a camp-site chosen by Despard so that fires could be lit and hammocks slung before dark.

Nelson and Despard shared a tent, where the latter wrote notes and drew rough charts of the river and they discussed the next day's journey. Ashore, it was not only the chill nights, heavy dew and damp mist that made life uncomfortable. Apart from the mosquitoes there were venomous insects and reptiles; once Nelson woke to find a snake coiled at the foot of his hammock. Fresh fish and meat were to be had for the taking: giant tarpon, which leapt from the smooth, swift surface and plunged back with a splash like a cannon-ball; turtles; big iguana lizards; rodents and wild duck. Once Nelson turned away from the food on offer although hungry, sickened at the sight of monkeys in a cooking-pot.

They had covered more than sixty miles when Indians who had been scouting ahead paddled their canoes swiftly downstream with news of the enemy. About six miles up-river, beyond some rapids, they had sighted a Spanish battery on an island and the fortress of San Juan was probably not far beyond. The vanguard halted just below the rapids and Polson decided to send a patrol led by Despard through what he called "these horrid woods" to observe the island from the bank, while the soldiers followed their trail and the Indians dragged the boats up the rapids. As the troops struggled through the undergrowth, thorns tore their skin and uniforms, tendrils of creeper tripped their feet and leeches began to swell with their blood. Once a scream startled the column; a soldier had been bitten in the eye by a dangling snake; he was left beside the trail to be tended later but, when the search-party returned a few hours later he was found dead and already putrefying. At last coming up with Despard they were told that on the island was a semi-circular breastwork mounting small cannon and that it was manned by Spanish soldiers. The island lay some eighty yards from the bank and the water was deep, so that an assault would have to be made by boats.

Together Nelson and Despard planned the attack. That night, one assault party should paddle quietly past the island in canoes, keeping within the shadows of the shore, ready to attack it from the rear and another would prepare to give covering-fire from the bank while the main attack, led by Nelson, would be a frontal assault from the cutter and pinnace; all timed to coincide at first light. The dispositions were made as planned, except that several canoes and one of Nelson's two boats ran aground. Then the noise of rowing startled the Spanish sentries. A challenge was shouted and, as Nelson ordered his men to pull hard for the shore, guns flashed and the river spouted with grapeshot and musket-balls. Two soldiers were hit and then Nelson sprang with drawn sword from the bows of the boat for the shore, sinking to his knees in mud. Leaving his shoes stuck fast, he scrambled up the steep bank beside Despard, into the gunsmoke and over the breastwork into the battery.

The Spaniards fled, running into the fire of the British, who had landed in their rear, and promptly surrendered. At a cost of two soldiers wounded, fourteen prisoners and four small cannon were captured on the island, which, they learned, was named Bartola and they now called St. Bartholomew. Nelson, excited by his first experience of land-fighting, would thereafter boast, "I boarded, if I may be allowed the expression, an outpost of the enemy, situated on an island in the river."

From the prisoners they learned that the castle of San Juan lay less than five miles upstream and Nelson urged Polson to press forward urgently since its garrison had almost certainly heard the attack on the island. After dark, the colonel wrote in his journal, "This night, Mr. Despard, Chief Engineer, and Capt. Nelson of the *Hinchinbroke*, took one of the prisoners with them in a pitpan and went up the river very near the fort . . ."

At dawn on 10th April, as the sun began to burn away the milky mist on the river, the two men rounded a bend in the river and saw what had been the object of so much speculation. The castle of San Juan stood, less than a mile distant, on a green, conical hill at the head of a wide reach of the river and above the white water of rapids. The walls of the castle, painted a sepulchral white, sloped slightly like the sacrificial pyramids of Central America and from its keep flew the flag of imperial Spain. The thatched roofs of a village clustered around the base of the hill and on its landward side was a jumble of ridges and hillocks from which it might be possible to bombard the castle. The jungle had been cleared on either bank of the river, except for a few gigantic trees, and plantations of banana trees could be seen. Other than the stirring of the flag and the tumult of the rapids, there was no movement or sign of life; if the castle was to be assaulted, now was the time.

Back at Bartola, they found Polson preoccupied with the unexpected arrival of Major Lawrie, who reported that the second division was now following up the river and should arrive within a couple of days. Had this not been so, the colonel might have been receptive to Nelson's urging that he emulate Wolfe and seize the castle with an immediate *coup de main*. But he was a cautious man and, rather than take that risk, decided to await reinforcements, then invest and besiege the fort in the traditional manner. He would, however, begin the advance immediately, landing his troops about three miles downstream of the castle and out of sight of it. From this beach-head the approach-march would be made through the jungle.

The landing was made without difficulty and the four little four-pounder cannon put ashore to be dragged on sledges. Meanwhile Polson ordered Captain Richard Bulkeley of the Liverpool Blues to take two subalterns and fifty men and go ahead as fast as possible in the hope of seizing the high ground behind the castle. They disappeared into the undergrowth but once the main body was ready to start with its heavy weapons, ammunition and stores, they faced matted jungle, fallen trees, swamps and gullies. At dusk the mosquitoes were the most virulent they had met and one of the soldiers was attacked and mauled by a jaguar. On the second day of hacking through thickening jungle and heaving loads over deepening ravines, Polson gave up and ordered his men back to their boats. The approach to the castle would have to be made by river after all, although any hope of surprise would, of course, have been lost.

So it was that on 11th April, the procession of boats rounded the bend and came in view of the long reach leading to the castle. El Castillo de la Inmaculada Concepción had been built more than a century before as a defence against buccaneers ascending the hundred and eleven miles of the Rio San Juan to Lake Nicaragua. It stood on its steep-sided little hill, one hundred feet high, above the fiercest rapids on the river and had been strengthened during the Seven Years War. The walls of its stone keep rose fifty feet and were surrounded by a rectangle of ramparts fourteen feet high and four feet thick, about two hundred and twenty-five feet long by one hundred and thirty-five feet wide and with bastions at each corner. It was armed with twenty cannon and a dozen smaller guns and its garrison amounted to about seventy regular soldiers, who together with the local population and their families and slaves, who now crowded within the walls, numbered more than two hundred and twenty. Strong as it looked, the castle had a weakness: there was no well, the cistern was almost empty at the end of the dry season and water had to be fetched from the river.

The commander of the fortress was Don Juan d'Ayssa, who had just been entertaining the President and the Bishop of Guatemala, in whose honour the walls had been freshly whitewashed. He had had news from them of the declaration of war on Britain so, when he had heard the gunfire from Bartola, he had sent a fast canoe to the fortified settlement of San Carlos at the junction of the river and the lake with a letter asking for reinforcements and taking his wife to safety at Granada. Now he could see the British boats rounding the bend of the river and the infantry scrambling ashore. He ordered some of the cattle to be herded into the courtyard, the rest to be shot and shut the gates to prepare for the siege.

Nelson was among the first ashore, supervising the lashing of the little cannon to sledges for dragging towards the castle, when he was seized with violent stomach-pains and dysentery. Others were similarly crippled with abdominal spasms of "the fluxes" and the Indian guides discovered the cause. Near the landing-beach, they had found a pool of clear water amongst the trees and there they had drunk and filled their water-bottles. Only then did the Indians notice a broken and twisted branch and fruit of the poisonous manchineel tree floating in it, presumably so placed by the enemy to contaminate the drinking-water. Even so, he managed to follow the vanguard, who had cleared and captured the high ground commanding the approaches to the castle, and there he and Despard directed the levelling of the summit and the building of a breastwork for the first gun position. Next day, on the morning of 13th April, Colonel Polson wrote in his journal, "At daylight, Captain Nelson opened his Battery of one gun, which played with great success."

Working as his own gun-layer, Nelson's shooting was accurate and with one of his first shots he brought down the flagstaff and the banner of Spain. The other three cannon had now been dragged to the crests of other heights but their shooting was so wide that Polson immediately ordered that all the artillery should be controlled by Nelson, noting later that "there was scarcely a gun fired but was pointed by him or ... Despard". The two officers, who shared a tent in the siege-camp once again, had tried to persuade Polson that an immediate assault could carry the castle, but he had pleaded the lack of scaling-ladders and the imminent arrival of reinforcements. These had not appeared, nor had the reserve stocks of ammunition so that, after two days, the bombardment had to stop for lack of shot and Polson asked Despard whether his engineers could tunnel beneath the castle walls to place a mine. The sappers struck solid rock and the siege became no more than an investment until, on the 20th, the boats of the second division began to arrive. Yet hopes were soon dashed when it was heard that three-quarters of the ammunition had been lost when boats had capsized on passage up the river and that all that had been saved were fifty-three cannon-balls.

An even worse problem was the breaking of the weather. This was later described by Dr. Moseley after hearing the accounts of those who had been camped before the castle: "During the Periodical Rains, which begin about the middle of April, the torrents of water that fall for weeks together are prodigious, which gave the river a tremendous aspect and from their suddenness and impetuosity cannot be imagined by an European to portend anything but a deluge. This bursting of the waters above, and the raging of the river below, with the blackness of the nights, accompanied by horrible tempests of lightning and thunder, constitute a magnificent scene of terror unknown but in the tropical world." None had seen anything like this: the downpour blotted out sight of the far bank of the river and even the looming bulk of the castle itself became no more than a faint, grey shape. Tents and huts were beaten down and even when a roof remained watertight the rain threw up a spray that soaked everything beneath. Misery mounted for those prostrated with dysentery, some of whom – including Nelson – began to show symptoms of fever which had taken the usual three or four weeks to incubate, after infection when the expedition had been on the Mosquito Shore a month earlier.

By now the whole of the second division had arrived and its commander, Major James MacDonald, was supporting Nelson's call for an assault; Polson at last agreed and ordered the carpenters to make scaling-ladders. The siege was approaching its climax and the colonel, considering his next move, ordered Lieutenant MacLean of the Jamaica Legion to take a canoe manned by a dozen Indians up-river beyond the castle in an attempt to reach San Carlos and the lake, and then report on what opposition might be expected. On the 28th, Major MacDonald reported that the scaling-ladders and the assault-parties were ready and Colonel Polson decided that, according to the formalities of siege-warfare, he would now summon the castle to surrender. The only officer able to speak Spanish, an American, was sick so the formal summons was written in French and just as this was about to be taken across to the castle gates under a white flag of truce, a canoe appeared on the river with despatches from the coast.

First came the welcome news that reinforcements had arrived there from Jamaica – five hundred troops commanded by Colonel Kemble – and that they were about to begin the ascent of the river. There was also a letter for Captain Nelson from Admiral Parker, telling him that he had been appointed to command the frigate *Janus* and was to hand over command of the *Hinchinbroke* to Captain Collingwood. But Nelson was stretched in his tent, broken with malaria and dysentery, and there were doubts whether he could survive a journey down-river to the sea. Yet if he remained in the camp it seemed certain that he would die. So, after regretful farewells to Polson and his officers – and especially to Edward Despard – he was given letters for Colonel Kemble and Governor Dalling and helped into a canoe. This was thrust out into the swollen river, caught by the current and quickly whirled downstream and out of sight beyond the trees.

Compared with the agonising ascent of the river, descent was easy. Riding the flood, the canoe soon passed the island of St. Bartholomew and the litter of abandoned British camps on the lower reaches, taking three days to make the journey that had lasted two strenuous weeks in the opposite direction. On 1st May, the canoe had reached the tall, wind-ruffled grass of the coastal savannahs, passed the wooded islands of the estuary and finally reached the anchorage and the open sea. Several ships lay at anchor, another frigate and a sloop as well as the *Hinchinbroke* and a number of transports, and there was now a large encampment ashore.

But there was a listlessness about the scene that was explained when the canoe ran alongside Nelson's frigate: half her crew were sick with fever. He met Cuthbert Collingwood and Colonel Kemble but their greetings combined pleasure with alarm. Until his arrival, no word had reached them from Polson and they had expected to hear that his expedition was already in command of Lake Nicaragua and even of Granada. They were shaken by the sight of a post-captain of the Royal Navy, shrunken in his blue, white and gold uniform; his face yellow and hollow from fever. They were even more shocked by what he had to tell them: that the castle of San Juan had not yet been taken, although, when he had left, a summons to surrender was about to be delivered; that the troops were debilitated and sickening with malaria and dysentery and that the conditions under which they lived were appalling. Colonel Kemble's optimistic anticipation of the advance into Nicaragua drained away.

Once the formalities of handing over the *Hinchinbroke* to Collingwood's command were complete, Nelson was helped aboard the sloop *Victor* for immediate passage to Jamaica. On arrival a few days later, he was so weak that he had to be carried ashore in his cot but his friend "Billy Blue" Cornwallis, now commanding the third-rate *Lion*, lying off Kingston, insisted that Nelson should not be taken to the hospital which he saw as the ante-chamber to the cemetery at Green Bay. Instead he was sent to the care of their Jamaican friend Cuba Cornwallis, who was renowned for her treatment of sick officers; instead of bleeding them she would use herbal remedies and such comforts as a heated brick to warm their feet during the chill spells of fever. Above all, she was cheerful and, not expecting them to die, inspired them with a will to live.

Ill as he was, Nelson had several interviews with Governor Dalling, leaving him in no doubt as to the reasons for the disastrous delays to the expedition, saying that "happy it would have been" if Colonel Polson had ordered an immediate assault on the castle. But he spoke warmly of the colonel and wrote to him on 2nd June that Dalling had "expressed himself very much pleased with your conduct on every occasion and expressed a very great regard for you". He was writing to congratulate Polson on news that had reached Jamaica that same day, when an officer arrived from Nicaragua to report that the castle of San Juan had surrendered. In his despatches, Polson had given a full account of the fortunes of his expedition since it had sailed at the beginning of February and, realising that Nelson might be critical of his conduct, wrote, "I am persuaded that if our shot had held out, we should have had the fort a week sooner," adding, "As Captain Nelson goes to Jamaica, he can inform you of every delay and point of service as well as I can do, for he knows my very thoughts ... He was first on every service, whether by day or by night." He wrote in reply to Nelson's letter, "Thank you, my friend, for your kind congratulations. To you, without compliment, do I attribute, in a great measure, the cause".

As soon as he was strong enough to be moved, he accepted an invitation from Admiral Parker to recuperate at his country house, Admiral's Mountain, on Cooper's Hill near Kingston. It was a large, cool house built of stone; its wide verandah commanding a fine view of the harbour mouth and Port Royal. But when he arrived the Parkers were absent and he was well enough to suffer from boredom, writing, in the silence of the empty house to Hercules Ross, "Oh, Mr. Ross, what would I give to be at Port Royal. Lady P. not here, and the servants letting me lie as if a log and take no notice." When Lady Parker did arrive, he proved a difficult patient, refusing conventional medicines until they were brought to him by his hostess's youngest daughter, who thereupon became his "little nurse".

Dr. Moseley visited him and dismissed the possibility that he could take command of *Janus*; indeed, he began to doubt if the weakened body could withstand further tropical infections and suggested a return to the climate of England. Nelson himself realised how lucky he had been to survive thus far. "Dame Nature never failed me," he told Ross. "Green Bay had very often its jaws open to receive me."

Yet he was reluctant to leave while there was still hope of playing a part in great events on the Spanish Main. On receipt of Polson's despatch, Dalling had written an euphoric letter to Lord George Germain: "Now, my Lord, the communicating door to the South Sea having been burst open, what hinders his Majesty, should he so please, to carry the force of his Northern Army to the destruction of the Spanish Power, co-operating with a Southern squadron ...?"

While he himself would command the Northern Army, which would, he claimed, be "equal to the most serious attacks, from Chile to the kingdom of Mexico", he formally proposed that Nelson command the squadron in the Pacific. After telling Germain that "I have hitherto neglected a piece of justice to the service of Captain Nelson", and summarising his part in the San Juan expedition, he added:

> I most humbly entreat that his Majesty will be graciously pleased thro' your Lordship to manifest a satisfaction of his conduct and, in case a co-operating squadron should have been determined for the Southern Ocean, that he may be employed on that service. As for the service under my direction on this Northern one, Captain Nelson's constitution is rather too delicate. But such minds, my Lord, are most devoutly to be wished for government's sake.

But no sooner had he written this and begun planning his Northern Army, based upon more than three thousand regular troops now on their way from England, and, perhaps, American volunteers, than terrible news arrived from Nicaragua. This was a letter written by Colonel Kemble from the castle of San Juan on 19th May, 1780, soon after his arrival at "the inland Gibraltar of Spanish America". Even Nelson's account had not prepared him for what he saw there. "I was greatly surprised to find the troops under Colonel Polson's command in a most deplorable state ... I found everything in the greatest confusion." Almost everybody seemed to be sick with fever, dysentery or both and many had died, including several officers. There was an almost total lack of medical supplies; although plenty had been landed at the mouth of the river, so many Indians had deserted that there were not enough fit men to ferry them up to the castle. Colonel Kemble's reinforcements began to sicken, too. Their weeks "amidst the pestilential vapours of the harbour ... laid the seeds of a variety of diseases, which, aggravated by the fatigue ... in working the craft up the river, soon broke out in fluxes, dysenteries and other terrible disorders, which swept them off with such rapidity as to baffle all the skills and attention of the Medical Gentlemen".

When this news arrived, Nelson was on his way home. He had taken passage in the *Lion* on 4th September, under the care of Cornwallis, passing the westward-bound convoy, carrying the expected reinforcements for Nicaragua, in an Atlantic storm. On arrival at Portsmouth on 1st December he was so weak and fit for no more than the short journey by coach to London, where he stayed first with Cornwallis and then at Captain Locker's lodgings in Gray's Inn. It was there that he heard the sombre news from the Rio San Juan. Although Captain Despard had twice taken a canoe up the river as far as the lake and on the second occasion been supported by troops for the storming of the battery at San Carlos, Colonel Kemble, who had succeeded Polson in command, had lost heart. Within sight of success, he had decided not to attack, giving the shortage of rations as his excuse, and retreated down the river to the castle. There the soldiers continued to sicken and die.

When a naval officer, Commander James Clarke, was sent up the river on Dalling's instructions to assess the chances of another attempt to break into the lake, he was appalled by the sights he saw. On his way up the San Juan he passed the wreckage of the expedition: "Barrels of beef lying in some places, flour in others, arms and camp equipment lay scattered on several parts of the banks from the river mouth to the castle." There he found Despard in command, with all but one of the other officers sick, and he took Clarke upstream to the lake. This convinced him that the original strategy had been sound and that failure had been caused by "the troops delaying too long at the castle, which they might and ought to have stormed in the first instance, according to the plan proposed by Captain Nelson".

Disease had completed the defeat. Of nearly two thousand men sent up the river between February and November only about a hundred survived. In addition more than a thousand sailors died in the ships that had anchored off the mouth of the river and Captain Collingwood reckoned that out of about two hundred men of his original ship's company only about ten were still alive when he gave up command of the *Hinchinbroke* just before Christmas. Dalling was sternly reprimanded by Lord George Germain writing, "I lament exceedingly the dreadful havoc Death has made among the troops ... especially as from the entire failure of the Expedition no public benefit has been derived from the loss of so many brave men." The Governor was arraigned before a Committee of Enquiry, which decided that, but for the delays at the outset, which were blamed upon Lawrie and Polson, the enterprise might have succeeded. All knew that had Nelson's advice been heeded, this might have been the outcome. "When they arrived at the castle," wrote Dr. Moseley who had prudently watched the tragedy unfold from the safety of Jamaica, "as prompt in thought as bold in action, he advised the carrying of it instantly by assault. He knew the seasons were at hand and that there was no time to be lost. That his advice was not followed, this recital is a lamentable testimony." As it was, he concluded, the San Juan expedition had "been buried, with many of its kindred, in the silent tomb of government".

At the beginning of January 1781, a survivor of the expedition, a Captain Harrison of the Loyal Irish, arrived in Bath to recuperate, tell tales of the horrors he had faced and perhaps add that if Captain Nelson had had his way the conquest of Spanish America might have been well advanced. So when on 22nd January, the *Bath Journal* announced his arrival on the London coach, there was a ripple of excitement among those taking the medicinal waters in the Pump Room and enjoying soirées at the elegant new Assembly Rooms on Lansdown Hill. The place immediately reminded Nelson of Jamaica: not the winter weather, of course, although that was mild by Norfolk standards, but because of the hectic social activity, the card-playing and balls, the gouty old men eyeing the pretty young women and, amongst them, rich planters on leave from the West Indies. He himself was too ill to join them, staying with his elderly father, who had taken to escaping the North Sea gales by hiring rooms at the house of a Mr. Spry, an apothecary, at 2 Pierrepont Street near the Pump Room. So weak and haggard was Nelson that he purposely avoided the crowds, visiting the medicinal baths in the early evening when most were at dinner, or preparing for the night's entertainment.

The first few days were miserable and he wrote to Locker: "I have been so ill since I have been here that I was obliged to be carried to and from bed with the most excruciating tortures, but, thank God, I am now upon the mending hand. I am physicked three times a day, drink the waters three times and baths every other night, besides not drinking wine, which I think the worst of all." But within a month he was writing: "I have the perfect use of all my limbs except my left arm ... From the shoulder to my fingers' ends are as if half dead; but the surgeon and doctors give me hopes it will all go off. I most sincerely wish to be employed and hope it will not be long ... I must wish you good night and drink your health in a draught of my physician's cordial."

By March, he was fit again and able to enjoy the pleasures of Bath, including performances by Mrs. Sarah Siddons at the theatre in Orchard Street near his lodgings, where she was appearing in a repertory season. But when he visited his doctor's consulting room in Gay Street to settle his medical bill, Dr. Woodward refused payment. "Pray, Captain Nelson, allow me to follow what I consider to be my professional duty," he said. "Your illness, sir, has been brought on by serving your King and Country and, believe me, I love both too well to be able to receive any more."

Early in April, he felt strong enough to travel: first to stay with his uncle, William Suckling, at Kentish Town, from where he could visit the Admiralty to enquire about his next appointment; then to join the rest of his family at Burnham Thorpe. He broke the journey near Newbury in Berkshire to visit Captain Locker, who was staying with a naval friend, and tell him about Nicaragua. There he was reminded of his half-finished portrait, still stored at Mr. Rigaud's studio, and it was suggested that it might now be completed; his uniform changed to that of a post-captain and the castle of San Juan painted into the background. Nelson agreed, joking that Locker should advise the artist "to add beauty to it" and adding, with truth that applied not only to his sallow complexion and the lines of experience on his face, "It will not be in the least like what I am now."

CHAPTER III

In Search of Love
(1781–5)

"You will smile ... and say, 'This Horatio is for ever in love'."
– Captain Horatio Nelson to William Suckling from H.M.S. *Boreas*
off Nevis, 14th November, 1785

For an ambitious young captain of the Royal Navy, returned from war and recovered in health, three aims would be uppermost. The first would be hope of a new command. The second would be to visit his home and family. The third might be marriage. Nelson knew that he was lucky to have survived the campaign in Nicaragua and that it might have permanently impaired his health, yet he was avid for activity.

In London, he was told by Lord Sandwich, the First Lord of the Admiralty, that he would be offered another ship but that none was immediately available and that, in any case, he should continue his convalescence. Indeed, he had suffered a succession of relapses, the most worrying symptoms being the occasional partial paralysis of his left arm and leg so that he had been under the care of Mr. Robert Adair, the Surgeon-General to the Army. While staying with his uncle in Kentish Town, he saw his elder brother Maurice, still a clerk at the administrative Navy Office in the Strand, and together they decided to visit Burnham Thorpe in the summer of 1781.

Little had changed at the Parsonage House or in the village except that his brothers and sisters were all adults save Catherine, who had grown into a pretty and vivacious child of fourteen. After mixing with the strong, or extravagant characters in the Navy and the West Indies for so long, the lives and personalities of his own family must have seemed mild indeed. William, now a curate, was as self-centred as ever and, jealous of his younger brother's adventures, was talking of going to sea himself as a naval chaplain. Edmund had hopes of becoming a lawyer but was currently employed in Ostend as an accounts clerk in the office of the Boltons, prosperous merchants living and trading from the little port of Wells-next-the-Sea a few miles from Burnham Thorpe. Suckling, now aged sixteen, was apprenticed to a draper in the Suffolk town of Beccles and showed no aptitude for anything beyond shop-keeping.

Of the girls, only Susannah was married. When her uncle's legacy had freed her from wage-earning in the Bath millinery shop, she had lived at home and there she had met Thomas Bolton of the Wells family. They had married in 1780 and now she was pregnant. It was a good match for a country parson's daughter, who was at once at the heart of a jolly, comfortable family within easy visiting-distance of her former home and able to entertain her dashing naval brother at their table, or her husband would take him for a convivial evening with the Wells Club, which met to play cards twice a week at the Royal Standard, or the Three Tuns.

Nelson was concerned about his two younger sisters. Anne, too, had had to work as a shop-assistant but, instead of the genteel town of Bath, she had been employed in London at the Capital Lace Warehouse in Ludgate Street. She had been seduced, borne a child and been abandoned by her lover, and, at the age of twenty, returned to live with her father and younger sister. Little Catherine – Kate, Katty or Kitty, as her brother called her – was the liveliest of the three, with curly hair, large eyes, a tip-tilted nose and a rosebud mouth, and Nelson already had ambitions for her. "Although I am very fond of Mrs. Bolton," he said with the formality appropriate to a married woman, "yet I own I should not like to see my little Kate fixed in a Wells society."

There were only a few weeks to wait before a letter arrived from the Admiralty with instructions to take command of the frigate *Albemarle* of twenty-eight guns then having her bottom sheathed with copper-plate at Woolwich dockyard. On 23rd August, he arrived with his brother Maurice and Captain Locker to look her over; the latter was critical, remarking on her narrow gun-decks, lack of headroom and the probability that she would prove difficult to handle. Nelson would have none of this, praising her lines as "clean and bold". In his euphoria he thought his new ship's company "as good a set of men as ever I saw" and that there was "not a man or officer in her I would wish to change". But as the war to hold the American colonies was making demands upon the Royal Navy to protect convoys from attack by the French, she had not enough trained men for active service. By October her refit was complete and Nelson was under orders to take two other ships under command and cross the North Sea to bring a convoy back from the Baltic to Yarmouth roads. Arriving at the Nore, where the other frigate and a fourth-rate were waiting to join him, he learned that they, too, were seriously undermanned. Just then he heard that four big merchant ships, East Indiamen, were arriving in the Thames Estuary bound for the London docks. They were sailing in company under full press of canvas as protection against both French privateers off-shore and, inshore, the Royal Navy, which might attempt to impress some of their prime seamen as so often happened when homeward bound and in sight of port.

This was exactly what Nelson had in mind. A decade before, after his voyage in a merchant ship, he would have sympathised with sailors snatched from the welcome of their waiting families and forced to sea again under the rough discipline of a King's ship. But now he did not hesitate to give chase to the East Indiamen, flying a signal ordering that they bring to. The big ships had no intention of complying for they were well manned and armed and together more than a match for a frigate. Nelson ordered a blank charge to be fired from a nine-pounder gun as a warning but this, too, was ignored and the ships, led by one named the *Haswell*, swept on. Probably the masters of the East Indiamen expected a shot across their bows before they shook off the frigate but they did not know her captain, in whom recent experience had implanted ruthlessness. As the *Albemarle* sailed parallel with the *Haswell*, the latter's master noticed that the frigate's gun-ports were open and her guns run out; a moment later the flame and smoke of a broadside burst from her and tossed water-spouts around the merchantman. A second broadside followed, also aimed to miss; then a single shot, falling close alongside. The *Haswell* hove to, as did her companions, and "finding the *Albemarle* yard-arm to yard-arm with them", as Nelson put it, "they submitted". After taking as many seamen as his three ships required, he noted in his log that he had fired twenty-six nine-pounder and one eighteen-pounder shot in the subduing of his own countrymen.

The ruthless mood persisted, for when his little squadron had crossed the North Sea and arrived off the Danish fortress of Elsinore they were accorded none of the expected civilities: no ensigns were dipped; no salutes fired; and a mere midshipman came aboard the *Albemarle* to ask the names of the British ships and their destination. Nelson took this as a deliberate slight arising from strained political relations between Britain and Denmark, so he himself received the midshipman and answered his questions: "The *Albemarle* in one of His Britannic Majesty's ships; you are at liberty, sir, to count her guns as you go down the side; and you may assure the Danish admiral that, if necessary, they shall be well served." After the boy had left, he sent a message ashore, saying that he would salute Kronenberg castle with nineteen of those guns provided the courtesy was returned. It was.

A month later he escorted a convoy of nearly three hundred sail across the North Sea, himself continuing south to anchor in the Downs roadstead, between the town of Deal and the Goodwin Sands, where his ship was to be based. Letters from his brother William continued to arrive, begging help in becoming a naval chaplain, and attempts to dissuade him seemed ineffective. "I hope you have lost all ideas of going to sea," Horatio had replied, "for the more I see of chaplains of men-of-war, the more I dread seeing my brother in such a disagreeable situation of life." But the pestering continued and Nelson tried to frighten him away by suggesting that vacancies sometimes occurred through death in battle: "I got my rank by a shot killing a post-captain and I most sincerely hope I shall, when I go, go out of the world the same way: then we go all in the line of our profession – a parson praying, a captain fighting." He made much, too, of the discomfort, for it was a foul winter of constant gales and the frigate was on continual convoy duty along what her captain described as "a coast full of wrecks – twice we have parted from our anchors; the North Seas are dreadful at this time of year." Indeed, at the end of January, 1782, while Nelson was ashore in Deal, an East Indiaman's cable parted in the anchorage and she was blown aboard the *Albemarle*, carrying away her bowsprit, bringing down her foremast and damaging her hull and rigging so severely that she had to struggle around the coast to Portsmouth for repairs.

While in the dockyard, ships began to arrive with news that their convoy had been attacked by a Spanish squadron after leaving Jamaica and among their passengers was General Dalling. Now Nelson learned of the full extent of the disaster in Nicaragua and of the fate of his friends; most of them had died but Polson and Despard had survived, the latter having been accorded the local rank of lieutenant-colonel and appointed governor of the island and dependencies of Rattan off the Mosquito Shore. Dalling himself had been cleared by the court of enquiry – the blame for the fatal delays being accorded to the senior surviving officers, Lawrie, Polson and Kemble – and had begun to plan another expedition to sieze the Dutch island of Curaçoa. These and political problems in Jamaica had led to a summons of recall from Lord George Germain which he had ignored until the end of the year, when, to forestall the expected letter of dismissal, he had boarded the ship for England. The day before he had sailed, General Cornwallis had had to surrender his garrison at Yorktown to the American rebels and the fall of the British Government, including Lord George Germain, followed in March as Dalling arrived at Portsmouth.

At the beginning of April, Nelson was ordered on more convoy duty, this time to cross the Atlantic again to what he called "the Grand Theatre of Actions", which was living up to its name. Ashore in America, the British were facing defeat – the fall of Yorktown had been accompanied by the loss of Charleston and Savannah – but there had been success at sea. On 12th April, Admiral Rodney, a veteran of the Seven Years War, had caught up with a French fleet under the Comte de Grasse, escorting a troop-convoy bound for another attempted invasion of Jamaica. The transports had escaped but de Grasse had been decisively defeated – and himself captured together with five ships of the line – off Guadeloupe at what was to be called the Battle of the Saints. Jamaica and, indeed, all the British islands of the Caribbean, had been saved but what caught Nelson's imagination were Rodney's tactics. Instead of taking his ships into action in the line of battle as laid down in the Royal Navy's *Fighting Instructions*, he had burst through the French line to fight a confused, ship-to-ship battle in which the more effective British gunnery was decisive.

His own task was to escort a convoy from Cork to the mouth of the St. Lawrence river and then cruise between Cape Cod and Boston in search of American or French shipping. Again he was to benefit from his aptitude for making friends. On 12th July, while cruising off Plymouth, where the Pilgrim Fathers had landed, he took a schooner, the *Harmony*, whose American skipper, Nathaniel Carver, proved to have pro-British sympathies and be a skilled pilot in these difficult waters. Nelson ordered that the schooner be converted into a tender for the frigate, to be used for scouting and boarding prizes, and that Carver should remain on board the *Albemarle* as a pilot. He was impressed by the stoicism and good humour with which the American accepted this and by his professional skill when, two days later, the sails of four French ships of the line and a frigate appeared on the horizon and gave chase.

At Carver's suggestion, Nelson ran his frigate among the shoals of the St. George's Bank and, although, as he said, the French "gave me a pretty dance for between nine or ten hours", the prospect of running aground in the darkness persuaded their captains to sheer away before dusk. The French frigate followed but, when her captain saw the *Albemarle*'s main-topsail backed so that she lost way and then turn to present her broadside, he, too, flinched from the prospect of fighting amongst shoals, turned and steered for the safety of deep waters. Nelson thanked his pilot, "You have rendered us, sir, a very essential service and it is not the custom of English seamen to be ungrateful. In the name, therefore, and with the approbation of the officers of this ship, I return your schooner and this certificate of your good conduct. Farewell and may God bless you!" He therefore gave Carver a note briefly describing his services, that he could show to any other British captain he might encounter under similar circumstances. So the *Harmony* sailed away and the *Albemarle* continued her cruise, which had become as uncomfortable as it was dangerous, for the ship had been without fresh meat and vegetables for more than six weeks and some of her crew were showing the early symptoms of scurvy. Carver had noticed this and, the day after he had been released, put out from Plymouth again, ran alongside the frigate and shouted for permission to come aboard. He had brought with him a gift of four sheep, poultry and sacks of vegetables.

As a remedy this seemed too late, for the ship's company was becoming increasingly listless and sick. There was no further prospect of action because the four French ships proved to have been fugitives from Rodney, chivvied into Boston by Rear-Admiral Lord Hood. The *Albemarle* was now ordered to Quebec, of which her captain had heard so much from friends who had fought there twenty-three years before. As the frigate entered the St. Lawrence river, her crew delighted in a climate that was new to most of them: dry, bracing air; warm, sunny days and crisply cold nights. They sailed past wooded hills, where the leaves were beginning to show their autumn colours of red, brown and gold. Quebec itself stood on a bluff high above the river, its fortifications suggesting a gigantic counterpart to the Castillo de la Inmaculada Concepción at the tropical extremity of the Grand Theatre of Actions. When the ship anchored below the citadel on 17th September, 1781, twenty-two of her men were sent ashore to hospital, while her captain, himself "knocked up with the scurvy", urgently ordered fresh provisions. The new diet and the stimulating air quickly took effect and, within a month, Nelson was writing to his father, "Health, that greatest of blessings, is what I never truly enjoyed until I saw Fair Canada."

There was a lively social life in Quebec, although society was split between the French, the British garrison and their families and newly arrived American loyalists, driven from their homes in the rebellious colonies. Soon after the *Albemarle*'s arrival, the twenty-second anniversary of the coronation of King George III was celebrated with the firing of salutes, parades and balls and it was then that Horatio Nelson fell in love. This was the first opportunity to turn his mind to the question of marriage since he had been promoted to post-captain; not only because his duties had relaxed and his health improved, but that suitable young women were not often met in seaports and the daughters of the British gentry in Jamaica were sent home for their education and to find husbands.

Mary Simpson, the daughter of Colonel Saunders Simpson, the Provost-Marshal of the garrison, was aged sixteen and something of a beauty, handsome rather than pretty in the manner of the French girls as was suggested by a hymn of praise published in the *Quebec Gazette*:

Sure you will listen to my call,
Since beauty and Quebec's fair nymphs I sing.
Henceforth Diana is Miss S—ps–n see,
As noble and majestic is her air . . .

She lived with her family in an imposing house near the St. Louis Gate, where some of the grey stone houses that recalled the architecture of the provincial towns of northern France had now been adorned with elegant, white-painted door-cases by the British. The liking between Nelson and Colonel Simpson was mutual and, while the former could talk about recent service in Nicaragua, the latter was yet another who could remember Wolfe and the battle on the Heights of Abraham, a few minutes' walk from his house. Mary herself was impressed by Captain Nelson, who, although only just past his twenty-fourth birthday, she found "erect and stern of aspect", but with considerable charm.

Nelson made another friend in Quebec of a shrewd, sharp-featured Scottish merchant, government contractor, shipowner and member of the city's legislative council, Alexander Davison, eight years his senior. Not being able to confide his longings for Mary Simpson to his own officers, he found a confidant in Davison and was soon discussing his prospects of marriage with mounting urgency as the girl showed no inclination to exchange her life as a belle of a garrison town for that of the wife of a young naval captain, whose old-fashioned uniform suggested that he was living on little more than his pay.

After the flamboyant autumn colours of the woods around Quebec, winter came early and sharp so that the St. Lawrence began to freeze in October and Nelson suddenly visualised his frigate ice-bound in the river until spring, while he attended Miss Simpson at the fireside of the house by the St. Louis Gate. Just as this could have become reality, orders arrived for him to escort a convoy of troopships to New York and he complained, "a very *pretty* job at this late season of the year, for our sails are at this moment frozen to the yards". On the 13th of the month, he dropped downriver to the anchorage to await a wind but, next day, Davison, walking to his office near the quay, was surprised to see one of the *Albemarle*'s boats alongside and her captain striding into the town. When the Scot asked his friend what had brought him back, he replied, probably in words less pompous than those that Davison recalled, "I find it utterly impossible to leave this place without waiting on her whose society has so much added to its charms and laying myself and my fortunes at her feet." Davison tried to dissuade him, saying, "Your utter ruin, situated as you are at present, must inevitably follow." "Then let it follow," snapped Nelson, "for I am resolved to do it." "And I also," replied Davison, "positively declare that you shall not." So a forlorn Captain Nelson returned to his ship to find that final orders had arrived; that he was to join Lord Hood's squadron off New York; and that was likely to mean excitement. Dreams of domesticity with Mary Simpson faded as he wrote to his father, "I think it very likely that we shall go to the Grand Théâtre of Actions, the West Indies."

A month after the decisive exchange with Davison, Nelson was shepherding twenty-three transports into the anchorage off Staten Island where Lord Hood lay with twelve sail of the line. His first call was upon Rear-Admiral the Honourable Robert Digby, who commanded the North American Station and was based at New York. "You are come on a fine station for making prize-money," said the admiral in greeting. "Yes, sir," replied Nelson, "but the West Indies is the station for honour." His priggish reply was a hint that he hoped to be allowed to join Rear-Admiral Hood's squadron, which was about to sail for Jamaica. His zest for glory had returned and he wrote to a friend, "My interest at home is next to nothing, the name of Nelson being little known; it may be different one of these days."

Soon afterwards he met Hood, an old friend of his uncle's, for the first time and, as he went aboard the flagship, he caught the attention of a seventeen-year-old midshipman. This was Prince William Henry,[1] the third son of the King, who had embarked upon a naval career. His first meeting with Nelson and his account of him explained the remarkable impression he made.

"Captain Nelson," recalled the prince, "appeared to be the merest boy of a captain I ever beheld and his dress was worthy of attention. He had on a full-laced uniform: his lank, unpowdered hair was tied in a stiff Hessian tail of an extraordinary length; the old-fashioned flaps on his waistcoat added to the general appearance of quaintness of his figure and produced an appearance which particularly attracted my notice; for I had never seen anything like it before, nor could imagine who he was, nor what he came about. My doubts were, however, removed when Lord Hood introduced me to him. There was something irresistibly pleasing in his address and conversation; and an enthusiasm when speaking on professional subjects that showed he was no common being."

The *Albemarle* moved up the East River and anchored half a mile from what her captain called "York Town" to make desertion more difficult, for here the rebel army was close at hand and offering sanctuary and a new life to refugees from the harsh life of the Royal Navy. Even so, two men managed to desert from boats sent ashore for provisions and fresh

[1] The future King William IV.

water; one of them a corporal of the Royal Marines, charged with the prevention of desertion. Nelson did not care for the company of his fellow-officers at New York, who emulated Admiral Digby's interest in prize-money; "Money is the great object here; nothing else is attended to," he said. Even when ordered south with Hood's squadron it was impossible to shake off this preoccupation. While cruising off Jamaica early in 1783, Nelson gave chase to a French merchantman which had sailed past the rest of the British squadron without attracting attention. Boarding her, he discovered that she was loaded with replacement masts and yards for the French fleet and, as Hood's ships were in urgent need of sixteen new topmasts, they had more than a hundred to choose from. Nelson estimated this cargo and the ship to be worth £20,000 in prize-money but his elation evaporated when Lord Hood let it be known that as the ship had been captured within sight of the squadron, he and his other captains would claim most of it.

To disappointment was added humiliation when, early in March, he was sent on detached duty with another frigate and two smaller ships under command to dislodge the French from Turk's Island at the south-eastern extremity of the Bahamas. On arrival he sent an officer ashore with a summons to surrender and, when this was refused, ordered an immediate assault on the fortifications by landing parties of marines and sailors. Confident that what should have been ordered at the castle of San Juan would succeed here, Nelson was startled to see the landing parties greeted with cannon-fire and well aimed volleys of musketry. Their commanding officer sent word that they could advance no further without heavy loss and asked for further orders. Realising that such casualties for so small a prize might not be acceptable when the war seemed to be ending in defeat for the British, Nelson ordered immediate evacuation and a final bombardment of the island before sailing away.

Blame for the defeat had to be accepted by Nelson. Boldness had not been enough; he had under-estimated the enemy's strength which turned out to have been some hundred and fifty French regular troops entrenched with guns manned by sailors and mounted on well-sited earthworks. Yet any reprimand for impetuosity from Lord Hood was set aside on his return to the squadron for news had arrived that a ceasefire had been agreed in January so that peace negotiations could continue. As a goodwill gesture, Prince William was to make an official visit to Havana, using the *Albemarle* as his royal yacht, while Hood's squadron cruised just over the horizon, and Nelson was to be his aide-de-camp. He basked in the patronage, writing to Captain Locker that the admiral "treats me as if I was his son and will, I am convinced, give me anything I can ask of him: nor is my situation with Prince William less flattering."

After two days ashore in Cuba with the royal midshipman, Nelson was ordered to carry dispatches to the garrison of St. Augustine in Florida and then cross the Atlantic to Portsmouth. On anchoring at Spithead on 25th June, he wrote to Locker, "After all my tossing about in various climates, here at last am I arrived, safe and sound." A few days later the crew of the *Albemarle* were paid off, although their captain was gratified when, to a man, they volunteered to follow him to another ship if one was to be offered him. Their loyalty was returned for some days after his arrival in London, he wrote to Locker, "My time, ever since I arrived in Town, has been taken up in attempting to get the wages due to my *good fellows* for various ships they have served in during the war. The disgust of the seamen to the Navy is all owing to the infernal plan of turning them over from ship to ship so that men cannot be attached to their officers, or the officers care twopence about them." But the war was over and Nelson felt that he had earned some relaxation ashore, writing to his friend Hercules Ross, who had returned from Jamaica to Scotland: "I have closed the war without a fortune: but I trust and, from the attention that has been paid to me, believe that there is not a speck on my character. True honour, I hope, predominates in my mind far above riches."

Ashore, Nelson's horizons were widening and he determined on further self-education by learning to speak French, taking the advice of Prince William, who was off to the Continent for that purpose. As a travelling-companion, he found an old shipmate from the *Bristol*, Captain James Macnamara and together they set out in mid-October, stopping at West Malling in Kent to spend a night with Captain Locker before embarking at Dover and crossing to Calais in three and a half hours. Originally, Nelson had thought of staying at Lille but, as he put it, "Mac advised me to go first to St. Omer, as he had experienced the difficulty of attempting to fix in any place where there are no English." The first stage of the journey, rattling over cobbles in a badly sprung coach, took them to Marquise where, as Nelson recalled, they were shown "into an inn – they called it – I should have called it a pigstye: we were shown into a room with two straw beds and, with great difficulty, they mustered up clean sheets; and gave us two pigeons for supper upon a dirty cloth and wooden-handled knives – *O what a transition from happy England!* After a good laugh we went to bed and slept very soundly till morning."

On the road to Boulogne, Montreuil and, finally, St. Omer, Nelson noted that there seemed to be "no middling class of people", for this was France on the eve of revolution. After squalid inns and dirty towns contrasting with splendid prospects of noblemen's estates and country houses, it came as a surprise to find St. Omer "instead of a dirty, nasty town ... a large city, well paved, good streets and well-lighted". Here a

Madame La Mourie kept a genteel lodging-house catering particularly for English guests and where the learning of French was made more agreeable by the vivacious daughters of the house who served breakfast to the two young officers and played cards with them in the evenings. "Therefore," declared Nelson, "I must learn French if 'tis only for the pleasure of talking to them, for they do not speak a word of English."

The town was crowded with English visitors, enjoying unrestricted peacetime travel. Two other naval captains, named Ball and Shepherd, were recognised by their uniforms, although Nelson considered that the newly introduced gold epaulettes on their blue coats made them "great coxcombs" because this was still regarded as a showy French fashion. A clergyman named Andrews and his family were also staying at Madame La Mourie's and one of his two daughters put an end to any serious plan to learn French. "I must take care of my heart, I assure you," wrote Nelson to his brother William after describing her as a beautiful girl of about twenty. She and her sister played the piano and sang to the two young officers, who lost interest in playing cards with French girls who could not speak English. A month after their meeting, Nelson was writing to his brother, "My heart is quite secured against the French beauties: I almost wish I could say as much for an English young lady, the daughter of a clergyman with whom I am just going to dine and spend the day. She has such accomplishments, that had I a million of money, I am sure I should at this moment make her an offer of marriage, and she has no fortune." Another month passed and he was again writing to William: "I must conclude as I am engaged to tea and spend the evening with the most accomplished woman my eyes beheld and when a lady's in the case, all other things they must give place."

Miss Andrews was not only pretty, musical and charming; she was sympathetic and sympathy was needed because, soon after his arrival at St Omer, Nelson received the shockingly unexpected news of the death of his sister Anne. She had accompanied their father to Bath for the winter and, as Nelson had heard, caught a chill "occasioned by coming out of the ball-room immediately after dancing", and, after nine days of illness, had died. "My surprise and grief upon the occasion are ... more to be felt than described," he wrote to his brother, then, turning his thoughts from the sad, wronged figure of Anne to her younger sister, asked, "What is to become of poor Kate? My income shall always be at her service and she shall never want a protector and sincere friend while I exist." Meanwhile in St. Omer, the clergyman and his daughter offered spiritual and emotional solace.

For all his talk about money, Nelson was well aware that he could not afford to keep a wife in the manner he considered suitable. The only member of his family from whom he could expect financial support was his surviving uncle, William Suckling, and to him he wrote in January 1784, in a style suggesting that preoccupation with Miss Andrews had allowed the streak of ruthlessness in his character to show without veneer of tact. "The critical moment of my life is now arrived," he wrote, "that either I am to be happy or miserable – it depends solely on you. You may possibly think I am going to ask too much. I have led myself up with hopes you will not ... There is a lady I have seen, of a good family and connexions but with a small fortune – £1,000 I understand. The whole of my income does not exceed £130 per annum. Now I must come to the point – will you, if I should marry, allow me £100 a year until my income is increased to that sum, either by employment or any other way? A very few years, I hope, would turn something up, if my friends will but exert themselves." Perhaps his uncle could help arrange a new appointment for him, he suggested, with the uncharacteristic proposal that this might be some sinecure, like commanding a guardship, where his personal presence might not be required, or that he might take service with the squadron maintained by the East India Company.

"You must excuse the freedom with which this letter is dictated," he continued. "Not to have been plain and explicit in my distress had been cruel to myself. If nothing can be done for me, I know what I have to trust to. Life is not worth preserving without happiness; and I care not where I may linger out a miserable existence. I am prepared to hear your refusal and have fixed my resolution if that should happen; but in every situation, I shall be a well-wisher to you and your family and pray that they, or you, may never know the pangs which at this instant tear my heart."

His uncle agreed to help, as Nelson discovered on his return to London later that month, but this was now needless as the girl was not herself contemplating marriage. The encounter ended sadly but gently – for Nelson remained friends with the Andrews family – and he could try to forget her by what he called "running the ring of pleasure". London, he discovered, "has so many charms that a man's time is wholly taken up". The excitement was not sexual but political. With the loss of the American colonies, England was in turmoil and a general election imminent. Even professional sailors caught the political fever; Lord Hood was standing for Parliament, as was Locker's friend, Captain Kingsmill, and young officers were infected by their seniors' enthusiasm. Nelson had no set opinions of his own partly because his father had always flinched from such worldliness and partly because of divided loyalties: the Nelsons and their kind in the middle classes were Tory by tradition and inclination, whereas their lordly kinsmen, such as the Walpoles and the Townshends were Whigs. He himself admired the robust patriotism of William Pitt, who had just been appointed Prime

Minister at the age of twenty-five and whose lanky looks recalled his hero, Wolfe. But the Walpoles remained the most powerful of his potential patrons and his brother William, recognising where his interests lay, had been quick to offer them his vote at Cambridge University.

The talk in London was all of the coming election, whether at the King's *levée* in St. James's Palace, whither he accompanied Hood, or in Alexander Davison's comfortable, panelled rooms at Lincoln's Inn where Nelson would go, shed his "iron-bound" naval uniform coat, don one of his host's silk dressing-gowns and talk long into the night. Dining at Hood's smart new house in Wimpole Street, he was so inspired by the possibilities of politics that for a few days he thought of trying to stand for Parliament himself, the problem being as much the difficulty of choosing which party to support as the practicalities of finding a constituency. It came to nothing. "I have done with politics," he sighed. "Let who will get in, I shall be left out."

He thought of returning to the Continent for the summer to continue learning French, telling William wistfully, "I return to many charming women but no charming woman will return with me." Instead he considered buying a horse and returning to Burnham Thorpe, where he was gratified to hear that young Kate was learning to ride, "that she may be no trouble to us", with an enthusiasm that matched his own. Whilst trying to make up his mind, he joined his father in Bath. As so often happened in his profession, the future was taken out of his hands by the Admiralty and on 18th March, 1784, he was appointed to command the *Boreas*, a frigate of twenty-eight guns named after the north wind. As a post-captain commanding such a ship he could take a few boys to sea with him, as his uncle Maurice had taken him, to train as officers; this gave him a chance to make a generous and gentlemanly gesture to the girl who had refused him. Her young brother George had wanted to emulate his sister's suitor, so he wrote to their father offering George Andrews a berth in his frigate and a chance of glory.

There was another, less welcome name to be added to the ship's muster-book: that of his brother William, whose enthusiasm for the prospect of life at sea as a chaplain was undimmed. Nelson tried to sound enthusiastic himself while limiting his invitation by stressing his brother's responsibilities ashore. Nothing would give him greater pleasure than to take him aboard, he wrote, but while their father was at Bath he could hardly leave Kate on her own in Norfolk; when he returned for the summer "there can be no possible objection to your taking a trip for a few months and to return by the winter to keep our father and sister company at that lonesome place". Irritation with his brother showed when answering what must have sounded like a boorish question. "You ask, by what interest did I get a ship?" he replied. "I answer, having served with credit was my recommendation to Lord Howe, First Lord of the Admiralty." He added, "Come when you please, I shall be ready to receive you. Bring your canonicals and sermons. Do not bring any Burnham servants."

This afterthought came as result of news that had reached him while his ship still lay at Woolwich, where he had joined her. Not only was he to return to the Caribbean – not the Indian ocean, as he had hoped – but he was to be loaded with passengers. He would have to take thirty midshipmen, most of them destined for other ships on the station; but that was no cause for resentment since he enjoyed the company of the young. They were to include a distant cousin of his own, Maurice Suckling, young George Andrews and a son of Rear-Admiral Sir Richard Hughes, his senior officer on the Leeward Islands Station, who would be accompanied by his mother and his sister. The ship, he noted, would be "pretty well filled with lumber".

Most of these embarked at Portsmouth in April, 1784, and his heart sank on meeting Lady Hughes and her daughter. Not only would he have to listen to the mother's "infernal clack" all the way to Barbados, but the daughter, Rosy, was animated but plain, clearly in search of a husband and had her eye on him. There was no escape in so small a ship and, when the rough spring weather moderated and they were in gentler seas towards Madeira, he made a list of those walking his quarterdeck at seven o'clock one May evening: headed by Lady Hughes, Miss Hughes, himself and his brother, it included the purser and his wife, and twenty-seven officers, non-commissioned officers and midshipmen. Once he had made it politely obvious that he was not interested in Rosy, he found mother and daughter "very pleasant good people: but they are an incredible expense". His temper was improving with the mid-Atlantic weather.

The captain's courtesy drew an admiring response from the admiral's wife, who, accustomed to the ways of the Navy, took note of the attention he paid to the thirty boys in his charge; particularly to those intimidated by the prospect of life aboard a small, cramped, lurching ship, always under threat of violence in some form. "The timid he never rebuked," she was to recall, "but always wished to show them he desired nothing of them that he would not instantly do himself: and I have known him say – 'Well, sir, I am going a race to the mast-head and beg I may meet you there.' No denial could be given to such a wish and the poor fellow instantly began his march." The captain never remarked upon the manner in which the mast was climbed and, meeting the boy at the top, "began instantly speaking in the most cheerful manner and saying how much a person was to be pitied who could fancy there was any danger, or even anything disagreeable, in the attempt. After this excellent example, I have seen the timid youth lead another and rehearse his captain's words".

Each morning he helped the boys with their lessons in navigation and "at twelve o'clock was first on deck with his quadrant" to calculate the position of the ship. As they approached the tropics, he lectured them on the importance of hygiene and diet in that climate but also when they reached the Equator, skylarked with them in the traditional horseplay of "Crossing the Line" ceremony. When, in the last week of June, they sighted the hills of Barbados and anchored in Carlisle Bay, he did not forget "my children", as he called them. Invited to join Admiral and Lady Hughes at dinner with General Shirley, the Governor of the Leeward Islands, he said, "You must permit me, Lady Hughes, to carry one of my aide-de-camps with me." On arrival at the Governor's residence, he introduced him: "Your Excellency must excuse me for bringing one of my midshipmen, as I make it a rule to introduce them to all the good company I can as they have few to look up to, beside myself, during the time they are at sea."

The company of his superior officers was not to be good by his own standards. "The Admiral and all about him are great ninnies," he thought and as for Hughes himself, "I do not like him, he bows and scrapes too much for me." Certainly the admiral seemed to have been cowed by the rich and powerful traders of the Caribbean into what Captain Nelson regarded as a dereliction of duty. The war had ended, leaving a difficult legacy in relations between existing British colonies and those that had rebelled and become the United States of America. As Nelson himself put it, "The Americans, when colonists, possessed almost all the trade from America to our West India islands; and on the return of peace, they forgot, on this occasion, they became foreigners and, of course, had no right to trade in the British Colonies." This embargo was supposed to have been made law by the Navigation Act under which such trading was to be stopped, when necessary, by the Royal Navy and that was exactly what the new arrival proposed to do. However, he found that "Our Governors and Custom-house Officers pretended that by the Navigation Act they had a right to trade; and all the West Indians wished what was so much for their interest." Even Admiral Hughes was "led by the advice of the islanders to admit the Yankees to a Trade; at least to wink at it."

Captain Nelson was unlikely to comply and was given the independence to do his duty because the Leeward Islands Station was split into two; Admiral Hughes controlling the southern waters from Barbados while Nelson was appointed senior officer in the northern, where he would be based upon the island of Antigua. Before leaving Carlisle Bay, the latter gave a brisk demonstration of his interpretation of duty and courtesy, writing in the log of the *Boreas*: "Sailed the French Schooner of

War. Fired two nine-pounders at the fort for not hoisting her Colours to the French King's vessel going out." Sailing for Antigua, he stopped at the French island of Martinique and gave the authorities there a stiff lecture on neglecting such courtesies to his ship, realising that to fire on their fort might start another war.

Frustration had shortened his temper. This was compounded of his outraged sense of duty; the knowledge that on arrival at Antigua he would have to lay up his ship during the three or four months of the hurricane season without opportunity to show his admiral how the Navigation Act was intended to be implemented; and sexual frustration since there was no outlet for romantic and libidinous love and Midshipman Andrews was a constant reminder of his desirable sister. The coming months held out no promise but of discomfort and deepening frustration since the "hurricane hole", where he would spend them, was English Harbour, an almost land-locked succession of deep basins among rocky, scrub-covered hills, dried by the wind and sun and renowned for the ferocity of the mosquitoes.

The *Boreas* arrived off the harbour mouth on 28th July in "hard rain", the downpour blotting out the view of the new fortifications nearing completion on the commanding heights. Without wind, the frigate had to be towed by her boats between the batteries at the harbour mouth and then warped into the inner basin by cables rove through the rings of great anchors embedded ashore and hauled by the ship's capstan. She anchored among several other frigates and smaller vessels off the dockyard and, as soon as the sky cleared, her sodden sails were loosened to dry. As his ship lay steaming in the sun, her captain went ashore to pay his respects to the Commissioner of the Navy, who administered the dockyard, and formally take command as senior officer of the northern division of the Leeward Islands Station.

Prospects for the coming months were depressing. The ship would have to be checked for flaws; some repairs would certainly be necessary, her decks would be caulked and her sides painted; possibly she would have to be heeled at the careening berth for her bottom to be scraped clear of barnacles and copper plates replaced to protect the hull from the wood-boring teredo worm. Stores and ammunition would have to be checked and replenished and the marines sent ashore to drill and exercise. Social life would be meagre. For most of the ship's company it would be limited to evenings spent sitting on the low wall surrounding the water-catchment just outside the dockyard, chatting, drinking cheap rum and consorting with negro slave-women. The officers might establish a mess ashore together with those of other ships in the hands of carpenters and painters but, for them, too, drinking would be the easiest way to pass the time. Cuthbert Collingwood, and his younger brother Wilfred, were both commanding frigates in the Caribbean and the former had been in Carlisle Bay on board the *Mediator* when the *Boreas* had arrived and told him something of the couple he was about to encounter as they had taken passage in his ship on their way to the Leeward Islands. They were, he said, charming and hospitable.

The Commissioner did not, however, seem to be the sort of man who would appeal to Nelson. Captain John Moutray was aged sixty-one and senior to Nelson by twenty-one years in the Captain's List, although he was now on half-pay and employed as a civilian. His record as a naval officer was, by Nelson's standards, deplorable. Throughout the Seven Years War, he had commanded a hospital ship and then been unemployed for seven years when, thanks to social and political influence, he had first succeeded Locker in command of a frigate and then been promoted into ships of the line. In 1780, he had commanded the close escort of the convoy of about seventy ships bound for Madeira, the East Indies and the Caribbean, which had been attacked by a French and Spanish squadron in the Atlantic. Fifty-five merchant ships had been lost but all the escorting warships had escaped. At the subsequent court of enquiry, Captain Moutray confessed that he had ordered the convoy to disperse on seeing the odds against them, "seven line of battleships and a frigate, being well up in the wake" of his own ship. Shipowners, merchants and insurers, who suffered by the disaster, blamed the government, which, in turn, "endeavoured by all means in their power to shift the principal cause of the misfortune", as a contemporary historian put it, "to the conduct of Captain Moutray".

As a result he had been relieved of his command but when the political wind shifted two years later, his connections won him command of another ship of the line and he had been present at Admiral Rodney's relief of besieged Gibraltar. On his return to England he had been offered the appointment at English Harbour, where he had been for about eighteen months. Despite his professional reputation, Nelson liked him, for he was a Lowland Scot of breeding and invited visiting captains to dine at his residence, a comfortable, wide-verandah'd house named "Windsor" on the hill behind the dockyard. But it was irritating that the Commissioner, a civil servant, still wore his post-captain's uniform and affected the rank he had done so little to achieve.

Feminine company was not to be expected at English Harbour. The capital, St. John's, and most of what little society Antigua had to offer, was twelve miles distant down a dusty track and what women might be met at the dockyard and neighbouring plantation houses would be a few wives, weathered by the tropics, for any girls like the Misses Simpson and Andrews would have been sent to England for their education and health.

So it was with delight that Nelson met the Commissioner's wife, Mary Moutray. She was a woman of fashion, witty and attractive, with manners and conversation to be expected in the drawing-rooms of fashionable London but not in a Caribbean "hurricane hole". She and her husband at once invited Nelson to regard their house as his own and to sleep there while his quarters in the frigate were being painted.

Mary Moutray was just past thirty – Nelson was now twenty-four – and as pretty as she was sophisticated; her wit suggested by wrinkles of amusement around the eyes. The daughter of a naval officer, Captain Thomas Pemble, and brought up in Berwickshire, she had met and married John Moutray, a widower from a family of Fifeshire lairds, when she was twenty. Moving to London, their connections with the Scottish aristocracy – she was a particular friend of Louisa, the daughter of the Marquess of Lothian, who had married General Lord George Lennox – won her the favour of smart society and, in particular, the Duke and Duchess of Richmond. She had borne twins – James, whose godfather was Lord Hood, and Kate – who were now aged eleven. Nelson – ready to fall in love again – was enchanted by her, forgot his irritation with her elderly husband and found life at English Harbour transformed, writing to Locker, "Was it not for Mrs. Moutray, who is *very, very* good to me, I should almost hang myself at this infernal hole."

Her presence softened the harsh life: the heat and seasonal storms; the boredom and the discipline. Soon after the *Boreas* arrived, an example had to be made to ships' companies, to whom cheap rum and even desertion seemed to offer escape, and a seaman was "flogged round the fleet": taken by boat, trussed upright, from ship to ship and lashed with the cat-o'-nine-tails alongside each. Thereafter, the number of floggings was below average and when Nelson had to order all hands to attend the hanging of a sailor from the *Unicorn*, he was able, while the noose dangled from the yard-arm, to read Admiral Hughes's letter of pardon. Otherwise, the time passed easily and the tempo of social activity increased at the end of August with the arrival of the Governor to inspect the new fortifications and barracks he had ordered to be built on what had been named after him Shirley Heights. It was no loss when, a month later, William Nelson, having found that life as a naval chaplain was not so romantic in the context of heat, mosquitoes and the cramped quarters and smells of a ship and human bodies, thankfully took passage for England. His brother wrote to him from the Moutrays' house before he can have been halfway across the Atlantic, with equal lightness of heart, "I hope you are quite recovered and drawing very near to old England. The weather here has been so very hot since you left us, that I firmly believe you would hardly have weathered the fever ... I have been living

here for this past week, whilst my ship has been painting ... Mrs.
Moutray desires her love to you."

The gales had died and the thunderclouds rolled away by the end of
October and, after "a grand dinner" on board one of his ships, Nelson
led his squadron to sea, on a mission to the Virgin Islands, where he was
to look for possible sites for the settlement of American loyalists. Soon
after his return to English Harbour, he saw the frigate *Mediator* enter the
harbour and knew that he would now have Collingwood's company.
"What an amiable, good man he is!" he declared. "All the rest are geese."

Collingwood and the Moutrays were, of course, already friends.
Indeed, Mary Moutray had not only overcome his initial hostility but
drawn his latent charm to the surface. When told that he would be
embarking the Commissioner and his wife as passengers, he had
complained sourly, "Those Moutrays will be an expense to me. I don't
mind that if they are pleasant and satisfied: their going to the country I
am to be stationed in will give them an opportunity of showing their
thankfulness for my attentions." But soon the delightful Mrs. Moutray
had brushed aside any defensive brusqueness and was later able to write,
"Although the vigour of his mind was soon discovered, there was a
degree of reserve in his manner which prevented the playfulness of his
imagination and his powers of adding charms to private society from
being duly appreciated. But the intimacy of a long passage in his ship
gave us the good fortune to know him as he was, so that after our arrival
at St. John's or in English Harbour, he was as a beloved brother in our
house."

Four years older than their hostess, Cuthbert Collingwood was on
such easy terms with her that he was admitted to her boudoir and, when
preparing for a dance, helped to curl her hair, or, as he put it, "frizzing
your head for a ball". Rid of his diffidence, he was a striking man, his tall,
well-built figure now accentuated by wearing his hair in a queue falling to
his shoulder-blades. Nelson, on the other hand, was not only slight and
sallow but had had his head shaved to ease the discomfort of sweating
during one of his recurrent bouts of malaria, and was wearing an
ill-fitting yellow wig. Mary Moutray made gentle fun of this, insisting that
they draw one another's portraits.

If Nelson felt a twinge of jealousy at Collingwood's unexpected social
success, more would have been aroused by the lady's husband, who might
be elderly but clearly commanded her affection and faithfulness. This
was accentuated by resentment over his wearing of a captain's uniform
which implied that he was the senior officer. Nelson had been angered by
receiving letters addressed to, "Horatio Nelson Esq., second in
command of His Majesty's Ships in English Harbour". Such feelings

could be contained but a serious confrontation developed from a misunderstanding of orders by both men.

The *Boreas* was making regular cruises amongst the islands and returning from one on 5th February, 1785, Nelson was surprised to see one of the frigates in English Harbour, the *Latona*, flying the broad pendant of a commodore. The captain of the frigate was junior to Nelson, who at once summoned him on board the *Boreas* and asked "Have you any order from Sir Richard Hughes to wear a broad pendant?" "No." "For what reason do you then wear it in the presence of a senior officer?" "I hoisted it by order of Commissioner Moutray." "Have you seen by what authority Commissioner Moutray was empowered to give you orders?" "No." "Sir, you have acted wrong to obey any man you do not know is authorised to command you." "I feel I have acted wrong but being a young captain did not think proper to interfere in this matter as there were you and other older officers upon this station."

Nelson reported this exchange verbatim in a letter of complaint to the Admiralty, adding, "I did not choose to order the Commissioner's pendant to be struck, as Mr. Moutray is an old officer of high military character, and it might hurt his feelings to be supposed wrong by so young an officer." Next day Commissioner Moutray sent Captain Nelson a written order to place himself under his command as that of a commodore. Nelson refused and wrote to object that Moutray was no longer an officer in commission in a letter to Admiral Hughes, sending a copy to the Commissioner with a stiff little covering note assuring him of his "personal esteem".

In fact, Admiral Hughes had given Moutray authority to exercise command in his absence, despite his civilian status, and, as result of this squabble, the Admiralty changed and clarified the position of Commissioners, who thereafter were to be serving officers on full pay. Although they acted on his objection, the Lords of the Admiralty rebuked Nelson for appealing to them over the head of Admiral Hughes, with whom he should have settled the matter. As for Commissioner Moutray, he was a sick man and the unpleasant encounter must have strengthened his resolve to return to a gentler climate and company. Soon afterwards, Collingwood was writing, "Commissioner Moutray has but ill health. I am afraid we shall lose them: they are very desirous to get home and if he is not recalled I think he will resign. I shall miss them grievously; she is quite a delight and makes many an hour cheerful that without her would be dead weight."

Nelson was equally stricken and later in February, he wrote to William Nelson, "You may be certain I never passed English Harbour without a call, but alas! I am not to have much comfort. My dear, sweet friend is going home. I am really an April day; happy on her account, but truly grieved were I only to consider myself. Her equal I never saw in any country or in any situation. She always talks of you and hopes, if she comes within your reach, you will not fail visiting her. If my dear Kate goes to Bath next winter, she will be known to her; for my dear friend has promised to make herself known. What an acquisition to any female to be acquainted with: what an example to take pattern from. Moutray has been very ill: it would have been necessary that he should have quitted this country had he not been recalled." Before the letter could be put aboard ship, he added a postscript, "My sweet, amiable friend sails the 20th for England. I took my leave of her with a heavy heart three days ago. What a *treasure* of a woman. God bless her."

When Collingwood took leave of her, she gave him a purse of netting that she had made for him and he responded with a verse:

> Your net shall be my care, my dear,
> For length of time to come,
> While I am faint and scorching here,
> And you rejoice at home.
>
> To you belongs the wondrous art
> To shed around you pleasure;
> New worth to best of things impart,
> And make of trifles – treasure.

When the Moutrays had sailed for home, English Harbour reverted to its former status of an infernal hole. "This country appears now intolerable, my dear friend being absent," wrote Nelson to his brother a few days later. "It is barren indeed; not all the Rosys can give a spark of joy to me. English Harbour I hate the sight of and 'Windsor' I detest. I went once up the hill to look at the spot where I spent more happy days than in any one spot in the world. E'en the trees dropped their heads and the tamarind tree died: all was melancholy. The road is covered with thistles; let them grow; I shall never pull one of them up. By this time I hope she is safe in Old England. Heaven's choicest blessings go with her."

Both the friends sighed for her, perhaps speculating sadly what might have been if she had been widowed in Antigua, instead of, as now seemed probable, in Bath. Both wrote to her and it is likely that the jealousy, if not the suspicions, of her ailing husband were aroused because Nelson noted that somebody had tampered with the sealing-wafers of her replies: "My first letter from her came to me with the wafer open, but it is very odd that both our letters should be in the same situation. They were welcome to read mine; it was all goodness, like the dear writer." Collingwood's affection seems to have been captured even more securely than Nelson's for, much later, in one of many letters in which he gave free rein to "the playfulness of his imagination" that she so enjoyed, he wrote to her, "I wish you had one of those fairy telescopes that can look into the hearts and souls of people a thousand leagues off, then might you see how much you possess my mind."

Neither was a man to mope for long and for Nelson, in particular, hopeless love could be replaced by patriotic and professional zeal. Visiting the island of St. Kitts, he refused an invitation from the President because Irish flags were flying over the town to celebrate St. Patrick's Day, hoisted by "these *vagabonds*". When he encountered a French frigate off the island of Nevis and suspected that she was engaged in espionage, he followed her and with elaborate courtesy told her captain that he "thought it his duty to accompany him in an English frigate, that attention might be paid to officers of His Most Christian Majesty." He disregarded the Frenchman's polite refusal of an escort as he was "not to be outdone in *civility*" and never lost sight of her until she returned to her base in Martinique.

More worrying were the ramifications of the Navigation Act and the determination of almost all the British authorities in the islands to disregard it. American traders would call at British ports ostensibly for provisions and repairs and ask permission to sell enough goods to pay for such services, then discharge and market their entire cargoes – exchanging their timber, fish, flour and grain for the islanders' sugar and rum – while the Customs officers pretended not to notice. "The residents of these islands are Americans by connexion and by interest and are inimical to Great Britain," declared Nelson. "They are as great rebels as ever were in America." When a formal petition from the President and Council of the Leeward Islands, demanding free access to their ports for the Americans, was sent to General Shirley and Admiral Hughes, Nelson left neither in any doubt that, whatever they replied, he would abide by the letter of the law. The Governor replied tartly that "old respectable officers of high rank, long service and a certain life are very jealous of being dictated to in their duty by young gentlemen whose service and experience do not entitle them to it." To this, Nelson's response was that he was as old as the Prime Minister, and as capable of commanding one of His Majesty's ships as William Pitt was of governing the country.

As a result, as Nelson put it, "the *dear Boreas* is quite forgot, very much disliked", neither he nor his officers were welcome ashore and invitations to dine in the plantation houses ceased. So they passed their evenings on board with music and dancing for the sailors and theatricals – one of Nelson's favourite shipboard entertainments – for the officers. For his part, he felt even freer than before from personal embarrassment in chasing, searching and seizing illegal American traders with cargoes bound, he knew, for the warehouses of merchants he had met across their mahogany dining-tables. The climax of his campaign came when he boarded four American ships lying in the roads off Charlestown, the capital of Nevis, where they were trading. This time the ships' masters, supported by friends ashore, reacted strongly, and sued him for assault and imprisonment, claiming damages at £40,000. Nelson was told that if he went ashore he himself would be arrested and imprisoned.

Nevis was unlike the other British islands in being richer, more fashionable and its merchants and planters more arrogant. Some eighty sugar plantations had been established on the thirty-six square miles around the fertile cone of Mount Nevis, an extinct volcano that stood more than three thousand feet above the sea. Yet with the islanders' self-confidence went a degree of integrity, for when the case against Nelson was heard in the little stonebuilt court-house at Charlestown, the judge upheld his right to seize the American ships and the President of Nevis, John Herbert, who himself stood to lose by the seizures, offered to stand bail for £10,000 should Captain Nelson decide to come ashore and face arrest. Indeed, the two men became friends and met ashore to dine.

"Herbert is very rich and proud," Nelson discovered. "Although his income is immense, yet his expenses must be great as his house is open to all strangers and he entertains most hospitably." This was Montpelier, a big house with wide verandahs and louvre'd walls standing across the lane from the sugar-mill and boiling-house of the estate on the southern slope of Mount Nevis more than six hundred feet above the sea. Sea breezes ruffled the flowering trees and blew the mosquitoes away, cooling the high-ceilinged rooms with polished hardwood floors and stirring the long curtains that shaded windows commanding idyllic views of greenery, blue sea and sky. Nelson had twice made the journey from the neat streets of stone houses and the new Bath House Hotel over the sulphur spring at Charlestown, up the deep, narrow lane to the church at Fig Tree, over a crest and down the drive and between the imposing gateposts of Montpelier, before he had come to the notice of Mr. Herbert's niece, Fanny, who had acted as his hostess since the death of his wife and in the absence of his daughter.

Frances Nisbet was herself a widow at the age of twenty-seven, a few months older than Nelson. Her father, William Woolward, had been the senior judge on Nevis, where she had spent almost all her life and had married the doctor who had attended him at his death, Josiah Nisbet. Her husband suffered from tropical ailments, notably sun-stroke, so they had retired to England and there, in Salisbury, he had died, leaving her with an infant son named after his father. Returning to her mother's family on Nevis, she made herself useful to her uncle in entertaining his guests and managing his servants. She was accomplished in such lady-like activities as sewing and playing the piano and could speak some French and her looks were refined rather than pretty: dark, clear eyes; an English complexion, well-shielded from the sun by parasol and bonnet; softly-curling brown hair; and a nose with bridge and nostrils delicately arched, giving her an air of genteel, if not aristocratic, breeding. In London or in Bath, she might have attracted little attention, but amongst the flowers and scents of the tropics, hers was a rare beauty.

Twice, when Captain Nelson had called at Montpelier, she had been away but a cousin staying on the neighbouring island of St. Kitts had met him and excitedly wrote about him to her, as the most sophisticated of her friends: "We have at last seen the little captain of the *Boreas*, of whom so much has been said. He came up just before dinner, much heated and was very silent yet seemed, according to the old adage, to think the more. He declined drinking any wine: but after dinner, when the president, as usual, has the three following toasts, the King, the Queen and the Royal Family, and Lord Hood, this strange man regularly filled his glass and observed that those were always bumper toasts with him; which having drank, he uniformly passed the bottle and relapsed into his former taciturnity. It was impossible, during this visit, for any of us to make out his real character; there was such a reserve and sternness in his behaviour, with occasional sallies, though very transient, of a superior mind. Being placed by him, I endeavoured to rouse his attention by showing him all the civilities in my power: but I drew out little more than yes and no. If you, Fanny, had been there, we think you would have made something of him; for you have been in the habit of attending to these odd sort of people."

In the late spring of 1785 when Captain Nelson paid his third visit to Montpelier, it was early and none of the family was about and a negro servant showed him into the drawing-room, where he found company in the small form of Josiah, Mrs. Nisbet's five-year-old son. When Mr. Herbert finally bustled in to greet his guest he was surprised to find the room empty. "Great God!" he reported later, "If I did not find that great little man, of whom everybody is so afraid, playing in the next room, under the dining-table with Mrs. Nisbet's child." Soon afterwards, the guest was introduced to the child's mother who thanked him for his attention to Josiah. He was at once reminded of the charm and poise of another: for "her manners are Mrs. Moutray's". But here, it soon became clear, there were no obstacles: Frances Nisbet had been a widow for four years, had no suitor and, although she might have no fortune of her own, seemed to have expectations. "Her uncle, although he is a man who must have his own way in everything, yet I believe he has a good and generous heart," decided Nelson. "Many estates in the island are mortgaged to him. The stock of negroes upon his estate and cattle are valued at £60,000 sterling and he sends to England (average for 7 years) 500 casks of sugar ... and, as he says and told me at first, that he looked upon his niece as his child, I can have no reason to suppose that he will not provide handsomely for her."

In that cool, elegant house and in its lovely garden, shaded by great trees and coloured by exotic flowers, birds and butterflies, it was easy to fall in love, particularly when each tentative word or gesture drew a shy but encouraging response. At last marriage and the delights of home-making and creating a family seemed a real possibility and, with her, one that would do credit to any officer. Often she reminded him of Mary Moutray and, when he received a letter from her in Bath, he had to tell his new love about her predecessor: "A more amiable woman can hardly exist. I wish you knew her; your minds and manners are so congenial that you must have pleasure in the acquaintance." Such tactlessness in praising another woman was part of his impulsiveness and he knew it, telling her soon afterwards, "My temper you know as well as myself, for by longer acquaintance you will find I possess not the art of concealing it." While he was still addressing her as "Mrs. Nisbet", he proposed marriage and was accepted.

Before Mr. Herbert had time to give formal approval to the match, the *Boreas* was at sea again, and her captain making his first attempt to write a love-letter by asking his future wife, "Don't think me rude by this entering into a correspondence with you." Fanciful phrases did not come easily and he wrote in this same letter: "Most sincerely do I love you and I think that my affection is not only founded upon the principles of reason but also upon a basis of mutual attachment. Indeed, my charming Fanny, did I possess a million, my greatest pride and pleasure would be to share it with you; and as to living in a cottage with you, I should esteem it superior to living in a palace with any other I have yet met with." Love in a cottage might, in fact, be all he had to offer and it would mean a marked change for one accustomed to the luxuries of Montpelier. "My dear boy," he told Collingwood, "I want some prize-money." As there was little prospect of this in peacetime, he wrote again to his uncle William Suckling, telling him of his intentions and adding, "I am as poor as Job". He had begun his begging letter with a little self-mockery, writing, "I open for business which perhaps you will smile at, in the first instance, and say, 'This Horatio is for ever in love' ", but was soon at his most demanding: "Who can I apply to but you? Don't disappoint me, or my heart will break." To his friend William Locker he could write untrammelled by etiquette or anxiety, "I think I have found a woman who will make me happy," and to his brother William he wrote, "We may not be a rich couple, yet I have not the least doubt but that we shall be a happy pair – the fault must be mine if we are not."

CHAPTER IV

On the Beach
(1785–93)

"If your Lordships should be pleased to appoint me to a cockle-boat I shall feel grateful."
 – Captain Horatio Nelson to the Board of Admiralty,
 from Burnham Thorpe, Norfolk, 5th December, 1792

As the sun came up over Shirley Heights and lit the lagoons of English Harbour, Captain Nelson stood naked, dripping and happy, while his servant, Frank Lepée, emptied another canvas bucket of water over his meagre body. While the *Boreas* was refitting in the dockyard in the summer of 1786, he was living alone at the senior officer's house, with only "mosquitoes and melancholies" for company from sunset to bedtime. "Most woefully pinched by mosquitoes", which were "devouring me through all my clothes", he complained, until he retired beneath his mosquito-net for the night in the hope of "English sleep, always barring mosquitoes, which all Frank's care with my net cannot keep out".

Despite the discomfort, loneliness and the worries of command, he was content. His engagement to Fanny Nisbet had illuminated his future so that he could tell her, almost truthfully, "my mind dwells on nought else but you". The early formalities had been abandoned and now he could write to "my dearest Fanny" quite flirtatiously: "As you begin to know something about sailors, have you not heard that salt water and absence always wash away love? Now I am such a heretic as not to believe that faith: for behold, every morning since my arrival I have had six pails of salt water at day-light poured upon my head and, instead of finding what the seamen say is true, I perceive the contrary effect."

This intimacy had brought out curiously feminine aspects of his character: pleasure in the exchange of social gossip and absorption in domestic detail. His letters, written from English Harbour and during the autumn, when he had returned to cruising amongst the islands, mixed scandal with news of friends and relations, the problems of the Navigation Act and protestations of love and esteem. The names of his brother-officers and their paramours were disguised with an initial or a dash, after the custom of newspaper gossip-writers of the day; occasionally he named them. Thus, while he was discreet about "Captain S., a gentleman well-versed in the business of carrying off young ladies", it is "a Miss –", whose "character is much hurt ... from her intimacy with Sir Richard". This was Admiral Hughes himself. "I should suppose him a bachelor instead of a married man with a family ... *Entre nous* the A. makes quite a – of himself in this business." The errant Sir Richard was "in high spirits of having left her Ladyship at Barbados", where, having married her Rosy to a major of infantry, she was preparing to leave for home in a ship whose crew were, wrote Nelson, "thirsty souls and I think she will either be lost or burned before she gets to England". Her husband was showing no inclination to see her off: "Common decency ought to have induced such a *polite* man as Sir Richard to have gone down", he declared. "What a blessed couple."

There were shopping errands to be discussed: notably for a red cage-bird and a riding-hat. "My endeavours for a red bird have been fruitless but I shall always remain upon the look-out till I get one," he wrote to Fanny from Barbados. "The strings I have got, but the hat and ribbon is not at present in this town." Eventually, he had to admit failure: "I have got a young grey parrot but am unable to get a red bird ... The hat I can't get. When I ask, they tell me ladies do not ride in this country." Even more troublesome was having to take Fanny's piano from Nevis to St. Kitts to have it tuned because this had to take place on board his ship and he complained, "All the news I shall tell you is that a man is cracking my head with tuning your pianoforte. However be assured there is nothing in this world I would not bear with to please my dearest Fanny."

His health was bedevilled by recurrent malaria and he worried about this, perhaps with fatherhood in mind; he was already referring to his future step-son as "my good little fellow" and liked to speak of the midshipmen in the frigate as "my children". So he ended one letter from English Harbour, "A pint of goat's milk every morning and beef tea will make me what I wish to be for your sake, for indeed I am with the most ardent affection, ever your Horatio Nelson." This worry was not unjustified because a doctor soon afterwards gave him much the same warning as had brought him home after the Nicaragua campaign: "An immediate removal to another climate is highly necessary."

One present and future pleasure was in introducing Fanny to his friends, for she had rekindled the enjoyment of polite society that had been aroused by Mrs. Moutray. The latter was presumably still in Bath but he was piqued at not having heard from her for more than six months: "Not a line from her ... I can't account for it. I know myself to be so steady in my friendships that I can't bear the least coolness or inattention in others." A month later, a letter did arrive, "full of affliction and woe" for her husband had died and the Admiralty had refused her a pension, despite the Duchess of Richmond arranging for her to plead her case with the King and Queen in person. Again Nelson stressed his attachment to Mary Moutray to a tactless degree in a letter to Fanny:

Dear soul, she desires I will say everything to you for her. Her kind wishes for our happiness equal to that what she enjoyed but *far, far* more lasting. Indeed, my dearest, I can't express what I feel for her and your good heart I am sure will sympathize with mine. What is so truly affecting as a virtuous woman in distress? But if partaking in grief is an alleviation of the sufferings of that all-amiable woman, she has many sharers. When you know her, you must love her.

Now Nelson himself was to become involved with the Royal Family. Prince William Henry, who had been a midshipman when they had first met at New York, was now a post-captain and in command of the frigate *Pegasus*. He was due in the Caribbean from Newfoundland and, since Admiral Hughes had himself sailed for England, Nelson was temporarily senior officer on the Leeward Islands station and would be expected to attend the royal visitor during his cruise. The prince had become an enthusiastic naval officer, although loud-mouthed and something of a martinet, but whatever reservations Nelson may have had about his overbearing manner were muted by his reverence for royalty. When the *Boreas* joined the *Pegasus* off Dominica and the two men renewed their acquaintance, it became clear that Nelson's duties were to be primarily social as they had been during their visit to Havana.

"Our young Prince is a gallant man," he wrote to Fanny from Antigua. "Some ladies at Dominica seemed very charmed by him. He is volatile but always with great good nature. There were two balls during his stay and some of the old ladies were mortified that His Royal Highness would not dance with them, but he says he is determined to enjoy the privilege of all other men, that of asking any lady he pleases." The bulging Hanoverian eyes found so much to dwell upon that, as Nelson put it, "I fancy many people were as happy to see His Royal Highness quit as they were to see him enter St. John's, for another day or two's racquet would have knocked up some of the fair sex. Three nights' dancing was too much and never broke up till near day. Miss Athill is the belle of the island and of course attracted His Royal Highness's attention." At first Nelson was surprised at his own resilience: "I have not more than twice or thrice been in bed till morning and have rode a great deal in the day, but so far from doing me harm everybody tells me they never saw me look so well. I am reconciled to the business as I really love to honour the

Prince, otherwise I could not have gone through it." But the round of dinner parties, balls, soirées, riding parties and cockfights was eventually too much even for him and, after two months of it, he was complaining: "Tonight I have to fag at the public ball. Oh, how I wish it over and that I was returned on board the *Boreas*."

It was not all social capers and the more tiresome of several professional problems that came his way as senior officer was the case of Lieutenant Schomberg. When Prince William Henry had been appointed to the *Pegasus*, he had been given an able first lieutenant to ease his task in command and Nelson was among those who thought highly of Isaac Schomberg. Perhaps his efficiency irritated the Prince because when his first lieutenant sent one of the ship's boats ashore on some errand without informing him, he accused him of the serious naval misdemeanour of "neglect of duty" and entered this reprimand in the frigate's General Order Book. Realising that this record would harm his chances of promotion, Schomberg appealed in the only way he could, by writing to the senior officer on the station and demanding that the case be tried by court martial. But there were not enough captains available to form such a court, so, pending that, or another, solution and feeling that he should take some action, Nelson had Schomberg placed under arrest in his ship. After some embarrassing weeks the lieutenant was returned to England and appointed to another ship and the whole question of reprimand and court martial was set aside. Later, Nelson wrote to the Prince asking for his indulgence towards an officer, who had been "too hasty":

> If to be truly great is to be truly good (as we are taught to believe it) it never was stronger verified than in your Royal Highness, in the instance of Mr. Schomberg ... Resentment I know your Royal Highness never had ... it is a passion incompatible with the character of Man of Honour. Schomberg was too hasty certainly in writing his letter; but now you are parted; pardon me, my Prince, when I presume to recommend that Schomberg may stand in your Royal favour as if he had never sailed with you; and that at some future day, you will serve him. There only wants this to place your character in the highest point of view.

For his part, the Prince enjoyed Nelson's company, dining together in one or other of their ships, when social engagements ashore permitted, and teasing him about his forthcoming marriage, once provoking a needless and tactless apology to Fanny. "His Royal Highness often tells me he believes I am married," he wrote, "for, he says, he never saw a lover so easy, or say so little of the object he has regard for. When I tell him I certainly am not, he says then he is sure I must have a great esteem for you and that it is not what is (vulgarly) no I won't make use of that word commonly called love. He is right, my love is founded on esteem, the only foundation that can make the passion last."

The Prince followed this banter with a command: "His Royal Highness . . . has told me that . . . if I am not married this time we go to Nevis, it is hardly probable that he should see me there again, that I had promised him not to be married unless he was present." Indeed, he insisted that he give the bride away at the ceremony. There could be no further delay and the marriage was arranged for 11th March, 1787, at Montpelier. The ceremony was to be conducted at the house by the Reverend William Thomas, rector of the parishes of St. John and St. Thomas, rather than in the little church at Fig Tree, with Prince William Henry, in full naval uniform, escorting the bride and Lieutenant Digby Dent of the *Boreas* attending the groom. It was an idyllic setting, the wedding party gathering in a cool room where the gleam of silver reflected on polished mahogany and gilt-framed portraits of English ancestors were lit by shafts of bright sunlight slanting through the louvres of the shutters and the filmy curtains. The words of the marriage service spoken, the Prince proposed a toast to the health and happiness of "the principal favourite of the island", Nelson declaring that "Till I married I never knew happiness". The guests, glasses in hand, strolled on the lawn among the flowering shrubs and beneath the shade of the spreading branches of a great silk-cotton tree. The only sombre thoughts were those of Captain Thomas Pringle, a friend of the groom's since his time at Quebec, who contained them until next day when he had to share them, saying, "The Navy, sir, yesterday lost one of its greatest ornaments, by Nelson's marriage. It is a national loss that such an officer should marry; had it not been for that circumstance, I foresaw Nelson would become the greatest man in the Service."

Certainly, the bridegroom's eyes were now upon married life, home-making and the raising of a family but, before the couple could leave for home, there were more professional duties. There was the final stage of the Prince's cruise to the Virgin Islands and Grenada to complete; there were allegations of widespread embezzlement amongst the Navy's contractors and officials in the Leeward Islands that had to be investigated; and there was a court martial for a capital offence. The accused was Able Seaman William Clark, who had deserted his ship, the *Rattler*, commanded by Cuthbert Collingwood's brother; he was clearly guilty and, less than a month after the happiness of his wedding-day, Nelson, as a president of the court, was having to condemn a man to death by hanging. But the Prince had not yet sailed and could be asked to grant a reprieve, which he did, and to which Nelson added immediate discharge from the Navy, letting Clark go ashore in Antigua, a free man. For this he was censured by the Admiralty on the grounds that he had only the power to suspend the sentence and certainly not to pardon or discharge. He was unrepentant, replying, "I was near, if not cutting the thread of life, at least shortening a fellow-creature's days. The law might not have supposed me guilty of murder, but my feelings would nearly have been the same," adding, when their Lordships still objected to the discharge of the pardoned sailor, "I had always understood that when a man was condemned to suffer death, he was from that moment dead in Law; and, if he was pardoned, he became as a new man; and, there being no impress, he had the choice of entering, or not, His Majesty's service."

The freeing of Able Seaman Clark was not quite his last action before sailing for home. That came at the beginning of June when the *Boreas* lay in Nevis roads and Nelson was taking leave of Fanny and her uncle, who were to follow in the comfort of the West Indiaman *Roehampton*; his ship's company had also been celebrating their imminent departure and he ordered three marines to be punished with a dozen lashes each for drunkenness. Thereupon the frigate sailed and, after brief calls at St. Kitts, St. Eustasia and St. Martin, crossed the Atlantic in a month, weathering a gale in mid-ocean. Nelson, who had been sickly on the voyage, had expected that his ship would be paid off on arrival at Portsmouth but he was ordered to lie at Spithead in readiness for sea because of the renewed risk of war with France.

In September, he was ordered to the Nore, where the *Boreas* was to act as receiving ship for men rounded up ashore by the press-gang, eleven hundred being pressed in a single night. The misery of these captives compounded the discontent of the crew and Nelson had to order three of his men to be flogged for "using mutinous language to their officers" and five more for "disobedience and neglect of duty". He himself was miserable because, although Fanny had arrived in London, he complained, "We are here laying seven miles from the land on the impress service and am as much separated from my wife as if I were in the East Indies." Fanny was equally miserable and her father-in-law, to whom she had written, told his daughter Kitty, "She has been unwell and in poor spirits. Hard, she says, is the lot of a sailor's wife."

The *Boreas* had become an unhappy ship and there was a spate of desertions, which had hitherto been rare in Nelson's ships. However, at the end of November, when she was at last paid off, the ratings were awarded an extra month's pay in recognition of this extra and unexpected service in peacetime and went on their way; this time, without any offer to follow the captain they had served for nearly four years. Nelson himself had been forwarding presents of wine, rum and tropical fruit to friends and relations but he had brought other, less agreeable, reminders of the Caribbean with him. The litigation over the seizure of the American ships off Nevis was now in the hands of London lawyers and he began to feel that some senior officers at the Admiralty were, as a result of his zeal in enforcing the Navigation Act, almost as hostile as those in the Leeward Islands. Pointedly, it seemed, none of the temporary promotions and appointments he had made, when in acting command of the squadron, had been confirmed.

At last Captain and Mrs Nelson could be reunited at Mr. Herbert's fine London residence, 5 Cavendish Square, and later took lodgings nearby at 10 Great Marlborough Street, then 6 Princes Street. Now, it seemed, they could relax and enjoy the pleasures that the capital could offer a well-connected captain and his lady. But, hardly had they settled into these urban comforts, when the uglier realities of his calling interrupted: one of his men, just discharged from the *Boreas*, had been accused of murder and his former captain was asked to give evidence at his trial. James Carse, the ship's cooper, had gone ashore with some fifty guineas in hoarded pay and travelled up-river to the shabby riverside district of Shadwell to meet a cousin at a tavern called The Ship in Distress. There he had met a young prostitute, Mary Mills, accompanied her to a bedroom and cut her throat. He had been caught literally red-handed so that the only evidence that might save him from the gallows would be a plea of insanity.

The case of *Rex v. Carse* was heard at the Old Bailey on 17th December, 1787, before Mr. Justice Heath and Captain Nelson was called to the witness box and asked about the character of the accused. "It seldom happens that any man can serve four years without being guilty of some sort of offence," he replied. "That man at times ... appeared melancholy, but the quietest, soberest man that I ever saw in my life. He appeared to be a man who had seen better days ... When I heard of this affair, I said, if it is true he must be insane for I should as soon suspect myself, and sooner, because I know I am hasty; he is so quiet a man, and never committed a fault during the time I knew him. Seamen I know perfectly; when they come home, the landlords will furnish them with raw liquors; I saw thirty or forty from that ship that were as mad as if they were at Bedlam, and did not know what they did. I know that when seamen are furnished with British spirits, it turns the brain. He is not a drunkard by any means ..."

But he did suggest a reason for insanity: "At the island of Antigua, I think it was, he was struck with the sun, after which time he appeared melancholy; I have been affected with it; I have been out of my senses; it hurts the brain." Was Carse a man likely to have committed murder? "I should as soon suspect myself, because I am hasty, he is not," he repeated. Nelson then explained that, as result of sunstroke, Carse had been sent ashore to hospital "with a fever which affects the brain" and, on his return, "I had thought to send him home as an unfit person to serve in that climate". This evidence was decisive and James Carse was declared guilty but insane and his life spared.

The Nelsons spent Christmas with Mr. Herbert but Fanny was already missing the warmth of Nevis because, although Cavendish Square was in a new residential suburb, with farmland a few minutes' walk away to the north, her husband could complain, "I fear we must at present give up all thoughts of living so near to London for Mrs. Nelson's lungs are so much affected by the smoke." So in January they took the coach to Bath, where Nelson left his wife in lodgings while he continued to Plymouth where Prince William Henry had invited him to join the celebration of the *Pegasus*'s homecoming. Gratified to find his royal friend "everything I could wish" and his ship "one of the best disciplined", he returned to Fanny and together they continued their holiday with an aunt of hers near Bristol and at Exmouth on the Devon coast. Even here it was impossible to shake off the trammels of West Indian troubles for official correspondence over the contractors' frauds continued as did the litigation over his seizure of American cargoes, although the worry of this was lessened by assurances that any costs would be borne by the Treasury. Happier connections were also renewed when a letter arrived from Hercules Ross, who had returned to his native Scotland to marry and enjoy his Jamaican fortune. Nelson replied heartily, asking whether there might be a chance of meeting in the Pump Room at Bath and then revealed something of the motives that drove his ambition.

"You have given up all the toils and anxieties of business," he wrote, "whilst I must still buffet the waves – for what? That thing called Honour is now alas! thought of no more ... I have invariably laid down, and followed close, a plan of what ought to be uppermost in the breast of an officer; that it is much better to serve an ungrateful Country than to give up his own fame. Posterity will do him justice: a uniform conduct of honour and integrity seldom fails to bring a man to the goal of Fame at last – but to what am I getting? Into a sermon."

It was beginning to look as if the country *was* ungrateful. Twice Nelson called at the Admiralty to see the First Lord – to establish his claim to another command should the likelihood of war increase and to ask for the reimbursement of expenses incurred during his investigation into West Indian frauds – but Lord Howe was otherwise engaged. He had hoped for a frank exchange with the old admiral he so much admired for his stern integrity, who had been close both to the elder Pitt and to his son, the present Prime Minister; instead, he had to write a letter, pointing out the expense of all those journeys between English Harbour and St. John's and declaring, "My zeal for His Majesty's Service is as great as I once flattered myself your lordship thought it."

It seemed increasingly probable that his upholding of the letter of the law prohibiting American trade and the greed and even corruption amongst senior officers and officials that this had exposed, had won him enemies not only in the Caribbean. But one friend, at least, would be above the admirals' prejudices: Prince William Henry. Fanny had suggested a way of both adding to their income and enhancing their social position and her husband wrote him a careful letter. "There may be a thing, perhaps, within reach of your Royal Highness; therefore, trusting to your goodness, I shall mention it," he began, diffidently. "The Princess Royal must very soon have a Household appointed her. I believe a word from your Royal Highness would obtain a promise of a situation in her Royal Highness's Establishment not unbecoming the wife of a Captain in the Navy; but I have only ventured to say this much and leave the issue to your better judgement." But whether or not the Prince responded to this, Fanny Nelson was not invited to become a lady-in-waiting.

The homecoming was not as joyous as he had so long expected. Even the welcome to Burnham Thorpe was cooled by Edmund Nelson's shyness of his daughter-in-law, who would, he feared, find the simplicities of the parsonage and the harshness of the weather that usually opened the year in Norfolk in brutal contrast to the Caribbean. When she wrote a letter of self-introduction to him from Cavendish Square, he noted, "My very polite correspondent ... seems to think it will not be many weeks before she visits these Arcadian Scenes: rivers represented by a puddle, mountains by anthills, woods by bramble bushes; yet all is taste, if not hid by snow. Forbid it Fate."

On further reflection he was even less enthusiastic, writing to Kitty, "To say the truth I am not now anxious to see them. Him for a day or two I should be glad of, but to introduce a stranger to an infirm and whimsical old man, who can neither eat nor drink, nor talk, nor see, is as well let alone." His shyness increased as he brooded upon the arrival of the fine lady from the West Indies and he wrote again to his youngest daughter:

I have requested him not to think of bringing his lady and suite to Burnham till his other visits are at an end. Indeed, I am in no haste to see and receive a stranger; perhaps you may introduce her by and by. I believe she will form a valuable part of our family connections and certain it is that he has a claim to all my affection, having never transgressed. But every power of mine is in decay. Insipid, whimsical and very unfit for society, in truth, and not likely to revive by practice.

Instead, her introduction to Norfolk and the family was to be gentle. First, little Josiah was to be escorted to Hilborough near Swaffham by Nelson's sailor-servant, Frank Lepée, to be put in the care of William Nelson and his wife at the rectory from whence he would be placed in a boarding school. Then, when the weather improved, the captain and his lady would visit his sisters: first, Susannah Bolton, whose family had moved from Wells to Cranwich near Hilborough; then his cherished Kitty. The year before, accompanying her father to Bath, she had met, at a ball, the most dashing and eligible of bachelors, George Matcham. Having followed his father into the service of the East India Company, he had made a modest fortune and indulged his taste for travel, returning to England overland and writing an account of the journey which had been published. Now a handsome man of thirty-four, he was charming, restless and energetic; they fell instantly in love and, two months later, were married by her father. They had taken a fine house, Barton Hall among the inland lagoons of the Norfolk Broads and, together, they and the Boltons could offer Fanny the style of entertainment to which she was accustomed.

At the Boltons' they met Nelson's younger brother, Edmund, who had been taken into partnership by his brother-in-law but was declining into illness and not expected to live. There was worrying news of the other two brothers: Maurice, still at his desk in the Navy Office, was in debt and Horatio made a special journey to London to "entirely liberate poor Maurice from the galling chain". Suckling was also a problem: he had been apprenticed to a draper but, on receiving his own legacy from their Uncle Maurice Suckling, had bought the village shop at North Elmham, between Burnham Thorpe and Norwich, where he sold groceries and cloth. But his principal interests were known to be greyhound-racing, hare-coursing and convivial drinking. His family were not optimistic but did what they could to help by buying from him. An indication of his inefficiency was given by Horatio when, during this tour of family and friends, he rode over to collect an overdue order for their brother William. "I was at Elmham yesterday," he wrote, "and your cloth was packed up but my brother waited till he got down the blue for turn-ups and lining ..."

Nelson rode on to visit his father, alone, to tell him that he would bring Fanny for a visit during the autumn, when the weather in Norfolk tended to be fine and bland, before they left for France. His wife spoke good

French and he was determined that his own attempt at learning it – interrupted by his longing for Miss Andrews – should now be completed. But before this, while they were staying with the Matchams at Barton, the newspapers announced the appointment of a new Board of Admiralty with Lord Chatham, the Prime Minister's elder brother, as First Lord and Lord Hood as one of the two Sea Lords. This was not an opportunity to be missed and Nelson at once wrote to his former commander-in-chief and, soon after, presented himself at the Admiralty.

"I saw Lord Hood this morning," he wrote to Fanny at the end of August. "He made many enquiries after you and was very civil. He assured me that a ship in peacetime was not desirable; but that should any hostilities take place, I need not fear having a good ship." Despite this, Nelson could not resist using other connections in the hope of another command and on hearing that his friend "Billy Blue" Cornwallis – now a commodore – was taking a squadron to the East Indies, twice wrote to him eager for an appointment. The reply was friendly but discouraging: there was no employment available. So, clinging to Lord Hood's promise, he returned to the social round in Norfolk and, finally, in December, took Fanny to Burnham Thorpe.

Edmund Nelson was delighted with his daughter-in-law and she with him. His diffidence, whimsical wit and generosity overcame any apprehensions of discomfort in the simple stone-flagged house around which winter fogs were already collecting. It was a bleak scene for the windows looked out upon the little river Burn running through marshy fields across the lane and the bare boughs of the trees about the house. The garden could not be expected to look well in winter but George Matcham had been urging his father-in-law to transform it from the cottage garden it had been to something befitting a country gentleman with the planting of a rose garden, the digging of a ha-ha and the diverting of the river into a newly dug pond. Calling his energetic son-in-law "Capability M.", the rector had given him a free hand but, once he had departed for his own house on the far side of the county, could not maintain the effort with only himself and his servant, Peter Black ("Poor, forlorn, tho' wise as ever," noted his master), as "Artists in Improvement" to "reduce chaos into order". They had begun a year before and in the following spring, while Horatio had still been in Bath, the old man had written to George Matcham, disguising his dismay with whimsy:

Nature, undisturbed, only begins to rear her head and, as the Sleeping Venus, shows an inclination to get up. But where she has been roughly handled by the indelicate hand of Peter, breaking in upon her retirements at the moment she was undressing for a winter night, tearing away her clothing, carrying her like an unfeeling assassin to a cold, inhospitable clime – no kind friend at hand to afford shelter, or nourishment – the worst is to be expected. She is ashamed to come forth, half naked in tattered clothes, exposed to the ridicule of every dirty boy – and therefore much, I fear, will die in obscurity. However, as yet, do not despair.

Nelson could no more depart for France and leave his father amid the chaos of his garden and to farm his thirty acres of land at the age of seventy-six, than he could have abandoned Colonel Polson at the mouth of the San Juan river. Whatever the reasons, plans for the holiday abroad were abandoned and the couple settled down for the winter at the Parsonage with the old rector who was delighted at the prospect of their company and of his son's help with the garden and the roses that George Matcham had promised to send from Barton. "Your bro' is happy in the thought of a future crop," he wrote to Kitty of Horatio. "I wish his good wife had her amusement; a little society and an instrument with which she could pass away an hour. Her musical powers I fancy are above the common sort. I am sure nothing on their part is wanting to make the winter comfortable and agreeable to me."

First, Nelson had to arrange for his half-pay of eight shillings a day – augmented by the annual allowance of £100 he and his wife each received from their uncles – and this involved formalities concerning the local magistrate. Thomas Coke of Holkham was much more than a magistrate for he had become the most influential landowner in the county, known simply as "Coke of Norfolk". Having inherited the enormous new palace of Holkham Hall and its vast estates from his uncle, the Earl of Leicester[1], he had brought imagination and enterprise to agriculture, transforming it from a means of making a living into an industry. Experimenting with the breeding of livestock most suitable for their environment, he had also, the year before, successfully grown wheat for the first time on what had always been regarded as poor farming land. He was approachable and generous, six years Nelson's senior, and would have been a natural friend despite his eminence in the socially stratified county, were it not for his politics. Thomas Coke had represented Norfolk in Parliament as a Whig.

The Nelson family's attitude to politics was confused, as middle class Tories distantly related to landowning Whigs. Edmund Nelson, unlike some of his fellow-parsons (Dixon Hoste of Tittleshall, for instance, expended more efforts on political campaigns than on his parish in the

---

[1] After twice refusing a peerage, Thomas Coke accepted an earldom in 1837 and took his uncle's former title, Earl of Leicester.

hope of a bishopric), flinched from politics. His son William leant towards the Whigs, for the better ecclesiastical appointments were usually in their gift; Horatio's sympathies were Tory, for he admired William Pitt's robust attitude to impertinent foreigners and he was appalled at the support the Whigs had accorded the rebellious American colonists. Thomas Coke, it was said, had drunk a toast to George Washington on every night of the American War as "the greatest man on Earth".

So Nelson rode the mile from the Parsonage, through the gates and along an interminable drive, through parkland that seemed a county within a county until Holkham Hall showed through the trees; a grim pile, built of pale yellow brick of local manufacture, giving it an institutional appearance. Coke received him in his study on the ground floor; a modest room, looking out on to the park arranged by "Capability" Brown to provide a distant view of an obelisk on the horizon. Above reared the oppressive bulk of the palace, the whole of its principal floor, immediately above Coke's quarters, given over to state apartments, enriched with red damask and gilding, paintings by Italian and Flemish masters in carved gold frames, antique statues from Rome, velvet hangings and tapestries, reached by a ceremonial staircase in a great hall supported by pillars of mottled marble. Captain Nelson had never seen anything like this before; beside this, St. James's Palace, where he had attended the King's levée, had been modest. Coke himself was friendly and businesslike but it was clear to the unemployed naval officer that the two of them, living a mile or so apart, belonged to different worlds.

They had hardly settled into the simplicities of life at Burnham Thorpe when, as often happens on that coast, winter weather arrived late but bitter. Parson Nelson welcomed the season as an ordeal decreed by the Creator to try him: "December has visited us in all the pomp and parade of winter, wind and storm and rattling hail; clothed with frosted robes, powdered with snow, all trimmed in glittering icicles; no blooming dowager was ever finer." Roads were closed by mud or snow and all visiting farther afield than the Burnhams stopped; certainly the warmth and comfort of Barton Hall was out of reach. Mid-way between the two, at the village of Weston Longville, the rector, James Woodforde, was writing in his journal on the last day of 1788: "The coldest night I ever felt (I think) in my life and this morning also the coldest with high wind and small snow. It froze and still freezes sharply almost in every place in my house. The thermometer was the lowest I ever remember tho' it stands in my study." It was much the same at the Nelsons' rectory.

Fanny Nelson, accustomed to only slight variations between warmth and heat in the West Indies, had never known anything like it. "Mrs. N.

takes large doses of the bed," noted her father-in-law with suppressed irritation, "and finds herself only comfortable when enclosed in moreen. Myself, more accustomed to the climate, give no heed to small illconveniences." Even her husband felt "a rheumatic twinge" but passed the time reading – Dampier's *Voyages* was a favourite – and poring over charts in the candlelight. Both huddled indoors and the rector confided to Kitty, "The severe season has affected both your brother and his lady. They are moving just out of the bedchamber but both are brought to acknowledge that they never felt so cold a place." He himself was ever-optimistic: "The sun is now at its farthest distance and we must wait his return for spring entertainment of the rose and hyacinth ..."

When this came, old Edmund's enthusiasm was infectious as he praised the benefit to health of "the charming open lawns and pure air collected from the large fields of Thorpe, mixed with fine parts of a clear, purling stream bordered with cresses, thyme and vervain". Yet with spring came restlessness. Nelson could walk up the muddy lane that ran from the Parsonage garden up the gentle slope behind and from the crest, looking north, he could see between two low hills the horizon of the sea, a short, straight line amongst the curves of landscape, woodland and cloud. Now it was more often blue than grey and sometimes he saw distant sails. He could ride a pony over another hill for a mile or so to the little seaport of Burnham Overy Staithe. There he could watch ships and sailors at work: cockle-boats and wherries and schooners of the coastal trade, sometimes warping up the creek that wound through salt marshes which, as summer neared, were colour-washed with sea lavender and pinks. Beyond, framed between two headlands of sand-hills, was the line of white water that marked the sand-bar and the open sea. As he looked north, he knew that no land lay between this shore and the ice-cliffs of the Arctic he remembered. He could watch boat-handling here and more at Wells to the east, where the Boltons had lived and where he would always find a rowdy welcome at the card-tables of the Wells Club. More appropriate company was within closer reach at Burnham Market, where the squire, Sir Mordaunt Martin, and his large family lived at Westgate Hall, and North Creake, just upstream along the Burn, where Canon Poyntz, the scholarly and well connected rector – his sister was Countess Spencer, mother of Georgiana, Duchess of Devonshire, the figurehead of fashionable society – was collecting a library. Farther afield lived the landowning families to whom the Sucklings were related or connected – the Walpoles, Townshends and Durrants – but only Lord and Lady Walpole of Wolterton offered the prospect of an annual visit from their cousin, the unemployed captain, and his wife. Then each year there would be an opportunity to meet polite society in the west and centre of the country at dinners, balls and soirées at the Lynn Feast and the Aylsham Assembly.

As the year progressed, the Nelson family was itself responsible for most of the events that affected the couple. The only celebration was for the birth of Kitty's first child, a boy; otherwise, his brother Suckling's attempts at making a living as a village shopkeeper had failed and Edmund had returned to die at his father's house. Nelson took charge of the funeral arrangements and his attention to detail for "this last sad scene" was immaculate: "The hearse is to come from Fakenham at 10 o'clock to receive the body, which will be met at the church gate by Mr. Crowe, who is ordered a scarf, hat-band and gloves. The body to be carried by the six oldest parishioners, who are to receive a crown a piece after the funeral and, instead of gloves, each man is to have a handker-chief for their wives of the same price." The problem of placing Suckling fell to his father, who recommended that, as a last resort, he study Latin with a view to going up to Cambridge University and taking holy orders. So the young man also returned home, penniless and taking all help and hospitality for granted, or, as his father generously put it, "Suckling is such a philosopher that he endures his change with absolute indifference and even cheerfulness, though the common necessities of life are scarcely in any prospect before him now."

It was not only the family itself that could expect kindness from the Nelsons of Burnham Thorpe. Since the trial of his ship's cooper for murder more than a year before, there had been some correspondence with the Admiralty over the formalities of committing "the unhappy object James Carse", as his former captain called him, to an institution for the insane. Nelson did not forget him and, in April, wrote to the Earl of Chatham, the First Lord of the Admiralty, offering further help: "I can assure your Lordship that until this dreadful disorder came upon him, there could not be a more orderly man. And if he is recovered I should certainly have no objection to receiving him, wherever I am employed, although he is an elderly man."

News that he hoped might affect his own prospects was read avidly by Captain Nelson in the *Norfolk Chronicle*, which arrived from Norwich every Saturday afternoon. There he read of political unrest in France and the threat to its monarchy. In the summer this came to a head when, on 14th July, 1789, the Paris mob stormed the Bastille prison and, the following month, the National Assembly adopted the Declaration of the Rights of Man, the revolutionary tract written by Thomas Paine, a fellow-Norfolkman, who had gone to America, supporting the rebel cause and so was regarded by Nelson as a dangerous subversive. Such upheavals could have repercussions that would necessitate the mobilisation of the Royal Navy, even as a precaution; and that could mean another command for him. So, between writing letters to the Admiralty and naval friends, he kept himself busy in the garden, completing the work started by his brother-in-law in diverting water from the Burn into the pond, and laid out flowerbeds, digging, it was said, "as it were for the purpose of being wearied". The farm that went with his father's living occupied him, too. "I am now commencing farmer," he wrote to Locker. "Not a very large one, you will imagine, but enough for amusement." But field sports did not interest him. "Shoot I cannot; therefore I have not taken out any licence." When he was persuaded to join a shooting-party, his efforts were remembered: "He once shot a partridge; but his habit of carrying his gun at full cock and firing as soon as a bird rose without bringing the piece to his shoulder, made him a dangerous companion." His father worded this more indulgently: "An enemy floating game is a better mark." But he did come to enjoy coursing hares, perhaps being introduced to it by Suckling, for the wide fields around and above Burnham Thorpe were suited to the sport, particularly a spread of high ground near the old Roman road south of Holkham, where a mounting-block had been set up so that the gentry could gather to watch and wager on dogs and hares. He was probably happiest walking in the woods, looking for birds' nests as he had when a boy and in this, so long as it was not too energetic and the weather was fine, he could be joined by his wife.

During 1789, there was a summons to Whitehall but it was only for him to give more evidence at the continuing enquiry into West Indian embezzlements. When a sudden dispute over trading rights in Nootka Sound, an anchorage on the coast of Vancouver Island, broke out between Britain and Spain there was even talk of war. Nelson heard about this at the same time as his Norfolk neighbours for, as he complained, "the retired situation, which I am placed in, seldom affords any other means of information than a newspaper". Now he read reports of ships being fitted for sea and officers recalled and at once took the coach for London, presented himself at the Admiralty and asked for an interview with the First Lord. But Lord Chatham was too busy and, determined to state his case to one of the Board, he sought out Lord Hood at his house in Wimpole Street. Ever since they had first met at New York, Nelson had regarded Hood as a friend and potential patron and so what passed in the tall house in that new and fashionable London street came as a shock all the more stunning. Indeed, Nelson could not bring himself to write of it for two years; then he confessed that when he had asked Lord Hood for an appointment at sea, "he made a speech never to be effaced from my memory, viz.: that the King was impressed with an unfavourable opinion of me."

It was not only the surprise and hurt of this unexpected blow that was so shattering but that it was added to what he described as "a prejudice at the Admiralty evidently against me, which I can neither guess at, nor in the least account for." He must have speculated that it was the result of his zeal in suppressing American trade in the Caribbean that had so displeased his superiors there; or it might have been linked with his friendship with Prince William Henry and the affair of Lieutenant Schomberg, because the relationship between the King and his sailor-son had been turbulent and he might have been seen as an undesirable friend. Worse still, although probably not recognised, was the damage to his quasi-religious reverence for the monarch, which had begun at the moment of inspiration in the South Atlantic. He had been spurned by his godlike patron, and that was not to be accepted, so it must be assumed that the King had been misled into this view by his advisers. "Neither at sea nor on shore, through the caprice of a Minister can my attachment to my King be shaken," he declared boldly. "That will never end but with my life."

In despair, he appealed to the Prince – now created Duke of Clarence – who had given him a generous testimonial to the First Lord, but without the usual flowery preamble: "Sir, my not being appointed to a ship is so very mortifying that I cannot find words to express what I feel on the occasion; and when I reflect on your Royal Highness's condescension in mentioning me to Lord Chatham, I am the more hurt and surprised."

The humiliation was worsened by the litigation over his seizures of cargoes under the Navigation Act coming to a head. One spring morning, he had gone to market where he hoped to buy a Galway pony when an unexpected and unwelcome visitor rode up to the Parsonage: a bailiff from the court at Walsingham. Demanding to see Fanny, he questioned her to make sure that she was the wife of Captain Nelson and then served her with a writ, notifying him of an action for damages assessed at £20,000 on behalf of two American captains. It was not so much the outcome of the case that infuriated Nelson on his return, riding his new pony, because any costs would, he had been assured, be borne by the Treasury, but the intrusion and the flustering of Fanny. "This affront I did not deserve!" he complained to the Admiralty, while at home he even talked of leaving England to become an exile in France and, Fanny recorded, "he once spoke of the Russian service" as a naval mercenary.

Not even the general election of that summer could divert him, although he was gratified that it returned William Pitt to power. Their magnificent neighbour, Thomas Coke, also stood for Parliament after a six-year absence from politics and was elected but his sympathy towards the revolutionary movement in France did not endear him to Nelson.

10 *Above left*: The fascinating Dr. Benjamin Moseley, authority on tropical diseases, sugar, black magic, sharks, coffee and much else, who prudently decided not to sail for Nicaragua, painted by John Hoppner.

11 *Above right*: The friend from Nicaragua: Captain Edward Despard of the "Liverpool Blues", the engineer officer on the Rio San Juan expedition with whom Nelson shared a tent, painted by George Romney.

12 *Below left*: The generous Hercules Ross, sugar-planter of Jamaica, who befriended the young Captain Nelson and remained his admiring correspondent when retired to Scotland, painted after a portrait by Sir Henry Raeburn.

13 *Below right*: First among Nelson's friends of West Indian years was Captain William Locker (here painted by Gilbert Stuart), the tough but cultivated captain of the *Lowestoft*.

14 *Above*: El Castillo de la Inmaculada Concepción – or, as Nelson knew it, St. John's Fort – on the Rio San Juan in Nicaragua as drawn in 1780, probably by Captain Despard.

15 *Below*: The castle of San Juan photographed by the author in 1978 from upstream on the San Juan river. In the jungle on the border of Costa Rica, it could still be reached only by boat.

View of English Harbour Antigua Bay.

16 *Above*: English Harbour as the principal British naval base in the northern Leeward Islands. The Naval Commissioner's House, "Windsor", stood on the hill above the dockyard.

17 *Below*: Nelson's Dockyard – as it is now known – as a yacht haven and a tourist attraction. The dockyard at English Harbour has been handsomely restored but "Windsor" no longer stands.

18 *Above left*: Love frustrated. Captain Nelson's romantic attachment to Mary Moutray (drawn in 1781 by John Downman in London) might have ended differently if her elderly husband had died in Antigua instead of Bath.

19 *Above right*: Love requited. After Mary Moutray had returned to England with her family, Captain Nelson met Fanny Nisbet in 1785 and married her two years later. This portrait was painted in 1798 by Daniel Orme.

20 *Below*: Home waters: the healing baths and convivial assemblies at Bath, where Nelson recuperated after Nicaragua and was often to stay with his wife and father, as seen at the time by Thomas Rowlandson.

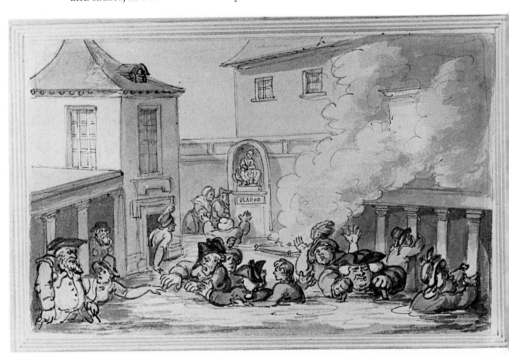

They had already brusquely refused an invitation to a Whig fête held some months before by Coke at Holkham to celebrate the anniversary of the landing of William of Orange at Torbay: "Captain Nelson's compliments to Mr. and Mrs. Coke and is sorry it is not in his power to accept their invitation for November 5th." Instead, his own political ambitions having faded, he agreed with his father who declared, "The noisy nonsense of elections does not disturb me, nor the neighbourhood in any great degree." Comparing his own activities with "the annual velocity ... nine-tenths of the country are moving with", the old man described himself as like "the poor snail that just creeps from shrub to shrub to spoil a rose" and his son now retreated further into the life of a modest gentleman-farmer.

Farming his land at Burnham Thorpe and near his father's other two churches at Burnham Ulph and Burnham Sutton; caring for his pony, Tycho, and buying a starved pointer as a pet rather than a gun-dog; putting the finishing touches to the garden and the little lake; all Nelson's tendency to be punctilious over detail was concentrated on such. He was ordering loose-covers for the furniture from Mr. Scott, the upholsterer: "A sopha cover of blue and white striped Manchester, of the pattern sent, or nearly like it. The price I cannot exactly tell ... A cover is sent, which fits very well except length; let the other be three inches deeper to hang over the legs ... Mrs. Nelson desires a handsome, rich *blue* – but not dark"; or Norfolk turkeys for Captain Locker; "Three very fine, large turkeys, also sausages sufficient to eat with them. Let the turkeys be ready for the spit, sewed up in separate cloths and securely packed up in a basket. If sausage meat is more convenient, let it be put in a jar and sent with them"; he was passing on social gossip: "Mrs. Nelson desires me to say that Miss Durrant is grown a very fine, tall young woman. Lady D. is quite the old woman; lost her front teeth!"

Whenever the *Norfolk Chronicle* reported a worsening of British relations with revolutionary France or with Spain, he would write again to the Duke of Clarence, or to the First Lord of the Admiralty. When in September, 1790, he had heard that his first ship was to be brought back into commission he asked: "If the *Raisonnable* is not given away, I should esteem myself highly honoured by the command of her." When a negative reply – or, worse, no reply – arrived, depression and irritability followed in "a sudden melancholy" or, as it was later described, a "tempest of his passions". Neither were Fanny, nor his father, easy to live with: she complaining about the cold, the lack of social activity, or both; he, irritating by the very sweetness of his temper and, since he regarded weak eyesight as God's judgement and so not to be questioned by the wearing of glasses, having to have the newspapers read aloud to him. Too conscious of his own real and imagined failings, Edmund understood this and suggested that it would be more convenient for him to move out of the remote Parsonage to a tiny, rented cottage up an alley near one of his churches, All Saints' at Burnham Ulph. It might have been built for a labourer but he planned to furnish "one clean, spruce room" for receiving visitors, lit by a pair of gilded girandole candle-brackets either side of the fireplace and with "an elegant tea caddy and tea" to hand. A neighbour would act as housekeeper, crossing the lane to the little church while he was preaching to whisper from the vestry door that dinner was ready. "*My town residence*," he told Kitty, "promises all that could be looked for. It is near my Chapel of Ease, warm and in the vicinity of what is useful in food, clothing and physic and most likely, by and by, a little social chat may take place."

The rector had moved by the end of the year, worrying about his daughter-in-law, as he told Kitty: "Your bro' is well and I hope fixed at Thorpe, a place he delights in; but I wish it was a little better accommodated to Mrs. N., as a woman who would sometimes choose a little variety." He did what he could to enhance the simplicities of village life, asking Kitty, "Be so good as to buy for Mrs. Nelson a plain, handsome bonnet such as she may wear at Wolterton if need be, or what you would for yourself buy for dining, visits, etc. Send it down and if any covering for the neck by way of a cloak is needful, add that also. Place them on my account."

Suckling was another worry but a place at Christ's College, Cambridge, had been found for him at further cost to his father's modest resources and there was hope that, with extra tuition, he might achieve ordination. "He will pass (no doubt) amongst a crowd of undistinguished preachers," noted his father with surprising acerbity, "and again some respect in the village of his residence from his quiet disposition, his liking to a little conviviality and his passion for greyhounds and coursing." The Match-ams, too, were leaving Norfolk and moving to Hampshire where they planned to build a house near Ringwood. The Boltons lived near William Nelson at Hilborough and the two families remained the principal source of company for those still living at the Burnhams. Otherwise, the year 1791 was remarkable for Captain and Mrs. Nelson only for a visit to King's Lynn for the annual jollities of the Lynn Feast and to Wolterton, where they dressed in black to mourn the death of their distant relation Lord Orford, whose title passed to "Mr H. Walpole of Strawberry Hill", although they had never been invited to his mansion at Houghton, near as it was to Burnham Thorpe.

Throughout the year, the news from France – reported in some detail by the *Norfolk Chronicle* – had been disturbing; in June, King Louis XVI had escaped from Paris but was recognised and arrested, together with his family, at Varennes near the frontier and returned to his capital, a prisoner. As 1792 began, the possibility of war became distinct: in February, Austria and Prussia formed an alliance against France, which declared war on the former in April and on the latter in July. But while Europe was convulsed with crisis that April, Nelson had to worry about moving his sheep from the water-meadows beside the little river in front of the Parsonage when it flooded: "The sheep have been until Wednesday last kept in the marshes since the grass began to spring ... and now the marshes are under water." In June, Nelson read a report from London that the Admiralty was beginning to prepare for war: "A fleet of observation is a measure at length determined on and yesterday orders were received at Portsmouth to fit out the guardships with all possible expedition." While no letter of recall reached him, it was galling to find that Norfolk neighbours – mere civilians, landowners, farmers and even labourers – were more actively employed than he, as when, at the end of the month, the Marquess Townshend, the Lord Lieutenant of the county, reviewed the Western Battalion of the Norfolk Militia on Stourton Heath near Dereham.

The weekly newspaper was published in Norwich on Saturday morning and that afternoon Nelson would be awaiting its arrival at the Burnham Market inn. Now that it included such full despatches from Paris and other European capitals as well as reports from London and Portsmouth, he needed time to read and consider the news. If he took the *Norfolk Chronicle* to the Parsonage, Fanny would want to hear the social gossip; if he took it to his father's cottage, the old man might embark upon some philosophical discourse; he had to find somewhere to read undisturbed. So he would ride over the low chalk hill to Burnham Overy Staithe and along the embankment that separated the creek from the meadows that had been reclaimed from the salt marshes; there, sheltered from the wind, he could read and think while an occasional sail, passing to or from the sea, would sharpen his awareness of what he was missing[1]. It was here he read the news from Paris: the storming of the Tuileries, the massacre of the Swiss guards and the imprisonment of the Royal Family. He read, too, of the advance of avenging Austrian and Prussian troops and then, in September, the reports became horrifyingly immediate and personal. Beneath the headlines DREADFUL MASSACRE IN PARIS and

[1] In 1960, the author was told by Mr. James Riches, whose family had kept the village shop at Burnham Overy Staithe for generations; "My people used to say that on Saturday afternoons Captain Nelson used to take his work down to the bank." Seeing him from a distance, engrossed in reading, shopkeepers might have thought this book-work with accounts or the study of documents.

HORRIBLE ACTS IN FRANCE were the hideous details of what came to be known as the September Massacres and the threat to the Revolution which ended when the foreign invaders were repulsed at Valmy. It was one thing to read about anonymous aristocrats being lynched by the Paris mob but another to read in the peace of a summer afternoon in Norfolk of the terrible death at their hands of the Princesse de Lamballe: "A fine rather than a beautiful woman; she was tall and most elegantly formed – her face brunette with most expressive sparkling black eyes. Her mental qualifications exceeded those of her external beauty and were stored with the richest acquirements from the *belles lettres*."

Although Nelson still wrote to the Admiralty begging for a command, he was resigned to neglect, remarking of one written in the autumn of that year, "I can hardly expect any answer to my letter, which has always been the way I have been treated." So he continued with the seasonal routine of farming and the round of social visits after the harvest and it was while staying at Wolterton that he was shocked by events much nearer home. The Walpoles were not stimulating company, their appeal as host and hostess being in their social status, but on this occasion there was plenty to excite and alarm: no less than the risk of revolution in England. It had not only been Thomas Coke and the Whigs who had given the first revolutionary stirrings in France a guarded, sometimes fulsome welcome; the new radical politics had become more than a talking-point and, throughout the country, radical clubs and corresponding societies had been formed to question the established order. On his return to Burnham Thorpe from Wolterton at the beginning of November, Nelson was worried enough by what he had heard to write about it to the Duke of Clarence.

He began:

> If I may judge from this county, where Societies are formed, and forming, on principles certainly inimical to our present Constitution both in Church and State, of which our Dissenters are the head, and in this county they have great riches ... I have been staying some time with my relation, Lord Walpole, near Norwich, at which place, and near it, the Clubs are supported by Members of the Corporation; and they avow that till some of the nobles and others in Parliament are served as they were in France, they will not be able to get their rights.

His anxiety has been strengthened by a letter from Cuthbert Collingwood, who was also on half-pay at his home in Northumberland, where he had recently married, reporting the same social unrest.

He had written:

There are great commotions in our neighbourhood at present. The seamen at Shields have embarked themselves, to the number of 1,200 or 1,400, with a view to compel the owners of the coal-ships to advance their wages; and, as is generally the case when they consider themselves the strongest party, their demand has been exorbitant. Application was made to Government for such assistance as the remedy of this evil might require. They have sent the *Drake* and *Martin* sloops to join the *Racehorse*, which was here before, and some troops of dragoons, whose presence, I hope, will dispose the Johnnies to peace without having occasion to act. But the times are turbulent; and the enthusiasm for liberty is raging even to madness. The success of the French people in establishing their republic has set the same principle, which lurked in every state in Europe, afloat.

Alarm was spreading through the country and particularly in Norfolk, the county of Thomas Paine, which had a radical tradition going back to Kett's rebellion of the seventeenth century and beyond. In his newspaper, Nelson read that the Mayor of Norwich, John Harvey, had addressed a gathering of "gentlemen, clergy, merchants and tradesmen" at the Maid's Head Inn near the cathedral with this warning:

Gentlemen! A more important or a more awful crisis than the present can scarcely be conceived, when various combinations of wicked and designing men are held in different parts of the kingdom expressly for the purpose of creating discontent and exciting suspicion and distrust ... Missionaries are sent from club to club to disseminate these detestable opinions ... God forbid that this nation should ever sink under that levelling system where every ruffian's hand may be put into his neighbour's purse to supply his own wants.

The rural gentry reacted in different ways: some wrote to their Members of Parliament; some joined the militia; most refused to believe that the English could ever become so over-excited as the French; Nelson sought a cause and a solution. He listened to the labourers talking on his farm; perhaps he called at the village inn, The Plough, to ask opinions. He was disturbed by what he was told and made notes of what he heard, putting them to constructive use. He had just received a reply from the Duke of Clarence to yet another letter asking for active employment in view of the possibility of war with France, saying encouragingly, "should matters between the two countries grow serious, you must be employed" and asking whether his rift with Lord Hood had healed. In his letter of thanks, Nelson repeated his warning to the Duke about political agitation in Norfolk and, in particular about a radical preacher, Joseph Priestley, and the use of village inns for such meetings. He trusted that the magistrates would annul the licences of "those public houses who allow of improper Societies meeting in them and take up these incendiaries who go from ale-house to ale-house advising the poor people to pay no taxes, etc. In this neighbourhood a person of the name of Priestley, a clergyman, has held this language to a circle of ten miles round him; and, a few days past, I asked a Justice of the Peace, 'Why, as such a man's conduct was known, that he was not taken up?' His answer was, 'that no Justice would render himself unpopular at this time by being singular; for that his life and property were gone if the mob arose: but that when the Justices all agreed to act in an uniform manner, this man should certainly be taken hold of.'"

Nelson had noted that, in his part of the county, farm labourers' wages had been raised by their alarmed employers and he set their plight and consequent attitudes in context.

That the poor labourers should have been seduced by promises and hopes of better times, your Royal Highness will not wonder at, when I assure you that they are really in want of everything to make life comfortable. Part of their wants, perhaps, were unavoidable from the dearness of every article of life; but much has arose from the neglect of the country gentlemen in not making their farmers raise their wages in some small proportion as the price of necessaries increased ... Their wages have been raised within these three weeks, pretty generally, one shilling a week: had it been done some time past, they would not have been discontented, for a want of loyalty is not amongst their faults ...

To his letter he attached a table of income and prices entitled: "An account of the earnings and expenses of a labourer in Norfolk with a wife and three children, supposing that he is not to be one day kept from labour in the whole year." Earnings for the man, including the busy harvest-time, and his wife's gleaning, came to a total of £23.1s.0d., while expenditure on clothes, which he listed garment by garment, soap, candles, coal and rent amounted to £8.13s.10d. "For food, five people – £14.7s.2d.", he concluded, adding, "Not quite twopence a day for each person; and to drink nothing but water, for beer our poor labourers never taste, unless they are tempted, which is too often the case, to go to the ale-house." He had been surprised and shocked by his own findings: "Hunger is a sharp thorn and they are not only in want of food sufficient but of clothes and firing."

It was a paradoxical time for, as sympathy with the egalitarian ideals of the French Revolution spread amongst the liberal-minded and the poor, so the likelihood of war with France increased. At the end of November, news arrived from Paris that the Jacobins had taken over the direction of the Revolution led by Danton; at the beginning of December, the trial of the King began and, on the 15th November, 1792, the *Norfolk Chronicle* published a report that he had been "beheaded before the eyes of the Queen, who was immediately hanged on the spot." It was reassuring, therefore, to read in the same issue that King George III had in his speech opening the new Parliamentary session, given the French a warning. Although he had "uniformly abstained from any interference with respect to the internal affairs of France", he had said, "It is impossible for me to see without the most serious uneasiness the strong and increasing indications which have appeared there of an intention to excite disturbances in other countries ..." Therefore, he concluded, "I have thought it right to take steps for making some augmentation of my naval and military force."

Although the first issue of the *Norfolk Chronicle* in 1793 announced that the King of France was still alive after all, its report from Paris began; "The fate of the unfortunate Louis engrosses all attention here" and there was news of warlike activity from London:

> Every public measure seems to announce that we are on the eve of war. Within the last few days contracts to a very large amount have been made for all kinds of naval and military stores, transports, etc. Indeed it is not improbable that some act of hostility may take place before the end of the present week for a small squadron of our ships have already weighed anchor from the Downs and sailed on Monday to the eastward.

Nelson knew that if his time was not come now it never would and he took the coach to London and on 6th January, 1793, presented himself in the ante-room of the First Lord's office at the Admiralty. What happened there excited him so that it was not until next day that he was able to compose himself to sit down and write to Fanny about it:

> *Post nubila Phoebus* – Your son will explain the motto: After clouds comes sunshine. The Admiralty so smile upon me that really I am as much surprised as when they frowned. Lord Chatham yesterday made many apologies for not having given me a ship before this time and said that, if I chose to take a sixty-four to begin with, I should be appointed to one as soon as she was ready; and, whenever it was in his power, I should be removed into a seventy-four ... Everything indicates war. One of our ships, looking into Brest, has been fired into: the shot is now at the Admiralty. You will send my father this news, which I am sure will please him.

Lord Hood, now friendly again, had told him that his ship would probably be either the *St. Albans* or the *Intrepid*, fourth-rates which were being brought forward from reserve at Portsmouth and Plymouth. This was a disappointment since he had hoped for one at Chatham because Captain Locker had also been recalled to service and, as a commodore, was Commander-in-Chief at the Nore, his flagship a few miles down-river from the dockyard. In any case, he had asked the Admiralty not to print recruiting posters for whichever ship these chose for him until his name could be included as her captain.

The Admiralty's decision would be made in a matter of days, perhaps weeks, so there would be time to return home for packing and making arrangements for the family. This time, his return from London to Norfolk was euphoric; there were congratulations from all, although Fanny's was tearful rather than enthusiastic. Now he could read with the excitement of a participant such news in the *Norfolk Chronicle* as "Orders have been sent to Portsmouth for the following ships of war to be fitted for commission with all possible dispatch ...", and, "The *Victory*, of 110 guns, was put in commission last Thursday." Then the issue of 26th January brought the expected news from Paris: "The unfortunate LOUIS is no more! He was beheaded yesterday morning in the Place de Louis Quinze. He died with the most heroic fortitude"; and, from London: "Last night a meeting of Cabinet Ministers was held at Mr. Pitt's house in Downing Street, in consequence of which several dispaches were sent off from the Admiralty and War Office. A war seems more certain than ever ..."

Orders to join a ship now arrived and, on this same day, Nelson wrote to Commodore Locker, "Lord Hood tells me I am now fixed for the *Agamemnon* at Chatham ... Lord Hood has been very civil indeed. I think we may be good friends again." Meanwhile he had arranged that a lieutenant and four midshipmen should tour Norfolk seaports in search of volunteers for the ship and that his friends amongst sea-captains trading between Wells and the northern ports had promised to send any they could find to the Navy's recruiting officers at Newcastle and Whitby. Nearer home, the sons of the rural gentry were being offered to him, together with those of three clergymen: William, son of Dixon Hoste, the worldly and political rector of Tittleshall; handsome John, son of Thomas Weatherhead of Sedgeford and his younger brother; and William Bolton, son of Susannah's brother-in-law, the rector of Hollesby. The future of Nelson's own stepson, Josiah, was also settled for he too would be going to sea at the age of thirteen. But Fanny was miserable and showed it, unable to share her husband's delight. Although Edmund Nelson at once assured her that he would be returning to the Parsonage, he worried about her: "Poor Mrs. Nelson will, I hope, bear up with a degree of cheerfulness." Farm labourers and seamen from the Burnhams, Wells and the neighbouring villages volunteered for the *Agamemnon* and were sent to Chatham. Meanwhile, in Burnham Thorpe, Nelson gave a farewell party for his neighbours from what he described as the "homesteads by the stream" at The Plough. While the little inn was noisy with talk and laughter a crowd of village boys – too young to be invited – had gathered outside and one of them, from the High family, was being teased for boasting that one day he, too, would be going to sea with Captain Nelson. A scuffle started and some of the men in the parlour, hearing the noise, came out into the forecourt, tankards in hand, Nelson following. The combatants were separated and Nelson remarked with a smile to the small boy who had been the cause of it that he had put up a valiant fight. Then and there the boy decided that, come what may, he would follow Captain Nelson to sea and his fellows, half-joking, half-admiring, at once gave him the nickname Valiant.

Two days before Nelson was due to leave, the last issue of the *Norfolk Chronicle* that he could expect to see for some time arrived and gave emphasis to the dramatic news it reported with a woodcut on its front page of the grim shape of "The Guillotine, or Beheading Machine". The horror that had taken hold of the French Revolution had swept aside most of the sympathy for its original ideals. Even radical or discontented Norfolkmen, who had listened so attentively to the republican agitators a few months before, now found as much satisfaction as did Nelson himself in reading that "Twenty more ships of the line will be put in commission as soon as possible with a proportionate number of frigates. Orders were sent on Saturday from the Admiralty Office to the Dockyards for that purpose ... There are now 104 ships in commission – 36 of the line."

On 1st February, 1793, France declared war on Britain. Four days later, Captain Nelson, accompanied by his stepson and Frank Lepée, left Burnham Thorpe bound for London and then Chatham, where he would commission the *Agamemnon* in three days' time. He was now aged thirty-four, physically strong and charged with pent-up energy and ambition. But his new-found zest was not reflected in the wife he left behind and she made little effort to disguise her feelings. "Poor Mrs. Nelson has indeed a severe trial," wrote her father-in-law, who had planned to share his house with her. "She will be with me here and in the Parsonage a week or two, then makes a visit to Hilborough and look out for a comfortable lodgings in Swaffham, where she means to reside ... If the warlike storm blows over, then most likely the course of matters will return to their old channel."

On 7th February, Captain Nelson trod the deck of one of His Majesty's ships for the first time for more than five years and smelled that pungent mixture of tar, hemp, wet wood and human bodies. After the formalities, he went to his cabin, opened her leather-bound log-book and wrote his first entry: "Fresh gales with wind at times. Went on board and put the ship in commission. Found the carpenter and joiner at work." He was happy with what he saw of the *Agamemnon*, although she looked little more than a hulk in the dockyard, and Commodore Locker had been collecting drafts of prime seamen and the best of the volunteeers for her. One of Nelson's first acts was to visit his old friend at Sheerness but both knew that this was likely to be their last encounter on board ship. Locker's health had never fully recovered from the illness that had put him ashore at Jamaica when commanding the *Lowestoft* and he was now about to leave the sea for the last time to become Lieutenant-Governor of Greenwich Hospital, the great institution which cared for naval pensioners and the sons of seamen. Nelson knew that he himself would only remain at Chatham as long as it took to make his ship ready for active service.

There was much to be done. First the trimming of the iron ballast in the bilges; then stepping a new foremast and bowsprit and rigging the ship. There were stores, salted meat and casks of fresh water to be loaded. Drafts of seamen arrived to be issued with working clothes and hammocks but, although Josiah had arrived with him, he remembered his own miserable introduction to the Navy at this very port, and decided that most of the boys who were to become his midshipmen should not join until the ship's company had "shaken down" and the *Agamemnon* was ready for sea. During February, all of March and much of April, work continued and Nelson's impatience showed in his irritation with Fanny, who was proving to be inefficient as well as self-pitying. "You forgot to send my things ... by the Sheerness boat," he wrote to her. "I have got a keg of tongues, which I suppose you ordered, and also a trunk from Wells, Norfolk, and a hamper of three hams, a breast of bacon and a face, not very well packed, there being no straw between them and the motion of the waggons has rubbed them very much. However, they will do."

By the middle of April he was satisfied with his ship: "I can say with truth she is getting into high order. Although we are upwards of 100 short of complement, yet I think we shall be far from ill-manned ... Josiah is in high glee to think we are going to sail." It was blowing a gale when the *Agamemnon*'s sails were set for the first time and Josiah was seasick before they had left the Medway estuary, but Nelson was happy. "My ship appears to sail very fast indeed and every day puts us in higher order," he wrote on the 18th. "In short, we are well officered and manned, the greatest comfort a captain can have. My orders are not yet on board, but I expect them every day."

In the Downs roadstead off Deal, where she awaited a convoy to be escorted down-Channel to Portsmouth, the *Agamemnon* swung at her anchor, tugging at her cable, in the wind, her captain pacing his quarterdeck. The frustrations of unemployment, domesticity and a childless marriage now belonged to the past; ahead stretched the promise and possibilities of the sea.

CHAPTER V

A Taste of Glory
(1793–7)

"Agememnon is as well known through Europe as one of Mr. Har-
wood's ships is at Overy."
— Captain Horatio Nelson to Fanny Nelson from H.M.S.
Agamemnon at Genoa, 13th November, 1795

Despite the April gales, there was a holiday spirit on board the
Agamemnon when she anchored in Spithead in the spring of 1793. "My
ship sails very well indeed," boasted her captain. "We think better than
any ship in the fleet." He was delighted with the zest of her crew, many of
them young Norfolkmen who had learned some seamanship in the sandy
creeks he knew. More were brought aboard by luggers that came
bouncing over the choppy water from Portsmouth and amongst these was
young William Hoste, whose father had travelled by coach down to
Hampshire, to be greeted by other Norfolk boys: the two Weatherheads,
Billy Bolton and Josiah Nisbet amongst them. Another visitor was
Maurice Nelson, who had taken a few days' leave from his desk in the
Navy Office, his money worries and his mistress, to come aboard his
brother's ship and satisfy his curiosity.

The *Agamemnon* was under orders for sea but the gale strengthened
and she could neither weigh her anchor, nor send her visitors ashore.
When it moderated, she was able to get under way but not hoist out a
boat, so that when she sailed, Maurice Nelson, who had already slept a
night in his brother's cabin, was still on board. Most of the boys were
seasick: Nelson himself suffered at first, but soon discomforts were
forgotten in the excitement of sighting the coast of France. There they
found the right quarry for the *Agamemnon*: four French ships – two of
them frigates – with less fire-power and little more speed. They lay off La
Hogue, protected by shoals, and as the *Agamemnon* tacked to and fro at a
distance where she might not be identified as the danger she was, all four
got under way and one frigate stood out to sea. Then her captain saw
what awaited him, changed his mind and, Nelson wrote in his log, "She
tacked and stood in again, making a number of signals to the other ships

who stood close inshore under a fort." Not to be thwarted, Nelson steered for Alderney, passing so close to Cherbourg that young Hoste "could perceive with glasses the people walking on shore", and made the signal for a pilot. Two came aboard but neither dare risk taking a big ship through the notorious shoals of La Hogue; so, as William Hoste wrote to his father at the end of the six-day cruise: "We were obliged to desist from any further attack on those dastardly Frenchmen amongst the rocks. Our time being stated to return, we were obliged to steer for Old England without a prize and are at this moment entering Spithead."

Putting Maurice ashore to take the coach to London, Nelson fumed with frustration. "I believe we are sent out for no other purpose than to amuse the people of England by having a fleet at sea," he wrote to Fanny. But there were two fleets at sea: one, under Lord Howe in home waters; the other, commanded by Lord Hood, bound for the Mediterranean, and it was the latter which the *Agamemnon* was ordered to join as part of the third division commanded by Vice-Admiral William Hotham. On Saturday, 11th May, 1793, a day of cloud and gales, she sailed in company with two other ships of the line and two frigates, one of them his old ship, the *Lowestoft*, bound for Cadiz and the straits of Gibraltar. Lord Hood was friendly still. "The Lord has just sent me a civil note," Nelson told Fanny, and, "We are all well, my ship remarkably healthy"; so, as he had said, after clouds it was indeed sunshine.

Since Spain was as much a traditional enemy as France, it was curious, but fascinating, to visit Cadiz and be greeted as an ally, albeit a temporary one by all the signs. Nelson was as admiring of the Spanish-built ships in the harbour as he was shocked by the slovenliness of their crews: "I am certain if our six barges' crews (which are picked men) had got on board one of their first rates they would have taken her. Therefore in vain may the Dons make fine ships; they cannot make men." Shore leave was granted in the white-walled town on the long spit of land that separated the wide anchorage from the Atlantic and there disgust was added to disdain when they joined the crowds in the bull-ring. "A bull feast, for which the Spaniards are famous and for their dexterity in attacking and killing of which the ladies choose their husbands, was exhibited in which we English had certainly to regret the want of humanity in the Dons and Donnas," wrote Nelson to Fanny, delicately choosing the word "husbands" rather than lovers. He continued:

The amphitheatre will hold 16,000 people, about 12,000 were present. Ten bulls were selected and one brought out at a time; three cavaliers on horseback and footmen with flags were combatants. We felt for the bulls and horses and I own it would not have displeased me to have had some of the Dons tossed by the enraged animal. How women can even sit, much more applaud such sights is astonishing. It even turned us sick and we could hardly sit it out. The dead, mangled horses with their entrails tore out, the bulls covered with blood, was too much. However, we have seen one and agree that nothing shall tempt us to see another.

It was a relief to return to robust British surroundings under a Spanish sun at Gibraltar to take on wine, which would be preferable to rum and beer during a Mediterranean summer. Lord Hood was there in his flagship the *Victory* and their restored friendship was confirmed. Indeed it was Hood who implemented the Admiralty's promise of a bigger ship. "The Lord has sent to offer me a 74," noted Nelson, "but I have declined it ... I cannot give up my officers." This was no sacrifice since not only was he delighted with his ship and "our Jacks" but the *Agamemnon* was to lead one of the three divisions of Lord Hood's fourteen sail of the line, over which he kept tight control through the signals constantly run up the halyards of the *Victory*. To this was added briefly a fleet of twenty-four Spanish ships of the line, which quickly returned to port on grounds of ill-health on board. News of their departure was given to Hood by a Spanish frigate and, as Nelson scornfully remarked, "The captain of the frigate said it was no wonder they were sickly, *for they had been sixty days at sea.* This speech appeared to us ridiculous, for from the circumstances of having been longer than that time at sea, so we attribute our getting healthy."

The task of Hood's fleet was to blockade French warships and commerce into the ports of Toulon and Marseilles, particularly the former, which was a fortified naval base, where about twenty ships of the line were believed to lie with others building or refitting. As they approached the French coast, the horrors of the French Revolution that Nelson had read about for so long in the *Norfolk Chronicle* were suddenly thrown into sharp relief by the realities ashore. "A master of a ship ... from Marseilles says there are now only two descriptions of people in France – the one, drunk and mad; the other, with horror painted in their faces, are absolutely starving." Yet England was still in his mind's eye, although faintly and, in the same letter, he wished his father well with the harvest and sent his compliments to "the Burnhamites." The Admiralty was in clearer focus and he wrote an exasperated letter when he heard that prize-money due to the ship's company of the *Boreas* was still held by the Collector of Customs of Nevis. After saying with sarcasm that not "every poor seaman can go to Nevis to receive his money", he wrote: "They look up to their Captain as their friend and protector, and it was my intention, if the money was paid to me to advertise the distribution of it in London, when every officer and seaman, or their relatives, would be on the spot . . . I humbly hope Their Lordships will be pleased to order it to England." To Fanny he wrote affectionately if with some formality, "I look back as to the happiest period of my life the being united to such a good woman", and there was constant news of her son: "Josiah is a very good boy and grown very much . . . He is now in fractions, preparing to learn navigation."

More than a month of cruising off the French ports was a thankless task since results could not be seen and the blockading ships were themselves starved of fresh food. "All we get is honour and salt beef," said Nelson, longing for action. When it was reported that the French were fitting their ships with furnaces for heating red-hot shot to start fires aboard their opponents, his response was, "We must take care to get so close that their red shots may go *through* both sides, when it will not matter whether they are hot or cold".

Then something extraordinary and unexpected happened: Toulon surrendered to Lord Hood. Marseilles tried to surrender, too, but was quickly occupied by a Republican army which took terrible revenge. Toulon was as strongly fortified against attack by land as by sea and its citizens were able to declare their loyalty to King Louis XVII – the Dauphin, imprisoned in Paris – and invite the British fleet to enter their great harbour. "What an event this has been for Lord Hood," wrote Nelson to Fanny. "Such a one as History cannot produce its equal. That the strongest place in Europe and twenty-two sail of the line, etc., should be given up without firing a shot; it is not to be credited." There were problems for Lord Hood too, because the perimeter defences of the city, strong and well-sited as they were, needed a garrison of at least 50,000 troops, a force stronger than the entire British Army. The admiral at once landed his marines and sent out urgent calls for reinforcements.

But when Hood's ships sailed between the forts into the two broad basins of Toulon harbour to take possession of the city and dockyard, the *Agamemnon* was not with them, much to her captain's disappointment. He and his ship had been chosen – because of his forcefulness and charm, and her speed – for an urgent diplomatic mission: to strengthen the eastern flank of operations against France by ensuring the support of the Kingdom of the Two Sicilies, which covered the whole of Italy south of Rome and the island of Sicily. This was ruled by the Spanish Bourbon dynasty and King Ferdinand IV was married to Maria Carolina, the daughter of the Empress Maria Theresa of Austria and sister of the imprisoned Queen Marie Antoinette of France. They were potential allies of great value (see map, page xiii).

After calling briefly at Oneglia to land despatches for the British

Consul at Turin and again at Bastia in Corsica with a letter for General Paoli, the patriotic leader who was resisting the French, Nelson captured a Ragusan brig bound for Marseilles from Smyrna and put a prize-crew aboard. Then, on the night of 10th September, 1793, he arrived in the Bay of Naples to an ominously spectacular eruption of Mount Vesuvius that brought all hands on deck to stare in wonder, their up-turned faces lit by the glare. "The throws of fire from Mount Vesuvius were grand," noted Nelson in his journal and young William Hoste, writing to his father in their remote Norfolk rectory, described the volcano "in all its glory, for now its eruptions are most splendid; the lava spreading from the top and rolling down the mountain in great streaks of fire." At two o'clock in the morning the *Agamemnon* anchored off the city.

Next morning the fiery display had changed to a rolling canopy of smoke and the magnificence of the bay, bounded by the silhouettes of the Sorrento peninsula and the dragon-back of Capri, could be seen. A boat came alongside from the Neapolitan flagship at anchor nearby with a message that King Ferdinand was on board and wished to receive the British captain. So Nelson was at once pulled across in his barge and for the first time met the Bourbon monarch. Ferdinand was a strongly-built man with a long, deeply-lined face and small, cunning eyes divided by the prominent, clownish nose that had won him the nickname *Il Rè Nasone*; "Old Nosey" to the British sailors. Nelson responded to his robust manner when the King told him that he had known for nearly a week about the capture of Toulon by the Spanish and he replied hotly that it had surrendered before the arrival of the Spaniards. "The King seemed surprised," noted Nelson, "but said he was glad to hear it." Although Hood's despatches were for the British ambassador, he then produced a list of the French warships at Toulon and said that more troops were desperately needed to hold the place. Nelson had not been authorised to approach the King directly, let alone ask him for practical military aid so it was gratifying when the royal reply was that he regarded the British as the saviours of Italy and of his kingdom in particular.

Only now did Nelson go ashore, carrying Hood's despatches for the ambassador. On landing, he made for the embassy, the Palazzo Sessa, through steep, narrow streets between the cliff-like walls of houses and palaces, encrusted with heraldic carving and balconies, sometimes giving a glimpse through an archway of courtyards, or the dark interior of a church, flickering with votive candles before gilded saints. The British Embassy was a tall building, standing on high ground behind the royal palace, its window commanding a panoramic view of the bay and the mountains at its rim. Through the courtyard and up stone steps he walked, to find himself in a treasure-house of the arts: paintings by Italian masters in heavy gilded frames, statuary and the strange black and ochre shapes of Greek vases. It was there that he met the British ambassador, Sir William Hamilton and delivered Lord Hood's despatches.

Like most educated Englishmen, who read the newspapers and listened to gossip, Nelson had heard about Sir William and his wife. Indeed, the couple had long provided a subject for piquant chatter and Nelson himself may first have heard it in Bath or at Wolterton Hall. Sir William, now aged sixty-two, had, he knew, married a famous beauty – an artists' model and the former mistress of rich young rakes, it was said – less than half his age. They proved to be a striking pair; he, lean and sun-burned with alert, intelligent eyes and an aristocratic, aquiline nose; she, handsome, plump and zestful. Nelson took to them at once. "Sir William, you are a man after my own heart," declared Nelson, and, when Hamilton quickly concentrated on the essentials of his mission, "You do business in my own way." He had suggested that they immediately call upon the prime mover of events in Naples, an expatriate Englishman, Sir John Acton. The heir to a Shropshire baronetcy, he had been born to a French mother, lived all his life on the Continent and, by ambition and an air of command, had risen to become Prime Minister to King Ferdinand. He received them at nine o'clock that night, having already been told by the King of Nelson's request for reinforcements. This was agreed, he told them, but as the allies in Toulon were probably short of provisions it might be best to wait until the troopships could sail accompanied by their rations. To this Sir William, himself an old soldier, said that two thousand men sailing in three or four days' time would be more use than three thousand leaving with their stores in a fortnight. Acton thereupon ordered that the two thousand should leave for Toulon four days hence with their provisions.

Nelson, invited to stay at the Palazzo Sessa, asked if his midshipmen could come ashore for some sightseeing and Lady Hamilton at once arranged this, herself paying particular attention to his stepson. "Lady Hamilton has been wonderfully kind and good to Josiah," he wrote to Fanny, adding, as no further explanation of his hostess's background was needed, "She is a young woman of amiable manners and who does honour to the station to which she is raised." The others were not accorded his personal attention and William Hoste told his father, "Captain Nelson was so kind as to present me with two orders of admission to the King's museum and the ruins of Herculaneum, which were well worth seeing; but it was a mortifying circumstance to us that our conductors would not speak either English or French, therefore our curiosity was more excited than gratified."

Nelson had no time for sight-seeing. Together with Hamilton, he dined with the saturnine Acton and was summoned by the King to visit him at Portici, his summer residence outside the city where he was told by a lady-in-waiting that only the Queen's advanced pregnancy prevented her from receiving him. There was also the *Agamemnon* to replenish with fresh food, water and wine and make ready for visits by the King and the Hamiltons. In the event, too heavy a swell was running for the King to be rowed out to the ship but Nelson dined with him ashore and was bidden to a parade of the troops about to embark for Toulon. And so, early on the morning of his seventh day at Naples, he and the Hamiltons watched King Ferdinand himself drill, and then lead the march-past of four thousand men, now under orders to sail within a week. Now, prompted by Hamilton's shrewd, sometimes sharp, assessments, Nelson was no longer so in awe of the King and he noted in his private journal, "The vanity of the —— of Naples is such that he wished to cut a great figure by sending his stipulated force all at the same time and to that vanity we are now indebted for the 4,000 instead of the 2,000 at first promised."

Later that day, while Nelson was entertaining the Hamiltons and several ladies of the court on board his ship, a message arrived from Acton that a French corvette and a British merchantman she had captured had been reported at anchor off the coast of Sardinia. It was an occasion for setting an example and Nelson decided that "although my ship was almost without water, casks on shore for wine, etc., yet I considered that the city of Naples looked to what an English man-of-war would do. I ordered my barge to be manned, sent the ladies ashore and in two hours my ship was under sail." The seven Neapolitan warships at anchor in the bay did not join him in pursuit of the common enemy, which, in the event, escaped.

The mission to Naples had, however, been a success. Significant reinforcements were bound for Toulon: Nelson had made a positive impression on the King and his Prime Minister and he had established a trusting friendship with the Hamiltons. He had responded to their help and hospitality by showing interest in Sir William's collection of paintings and even asked his advice in choosing some inexpensive pictures for himself, although a planned shopping expedition was cut short by his sudden departure. "The sending off of the prints adds to the kindness I have already receiv'd from you and Lady Hamilton," he wrote from the *Agamemnon* a few days later. "I have sent 20 dollars, I do not know if I am right in my calculation."

In contrast to the ebullience of the Hamiltons came a fussy and discontented letter from Fanny, to which he replied irritably, "Why should you fret yourself? I am well, your son is well and we are as comfortable in every respect as the nature of our service will admit." She had taken lodgings at Swaffham but could not settle and her father-in-law, about to leave for Bath, wrote to her suggesting alternatives: "Swaffham you are not perfectly pleased with; can you fancy any other place? Spending the winter months with me at Bath, you have said no word about it. To leave you in an unpleasant or unsettled state I shall regret. Though my intention is to leave Burnham early in the next month, yet to accommodate you in any way that scheme shall be altered."

On 5th October Nelson was back in Toulon harbour, where the scene was now dramatically changed. "Shot and shells are throwing about us every hour," he wrote in his journal. "The enemy have many strong posts on the hills which are daily augmented with men." Ashore the allied garrison of British, Spanish, Sardinian, French royalists, and now Neapolitan troops, were hard pressed; the latter, inexperienced in war, suffered heavily as the French assaulted one redoubt after another. Increasingly accurate fire was being brought to bear on ships in the harbour, directed by a young artillery officer, Napoleon Bonaparte, a Corsican; but the *Agamemnon* was at sea under orders to join Commodore Linzee off the coast of Sardinia on 16th October. On that day Queen Marie Antoinette was beheaded in Paris, and when the news reached the Mediterranean, it stiffened the alliance against France; particularly in the Kingdom of the Two Sicilies where Queen Maria Carolina, alternately demented and depressed by grief for her sister, vowed vengeance. Forgetting her determination never again to speak French – "that murderous language" – she hung a placard beneath her sister's portrait inscribed, *"Je poursuiverai ma vengeance jusqu'au tombeau"*.

At two o'clock in the morning of 22nd October, while on passage for Sardinia, lookouts in the *Agamemnon* reported signal rockets in the darkness and then sighted five ships in the moonlight. Two hours later, she was within hailing distance of one, a big frigate, which was found to be French, accompanied by two more frigates, a corvette and a brig. Nelson now had his first chance of fighting enemy ships but it was not one that many captains would have welcomed: there would be none of the acclaim aroused by a duel between ships of equal weight for each of the frigates was smaller than the *Agamemnon*. But together the French ships could out-gun the British ship, which was under-manned as a third of her company had been left ashore to fight at Toulon.

Nelson gave chase to one of the frigates, the *Melpomène*, and action was joined at daylight, the French ship being expertly handled; firing her stern guns at the *Agamemnon*'s masts and rigging to slow her and yawing to loose a broadside. At nine the wind dropped, and the French frigate, badly battered, was joined by her consorts. But they forebore from closing with the British ship, which was too crippled aloft to make sail in pursuit. And so the French drew away and the *Agamemnon* – with one man dead and six wounded – limped on to Sardinia. On joining Linzee, Nelson sent him a brief account of the action and his despatch to Lord Hood, claiming that the *Melpomène* had been reduced to a sinking condition; but, shrewdly, he sent another account to his brother Maurice. In this he listed the comparative armaments and manpower of the opponents – giving the French 170 guns and 1,600 men against his own sixty-four guns and 345 men – in the sure knowledge that the letter would be passed round the Navy Office and counter any suggestion that his ship of the line had failed to beat a frigate.

The *Agamemnon*'s foremast and rigging were repaired by carpenters and riggers working all night so that she could join Linzee's squadron which was leaving on a mission to Tunis. The Bey had been favouring the French – indeed a French squadron was lying in the harbour when they arrived, waiting to escort a convoy to Marseilles – and the commodore's task was one of diplomatic persuasion. This proved difficult, for the Bey was wily and sophisticated: when Linzee described the horrors of the French Revolution and the execution of the King, he replied, "Nothing could be more heinous than the murder of their sovereign and yet, sir, if your historians tell the truth, your own countrymen once did the same." Nelson had no time for such teasing diplomacy: "I should have taken every Frenchman here without negotiating; even had the negotiations taken place, I would have had the French men-of-war and believe that the people of England will never blame an officer for taking a French line of battle ships."

Then came orders from Lord Hood for Captain Nelson to sail for Corsica and take command of the frigates cruising in those waters. Soon after his arrival he heard the shocking and unexpected news that Toulon had fallen. The French besiegers had stormed one allied fortification after another until all of the harbour was commanded by their fire. On the night of 17th December a general assault was launched on the defences and the Spanish and Neapolitan troops broke and ran. The British fell back on the town and the defences around the harbour but it was obvious they could not hold for long and Hood ordered the evacuation to begin. Meanwhile he sent an active officer, Captain Sir Sidney Smith, to burn the French ships that could not be towed out of the dockyard.

"Everything which domestic wars produce usually, is multiplied at Toulon," Nelson wrote to Fanny. "All is horror ... I cannot write all: my mind is deeply impressed with grief. Each teller makes the scene more horrible." Lord Hood had managed to evacuate some 15,000 Toulonese by sea but, as the Neapolitans panicked and the Spanish stopped fighting only the British tried to make a stand; the last defences collapsed and thousands had to be abandoned to the inevitable slaughter. Although the British managed to extract four French sail of the line and a dozen frigates, Captain Smith only managed to burn nine of those that had to be left – due largely to the failure of his Spanish incendiary parties to do their duty in the pandemonium; so that eighteen sail of the line escaped their attention, enough to provide the Revolution with a fleet to challenge the British in the Mediterranean. Nelson, who probably recognized something of himself in the ambitious, volatile Smith, awarded him the blame, remarking, "Lord Hood mistook the man: there is an old saying, *Great talkers do the least, we see.*"

When the end came, the *Agamemnon* was at Leghorn, taking on provisions and water, sailing on the third day of 1794 to rejoin Hood for the next essential stage of operations: the securing of a new base. The obvious place was the island of Corsica, which was in revolt against the French under its nationalist leader, the elderly Pasquale de Paoli, who had known Dr. Johnson and Boswell during a spell of exile in London. A mission had been sent to negotiate with the Corsicans, led by Lieutenant-Colonel John Moore and Lieutenant George Andrews, Royal Navy, whose sister Nelson had failed to win at St. Omer ten years before. In the event, the Corsican partisans did little to help but British troops landed and captured the port of San Fiorenzo with its fine anchorage on the north-west coast, sheltered by the long, rocky ridge of Cap Corse. Nelson himself was involved in harrassing attacks on the coast by British ships; one of the most difficult being at the fort in Martello,[1] which withstood close-range naval bombardment for two days.

The keys to Corsica were the two fortress-cities of Bastia and Calvi on the east and west coasts, both of which were more vulnerable to attack from the sea than by troops struggling over the tortuous tracks through the mountains from San Fiorenzo; in any case, General Dundas, the British commander there, was reluctant to try until reinforcements reached him from Gibraltar. The French were also expected to send reinforcements to the island so that Nelson's first task was to prevent this by blockade. Often close inshore and under fire, sometimes landing for a raid and at sea chasing and boarding suspected blockade-runners, he could write to Fanny: "My ship's company behave most exceedingly well. They begin to look upon themselves as invincible, almost invulnerable. They really mind shot no more than peas." No wonder then that he urged Hood to launch an assault on Bastia from the sea with marines, seamen

---

[1] This round, flat-topped tower, mounting a heavy gun, was to be copied and give its name to the scores of Martello Towers that were to be built along the south-east coast of England as a defence against invasion at the beginning of the 19th century.

and soldiers, who were embarked as marines, in the absence of regular soldiers. Such was his zeal that when he heard that the French garrison of the town was far stronger than expected and at least three times the size of the force that could be assembled for an attack, he kept the information to himself in the belief that it would deter Hood from making the attempt. Disingenuously, he kept up the pretence that the capture of Bastia was well within the capabilities of the force at Hood's disposal, using scorn to make further hesitation difficult. "When was before the time that 2,000 British troops, as good as ever marched, were not thought equal to attack 800 French troops, allowing them to be in strong works? What would the immortal Wolfe have done? As he did, beat the enemy, if he perished in the attempt."

Nelson was as diligent in introducing his midshipmen to war as he had been to the curiosities of Naples. On one coastal raid to "cut out" a French ship that had taken shelter in a cove near Bastia, Nelson took the thirteen-year-old William Hoste with him in his boat. "We instantly carried the vessel," wrote the boy to his father afterwards, "and killed several of the French, an officer among them." His captain also wrote to the Norfolk rectory: "Your son ... is a strong proof that the greatest gallantry may lie under the most gentle behaviour. Two days ago, it was necessary to take a small vessel from a number of people who had got on shore to prevent us; she was carried in high style and your good son was at my side." Yet when the landings eventually began on 4th April, he left young Hoste on board ship, telling his father, "Your dear boy wishes much to come on shore with me and, if I had not thought the danger too great, I should have brought him."

Bastia, defended by high walls, bastions and a citadel on low cliffs above the sea with mountainsides sweeping steeply to rugged peaks inland, was difficult to attack. To the south were swamps so it was to the north that the landings had to be made and there on a shingle beach at Miomo, three miles north of the town, more than two thousand soldiers and marines landed under the command of Colonel Villettes and Captain Nelson. While the troops marched south to make camp a mile from their objective, the sailors worked all night cutting down trees, clearing rocks and preparing to drag guns on roughly made sledges to batteries which had to be dug into the hillsides. Their technique, an adaptation of a familiar evolution, was described by an admiring landsman, Sir Gilbert Elliot, a lawyer and Member of Parliament, who had been evacuated from Toulon, where he had been civil commissioner during the British occupation. "They fastened great straps round the rocks," he noted. "They fastened to the straps the largest and most powerful purchases, or pulleys and tackle that are used on board a man-of-war. The cannon were placed on a sledge at one end of the tackle, the men walked down the hill with the other end of the tackle. The surprise of our friends the Corsicans and our enemies the French was equal to the occasion." It was more strenuous than it seemed for the way to Bastia lay across the face of steep, rocky hillsides, covered with thorny scrub and seamed with deep ravines; strange for sailors accustomed to the cramped environment of a ship, its familiar smells replaced by the pungent scent of wild herbs and pine. "It is very hard service for my poor seamen, dragging guns up such heights as are scarcely credible," recorded Nelson with satisfaction. "The expedition is almost a child of my own," he told Fanny, "and I have no fears about the final issue. It will be victory. Bastia will be ours."

The siege batteries complete, Lord Hood sent his barge ashore from the *Victory* on 11th April with a summons to surrender. In his private journal Nelson recorded the reply from Le Comte St. Michel, the Commissioner of the Convention in the city that "he had hot shot for our ships and bayonets for our troops, that when two-thirds of his troops had been killed he should then trust to the generosity of the English". On receiving this, "Lord Hood hoisted a red flag at the main top gallant masthead of the *Victory*,[1] when our batteries opened on the town, citadel and redoubt ... (first hoisting English colours on the rock over my tent and every man giving three strenuous cheers)". The bombardment and counter-bombardment thudded and echoed against the mountains, and smoke drowned the scent of wild rosemary. The besieged suffered far more than the besiegers, a walled city being an easier target than well-sited batteries behind breastworks; British losses were few, although Nelson himself was lucky to escape. He had been entertaining his friend Captain Thomas Fremantle of the *Tartar* to dinner in his tent and had taken him forward to see a new battery, returning by a short cut. "Walking with Nelson from thence," wrote Fremantle in his diary, "a shot knocked him down and covered me all over with dirt. Determine never to go the short way again."

But it was not gunfire, nor the threat of a general assault, which Nelson planned to lead himself, that brought victory, but hunger: the naval blockade had been entirely effective. After a final cannonade from the ramparts, a message came from the city that negotiations for surrender could begin next day, 19th May. That evening, the British troops from San Fiorenzo – three battalions of infantry, a regiment of dragoons and a hundred guns – finally appeared in the pass through the mountains behind the city to share the glory. Next evening, Nelson recorded: "Our

[1] The author saw this same signal hoisted on board H.M.S. *Victory*, when she was in commission as flagship of the Commander-in-Chief, Portsmouth, as the dockyard came under attack by VI flying-bombs in June, 1944.

troops marched from their posts, the band playing *God Save the King* and *The Grenadiers' March.* At seven, the French colours were struck ... and the British colours hoisted under three cheers from every seaman and soldier." Two days later, he continued: "At daylight this morning, the most glorious sight which an Englishman, and I believe none but an Englishman, could experience, was to be seen: 4,500 men laying down their arms to less than 1,000 English soldiers." The losses of the besieged were ten times heavier than those of the besiegers, whose health had been good although, as the weather grew hotter, they were plagued by mosquitoes from the swamps to the south of the city each night; but that was regarded as no more than an acceptable discomfort, as it had been on the expedition up the Rio San Juan. For Nelson himself the greatest hardship of the campaign was shortly to follow, when he read Lord Hood's despatch. When they met, Hood had been fulsome in his praise. "Lord Hood's thanks to me, both public and private, are the handsomest that man can pen," he told Fanny, "having ever since our leaving England been in the habit of getting thanks and applauses, I look for them as a matter of course." But in his report to the Admiralty, Hood had merely commended him for his part in landing the guns and stores, giving others the principal credit. "The whole operations of the siege were carried on through Lord Hood's letters to me," he complained to his uncle, William Suckling. "I was the mover of it – I was the cause of its success ... I am not a little vexed, but shall not quarrel."

Now it was the turn of an even more formidable French fortress and, on the day after the surrender of Bastia, he was writing to his new friend, Sir William Hamilton, "We shall now join heart and hand against Calvi". That this would be difficult, if not impossible, became apparent on the first sight of the fortified city on the headland on the west coast of Corsica. On three sides, the great granite walls rose sheer from the rocks on the shore and towering bastions guarded the fourth, on which a neck of open ground connected the citadel with the mainland. Other than starvation – and there was no evidence that the city was short of food – only prolonged bombardment by heavy artillery could reduce such a fortress. A sandy beach over which the guns could be landed close to the city was commanded by its batteries and otherwise the coast was rocky, pounded by seas whipped by westerly winds; the sea off-shore so deep and its bottom so rocky that it was difficult for ships to anchor.

On 17th June, a fine, almost windless day, the *Agamemnon* lay at anchor in fifty-three fathoms a mile from the only break in this rock-bound shore, a little inlet named Porto Agro, and this Nelson determined to explore. At half-past three the next morning, he was pulled ashore in one of the ship's boats, accompanied by Lieutenant-General the Honourable

Charles Stuart, who had relieved the timid General Dundas in command of the land forces, to assess the possibilities. He found Porto Agro "by no means a convenient place for landing guns or stores as sunken rocks lay twenty feet from the shore with deep water between them and with a common sea breeze such a sea sets in as to prevent boats landing". Indeed the clear, deep water between the rocks at the mouth of the inlet was only just wider than the span of his boat and its oars. There were more rocks beyond, but the inlet widened to a beach of stones and shingle about a hundred yards in width, where a landing could be made. Here worse difficulties began for the hillsides rose on all sides and the terrain was rough and rocky all the way to Calvi, three and a half miles distant. But it was already apparent that there was no alternative.

It remained calm next day and by seven o'clock in the morning the advance-guard had been put ashore in Porto Agro and, while they struggled up the hillsides, seamen dragged six field-guns on sledges up from the beach. That afternoon, two hundred and fifty seamen landed and camped on the shore to unload the weapons, ammunition and stores that would have to come this way and that night rigged sheerlegs and tackle to swing twenty-six-pounder guns from boats on to their sledges on the beach. But next day, recorded Nelson, "it blew so strong with a heavy sea as to preclude all intercourse with the shipping. By the morning of the 21st every ship had put to sea. We were employed in making roads for our guns and getting up three twenty-six-pounders to the Madonna [a hill-top chapel by a figure of the Virgin Mary standing on a prominent rock] about two and a half miles from the landing place. The road for the first three-quarters of a mile is up a steep mountain and the other part is not very easy in the heavy rains with much thunder and lightning." The next fortnight was hard labour, man-handling and dragging guns, shot, barrels of powder and rations up the steep slope from the beach and over the broken, boulder-blocked ground along a rough track torn through the scrub to the forward dump at the Madonna. That was not the end of the heavy manual work because batteries had to be built and naval officers – amongst them Lieutenant James Moutray, the son of Mary Moutray, once of English Harbour, Antigua, took charge of sailors working as gangs of labourers, "carrying junk for mortar platforms and placing the mortars on their beds all night", wrote Nelson in his journal. "A hundred seamen employed in getting forward things for the advanced battery. Lieut. Moutray made a battery for two eighteen-pounders ... with twenty-five men." He himself accompanied the parties hauling the guns and a routine was established: "It was General Stuart's orders for the working parties to move forward with sandbags, casks and platforms and, as soon as they were got forward, I was to move with the guns." At last, early in the morning of 4th July, the Royal Louis battery, manned by French artillerymen from Toulon, opened the bombardment.

Manning and fighting the guns was dangerous work since the batteries were within range of those mounted on the walls of the citadel. Each day, several of the besiegers were killed or wounded and among the dead was a captain of the Royal Navy; on 8th July, Nelson noted: "They destroyed two of our guns and much damaged another and the works. One shell burst in the centre of our battery amongst the General, myself and at least a hundred of us, but wonderful not a man was hurt, although it blew up our battery magazine." Then, on the 12th he was wounded. He had been watching the bombardment from a vantage point by an enormous flat-topped rock which commanded a view of the whole battlefield and the besieged city, when a shell burst on the rampart of the sandbags in a shower of stones and sand. Blood poured down his face from cuts; the deepest on the right brow which had narrowly missed his eye; but it had affected his sight. Although he wrote to Lord Hood, "I got a little hurt this morning: not much, as you may judge from my writing", and only noted in his journal, "At seven o'clock was much bruised in the face and eyes by sand from the works struck by shot", it proved more serious. Four days later, he was writing to William Suckling: "My right eye is entirely cut down; but the surgeons flatter me I shall not entirely lose the sight of that eye. At present I can distinguish light from dark, but no object ... I feel the want of it; but, such is the choice of war, it was within a hair's breadth of taking off my head." At first he made light of it to Fanny as "a very slight scratch towards my right eye, which has not been the smallest inconvenience", but three weeks later admitted that his eye was "as far recovered as to be able to distinguish light from darkness, but as to all the purpose of use it is gone ... The pupil is nearly the size of the blue part, I don't know the name ... the blemish is nothing, not to be perceived unless told." He could even joke, "So my *beauty* is saved."[1]

---

[1] "At Calvi, Nelson received a simple contusion injury to the right eyeball, damaging the iris diaphragm and resulting in a dilated pupil, which in time returned to normal. It is quite probable that there was also some bleeding behind the lens into the vitreous in the back part of the eye and this would cloud the vision, taking a bit longer than the pupil to recover by absorbing and clearing, but whether or not there was any damage of a lasting nature which could have resulted in a permanent loss of sight is highly conjectural," writes Mr. T. C. Barras, author of a study on Nelson's eyesight in *Transactions of the Ophthalmological Societies of the United Kingdom* (1986). "There was probably no lasting damage to the eye but he had also developed a pterygium (growth on the surface of the eye often due to exposure to sun and wind) in both eyes. Inflammation caused by this combined with deterioration in his eyesight, due to ageing, contributed to his fear of blindness often mentioned after 1800." On 31st August, 1803, Nelson wrote to Captain George Murray, "I am almost blind."

The dangers were not only those of war. There was the exhaustion of hauling heavy loads in the summer heat and the risk of dysentery or typhoid from tainted drinking-water, and, a month after they had camped near the swamps of Bastia – and the irritating mosquitoes – men began to sicken with fever. "The climate here from July to October is most unfavourable to military operations," wrote Nelson to his royal friend the Duke of Clarence in London:

It is now what we call the dog-days; here it is termed the Lion Sun; no person can endure it: we have upwards of one thousand sick out of two thousand and others not much better than so many phantoms. We have lost many men from the season, very few from the enemy. I am here the reed among the oaks: all the prevailing disorders have attacked me, but I have not strength for them to fasten upon. I bow before the storm, whilst the sturdy oak is laid low.

He was, in fact, lean and resilient, weathered and seasoned by nearly a quarter of a century of seafaring in all climates, and had survived the lethal embrace of the tropics. But a hundred and fifty of the *Agamemnon*'s crew including several midshipmen, Bolton and Weatherhead among them, were sick with malaria, heat-exhaustion, dysentery and, probably, typhoid, and, wrote their captain, "Poor little Hoste is also so extremely ill that I have fears about him". These survived but another, aged twenty-one, did not. "You will be sorry to hear young Moutray is dead," he wrote to Fanny. "I wrote you he was ill with Calvi fever. He was second lieutenant of the *Victory* and at this moment would have been a captain. What a shock it must be to his poor mother, who was all expectation of hearing of his promotion when a very different account will be told of her. His own amiable disposition will never be forgot by those who knew him." Nelson himself had a memorial to him carved for the church at San Fiorenzo, reading: "This stone is erected by an affectionate friend, who knew well his worth as an officer and his accomplished manners as a gentleman." By the end of July, the besiegers were so sickly – with less than a thousand men fit for active duty – that it seemed possible the city could survive their efforts.

Certainly Stuart's demands for surrender were ignored until, on the 28th, the French commander sent a letter announcing with eighteenth-century formality, rare in war with the new revolutionaries, that if no relief reached him within twenty-five days he would negotiate a capitulation. But General Stuart realised that his enfeebled troops were unlikely to withstand another month's ordeal and told Lord Hood that after another ten days he would have either to attempt an assault on the citadel or raise the siege. That night, four small ships slipped through the blockade and next morning could be seen discharging their cargoes at Calvi. As a result, it seemed, Stuart's latest ultimatum was in vain and the guns of Calvi opened another cannonade; the siege, it seemed, was a failure.

The British had not realised that the four blockade-runners had brought food, of which the garrison was not in desperate need, instead of ammunition, which was almost exhausted. On 1st August, the French sent word that they would be willing to negotiate on the 10th, if no further succour had arrived. So on that day, when Stuart found that he had not even four hundred men fit for duty, the French surrendered and some six hundred defenders marched out of the city – half of them regular French soldiers – past half that number of the victors. Meanwhile Nelson boarded two French frigates, which had lain under its guns throughout the siege; one of them, the *Melpomène*, he had fought off Sardinia.

Recognition was more important than prizes and that would have to wait until General Stuart's despatch was published in the *London Gazette*. "What degree of credit may be given to my services I cannot say," wrote Nelson to Fanny, but he was hopeful that it would be generous because, at his own accounting, "One hundred and ten days I have been actually engaged, at sea and on shore, against the enemy; three actions against ships, two against Bastia in my ship; four boat actions, and two villages taken and twelve sail of vessels burnt. I do not know that anyone has done more." When Stuart, whom he regarded as a friend, did not even mention his name, he was shattered. "My diligence is not mentioned," he wrote to William Suckling. "Others, for keeping succours out of Calvi for a few summer months are handsomely mentioned. *Such things are.* I have got upon a subject near to my heart, which is full when I think of the treatment I have received: every man, who had a considerable share in the reduction, has got some place or other – I, only I, am without reward ... Nothing but my anxious endeavours to serve my Country makes me bear up against it; but I sometimes am ready to give all up." A spark of optimism remained and, calming his anger, he remarked, "But never mind, some day I'll have a *Gazette* of my own".

Despite this lack of public acclaim, his qualities were recognised. Not only had Hood taken his advice on attacking Bastia without the army's support, but he had made success possible at Calvi by the vigour with which he had handled the landing and the heaving of the heavy weapons and stores over appallingly rough terrain. His energy and ability to act upon immediate and original ideas had also been noted by a new friend, whose political acumen and influence would be valuable: Sir Gilbert Elliot. A shrewd, witty Scot, a few years older than Nelson, with the self-confident determination of a Border laird of learning and some wealth, he was about to be appointed Viceroy of Corsica and rule the island as a colonial possession. It was probably his advice that prompted Hood to choose Nelson for another diplomatic mission.

Success in Corsica had been marginal compared with the disasters suffered by the allies in 1794: the armies of Britain, Austria and Holland had been driven out of France and Belgium; the Austrians and Prussians had fallen back to the Rhine; Spain was unable to halt the French advance through the Pyrénées. That summer the British had hailed a successful action in the Atlantic by Lord Howe as a great victory and named it, after the date, the Glorious First of June but he had only defeated the fleet escorting a large convoy of grain ships, which had safely reached France to relieve the famine. The only allies as yet unbroken were the Italian states and these were about to come under attack; so Nelson's mission was to arrange for the use of Genoa by the British fleet as a forward base from which to harry a French advance down the coast towards Rome and Naples. It was a success and he was particularly gratified at his reception in a city he thought "the most magnificent I ever beheld, superior in many respects to Naples; although it does not appear quite so fine from the sea, yet on shore it is far beyond it ... I was received in some state, the Doge advancing to the middle of the room to receive me".

No sooner had Nelson reported that Genoa could be used for replenishment, than he heard that Lord Hood, whose health had also suffered during that arduous summer, had been recalled to London: until his expected return in the spring, his place would be taken by Admiral Hotham, with whom Nelson had sailed for the Mediterranean. The *Agamemnon* was worn out by continuous sea-keeping and many of her crew had been sent ashore to hospital, some to die, but hopes of accompanying Hood were quickly set aside for there was immediate danger that the French might burst out of Toulon in an attempt to recapture Corsica. So the ship was sent for urgent repairs to Leghorn and there her captain lived ashore, worrying that the attempt might be made and the climactic battle fought in his absence between the two well-matched fleets, each of about fourteen sail of the line. "My ship and ship's company are not half the strength as when I left Spithead," he wrote to Fanny. "Yet I am sure this ship's company feel themselves equal to go alongside any seventy-four out of France."

By Christmas, the ship was ready for sea and joined Hotham off Toulon, waiting for the French to come out. They did not and lay safe at their moorings while the blockading ships plunged through heavy seas, battened down and under storm stay-sails. At first, Nelson found this exhilarating, writing to Fanny during a call for water and provisions at

San Fiorenzo during the third week of January, 1795: "We have had nothing but gales of wind, but in *Agamemnon* we mind them not; she is the finest ship I ever sailed in." A second cruise in worse storms tempered his enthusiasm and, a fortnight later, he was writing to Sir William Hamilton at the Palazzo Sessa, where the long curtains were being ruffled by unusually sharp draughts: "We have had the most tremendous weather, such as I have never experienced before in any seas; it blew a perfect hurricane." Although the ship herself was still seaworthy, her crew was not and their captain wrote to Lord Hood, now back in England, that "Poor *Agamemnon* wants almost a new ship's company ... nor is myself free from complaints. I have been so low with flux and fever this last cruise that I thought I shall hardly get over it".

Discomfort and discontent were now forgotten when news arrived that the French were at sea. On 8th March, Admiral Hotham heard that Rear-Admiral Pierre Martin had left Toulon with fifteen sail of the line with the intention of covering the passage of a troop convoy bound for the invasion of Corsica and with his own fleet, one less in number, gave chase. Sighting the British advance under full press of canvas, the French – their ships' companies debilitated by the loss of officers and senior seamen and gunners in revolutionary purges – put their helms over and ran. Two ships of the line, the *Ça Ira* and the *Jean Bart*, collided in the confusion; the former losing her fore and main top-masts when their stays and rigging were broken loose. The *Ça Ira*, a big ship of eighty-four guns, lost way and fell astern of the retreating French, although two, the *Jean Bart* of seventy-four guns and the *Sans Culotte*, a huge, first-rate mounting 120 guns, closed to take her in tow. Sea-worn as she and her crew were, the *Agamemnon* was still a fast sailer and her guns' crews perfectly drilled. Nelson saw his chance, pulled away from the British line and steered for the crippled ship. His ship's agility would allow him to rake her, loosing broadsides through her stern windows while keeping clear of her own tiers of guns. "At a quarter before eleven a.m., being within one hundred yards of the *Ça Ira*'s stern, I ordered the helm to be put a-starboard and the driver and after-sails to be braced and shivered," reported Nelson afterwards. "As the ship fell off, gave her our whole broadside, each gun double-shotted. Scarcely a shot appeared to miss. The instant all were fired, braced up our after-yards, put the helm a-port and stood after her again. This manoeuvre we practised till one p.m., never allowing the *Ça Ira* to get a single gun from either side to fire on us ... At this time the *Ça Ira* was a perfect wreck, her sails hanging in tatters, mizzen topmast, mizzen topsail and cross-jack yards shot away."

The French fleet had now turned to join battle, but Hotham, fearing that the *Agamemnon* and other ships in his van might be cut off, signalled

Nelson to break off the action and he obeyed. Next morning, the *Ça Ira* was sighted in tow of the *Censeur*, another "seventy-four", and, although an attempt by two British ships to take her was avoided, Hotham managed to cut off both ships and after a fierce exchange of broadsides in which the *Ça Ira* was dismasted and the *Censeur* lost her mainmast, both struck their colours. Nelson sent Lieutenant George Andrews across to the shattered ships to accept their surrender and hoist British colours. He found fearful carnage on their gun-decks and reckoned that the *Ça Ira* had lost 400 men killed and wounded and the *Censeur*, 350. Other parties were sent aboard to plunder their magazines of powder and shot, for the *Agamemnon* was running short of ammunition and Nelson hoped that the action would be continued. When he was rowed over to the flagship to urge the pursuit of the French, Hotham, thankful that his under-manned ships had thwarted the attempted invasion of Corsica at so little cost, replied: "We must be contented. We have done very well."

Although Nelson understood the admiral's reasons for refusing to risk his ships further, his blood was up and his excitement edged with frustration. The vivid accounts he wrote of his duel with the *Ça Ira* ended with his disappointment at not achieving more. To his brother William he described his adversary as "absolutely large enough to take *Agamemnon* in her hold. That Being who has ever in a most wonderful manner protected me during many dangers I have encountered this war, still shielding me and my brave ship's company. I cannot account for what I saw: whole broadsides within half pistol-shot missing my little ship, whilst ours was in the fullest effect ... Had our good Admiral have followed the blow, we should probably have done more." To Fanny, he described Hotham as "much cooler than myself" then gave vent to his frustration:

> I wish to be an Admiral and in command of the English Fleet; I should very soon either do much, or be ruined. My disposition cannot bear tame and slow measures. Sure I am, had I commanded our Fleet on the 14th, that either the whole French Fleet would have graced my triumph, or I should have been in a confounded scrape ... Now, had we taken ten sail and allowed the eleventh to escape, when it had been possible to have got at her, I could never have called it well done.

He recognised that his zest for glory and recognition had so swept aside fear that opportunity to show his worth in war was now a necessity. "May I venture to tell you," he wrote to Fanny with arch humour, "but as a secret, that I have a mistress given to me, no less a personage than the Goddess Bellona; so say the French verses made on me and in them I am so covered in laurels that you would hardly find my little face ... I am 'the dear Nelson', 'the amiable Nelson', 'the fiery Nelson': however nonsen-

sical these expressions are, they are better than censure and we are all
subject and open to flattery."

But his mistress was not only the goddess of war. He wrote fondly to
Fanny and, in depressed moments, even began to dream about settling
down in "a neat cottage" with her when peace came but from her he did
not receive what he craved: admiration and encouragement. Her letters
were full of the social gossip from Norfolk, London and Bath but
reflected her worries about his health and safety instead of glorying in his
success. As her father-in-law put it: "His poor wife is continually in a
hurry and fret about him ... In such a state, the blessings of a marriage
union are thus made a torment and most likely the health is destroyed, or
the temper soured so as never to be recovered." So when packets of
letters from home were opened on board the *Agamemnon*, back in port
after another storm or battle, her husband would read: "This winter will
be another anxious one. What did I not suffer in my mind, the last!" To
one yearning for an echo of his own enthusiasm, this was irritating, as
occasionally showed in his replies: "Why you should be uneasy about me
so as to make yourself ill, I know not."

Nor was Fanny the representative he would have wished amongst the
influential in London and Bath. Lord Hood had been staying in both
places and wrote to Nelson, saying that he had met "your good little
woman" and that she was as "contented and happy as she can be in your
absence". Lady Elliot, Sir Gilbert's wife, was also in Bath and of
her he wrote, "a charming woman; we talk matters over daily." One
of the few women that Nelson seems to have known and accepted as an
equal in terms of intelligence and *savoir-faire* was Mary Moutray; others
being approached cautiously as unattainable objects of desire, chatter-
boxes or feline in their wiles. "They will always do as they please," he
wrote at this time, when ending a letter. "Orders are not for them; at least
I never knew one who obeyed your most faithful – Horatio Nelson."

Like other naval officers, Nelson had come to accept that marriage
vows need no longer be binding east of Gibraltar. Leghorn had become
his principal port for repair and replenishment, being well-placed for
operations against the French advance into Italy; a useful Admiralty
contractor, Thomas Pollard, was there and a consul, John Udney, who
would introduce lonely naval officers to friendly Italian ladies. It was
probably through him that Nelson met Adelaide Correglia, an opera-
singer with some reputation for promiscuity; a source of political and
social gossip and sexual satisfaction. A liaison, rather than a love affair,
began and continued whenever the *Agamemnon* returned although there
is no hint of this in a letter to her in his stilted French: "*Ma Chére
Adelaide, Je suis en cette moment pour la mère. Une vaisseau Neapolitan partier*

avec moi pour Livorne. Croire moi toujours. Votre Chère Amie, Horatio Nelson. Avez vous bien successe" (sic). Some of his brother officers were uneasy about his involvement, perhaps because he had hitherto seemed a martinet in matters of propriety. Even Captain Thomas Fremantle, a bachelor who enjoyed taking a drink and a woman when in port, sounded slightly shocked when recording his meetings with the couple. "Dined at Nelson's and his dolly," he noted at Christmas, 1794, and, in the following summer, "Dined with Nelson. Dolly aboard ... he makes himself ridiculous with that woman", and soon after, "Dined with Nelson and Dolly. Very bad dinner indeed". Nelson himself referred to her obliquely when writing to Sir Gilbert Elliot, and passed on political gossip with the jocular note, "One *old* lady tells me all she hears, which is what we wish."

The recognition accorded him in June, 1795, was appropriate: the courtesy rank of Colonel of Marines carried additional pay but no further duties and he was still involved with operations ashore. His activity on the coast of Corsica a year earlier made him the obvious choice to command an inshore squadron charged with supporting the Austrian army defending Italy against the French advance along the coastal road. He had no confidence in the capabilities of the Austrians any more than in those of the Spanish, Corsicans, Sardinians or the Italian states: "The allies," he wrote to Hamilton, "are a rope of sand." This assignment started frustratingly for, on passage from San Fiorenzo to Genoa, on 6th July the *Agamemnon*, accompanied by four frigates, suddenly came upon the French fleet – seventeen sail of the line under Admiral Martin – and at once turned back for the Corsican anchorage where Hotham's main force lay. The French gave chase, then, when Hotham emerged from San Fiorenzo to support Nelson, turned and ran for the French coast. Then the wind changed and dropped and the expected battle became a series of spasmodic encounters over many miles of calm sea. Hotham's flagship, the *Victory*, had dropped eight miles astern of the *Agamemnon* and a few other ships in action with the rear of the French line, when Hotham decided that they were too close to the coast of France for safety and made signals to retire. "Thus ended our second meeting with these gentry," wrote Nelson to the Duke of Clarence, and, although he added that "in the forenoon, we had every prospect of taking every ship in the fleet", he was tactful in his criticism of Hotham: "If he has a failing, we are none of us without them, it is taking too much time to deliberate whereby opportunities are lost. We have felt this on more than one occasion." Privately he agreed with the officer in the *Victory*, who put it more bluntly that "had the British fleet only put their heads the same way as the enemy's and stood inshore ... the whole of the French line might have been cut off ... taken or destroyed."

Once he had made contact with the Austrian commander, General de Vins, it was obvious that frustration with timid leadership would continue. His own activity at sea contrasted with sloth ashore and it came as no surprise when the Austrians were routed outside Genoa, their general retiring for reasons of health on the first day of the battle. But, at the beginning of 1796, the problem of effective leadership was resolved when Nelson met his new Commander-in-Chief. Lord Hood had not, after all, returned; he had quarrelled with the new Board of Admiralty, under Lord Spencer, over a strategy that starved the Mediterranean of reinforcements and had been ordered to relinquish his command. In the Mediterranean, his indecisive deputy, Hotham, had been replaced temporarily by another cautious admiral, Sir Hyde Parker, before the Board chose as his successor Admiral Sir John Jervis.

The two men had met once before in London, when Captain Locker had introduced them at the House of Commons, where Sir John represented Yarmouth when not at sea. At sixty, Sir John cut a formidable figure: a hard, handsome face in which determination and command were occasionally relieved by a glimmer of humour and kindliness; his head set low on heavy shoulders that gave him a bull-like build. As a boy, he had made his way in the Navy despite extreme poverty and lack of patronage, to become a post-captain in the Seven Years War, when he had accompanied Wolfe to Quebec, joining him on his reconnaissance of the beach below the Heights of Abraham and, on his death on the battlefield, taking his dying message to the girl he had hoped to marry in England. A formidable fighting sailor (he had received his baronetcy for his capture of a French first-rate in the American War), he was already known for his practical innovations in improving the health of ships' companies: cleanliness, the ventilation of lower decks and obligatory doses of citrus juice as protection against scurvy. Amongst his men, he was revered, rather than loved, as a just disciplinarian and recognised by his officers as a perceptive judge of character and worth.

When he met Nelson again on the quarterdeck of the *Victory* in San Fiorenzo Bay on 19th January, 1796, they took to each other at once. Jervis found Nelson a source of frank and well-informed opinions about the state of war in the Mediterranean and brimming with confidence and energy for, as he now said, "my health was never better". They discussed the possibility of Nelson's early promotion to rear-admiral – for he was now high in the Captains' List – and Jervis offered him command of a ninety-gun ship if he was so inclined. They parted on such easy terms that a less-favoured captain complained to Nelson: "You did just as you pleased in Lord Hood's time, the same in Admiral Hotham's and now again with Sir John Jervis. It makes no difference to you who is

Commander-in-Chief." But it had, for mutual confidence had been established; as Nelson was to tell Jervis, "The moment I knew of your arrival, I felt perfectly at ease".

Although the war was going badly for the allies on the land, the arrival of Jervis transformed the spirit of the Mediterranean Fleet. When instructions for Nelson's promotion to rear-admiral did not arrive, he was given the rank of commodore to exercise an admiral's duties and Jervis ordered him to continue his blockade of enemy ports and harassing them along the coast, treating him "more like an associate than a subordinate officer". Nelson responded to this recognition with a burst of activity, capturing a convoy of five French ships laden with the siege-train of heavy weapons bound for the *Armée d'Italie*, which was now commanded by General Napoleon Bonaparte, aged only twenty-seven but celebrated for his part in the taking of Toulon. In June, Jervis ordered that the worn-out *Agamemnon* should escort a convoy to England but that Commodore Nelson should shift his broad pendant to the seventy-four-gun *Captain*. Most of the ship's company with whom he had sailed for the Mediterranean three years before were dispersed – a few killed in action, dozens dead of fever or disease, others invalided or drafted to other ships – and he was sad to part with the "poor old *Agamemnon*", but now his drive was more deeply embodied in himself than in a ship or squadron. At the end of 1795, he had boasted to Fanny, "*Agamemnon* is as well known through Europe as one of Mr. Harwood's ships is at Overy", referring to coasters that regularly called at the little Norfolk seaport. Now, he told her a story that he admitted was "all vanity to myself" about a letter addressed simply to "Horatio Nelson, Genoa". The writer of the letter "on being asked how he could direct in such a manner, his answer, in a large party, was, 'Sir, there is but one Horatio Nelson in the world'. I am known throughout Italy: not a kingdom, or state, where my name will be forgotten. This is my *Gazette*."

His own successes were more than matched, however, by Bonaparte's. The latter took Leghorn, the former arriving as the city fell and able to do no more than blockade the port; but he was able to land British troops to occupy Elba and prevent its immediate use as a base for another French attempt to recapture Corsica. The tide of war was set too strong to stem and French success in Italy impelled Spain to change sides in October; the British fleet was now heavily out-numbered by the newly combined French and Spanish squadrons and dependent on a few islands for bases. Nelson, whose promotion to commodore had been confirmed by the Admiralty was intensely active with his squadron. "I cannot, if I am in the field for glory, be kept out of sight," he told Fanny. "Probably my services may be forgotten by the great by the time I get home; but my mind will not forget, nor cease to feel, a degree of consolation and of applause superior to undeserved rewards." But his wife's applause was always conditioned by worry: "I pray God to protect and grant you a continuance of your great successes." Yet his health had never been better for it was often conditioned by the degree of his activity; as he wrote that August: "If I ever feel unwell, it is when I have no active employment, that is but seldom."

On 29th September, orders arrived from Jervis that the British Government had decided the Mediterranean was untenable and must be abandoned; Nelson was to organise the evacuation of Bastia. "At home they know not what this fleet is capable of performing, *any and everything*," he complained. "Much as I shall rejoice to see England, I lament our present orders in sackcloth and ashes, so dishonourable to the dignity of England, whose fleets are equal to meeting the world in arms." Next there was Elba to evacuate and for this duty he shifted his pendant to the frigate *La Minerve*, which had been taken from the French. In her and in company with another frigate, the *Blanche*, he engaged two Spanish frigates and captured both, although the prizes had to be abandoned on the appearance of an enemy squadron. His final task in the Mediterranean came at the end of January, 1797, when he left Elba and carried Sir Gilbert Elliot, the Viceroy of Corsica, to Gibraltar and beyond.

Passing Cartagena he saw that the port was empty and heard that the Spanish fleet had sailed on 1st February and on reaching Gibraltar was told that it had passed through the straits into the Atlantic four days earlier. As he followed, two of their big ships, still at anchor off Algeciras, gave chase. The frigate made sail but one of her seamen fell overboard and a boat was lowered to pick him up. The man had, in fact, already drowned but the search took so long that the boat, commanded by the first lieutenant, Thomas Hardy, was in danger of being overhauled and taken by the pursuing Spaniards. Seeing this, Nelson exclaimed, "By God, I'll not lose Hardy!" and ordered the topsails to be backed to check the frigate's way. The Spanish captains, seeing this, assumed that she was prepared to give battle and that, such was their overwhelming superiority in weight of broadside, must mean she could sight the topsails of an approaching British fleet on the horizon. So the Spaniards, too, backed their sails and this gave Hardy time to pull alongside *La Minerve*, which then made sail and escaped.

That night fog came down and, when it began to lift, Nelson saw the shadowy shapes of huge ships and realised that he was sailing through the Spanish fleet. If he could escape, there were two actions he could take. One was to search for Jervis and his main fleet, which would be somewhere between Gibraltar and Cadiz, and give him the news that the

Spanish were also in the Atlantic. The other would be to make sail for the West Indies to bring warning that they might be the enemy's destination and so to prepare. He chose the former and, as the Spanish ships faded in the fog without having learned the identity of the frigate that had glided through their midst, found Jervis off Cape St. Vincent with fifteen sail of the line on 13th February. Commodore Nelson went on board the *Victory* early that morning with his news; Jervis listened with stern satisfaction then, as a fleet action seemed imminent, ordered him back to his own ship, the *Captain*, which would take her place in the line of battle. The importance of intercepting the Spanish before they could reach Cadiz, which was probably their aim, was obvious to all. Not only had the British been driven from the Mediterranean but the whole of continental Europe was now dominated by France. At home, the scene was as dark for the war had brought the nation's commerce to the brink of bankruptcy; Ireland was near to rebellion and there were even rumours of simmering mutiny in ships of the Royal Navy. As Admiral Jervis was heard to say: "A victory is very essential to England at this moment."

The British were sailing in two columns and throughout the night they could hear the signal-guns of the Spanish fleet; faint at first, then louder. Dawn on St. Valentine's Day – 14th February, 1797 – was raw and misty but, as it cleared, distant shapes of ships took substance to the south-west seeming more gigantic as the distance closed. "By my soul, they are thumpers!" a British signal lieutenant called out. "They loom like Beachy Head in a fog." On board the *Victory*, Sir Robert Calder, the captain of the fleet, reported to Jervis: "There are eight sail of the line, Sir John." "Very well, sir." "There are twenty sail of the line, Sir John." "Very well, sir." "There are twenty-seven sail of the line, Sir John; near double our own!" "Enough, sir, no more of that," said Jervis. "The die is cast and if there are fifty sail of the line, I will go through them." It was through them that he meant to go, for it could now be seen that the Spanish ships were sailing in two loose formations between which the British could pass, fighting the foremost on equal terms and destroying it before meeting those coming up from astern. It was a perfect day for sea-fighting, calm but with a light breeze; and Jervis ordered his fleet to form a single column and steered for the gap between the two masses of Spanish ships. Once through, his fifteen ships would put about and, running before the wind, split into two divisions; one to engage the enemy's van; the other to keep the rear at bay until all his ships were able to concentrate their fire upon them.

The *Captain* sailed last but two in the British line and as soon as these were through to the west of the enemy fleet, Nelson saw signal flags hoist on the *Victory*'s halyards making the order to put about. But instead of ordering his ships to turn simultaneously – so making the *Captain* two from the head of the British line, which would be in action almost immediately – Jervis ordered them to tack in succession. This meant that the whole line would turn and follow its van into action; a much lengthier process. From his vantage-point at the rear of the line, Nelson saw that this would take so long that it would give the two Spanish divisions time to join together. This had to be stopped and there was only one action to take. He gave the order to Captain Miller, the American-born captain of his ship, to haul out of the line and steer directly for the head of the larger division of the enemy fleet. If he could force them to give battle, this would hold open the gap between the two divisions long enough for the turning British to carry out Jervis's plan. In giving the order, Nelson knew that he would face enormous odds and that he was flouting the cardinal principle of British naval tactics by leaving the line of battle without orders. He was not to know then that Jervis was watching his action with delight at his initiative.

Alone, the *Captain* joined action with seven Spanish ships, her seventy-four guns against three of 100 guns and another, the biggest warship in the world, the *Santissima Trinidad* of 140 guns mounted on four decks. Seeing her disappear in billows of gun-smoke, Jervis at once signalled the last ship in his line, the *Excellent*, commanded by Cuthbert Collingwood, to support Nelson. He was followed by Tom Troubridge in the *Culloden* and Captain Frederick in the *Blenheim*. It was the *Captain*'s battle with only smoke to shield her from Spanish broadsides that should have shot her to splinters. But Nelson's daring was not reckless: he knew that the Spanish crews were so inexperienced that their rate of fire might be only a tenth of his own, which could be three broadsides every two minutes.

For an hour, the *Captain* fought at pointblank range with five Spanish ships of the line until all her sails and rigging were shot away and her fore-topmast gone. He did not fight alone for long because Collingwood steered through the smoke to join him. As Nelson put it, "disdaining the parade of taking possession of beaten enemies, he most gallantly pushed up to save his old friend and mess-mate, who was to all appearance in a critical situation", both the *Culloden* and the *Blenheim* having been beaten back by Spanish broadsides. Realising that his own ship was now incapable of manoeuvre, Nelson decided on even closer action, and ordered Captain Miller to put the helm a-starboard to ram the eighty-gun *San Nicolas*, which had herself become entangled with the first rate *San Josef* of 112 guns. The *Captain*'s bow crashed into the stern of the *San Nicolas* and the two ships were at once locked together by spars and rigging. Calling for boarders – soldiers of the 69th Regiment, serving on board as marines; sailors armed with pistols, pikes and cutlasses – Nelson drew his sword and ordered the assault. Some sprang from bulwark to bulwark, others ran along the *Captain*'s yards and jumped for the enemy's rigging. An agile soldier of the 69th scrambled along the bowsprit, with Nelson following, and jumped for the stern of the *San Nicolas*. "Two men left the ship with me, but one fell into the sea," said Nelson, who was the second man to board the enemy:

A soldier of the 69th Regiment having broke the upper quarter-gallery window, jumped in, followed by myself and others, as fast as possible. I found the cabin doors fastened and the Spanish officers fired their pistols at us through the windows, but, having broke open the doors, the soldiers fired ... Having pushed on the quarterdeck, I found ... the Spanish ensign hauling down. The *San Josef* at this moment fired muskets and pistols from the admiral's stern-gallery on us. Our seamen by this time were in full possession of every part: about seven of my men were killed and some few wounded, and about twenty Spaniards

Having placed sentinels at the different ladders and ordered Captain Miller to push more men into the *San Nicolas*, I directed my brave fellows to board the first-rate, which was done in a moment. When I got into her main-chains, a Spanish officer came upon the quarterdeck rail, without arms, and said the ship had surrendered. From this welcome information, it was not long before I was on the quarterdeck, when the Spanish captain, with a bended knee, presented me with his sword and told me the admiral was dying of his wounds below. I gave him my hand and desired him to call to his officers and ship's company that the ship had surrendered which he did; and on the quarterdeck of a Spanish first-rate, extravagant as the story may seem, did I receive the swords of the vanquished Spaniards, which as I received I gave to William Fearney, one of my bargemen, who placed them with the greatest sang-froid under his arm ... Thus fell these ships. The *Victory* passing saluted us with three cheers, as did every ship in the fleet. At dusk, I went on board the *Victory*, when the Admiral received me on the quarterdeck and, having embraced me, said he could not sufficiently thank me and used every kind expression which could not fail to make me happy.

Then Nelson added to his own account: "There is a saying in the Fleet too flattering for me to omit telling – viz. 'Nelson's Patent Bridge for boarding first-rates', alluding to my passing over an enemy eighty-gun ship; and another of a sailor's taking me by the hand on board the *San*

Josef, saying he might not soon have another place to do it in and assuring me he was heartily glad to see me."

To this he added a joke that was circulating in the British fleet, *Commodore Nelson's receipt for making an Olla Podrida*:

Take a Spanish first-rate and an eighty-gun ship and after well *battering* and *basting* them for an hour, keep throwing in your *force balls* and be sure to let these be well *seasoned*. Your *fire* must never slacken for a moment, but must be kept up as brisk as possible during the whole time. So soon as you perceive your Spaniards to be well stewed and blended together, you must then throw your own ship on board the two-decker, back your spritsail yard to her mizzen mast, then skip in to her quarter-gallery window, sword in hand, and let the rest of your boarders follow as they can. The moment that you appear on the eighty-gun ship quarter deck, the Spaniards will all throw down their arms and fly. You will then only have to take a hop, skip and jump from your stepping-stone and you will find yourself in the middle of the first-rate quarterdeck with all the Dons at your feet.

Your Olla Podrida may now be considered as completely *dished* and fit to be set before His Majesty.

Nelson his art of cooking Spaniards.

At last Nelson was accorded the recognition he craved. Jervis had applauded him and when Captain Calder suggested to the admiral that his action in hauling out of line had been in defiance of instructions, he replied: "It certainly was so, and if ever you commit such a breach of your orders, I will forgive you also." While Jervis was created Earl St. Vincent for his victory, Commodore Nelson was made a Knight of the Bath and, a week after the battle, he heard that he had been promoted to rear-admiral. When news of the victory and eye-witness reports reached a worried and depressed England, his exploit thrilled the nation and his father, hearing the news in Bath, declared: "The name and services of Nelson have sounded throughout the City of Bath from the common ballad-singer to the public theatre. Joy sparkles in every eye and desponding Britain draws back her sable veil and smiles."

Fanny, also writing from Bath, told him he was "universally the subject of conversation" but, as the first reports of the battle had reached her, "My anxiety was far beyond my powers of expression ... my sufferings were great". Dutifully reporting the congratulations of friends, her own were muted by her fears: "I shall not be myself till I hear from you again," she concluded. "What can I attempt to say to you about boarding? You have been most wonderfully protected. You have done desperate actions enough. Now may I, indeed I do beg, that you never board again. *Leave* it for *captains.*" In her next letter, she repeated her plea: "I sincerely hope, my dear husband, that all these wonderful and desperate actions, such as boarding ships, you will leave to others. With the protection of a Supreme Being, you have acquired a character, or name, which all hands agree cannot be greater, therefore rest satisfied."

CHAPTER VI

Disaster at Tenerife
(1797–8)

"I shall come, one day or other, laughing home."
— Rear-Admiral Horatio Nelson to Mrs. Nelson from H.M.S.
Irresistible, off Lisbon, 3rd March, 1796

"As to fortune," wrote Nelson to Fanny from his cabin in the *Captain*, rocked on an Atlantic swell off Cadiz at the beginning of April, 1797, "we must be content with a little and the *cottage*. Near Norwich, or any other place that you like better, will, I assure you, content me ... My chains, medals and ribbons, with a contented mind, are all sufficient." Now that he was Rear-Admiral Sir Horatio Nelson, K.B., he relaxed and busied himself with the detail of his new coat of arms and the compliments received, sending his wife a ballad by "an old sailor", about what was now known at the Battle of Cape St. Vincent fought on St. Valentine's Day, which ended:

> "This hero brave, old England's boast,
> Grappled two ships along,
> Forced them to strike on their own coast
> and lasting laurels won.
>
> Long will this fact in history shine;
> 'Give me', the fair sex say,
> 'A Nelson for my valentine
> on this auspicious day.'"

He sent presents that reflected his triumph: for Fanny "some Naples sashes ... and a gown, also five elegant drawings of the action"; and he told her: "I intend my next winter's gift at Burnham to be fifty good, large blankets with the letter N wove in the centre that they may not be sold. I believe they may be made for about fifteen shillings of the very best quality and they will last some person or other for seven years at least ... I believe they are made at Frome. They are to be at my father's disposal in November."

Such comfortable words as these, full of affection and plans for a cosy future in Norfolk – "I shall, one day or other, come laughing home, when we will retire from the busy scenes of life" – were rudely interrupted when a much shorter letter arrived at Fanny's lodgings in Bath. It had been written on 27th May on board his new flagship, the seventy-four gun *Theseus*, and it told her briskly: "We are to anchor off Cadiz, in sight of the whole Spanish Fleet. I am barely out of shot of a Spanish rear-admiral." His squadron was part of Lord St. Vincent's fleet blockading the port and ready to give battle should the enemy's fighting ships emerge. To young William Hoste's father in Norfolk, he wrote a longer and less alarming letter: "We are looking at the ladies walking the walls and Mall of Cadiz and know of the ridicule they make of their sea-officers. Thirty sail are now perfectly ready and, the first east wind, I expect the ships from the Mediterranean, which will make them forty sail of the line. We are now twenty; some of our ships being always obliged to be absent for water, provisions, etc."

Nelson commanded the inshore squadron off the harbour mouth and he had no intention of limiting his activity to close blockade. On the morning of 3rd July, St. Vincent ordered his captains: "All the barges and launches ... with their carronades properly fitted and plenty of ammunition and pikes are to be with Admiral Nelson at half-past 8 o'clock this night for a particular service." This could have only one meaning and that was, as Nelson expressed it, "I wish to make it a warm night at Cadiz".

The plan was to bombard the city with a mortar mounted in a bomb-vessel in the hope of provoking the Spanish fleet to make a sortie so that it could be brought to battle before further reinforcements arrived. What was unusual about the operation was that the flotilla of British boats, which were to protect the ship against the swarm of Spanish oared gunboats that would certainly come out of harbour to attack her, would not be commanded by a captain, as would be expected, but by Admiral Nelson himself. Moreover, he decided to take with him in his ten-oared barge Captain Thomas Fremantle, his friend, who was commanding the frigate *Seahorse*. Their boat's crew would, like the others, be armed with pikes, pistols and cutlasses, while they would wear their elegantly chased and engraved fighting swords because hand-to-hand combat was almost inevitable.

After dark on 3rd July, the bomb-vessel *Thunderer* was towed into position a mile off the white sea-wall of the city and began to toss mortar-bombs, trailing plumes of smoke and sparks from their burning fuses, high into the air before plunging into the cluster of domes, towers and flat-roofed mansions beyond. It was a fine, clear night and for half an hour Nelson could sit in the stern of his barge watching the arching bombs. Then the enemy gunboats attacked. In the light of moon and stars visibility was clear and the Spanish commander, Don Miguel Tyrason, quickly identified the British commander's boat and ordered his own, which was more than twice the size, to pull for it. The two craft collided and their crews fought; the British outnumbered by two to one. "This was a service hand to hand with swords," said Nelson afterwards, "in which my coxswain, John Sykes, twice saved my life." One of the British crew remembered:

> John Sykes was close to Nelson on his left hand and he seemed more concerned with the Admiral's life than his own: he hardly ever struck a blow but to save his gallant officer. Twice he parried blows that must have been fatal to Nelson ... It was cut, thrust, fire and no load again – we had no time for that. The Spaniards fought like devils and seemed to resolve to win from the Admiral the laurels of his former victory; they appeared to know him and directed their particular attack towards the officers.
>
> Twice Sykes saved him; and now he saw a blow descending that would have severed the head of Nelson. In that second of thought that a cool man possesses, Sykes saw that he could not ward the blow with his cutlass ... He saw the danger; that moment expired and Nelson would have been a corpse: but Sykes saved him – he interposed his own hand! We all saw it ... and we gave in revenge one cheer and one tremendous rally. Eighteen of the Spaniards were killed and we boarded and carried her: there being not one man left on board who was not either dead or wounded.

Nelson, supporting his bleeding coxswain, thanked him: "Sykes, I cannot forget this." Nor did he, and it was not only Sykes's bravery that he remembered for he was to recall without modesty that "my personal courage was more conspicuous than at any other period of my life". He knew, too, that the story of the admiral fighting hand-to-hand alongside his sailors would spread quickly through the fleet and this was one of his reasons for taking the unnecessary risk. He knew, as did every other officer, that the lower-deck ratings of the Royal Navy were in a ferment of political agitation and personal grievance. The trouble had arisen through the confluence of two currents of discontent. Conditions of service were appalling, even by wartime standards, and the men demanded more pay than the current rate, which had not risen for a century; a fairer division of prize-money; better food; and more humane care for the sick and wounded. This had been joined by the strong radical tide that had reached Britain from France and, indeed, from America. To these had been added the undertow of Irish agitation for Ireland was near the brink of insurrection and many Irishmen were serving on the lower deck.

Mutiny had first broken out at Spithead in April but had been orderly and, when its reasonable demands had been met, normal loyalties and discipline were restored by the mutineers themselves after a visit to the ships by the elderly Lord Howe, whom they trusted. An uglier uprising had followed at the Nore in May and this had had to be suppressed with hangings at the yard-arm. The Admiralty had done everything possible to prevent news spreading to ships abroad, but spontaneous acts of mutiny had already occurred in the Mediterranean Fleet and, of course, ships – some of them recently mutinous – came out as routine replacements. In St. Vincent, the mutineers met a formidable opponent for he could be a ferocious disciplinarian: on the day before Nelson's boat action off Cadiz, he had had to send an officer to the *St. George* as witness to the execution of two homosexuals, "hanged for an unnatural crime", who might have expected to get away with a hundred or two lashes on the lesser charge of "going to another man's hammock". Mutiny had broken out in the same ship and, when the four ringleaders were condemned to death, St. Vincent insisted that they be hanged the following day, although it was a Sunday. When his deputy, Vice-Admiral Charles Thompson, protested that this was "profaning the Sabbath", he was at once sent home to England. Nelson thought otherwise, sending St. Vincent a note to say, "I very much approve of its being so speedily carried into execution, even though it is *Sunday*. The particular situation of the service requires extraordinary measures". He added to the flag-captain, Sir Robert Calder: "Had it been Christmas Day, instead of Sunday, I would have executed them." To him mutineers were comparable with revolutionaries who had become regicides in France, so offending his near-deification of monarchy.

His own ship had not been without trouble. Captain Fremantle's bride, Betsey, who had accompanied him to sea in his frigate, had noted, "the *Theseus* men, the most tiresome, noisy, mutinous people in the world". Yet it was on the quarterdeck of this same ship that a note had been left and shown to Nelson, reading: "Success attend Admiral Nelson! God bless Captain Miller! We thank them for the Officers they have placed over us. We are happy and comfortable and will shed every drop of blood in our veins to support them and the name of the *Theseus* will be immortalised as high as the *Captain*'s." It was signed: "Ship's Company". One reason for Nelson's popularity was that it had become known that he sympathised with the plight of the sailors as strongly as he condemned mutineers. "I am entirely with the seamen in their first complaint," he had written of their poor pay to Dixon Hoste. "We are a neglected set and, when peace comes, are shamefully treated; but, for the Nore scoundrels, I should be happy to command a ship against them." His men would have manned it, too, for they knew he would share their risks; indeed, take more.

It was not only the approval of his men that he sought. "My late affair here will not, I believe, lower me in the opinion of the world," he wrote to Fanny a week after the action off Cadiz. "I have had flattery enough to make me vain and success enough to make me confident." But he needed a more robust recognition than another timid letter that now arrived from her: "I am very anxious. God Almighty protect you and Josiah. The time draws near when you thought of returning, it seems just at hand, which most probably increases my feelings and anxiety." It was only after such expressions of worried yearnings that she wrote what he wanted to read: that neighbours now "talked of our 'Norfolk hero'".

There was now a new opportunity for glory in the offing. Since April, Lord St. Vincent, eager to take the offensive had been considering an attack on the Spanish port of Santa Cruz on the island of Tenerife, where homeward-bound treasure-ships from Havana or Manila would call and might be vulnerable. Two such ships had, in fact, been sighted in the roadstead in April and two British frigates had attempted to cut them out: one – laden with a mixed cargo – had been taken, but the other, a bullion ship from Manila, had been mistaken for a warship and the attacking boats had sheered away. A month later, two more British frigates attacked Santa Cruz and succeeded in cutting out a fine French corvette, *La Mutine*, which had been put to use as a despatch-vessel for the Mediterranean Fleet. Now a further report reached St. Vincent that another cargo of bullion had arrived at Santa Cruz from Manila in *El Principe d'Asturias*, and, on 14th July, he sent orders to Nelson that began, "You are hereby required and directed to take the ships named in the margin under your command ... and to proceed with the utmost expedition off the Island of Tenerife and there make your dispositions for taking possession of the Town of Santa Cruz by a sudden and vigorous assault." The ships named were four of the line, three frigates and a cutter, the familiar tender of the Mediterranean Fleet, the *Fox*, commanded by an old sea-farer named Gibson.

On 15th July, Nelson's squadron left Cadiz for Tenerife and for six days ran before the wind, swooping over a gentle Atlantic swell, while the ships' companies trained at the guns and with small arms and carpenters made scaling-ladders for the assault. Then, late on a Thursday afternoon, masthead look-outs sighted a faint outline in the sky to the

south-west, like distant storm-clouds, and knew it to be the silhouettes of
the volcanic peaks of Tenerife. Although the British believed Santa Cruz
was defended by a small number of regular soldiers and ill-trained
militia, its fortifications were known to be strong: the mole-head below
the town was commanded by the castle of San Cristobal and sixteen stone
strong-points faced the sea along six miles of coast, mounting about a
hundred cannon. The Spaniards must not be allowed time to man these
defences, so a surprise attack was essential.

Keeping below the horizon, the squadron lay to and landing parties
and marines from the ships of the line were sent across to the frigates
together with boats in which they would be towed towards the coast. That
evening at dusk the frigates steered for Santa Cruz, with the big ships
following three hours later. The plan was that a thousand men were to be
landed at dawn, to the east of the town, between it and the strongest
shore-battery, the Paso Alto, under the command of Captain Troubridge. But when the sun came up over the ocean to light the black,
jagged peaks, the towers and colour-washed houses of Santa Cruz and
the beaches of black sand, watchers in the frigates were dismayed to see
the crowded boats still labouring out at sea. An inshore current,
unexpectedly strong, had demanded all their efforts to prevent them
being swept down the coast and, hearing alarm guns fired ashore,
Troubridge knew that surprise had been lost and ordered his coxswains
to turn their boats and pull back to the ships.

When Nelson came up in the *Theseus* and heard what had happened,
he ordered a second attempt to be made immediately under cover of a
bombardment by his big ships. So the tired boats' crews, who had been
awake all night and had already spent exhausting hours at their oars,
again pulled for the shore. This time they reached it and struggled up a
steep slope in the hot sun under fire from the Spanish who held the
higher ground. But they had neither the energy nor the numbers to
attempt a frontal attack on the fortifications, let alone the fortified town,
and at dusk Troubridge ordered his men back to the boats and to the
ships out at sea. Next day, the squadron lay off-shore and out of range of
the twenty-four-pounder guns in the shore batteries, while Nelson called
a council of war. A gale was now blowing and, while the ships tacked to
and fro under close-reefed topsails, the admiral and his captains assessed
the situation. Surprise might have been lost but encouraging news had
arrived on board with a German deserter from the town, who maintained
that it was still vulnerable to attack. Hearing his report from her husband,
Mrs Fremantle wrote in her diary on 23rd July: "A German that was
brought off yesterday says the Spaniards have no force, are in the greatest
alarm, all crying and trembling, and that nothing could be easier than to

take the place; only 300 men of regular troops, the rest are peasants who are frightened to death."

It was still blowing hard on the 24th, but when Nelson summoned his captains to a conference in his cabin on board the *Theseus* that afternoon, he gave them the surprising news that he had decided upon a direct assault on Santa Cruz by night. A thousand sailors and marines would be landed on the mole that jutted into the sea from the centre of the town that very night: the first wave of assault being put ashore from ships' boats; the second, from a captured Spanish ketch and the cutter *Fox*, which would embark nearly two hundred men. He himself would command the attack, leading one of six divisions of boats, the other five being commanded by post-captains: Troubridge, Miller, Hood, Waller and Thompson. After the conference, Nelson changed into clean clothes as was prudent before action, to reduce the risk of an infected wound; relaxing formality slightly by pulling on a pair of stockings striped with blue instead of the plain regulation white. He then dined quietly on board the *Seahorse* with his captains and Mrs. Fremantle, whose husband was to accompany the assault. Such was the calm confidence of the occasion that when the officers were called at 10.30 that night and clambered down the ship's side into their boats, tossing in the darkness alongside, Betsey Fremantle went to bed and to sleep.

The sea was choppy, the wind blustering, but the boats were pulled into their formations around the captains' barges, identified by large Union flags of flapping sailcloth upon which the names of their ships had been painted in large yellow letters across the broad, red, horizontal stripe. In the stern of the admiral's boat sat Josiah Nisbet, proud to have overcome his step-father's objection that "Should we both fall, what would become of your poor mother?" with his reply: "I will go with you tonight, if I never go again." The divisions of boats were then loosely roped together and the flotilla pulled for the shore across two miles of leaping water. They were to land on the mole, a broad pier of lava-blocks that jutted eighty yards into the sea, spike the guns upon it, then, manhandling their scaling-ladders, race for the walls of the castle of San Cristobal. Once the castle had been stormed, the town beneath its guns would surely fall, too,

Ashore, their arrival, now or later, was expected: Don Antonio Gutierrez, the Commandant-General of the Canary Islands, although aged sixty-eight, was a seasoned soldier who had fought the British in the American war. True, his force of regular soldiers numbered less than a hundred, but he could deploy five regiments of militia, whose training and resolution were of a higher order than could have been expected, and, amongst others, the French crew of the captured *La Mutine*. Since the first attack in April and the arrival of this squadron two days before, a direct attack had always seemed possible, particularly so when Gutierrez had received the ultimatum and realised that his opponent was Admiral Nelson, whose reputation had preceded him. And so the sentries on the ramparts and the look-outs on board the Manila bullion-ship were awake and staring into the darkness when, soon after one in the morning, one of the latter sighted a bow wave and the lift of oars out on the white-flecked waves and a sentry on the Paso Alto battery saw the shape of a ketch mask the white-horses out at sea. The first gun was fired.

In one of the boats of the *Zealous*, Lieutenant William Webley saw what had happened:

> We proceeded in four lines, Captains Troubridge, Hood, Miller and Waller leading the boats; Captains Bowen, Thompson and Fremantle attendant on the Admiral in their boats. We proceeded on until one o'clock ... when we were ordered by Captain Bowen to lay on our oars as we had *just passed* the mole, the intended place of landing. At this instant the cutter was discovered and fired upon – and, before the boats could pull round in order, the Admiral pulled in for the mole with orders to follow. The alarm now became general and they opened a cross-fire from all sides of cannon and musketry *so truly warm*!

As Nelson's barge tossed against the wet stone, he drew his sword – the fighting sword worn by Galfridus Walpole, given him by Captain Suckling – and scrambled ashore; then reeled and staggered back into the boat. He grabbed his sword with his left hand, his right arm pumping blood, and he collapsed, Josiah catching him as he fell. "I am a dead man," he muttered as his stepson laid him on the bottom-boards, tore the black silk stock from his own neck and tied it as a tourniquet around the arm above the wound. Some men had already jumped ashore and were running down the mole towards the Spanish guns, but Josiah Nisbet saw that the admiral's life depended on an immediate return to a ship and a surgeon. Ordering the crew to pull away from the mole, he steered along the shore, hoping that the cannon could not be depressed sufficiently to hit them, while one of the bargemen stripped off his shirt and made a sling for the Admiral's arm. The enemy batteries safely passed, Josiah, himself pulling at an oar, shouted to the coxswain to steer for the darkness of the open sea. As they turned, he saw in the light of gun-flashes men struggling in the water all around them and Nelson, now sitting at the stern of the boat, insisted that, whatever the risk, they must be saved. Some were hauled aboard, survivors from the cutter *Fox*, which had been hit by a heavy shot below the waterline and sunk as she approached the shore. Eventually a ship towered above them: it was the *Seahorse* and

Josiah ordered his boat alongside her. Nelson at once ordered him to continue and find another, even when Josiah pleaded that his life was at risk. "Then I will die," he replied, "I would rather suffer death than alarm Mrs. Fremantle by her seeing me in this state when I can give her no tidings of her husband."

So the barge sheered away to find the *Theseus*. On her upper deck, Midshipman Hoste – too young to join a landing-party – watched as the boat came bouncing alongside, curiosity turning to shock as he saw Nelson, "his right arm dangling by his side while with his left he jumped up the ship's side and, with a spirit that astonished everyone, told the surgeon to get his instruments ready for that he knew he must lose his arm and the sooner it was off the better". The amputation was agonising; the cutting of the flesh with a cold knife was worse than the sawing of the shattered bone: in future, Nelson decided, surgeons should heat the blade before operating. It was quickly over and the surgeon, Thomas Eshelby, entered in his medical log: "1797. July 25. Admiral Nelson. Compound fracture of the right arm by a musket ball passing through a little above the elbow, an artery divided: the arm was immediately amputated and opium afterwards given."

Back on the beach, all was danger and disaster. Most of the boats heading for the mole had been swept past by the current and crashed on to the rocky shore; some smashed to splinters. Order was lost and men scrambled ashore to make a dash for cover from musket-fire among waterfront buildings. With Captain Hood and landing-parties from the *Zealous* was Lieutenant Webley and, when their boats were carried past the mole and the Spanish batteries opened fire, as he said, "The word was then given to pull in and as soon obeyed, cheering and shouting under the heaviest fire I ever remember to have seen both of cannon and musketry, notwithstanding which we landed 500 men in very bad surf, which were with difficulty collected. Unfortunately many boats did not land owing to mistaken orders, darkness, confusion, etc., attending such expeditions." Those who got ashore and into the alleys, between two-storey houses with balconies or over-hanging lattice windows, began what Webley described as "skirmishing in the streets and the satisfaction of the inhabitants firing at us from holes and corners – *vastly uncomfortable!*"

Far from being "all crying and trembling", as the German deserter had reported, the defenders of Santa Cruz were full of fight. Since the British squadron had first appeared, the militia had been summoned from all parts of Tenerife so that the garrison now numbered something like eight thousand, including those manning the hundred guns of the shore batteries and French artillerymen serving forty field-guns. The

British, who had jumped on to the mole, were almost wiped out, but not before they had driven the gunners from their battery at the mole-head and spiked the cannons' touch-holes. Bowen, who had landed when Nelson was hit, was killed there and both Thompson and Fremantle wounded. Troubridge and those who had missed the mole and struggled ashore through the surf found that most of their powder was wet and they would have to fight with cutlasses, swords and pikes. Under sniper-fire from windows, they ran from door to door along the Calle de la Caleta to the Plaza de l'Iglesia, beneath the tower of the church of the Concepción, and from there to the Atrio and the Plaza de Santo Domingo, hoping to find Nelson and those who had landed on the mole. The defence stiffened and whenever the British emerged into a wider street or square, these were swept with grape-shot from hidden guns. A Spanish officer of Irish descent, Don Bernardo Cadogan, described the scene: "Our people threw themselves into all the alley-mouths leading into these streets, in bands of from forty to sixty soldiers, having, some of them, a wheel-piece discharging grape. As soon as the enemy showed his face, these were let go and made them fall in numbers." Then, at daybreak, he continued: "After several such salvoes, the English, assailed on all sides and in places without any ammunition, held aloft a flag of parley, as we supposed, in order to capitulate". But this was not the case: Troubridge and Waller, with some 340 exhausted men, their powder wet and without scaling-ladders to attempt an assault on San Cristobal, decided on bluff and sent an imperious ultimatum to the Commandant-General by a sergeant of the Royal Marines: unless the castle was instantly surrendered they would burn the town. Gutierrez was not impressed and the fighting continued. So Troubridge tried again; he had now joined forces with parties commanded by Hood and Miller of the *Theseus*, and sent the latter with a more formal summons. Still the Commandant-General refused to be bluffed.

Now the British took cover in the convent of Santo Domingo, which, with its thick walls, no windows on the ground floor and only narrow windows on the first floor, could be defended. From here, they noticed a flurry of activity among their assailants as if another British assault was approaching from the sea: but it was only the sight of stricken boats of the original landing still wallowing offshore. Even so, Troubridge tried again; this time sending two of the friars with his offer that, in return for the surrender of the contents of the Royal Treasury and that of the Royal Company of the Philippines, the British would be willing to return to their ships. This too was spurned and, as the sun came up and the plight of the invaders became apparent – besieged by thousands of enemies in the centre of a hostile town strewn with their own dead and wounded and with no hope of rescue – all hopes of victory by bluff were abandoned. Finally, Captain Hood, accompanied by Lieutenant Webley, was sent to request terms of surrender – instead of *vice versa* – proposing that they should be permitted to return to their ships without loss of military honour and, in return, would refrain from further attacks on the Canary Islands. The Commandant-General accepted the offer.

"At six in the morning," recorded a Spanish officer, "The English troops fell in from the square in front of the church to the house of the Viceroy. On the beach by the butchers, they were made to give up their arms." Another gleeful spectator was Cadogan: "Hearty *vivas*, many times repeated, and our men drew up in solid files along the Plaza de la Pila with bands playing. The English, obeying orders, emptied their muskets by firing them into the sea and forming up afterwards, according to their various divisions, marched between our bands, receiving the honours of war; that is, still bearing their weapons, their drums and fifes and so going over the wall to their boats to cries of '*Viva la Republica! Viva la Libertad!*'" As the columns of some seven hundred British sailors and marines, dirty and dishevelled, swung through the streets behind their officers, Spanish courtesy gave way to mockery as they passed; French sailors from *La Mutine* jeered and only shouted commands from Hood and Webley stopped their men breaking ranks.

Meanwhile Cadogan had been helping to clear the battlefield of dead and wounded. "The mole was sprinkled with dead bodies, which were being removed, not to offend the eye"; amongst them Captain Bowen, "a goodly corpse to look upon, lay dead by his first lieutenant and many of their best fellows". Nearby he found "three lieutenants, mortally hurt: Mr. Crusham [Basham] and Mr. Whelther [Weatherhead], handsome youths indeed. I am glad to have somewhat succoured these poor boys, having stripped away my shirt for them to furnish wherewithal to wipe their faces and make bandages to stay the blood which covered the guardhouse steps ... the shore was cumbered with dead. We behaved handsomely to them after our victory. We gave them all round a regale of bread, wine and fruit."

While the bulk of the British were ferried out to the squadron in Spanish boats – their own having been sunk in the landing, or later stove in by the defenders – the officers were invited to dine with the Commandant-General, but, recorded one of their hosts, "at table they hardly raised their eyes and one could see that their faces were very sad." Not only had the attack failed but British casualites had been heavy. One hundred and fifty-three men, including seven officers, were killed, drowned or missing and some of the many wounded were to die later. Amongst the latter was John Weatherhead, who was taken out to the

Theseus to die four days later; "the darling of the ship's company," mourned William Hoste, who took his place as lieutenant. Watching from Santa Cruz, the Spaniards were awed, even grieved, at the scale of their victory: "All the enemy ships flew flags and pennants at half mast," one noted, "which makes us think that many of their officers had died."

The Spanish response was generous. Twenty-five British wounded were ferried out to the ships from the hospital and Nelson exchanged letters of flowery gratitude and presents with Gutierrez: a barrel of English ale and a cheese from the former and two demijohns of the best Canary wine from the latter. As a final courtesy, Nelson offered to take the Commandant-General's despatches reporting his victory and send them ashore at Cadiz. Then, on 27th July, when the last salute of guns echoed from the black mountainsides of Tenerife as the corpse of a British officer was committed to the sea the squadron made sail and was gone. As the *Theseus* lifted over the swell towards Cadiz, Nelson dictated his own despatch, telling St. Vincent in a short covering letter, "Although I am under the painful necessity of acquainting you that we have not been able to succeed in our attack, yet it is my duty to state that I believe more daring intrepidity was never shown than by the Captains, Officers and Men you did me the honour to place under my command."

The attack on Tenerife had failed because of its commander's over-confidence, induced by his contempt for the Spaniards as opponents and by his own spectacular feats of arms against them earlier in the year. Intelligence reports had under-estimated the defences and, when Troubridge's first attempt had failed, pride dictated that he try again, trusting in his own magical powers of leadership and the Providence in which he had such faith. As he confessed later to a friend: "Had I been with the first party, I have reason to believe a complete success would have crowned our endeavours. My pride suffered; and I felt the second attack was a forlorn hope, yet the honour of our country called for the attack and that I should command it. I never expected to return."

Although elated by the battle, there was soon a reaction and on the day he prepared his report for St. Vincent, he wrote a letter to him in spidery, angular script with his left hand. "I am become a burthen to my friends and useless to my country," he despaired. "When I leave your command I become dead to the world; I go hence and am no more seen . . . I hope you will give me a frigate to convey the remains of my carcass to England." He was still able to suggest that Josiah might be promoted to captain: "The boy is under obligations to me but he repaid me by bringing me from the mole of Santa Cruz." To this letter he added a postscript as St. Vincent's flagship came in sight: "A left-handed admiral will never again be considered as useful, therefore the sooner I get to a very humble cottage the better and make room for a better man to serve the state." St. Vincent's reply was generous: "Mortals cannot command success: you and your companions have certainly deserved it by the greatest degree of heroism and perseverance that was ever exhibited ... Give my love to Mrs. Fremantle. I will salute her and bow to your stump tomorrow morning if you will give me leave." When he did so, he arranged for Nelson to sail for home in the *Seahorse* with the wounded Captain Fremantle and his wife.

In his depression, Nelson was not prepared for the welcome he was to receive. It had been a dark year for Britain. On the Continent, Napoleon Bonaparte had defeated the Austrians at Rivoli and conquered the whole of northern Italy, including the Venetian Republic and Genoa. At home, the Royal Navy, the foundation of British power and prosperity, had mutinied and the nation was still in a state of shock. Amid these clouds of trouble the one gleam of inspiration had been Nelson's dash and courage in action off Cape St. Vincent and Cadiz, followed by his gallantry at Tenerife, fruitless as it had been. Arriving at Spithead on Friday, 1st September, he was avid to get ashore and, although it was blowing hard, ordered a boat as soon as he had dined with the Fremantles and was in Portsmouth before dark. There his welcome began and was such that he was soon writing to St. Vincent, "My general reception from John Bull has been just what I wished."

Fanny Nelson had heard of his wounding at her lodgings in Bath. She had first read in the *Bath Chronicle*, amongst news of the war, that "Rear-Admiral Sir Horatio Nelson had been dispatched with three sail of the line either for Tenerife or the Madeiras". Then a letter had arrived from a ship at sea – as could be seen by the franking – but in a strange handwriting so that, fearing the worst, she dared not open it and her father-in-law, who lodged nearby, asked his daughter, Susannah Bolton, who was visiting them, to do so. To their shocked surprise the letter had been written by her husband. "I am so confident of your affection that I feel the pleasure you will receive will be equal whether my letter is wrote by my right hand or left," he had written in the *Theseus* while on passage from Santa Cruz to join St. Vincent. "It was the chance of war and I have great reason to be thankful and I know it will add much to your pleasure in finding that Josiah, under God's providence, was principally instrumental in saving my life ... The cottage is now more necessary than ever." Then he had added, "Just joined the fleet, perfectly well and shall be with you perhaps as soon as this letter."

On Sunday, 3rd September, a bland, sunlit day, Fanny accompanied Edmund Nelson and Susannah to church and returned to dine at her lodgings. She had taken rooms at 17 New King Street in the south-western outskirts of the town; a long street of stone houses dignified with pediments and pilasters around their front doors to befit the status of their genteel residents of moderate means; and her father-in-law's rooms were round the corner in Upper Charles Street. That evening as the three of them, together with Susannah's daughter, Kate, sat in the drawing-room, they heard horses' hooves and iron-rimmed wheels on the paving outside; then a once-familiar voice calling the coachman to halt. A moment later Horatio Nelson was amongst his family again, "come laughing home".

He was changed. More than the milky blue of his half-blinded right eye, or the empty sleeve of his coat hooked across his chest, or the hair that was now grey. He smiled, rather than laughed, to hide the loss of teeth that had caused his lined cheeks to sink. His manner was different, too: high-mettled, an air of command, an aura of experience and an expectancy that seemed to demand reaction to his presence. She had changed, too: nearly five years older, of course, and marked by anxiety; loving but apprehensive. Only old Edmund Nelson, now in his seventies, appeared the same: wise, saintly and self-effacing. Next day, the *Bath Chronicle* announced that Admiral Nelson had "arrived in this city on Sunday evening in good health and spirits to the great joy of Lady Nelson and his venerable father". Only his family realised that he was still in pain from his wound, which had not healed, and Bath doctors – more accustomed to the problems of liver and gout than gunshot wounds – were summoned. "I am beset with a physician, surgeon and apothecary," he wrote a few days later, "and, to say the truth, am suffering much pain with some fever." Troublesome as this was to him it gave Fanny the opportunity to demonstrate her devotion by stifling her scruples and washing and dressing the inflamed stump of his arm in which a septic sore centred on one of the silk ligatures. At night, she gave him opium to induce sleep.

Plans to spend the winter in Bath were quickly dropped in favour of a move to London to consult surgeons and to take up with their useful naval and political connections. The Duke of Clarence had written to ask that, when they came to London, he wished to be "one of the first to shake you by the hand" and Nelson wrote assuring him that "not a scrap of that ardour with which I have hitherto served our King has been shot away". So by the middle of September, they were in London, where Maurice Nelson had arranged lodgings at 141 Bond Street, and a series of medical consultations began, one of them with Dr. Benjamin Moseley, who had been in charge of what medical precautions had been taken for the expedition into Nicaragua and had since written a dramatic account of the disaster that he had been so prudent to avoid himself; he was now physician to the old soldiers' Royal Hospital in Chelsea. None of the doctors could suggest much more than allowing "time and nature" to heal the wound.

This it did. Despite the busy social life of the fashionable residential district of Mayfair all around them and the proximity of the theatres, the Nelsons went to bed early and only once were they disturbed. For two years past – even during the mutiny at the Nore – Admiral Duncan had been keeping the sea off the Texel, blockading the Dutch fleet that was allied with France. In October, when Duncan's main fleet was away refitting in Yarmouth roads, the Dutch came out; Duncan immediately made sail and intercepted them on the 11th. Without bothering to form a conventional line of battle, the British bore down upon them, broke through their line and a furious battle began at pointblank range in which the superior British gun-drill soon told. By mid-afternoon, thirteen ships had been captured. When news reached London, church bells pealed, crowds thronged the streets and candles were lighted in front windows. The Nelsons had gone to bed and the house in Bond Street was dark. Suspecting unpatriotic lack of enthusiasm, a crowd hammered on the door and, when it was opened by a servant, demanded that the windows be lighted. But when told who was lodging there and was trying to sleep, the ringleader quietened the crowd and announced, "You will hear no more from us tonight". Time and nature, aided by Fanny's devoted nursing, achieved what medication could not and at some time in November the troublesome ligature came away from the wound, which quickly healed. During the first week of December, the Nelsons walked round the corner from Bond Street to their local church, St. George's, Hanover Square, and left a brief thanksgiving prayer for the parson to read aloud on the following Sunday: "An officer desires to return thanks to Almighty God for his perfect recovery from a severe wound and also for the many mercies bestowed upon him."

The long convalescence had allowed daytime social activity, however. At the end of September, Admiral Nelson, accompanied by his elder brother and Captain Edward Berry, who had been his first lieutenant on the *Captain* and was also a Norfolkman, attended a *levée* at St. James's Palace. When his own turn to be presented to his sovereign came he was able to turn a tactless gaffe by King George into a graceful compliment to the shy, twenty-nine-year-old naval officer at his side. "You have lost your right arm!" exclaimed the monarch to the hero of the hour, who quickly replied, "But not my right hand, as I have the honour of presenting Captain Berry." To this, the King was quick enough to respond, "Your country has a claim for a bit more of you." His rank and title had given him social confidence and packets of prize money had accumulated and this, together with a rear-admiral's pay and now an annual disability pension of £1,000, enabled him to maintain an appropriate standard of living, which could now include having his portrait painted again and buying a house in the country.

Among the first reunions on his return to London had been with his old mentor Captain Locker, now Lieutenant-Governor at Greenwich Hospital, where Lord Howe was Governor. Locker had a sense of history: he was collecting biographical details of contemporary naval officers and had, of course, prompted Nelson to have his portrait painted by Rigaud before he had left for the Caribbean. Now, he suggested, it was time for his portrait to be painted again; not only had the subject changed in appearance almost beyond recognition but had been touched by what he called "winged, long-tongued fame". The artist he recommended this time was Lemuel Abbott, himself a clergyman's son, who earned a precarious living painting the portraits of sea-officers on leave, but had never mastered the portraiture of women, nor of the full figure, to achieve the reputation that Locker thought was his due. Although Abbott lived in Bloomsbury the chance of painting the celebrated Admiral Nelson was so valuable that he agreed to bring his materials to the Lieutenant-Governor's house at Greenwich and paint his subject there.

The Nelson that was recorded by his eye and brush was vibrant with contradictions: commanding yet vulnerable; experienced but innocent; his sensual mouth compressed with determination. This was not only the Nelson seen by the artist, or by his small circle of intimates; this was the face that was capturing imagination and hearts everywhere. Hitherto, naval heroes had been distant images, seen only in the windows of print shops, or, after death, carved in marble and perhaps dressed as mythological Romans; on retirement they might be glimpsed red-faced and white-wigged, on the steps of their London club, or at an assembly in Bath. Brave, perhaps, but also beings apart, with few, if any, attributes with which the populace could identify. Now all had changed. Here was a naval hero, who could be seen to have lost an arm and the sight of an eye, just as had the destitute sailors begging in the streets. Word had got about that he was as kind and humorous as he was brave and he was loved for it by sophisticated society as much as the London crowds. Even when on leave, it was known, he was keeping a kindly eye on the welfare of his men: writing a letter about financial support for the family of a sailor from the *Theseus* drowned off Tenerife, for example. In this case, he insisted to the authorities that no distinction could be made between "those who are cut in twain by a shot and those who are drowned by a shot from the enemy. Having lost their lives in battle is sufficient to entitle the relatives to the gratuity viz. one full year's pay."

Even a tart-tongued *grand dame* like Lady Spencer, wife of the new First Lord of the Admiralty, fell under his spell. "The first time I saw him was in the drawing-room of the Admiralty and a most uncouth creature I thought him," she declared. "He had just returned from Tenerife, after having lost his arm. He looked so sickly it was painful to see him and his general appearance was that of an idiot; so much so that, when he spoke and his wonderful mind broke forth, it was a sort of surprise that riveted my whole attention."

Among the social activities – the thanksgiving service at St. Paul's; the granting of the Freedom of the City of London; the dinner-parties and soirées; and visits to the College of Arms to consult the heralds about his new coat of arms – he still commanded the attention of the Admiralty and was relieved to hear that St. Vincent was asking for his return. While a flaghip was made ready, he received the customary invitation, accorded to all outward-bound officers of his rank, to dine with the First Lord and on this occasion took the unusual liberty to add to his acceptance that it would make him "the happiest man alive" if his wife could accompany him. The surprised Lady Spencer noted:

> He said he was convinced that I must like her. That she was beautiful, accomplished; but, above all, that her angelic tenderness towards him was beyond imagination. He told me that his wife had dressed his wounds and that her care alone had saved his life. In short, he pressed me to see her with an earnestness of which Nelson alone was capable. In these circumstances I begged that he would bring her with him that day to dinner. He did so, and his attentions to her were those of a lover. He handed her to dinner and sat by her; apologising to me, by saying that he was so little with her that he would not voluntarily lose an instant of her society.

These were the happiest weeks that Fanny had known. Physical intimacy with her husband had been brought about by his wound rather than sexual desire: first, dressing the ugly red stump and, even when it had healed, inspecting it for a recurrence of the inflammation and helping him to manage in their daily life with only one hand; even at Lady Spencer's dinner-table, cutting up food for him on his plate. Their old dream of "a neat cottage" could now become a reality, too; although something more substantial would be necessary for an admiral and his lady. So when Susannah Bolton's brother-in-law, Sam Bolton, wrote to recommend "a gentleman's house" near his own outside Ipswich, Nelson was ready to take his word for its suitability and, without seeing it, to buy. This was "Roundwood", a substantial, plain house of eleven rooms, including "two genteel parlours" and four principal bedrooms, standing in fifty acres of grounds. The house was sold by auction at the White House tavern in Ipswich and bidding on the Nelsons' behalf was successful at £2,000. For Fanny, the pain of parting on his return to sea would be lessened by the pleasure of preparing an idyllic home for his next return.

Meanwhile, delays in refitting his flagship allowed time for another visit to Bath, although the perambulations of Norfolk that had long been planned had to be postponed. Now that he was again under orders for sea, there was a tightening and hardening in his thoughts and attitudes: in discussing the court-martial of a captain accused of misconduct in the Camperdown action, he suggested that only one sentence was appropriate – presumably the death penalty – but added "it is a virtue to lean on the side of mercy". Also, the sailor's eye that had roved in Leghorn was again susceptible to a pretty face; when a peer of their acquaintance gave them the use of his box at the theatre, he confessed to a male friend: "His Lordship did not tell me all its charms; that generally some of the handsomest ladies at Bath are partakers in the box and, was I a bachelor, I would not answer for being tempted. But as I am possessed of everything that is valuable in a wife, I have no occasion to think beyond a pretty face." Fanny possessed other qualities and a gentility that did credit to a sea-officer without much courtly polish; she would now, for the first time, be mistress of her own house. "It is right that you should be in your own cottage," her husband declared, urging her to leave Bath society and take up residence at their new home.

His own home would again be a ship. Originally, the new *Foudroyant* was to have been his flagship but she was not yet completed, and he was given the ten-year-old *Vanguard* of seventy-four guns. Edward Berry was to be her captain and he would take responsibility for the fitting out, the replenishment and the working-up of the ship's company for sea. He had then to take her round from Sheerness to Portsmouth where Admiral Nelson would embark. This he did on 29th March, 1798, after a final, gratifying leave-taking audience with the King. His flagship lay at anchor in the roads off St. Helens, in the lee of the easterly tip of the Isle of Wight, to await a wind that would carry her, and the convoy she was to accompany, down Channel and into the Atlantic.

Departure was beset by petty irritations: there were difficulties in living aboard ship with only one arm that had not been apparent when he had been an invalid on his way home from Tenerife. There was money owing to him from the fathers of some of the boys he was taking to sea under his patronage. Finally, Fanny had made a muddle of packing his luggage and this brought out all his fussy punctilio. On arrival at Portsmouth he had written to her that he had "with great difficulty found *one* pair of raw silk stockings"; a few days later he was writing from his ship: "My black stock and buckle has not yet appeared, nor are the keys of my dressing-stand sent," adding with blunt honesty, "I can do very well without these things but it is a satisfaction to mention them." Two days later, he wrote again:

I have looked over my linen and find it very different to your list in the articles as follows: thirteen silk pocket handkerchiefs: only six, new; five, old. Thirteen cambric ditto: I have sixteen. Twelve cravats: I have only eleven. Six Genoa velvet stocks: I have only three. You have put down thirty huckaback towels: I have from 1 to 10. Eleven is missing from 11 to 22, that is Nos. 12 and 21; therefore there is missing Nos. 11–22 and to 30: ten in all. I only hope and believe they have not been sent. I do not want them. Have you the two old pieces of gold which my father gave me, for I have them not? and yet I am pretty positive I brought them home: if you have them not, they are lost.

Fanny had not managed to prove herself an efficient housewife any more than she had been able to give her husband a family of his own.

On 10th April, the awaited wind blew and the *Vanguard* and her convoy made sail and were away down-Channel. His destination was Lisbon, where the mouth of the Tagus offered a convenient base for the continuing blockade of Cadiz, and there he arrived at the end of the month. "The arrival of Admiral Nelson has given me new life," wrote St. Vincent to Lord Spencer, for he realised that his zeal and popularity with the ships' companies were an essential ingredient of his fleet. In his absence, the men had become restless under the hard discipline that he had felt necessary since the mutinies of the preceding spring. There was urgent and dangerous employment awaiting his arrival.

The presence of the British fleet in the Tagus illustrated the British predicament. Portugal was the only ally able and willing to offer St. Vincent a base. East of Gibraltar, the Mediterranean had been a hostile sea since the British withdrawal eighteen months before and the French were taking advantage of their dominance there. Reports had been reaching London throughout the spring that a major expeditionary force, together with its fleet of transports and escorting fleet of warships, was preparing to leave Toulon and the ports of that coast, including Marseilles and Genoa. General Bonaparte was in command, it was known, but his destination was not. He could be bound for any country bordering the Mediterranean – including the now neutral Kingdom of the Two Sicilies – or preparing to attack Portugal through Spain, or, by breaking out into the Atlantic, for a descent upon Lisbon, or even upon Ireland which was now in open revolt against the British. It would be Nelson's task to find out. Taking two other seventy-four-gun ships –

Captain Sir James Saumarez's *Orion* and Captain Alexander Ball's *Alexander* – and three frigates under command, he was to sail on a dangerous reconnaissance mission into the Mediterranean. The Admiralty's reasons for their choice of commander were explained by Lord Spencer: "The appearance of a British squadron in the Mediterranean is a condition on which the fate of Europe may at this moment ... depend ... I think it almost unnecessary to suggest ... the propriety of putting it under the command of Sir H. Nelson, whose acquaintance with that part of the world, as well as his activity and disposition ... qualify him in a peculiar manner for that service." The First Lord now went further, and after Nelson's departure instructed St. Vincent to give him a striking-force, rather than a scouting squadron, of not less than ten sail of the line. Without waiting for promised reinforcements from home, the Commander-in-Chief at once detached ten of his "seventy-fours" and one fifty-gun ship commanded by "choice fellows of the inshore squadron" off Cadiz and sent them after him into the Mediterranean under full press of canvas.

Meanwhile all that the reconnaissance squadron could do was make for Toulon in the hope of intercepting the French armada, then shadowing it to discover its destination. Bound for the enemy's coast on 17th May, Nelson's frigate, the *Terpsichore*, chased and took a French corvette, which had left Toulon the night before, and he learned from prisoners that General Bonaparte was about to embark and the great expedition to set sail. Fifteen enemy sail of the line were, he was told, ready for sea and about 12,000 troops had already embarked with more assembling ashore. The escorting warships were apparently to be commanded by Vice-Admiral François Brueys, a former royalist officer, who had fought the British in the American War and been reinstated on Bonaparte's instructions, flying his flag in the gigantic *l'Orient* of 120 guns. "But no one knows to what place the Armament is destined," Nelson wrote to St. Vincent. "Reports say that they are to sail in a few days and others that they will not sail for a fortnight." In any case, he himself would soon see their mast-heads and then find out for himself.

Three days later, on a Sunday, the squadron was in position to watch and wait. Morale was high; indeed, as Nelson's flag-captain, Edward Berry, said "elated beyond description". The squadron itself, "though small, being very choice"; the weather, fine; "We thought ourselves at the height of our glory: what more could we wish for?" But that evening, Berry noted, "towards sunset, the weather did not appear so promising ... before 12 at night, the gale came on". What happened then was described in appalled retrospect by Nelson in a letter to Fanny four days later:

I ought not to call what has happened to the *Vanguard* by the cold name of accident: I believe firmly that it was the Almighty's goodness, to check my consummate vanity. I hope it has made me a better officer, as I feel confident it has made me a better man. I kiss with all humility the rod.

Figure to yourself a vain man, on a Sunday evening at sunset, walking in his cabin with a squadron about him, who looked up to their chief to lead them to glory, and in whom this chief placed the firmest reliance ... Figure to yourself this proud, conceited man when the sun rose on Monday morning, his ship dismasted, his fleet dispersed and himself in such distress that the meanest frigate out of France would have been a very unwelcome guest.

A tornado had struck the ships and Berry, unaccustomed to handling a ship of the line in a storm, probably did not react as quickly as Nelson would have done. Sails were hastily furled but not quickly enough: first the main-topmast went over the side, the topsail yard, crowded with men, hurtled to the deck; next the mizzen topmast went and then the foremast "gave an alarming crack ... and went by the board with a most tremendous crash". With masts, sails and rigging swinging and battering against the hull, dragging her into the thundering seas, the ship seemed lost. She would have been for, when the tangle of ropes, spars and splintered masts were hacked free, the gale and westerly swell drove the hulk shorewards until they could hear the roar of surf above the howl of the gale. Only the grim persistence of Ball and Saumarez – the former taking the crippled ship in tow – saved her from foundering, or destruction on the rocks.

Amazingly, the *Vanguard* had lost only two men when the topsail yard crashed – one of them a Norfolk midshipman – and, more surprisingly, her riggers and carpenters found enough spare spars, rope and canvas to re-rig the ship and, in only four days, she was again cruising with her consorts. But the gale that had come close to wrecking the British flagship had carried the French fleet out of Toulon, driven them past the storm-wracked British ships in the dark of that Sunday night and carried them far over the horizon before Nelson could try to deduce where they had gone. His own frigates had been swept away, too; when the storm moderated, their captains assumed that the admiral would retire to repair his ships at Gibraltar and made their own way thence, so depriving him of his fast scouts. "I thought they would have known me better", was Nelson's comment.

Yet the delay brought one compensation. At dawn on 5th June, a sail sighted to westward proved to be *La Mutine* and soon Captain Hardy was boarding the *Vanguard* with news that three days' sailing-time behind him were the ten ships of the line that would transform Nelson's squadron into a fleet. He also heard from a merchant ship the first report that the French had broken out of Toulon and that they had last been sighted steering south-east, passing north of Corsica and towards Italy, this suggesting a descent upon Naples and the Kingdom of the Two Sicilies. When reinforcements arrived and greetings had been exchanged on the quarterdeck of the *Vanguard*, Nelson followed, sailing in three divisions, having instructed his captains that, should they catch the enemy, two would engage their fleet and the third attack the troopships. Whenever the sea allowed, the captains crossed to the *Vanguard* for tactical conferences, discussing exactly what they would do if the French were met under these circumstances or those. Some were already old friends; the rest soon seemed so. The newcomers were Troubridge of the *Culloden*, Miller of the *Theseus*, Louis of the *Minotaur*, Hallowell of the *Swiftsure*, Gould of the *Audacious*, Peyton of the *Defence*, Hood of the *Zealous*, Foley of the *Goliath*, Westcott of the *Majestic*, Darby of the *Bellerophon*, Thompson in the fifty-gun *Leander* and Hardy with the brig *Mutine*. Together, these men inspired Nelson to paraphrase a famous Shakespearean quotation from *King Henry V* when he later declared, "I had the happiness to command a Band of Brothers".

An attack on Naples itself might not be the principal danger because it could be reached more easily overland. But an ultimatum delivered to King Ferdinand threatening an invasion of Sicily was quite probable; another possible destination was Malta, the island dominating the central Mediterranean narrows, which had been held for centuries by the Knights of the Order of St. John of Jerusalem, who had arrived there as Crusaders. But an army of 35,000 men – as Bonaparte's strength now seemed to be – was unnecessary for such an operation and Malta might be taken only to guard the rear of a far more ambitious undertaking such as a move into Turkey, the Levant or even Egypt and then an advance on India, where France still had a powerful and active ally in Tippoo Sahib. More news reached Nelson off the island of Ponza and, on 15th June, he wrote to Lord Spencer:

The last account I had of the French fleet was from a Tunisian cruiser, who saw them on the 4th off Trapani in Sicily, steering to the eastward. If they pass Sicily, I shall believe they are going on their scheme of possessing Alexandria and getting troops to India – a plan concerted with Tippoo Sahib, by no means so difficult as might at first view be imagined; but be they bound for the Antipodes, your Lordship may rely that I shall lose not a moment in bringing them to action.

Two days later, Nelson was back in the Bay of Naples, the splendid sight of his ships in line ahead sending a thrill through one of the excited spectators at the windows of the Palazzo Sessa. Nelson did not leave his flagship but sent Troubridge and Hardy ashore to see Sir William Hamilton and Sir John Acton and deliver a letter to Lady Hamilton. "As soon as I have fought the French fleet," he told her, "I shall do myself the honour of paying my respects to your Ladyship at Naples and I hope to be congratulated on a victory ..." She wrote in reply, "God bless you and send you victorious and that I may see you bring back Bonaparte with you ... I shall be in a fever with anxiety ... I will not say how glad I shall be to see you. Indeed I cannot describe to you my feelings of your being so near us." Immediately afterwards she sent a second, enclosing a letter she herself had just received from Queen Maria Carolina, instructing him, "*Kiss it* and send it back ... as I am bound not to give away any of her letters." Her husband was as glad to see the British ships and meet Nelson's two envoys, Troubridge and Hardy, and had taken them at once to see Acton at the Palazzo Reale. There was little more he could do for the Neapolitans were paralysed with fear of the French, dared not risk offending them and the Prime Minister instantly refused the British request for the loan of frigates to help in the search for Bonaparte's fleet. But he did sign an order allowing the ports of the Kingdom of the Two Sicilies to furnish the British with supplies and fresh water. So Nelson sailed away without seting foot ashore, or meeting the Hamiltons, realising that his presence was an embarrassment, or, as he put it in a letter to Sir William, "The best sight (as an Irishman would say) was to see me out of sight". But, having stressed his need for more active support and particularly his desperate need of frigates, he added a gallant message for the ambassador's wife: "Pray present my best respects of Lady Hamilton. Tell her I hope to be presented to her crowned with laurels or cypress."

On 20th July, the fleet passed the Straits of Messina and, two days later, off Cape Passaro, hailed a Genoese brig, whose master shouted his answers to their urgent questions: he had, he said, left Malta the day before. Yes, the French had been there; the island had surrendered on the 15th. No, they were now gone and were bound for Sicily. But Nelson knew that the enemy fleet had already passed down the east coast of Sicily without any news of an invasion, so could that supposition be wrong? Nelson summoned four captains – Saumarez, Troubridge, Ball and Darby – to join him and Berry in the *Vanguard* for a council of war and summed up his reasoning based upon all the scraps of intelligence that had reached him at Naples, off the Sicilian coast and now from the Genoese brig, in a memorandum to St. Vincent. Might the enemy have

21 *Above*: Triumph in Corsica. The fortified city of Bastia, which fell in 1794 after Nelson supervised the landing and fighting of naval guns. During the siege, the British were exposed to malarial mosquitoes from the nearby swamps.

22 *Below*: The way to Calvi. The only beach where guns could be landed on the exposed and rocky coast for the siege of this second fortified town was in the little inlet of Porto Agro. From the beach the guns had to be manhandled for more than two miles.

23 *Above*: Disaster at Tenerife. Admiral Nelson, using the hand he was about to lose, drawing up plans for an attack on Spanish fortifications. Probably sketched by an officer on board his flagship.

24 *Below*: The daylight attack. The first assault on Tenerife, led by Captain Troubridge, failed when surprise was lost. It was sketched by Lieutenant William Webley of the *Zealous*; the only known contemporary picture of the actions.

25 *Above*: Blockade at Cadiz. The Inshore Squadron commanded by Rear-Admiral Sir Horatio Nelson, whose flagship, the *Theseus*, lies third from the left in the foreground, wait within sight of the Spanish fleet lying at anchor in the roads.

26 *Below*: Triumph in Aboukir Bay. The French flagship *l'Orient* explodes at the climax of the night battle that began at sunset on 1st August, 1798. A favourite subject for dramatic battle-pictures, this one was painted by George Arnald.

27 *Above*: The new hero, confident and serene. Admiral Nelson painted by Lemuel Abbott while recuperating from the loss of his arm and being nursed in London by his wife.

28 *Left*: The waiting wife. When her husband returned to the Mediterranean, Lady Nelson waited faithfully in London, Bath, Norfolk and finally at their new house near Ipswich with his portraits to remind her of past devotion. This portrait is attributed to Henry Edridge.

attacked Sicily? "It was certain the Sicilian Government were not alarmed, or they would have sent off to me. I recalled all the circumstances of this Armament before me: 40,000 troops in 280 transports, many hundred pieces of artillery, waggons, draught-horses, cavalry, artificers," and, as he had now heard, "naturalists, astronomers, mathematicians, etc... This armament could not be necessary for taking possession of Malta. The Neapolitan ministers considered Naples and Sicily safe; Spain, after Malta, or indeed any place to the westward, I could not think their destination, for at this season the easterly winds so strongly prevail between Sicily and the coast of Barbary that I conceive it almost impossible to get a fleet of transports to the westward. It then became the serious question, where are they gone?"

It was agreed that the French must be heading east. Their destination might be the island of Corfu, or Constantinople, where the power of the Turkish empire could be broken at its heart. But the possibility that presented the greatest threat to British interests was Egypt, and Nelson concluded: "I therefore determined, with the opinion of those captains in whom I place great confidence, to go to Alexandria." His imagination darting ahead, Nelson foresaw that once Bonaparte landed on the Egyptian coast he could "with great ease get an army to the Red Sea, and, if they have a concerted plan with Tippoo Sahib, to have vessels at Suez; three weeks, at this season, is a common passage to the Malabar Coast when our Indian possessions would be in great danger". Only Egypt and India with their ancient and mysterious civilizations would be destinations warranting the inclusion of scholars and scientists in the expeditionary force. So the fleet again steered south-east and Captain Saumarez noted, "Some days must now elapse before we can be relieved of our suspense and if at the end of our journey we find we are upon a wrong scent, our embarrassment will be great indeed. Did the chief responsibility rest with me, I fear it would be more than my too irritable nerves would bear."

Already the French lead in time had been reduced from three weeks to three days and, crowding sail, Nelson hoped to catch Bonaparte either before, or during, the landing of his army. On 26th June, when 250 miles from Alexandria, he sent *La Mutine* ahead, bracing himself for imminent action. Two days later, the minarets of the city, the great lighthouse and masts of ships in the harbour were sighted from the mast-heads of the British fleet. The port of Alexandria lay before them, shimmering in the heat, but the French fleet was not there. The masts belonged to a few Turkish warships and merchantmen loading or discharging cargoes. Perhaps the enemy had landed farther east? So Nelson led his line of battle past Alexandria and the long, sandy coast; past the mouths of the

Nile delta and then northward up the eastern shore of the Mediterranean to the misty mountains of the Levant and Asia Minor. The French were not there; there was no sign, nor word, of them; Nelson had, it seemed, been wrong. "It is an old saying, 'The Devil's children have the Devil's luck'", he mused. "I cannot find, or to this moment learn, beyond vague conjecture, where the French fleet are gone to."

The most worrying possibility was that the master of the Genoese brig had been right after all and that Bonaparte was now in occupation of Sicily, so Nelson beat westward with day after uneventful day to brood. Off Crete, he learned that the French were not at Corfu, so with deepening dread he feared that the whole Kingdom of the Two Sicilies might have fallen to the French and that his failure was complete. It had been one thing to fail at Tenerife, but that had been a gallant failure, and his reputation still stood high from his feat of arms at St. Vincent; this, however, was a failure of judgement unredeemed by bravery in battle. Then, at last, on 19th July, the brown hills of Sicily came over the horizon and he sent a boat into Syracuse for news. There was none: the French had not landed in Sicily either.

"Bonaparte ... commands the fleet as well as the army," Nelson wrote to Fanny next day, but his efforts were not over for, he added, "Glory is my object and that alone". To the Hamiltons he wrote: "We must have a victory. We shall sail with the first breeze and be assured I will return either crowned with laurel, or covered with cypress." He wrote to St. Vincent, too, blaming his failure on the lack of frigates for scouting and his intention of heading east again to hunt the French off Greece, Turkey, Syria and, once again, Egypt. He wrote with a fierce, forced optimism, knowing that even when he had found Bonaparte's destination, he would no probably be too late: the French army would be ashore and the French fleet safe in harbour. Already, while on passage for Syracuse, he had written a long letter to St. Vincent justifying his decision to make for Egypt. "Was I to wait patiently till I heard certain accounts?" He concluded:

> If Egypt was their object, before I could hear of them they would have been in India. To do nothing, I felt, was disgraceful: therefore I made use of my understanding and by it I ought to stand or fall. I am before your Lordship's judgement (which, in the present case, I feel is the Tribunal of my Country) and if, under all circumstances, it is decided that I am wrong, I ought, for the sake of our Country, to be superseded ... However erroneous my judgement may be, I feel conscious of my honest intentions, which I hope will bear me up under the greatest misfortune that could happen to me as an officer – that of your Lordship's thinking me wrong.

CHAPTER VII

The Victor of the Nile
(1798)

"If I was King of England, I would make you the most noble, puissant
Duke Nelson, Marquis Nile, Earl Alexandria, Viscount Pyramid,
Baron Crocodile and Prince Victory that posterity might have you in all
forms."
– Lady Hamilton to Admiral Nelson, from Naples, 26th October,
1798

Blinded by lack of frigates but still convinced that the French armada had
not tried to beat westward against the prevailing winds, Nelson steered
for Greece. There, perhaps, he might hear reports to suggest Bonaparte's
destination, if only by a process of elimination. Sailing east across the
mouth of the Adriatic to the peninsulas of the Peloponnese, he would
detach ships to visit a port, or stop a merchantman, and then rejoin the
fleet. On 28th July, it was Troubridge who was ordered into the little
Greek port of Koroni to question the Turkish governor. Three hours
later, he was sighted, returning with all sails set. The *Culloden* had a prize
in tow – a French brig, laden with wine – but that was not the occasion for
the urgent signals flying from her halyards, nor of Troubridge's excited
message for the admiral. This was that four weeks before, the French –
more than twenty warships and about three hundred transports – had
been sighted from Koroni and, much to the relief of its people, had sailed
past and disappeared over the horizon towards the south-east, the
direction of Egypt.

Nelson had been right, after all; he had out-sailed the French on a
different course to the coast of Egypt, or the Levant; and he had missed
them again on his return westward to Sicily. There could be no mistake
this time, as Ball confirmed when the *Alexander* stopped another merchantman later that day and heard the same story. Such was his
excitement that Nelson could hardly eat or sleep. There was no need for
further tactical conferences with his captains for these had been held in
the *Vanguard* whenever weather permitted during the past two months.
Should the French be intercepted at sea, the British would attack in three

divisions: two, under Nelson and Saumarez, would engage the enemy's line of battle while a third, commanded by Troubridge, would attack the transports. It was now unlikely that they would be caught at sea; if they were already safe in harbour – in Alexandria, for example – the British could do no more than blockade. But if they were found at anchor, the tactics would be to concentrate overwhelming force on one end of their line, destroy it and then move on to destroy the rest. The awful possibility – indeed, probability – was that they were already snug under the batteries of a port, or that the troops had been landed and the warships again disappeared into the maze of the Mediterranean.

Four days later – at ten o'clock in the morning of 1st August – the long sandy shore of Egypt lay along the southern horizon and two ships – the *Alexander* and the *Swiftsure* – scouting ahead of the main force, signalled that the minarets and lighthouse of Alexandria were again in sight. On their quarterdecks, Ball and Hallowell waited for their lookouts' shouted reports from the mastheads. Yes, the harbour was thick with masts! No, they were not the masts of ships of the line. The port of Alexandria was crammed with French transports and the French flag was flying above the citadel, but Bruey's line of battle was nowhere to be seen. In an agony of disappointment, Nelson gave the only possible order: to steer east along the coast on another sweep towards the Levant in the hope that the enemy had not sailed for refuge, at Malta or Corfu.

So eastward they sailed towards the peninsula of Aboukir and, beyond, the delta of the Nile; in the van, Hood's *Zealous* and Foley's *Goliath*. Perched on the latter's royal yard was Midshipman George Elliot – son of Nelson's friend Sir Gilbert Elliot – scanning the horizon ahead through his telescope. Soon after two o'clock, he saw, standing across the skyline above the sandy spit that ended in the little town and fort of Aboukir, something with the appearance of a picket-fence. This was the masts and yards of a fleet at anchor. It was the French fleet. A shout to the quarterdeck would have alerted watchers in the *Zealous*, sailing close alongside, so Elliot swung from the yard to a backstay and slid down it to the deck and ran to Foley with the news. Immediately the captain ordered the signal "Enemy in sight" to be hoisted, but the stopper on the hoist of flags came adrift; before this was fastened, the same signal flew up the halyards of the *Zealous*, for their lookouts had seen the enemy, too. All eyes strained ahead and men raced into the rigging for a view of the ships they had hunted so long. In the flagship, Berry noted, "The utmost joy seemed to animate every breast". In the *Orion*, the officers heard the news at their dinner table with Saumarez, when, as he put it, "Judge what a change took place – all sprang from their seats and, only staying to drink a bumper to our success, we were in a moment on deck." As for Nelson, his "pleasure ... was perhaps more heightened than that of any other man", as one of his officers said. Knowing that a decisive action was now a certainty, he remarked: "Before this time tomorrow, I shall have gained a peerage, or Westminster Abbey." Then, having calculated that, even with a north-westerly breeze filling their sails, his fleet would not be within gunshot of the enemy for about four hours, he ordered his own dinner to be served.

Such was his excitement that he could not sit still. "When I saw them, I could not help popping my head every now and then out of the window, although I had a damned toothache," he recounted. "Once, as I was observing their position, I heard two seamen quartered at a gun near me, talking and one said to the other, 'Damn, look at them. There they are, Jack. If we don't beat them, they will beat us'. I knew what stuff I had under me ..."

Until this moment, he had known nothing of his quarry beyond reports and rumours and nothing whatsoever of his enemy's intentions. Nelson could not know that their presence at anchor in Aboukir Bay was the direct result of General Bonaparte's decision to postpone an invasion of England until the French could hope to seize command of the Channel; instead, he had recommended an expedition to Egypt and then, perhaps, India, as Nelson had guessed; or, turning north into the Levant, advancing on Constantinople and invading Europe from the east. The aims of the expedition had only been agreed in Paris in mid-April and, six weeks later, his army of more than 35,000 men had sailed, escorted by thirteen sail of the line – two of them eighty-gun ships and one the huge *l'Orient* of 120 guns – and four frigates. Confident that only a small British squadron might have returned to the Mediterranean, they descended upon Malta and took it without difficulty from the Knights of St. John, filling their army's coffers with gold and silver ingots from the melted treasures of the churches and palaces. Leaving a small garrison to hold the island, they had sailed for Egypt and, on the night of 22nd June, had heard with alarm the distant thud of signal guns. These had been fired from Nelson's fleet sailing on a parallel course for Alexandria but, unencumbered by a convoy, sailing faster so that by dawn they were out of sight.

On 1st July, off the Egyptian coast, Bonaparte heard that two days earlier a British squadron had been sighted, so he decided to land at once and next day his army was ashore and their transports safe in harbour. No time was lost in advancing on Cairo and, three weeks after landing, Bonaparte drew up his troops in battle order within sight of the Pyramids: there, in defensive squares, they met the onslaught of the army of the Mameluke rulers of Egypt and destroyed it with rolling volleys of musket-fire. As the sun had lit the desert that dawn, Bonaparte had ridden along the ranks of his waiting infantry and, inspired by his sense of history, shouted to them, "Soldiers, from the tops of these monuments, forty centuries look down!"

Meanwhile, Admiral Brueys had decided against taking his big ships into Alexandria as the harbour entrance was narrow, and against Bonaparte's recommendation to take refuge from the pursuing British at Corfu. Instead, he decided to anchor in a tight defensive line between the shoals and the shore in Aboukir Bay and it was the sight of this that stimulated Nelson's own sense of history. He remembered actions in which a moored line of warships had proved as impregnable as fortresses and knew that his captains understood his plan to prevail by the concentration of force against one end of the line. So there was no need for more orders than one at three o'clock: "Prepare for battle and for anchoring by the stern"; another at five: "I mean to attack the enemy's van and centre"; and at half-past five: "Form line of battle as convenient." Only one final signal would then be necessary.

Seen from the quarterdeck of *l'Orient*, the British appeared to be sailing in a loose pack and Brueys expected them to sail past his line, perhaps fire a few broadsides at extreme range and then haul away to assess the prospects of various tactics for an attack next day. At first he considered putting to sea and, having the advantage in weight of broadside, fighting them fleet-to-fleet. But, when his topsail yards were already being hoisted and braced, he realised that, as he had parties ashore from all his ships, digging wells and guarding the working-parties against marauding bedouin, he had not enough men aboard to man the guns and work the ships. And so, confident in the strength of his position, he decided to fight it out at anchor (see plan, page xiv).

The British were cleared for action with port-lids open and guns run out. Hammocks were packed in tight rolls in nets along the bulwarks as a shield against splinters and musket-shot, netting rigged to keep boarders off the decks, rolled sails wetted to reduce the risk of fire; all but two hatches, needed for the powder-boys to bring up gunpowder, battened down; damp sand strewn on the gun-decks to prevent bare feet slipping on blood. The captains took their places on the quarterdecks, the gunners on the gun-decks, the surgeons in the cockpit, the carpenters and their repair parties to the orlop deck, the marines with their muskets trooped to the upper-deck and the lieutenants with drawn swords to the gun-decks where the gun-crews, stripped to the waist, stood by the gently convex line of cannon along either side of the ship. One officer heard excited banter amongst his men as they looked out of the gun-ports towards the line of enemy ships: "There are thirteen sail of the line and a whacking lot of frigates and small craft. I think we'll hammer the rusk off ten of them, if not the whole boiling." Then talk turned to prize-money: "I'm glad we've twigged 'em at last. I want some new rigging damnably for Sundays." "So do I. I hope we touch enough for that and a damned good cruise among the girls besides." At forty minutes past five, Nelson made the final signal for close action.

From the open sea, the French line looked impregnable, curving from the shoals, where the sea broke beyond the little island off the Aboukir peninsula, southward towards the sandbanks off the shelving shore. Nelson planned to attack the northerly end of the line first; two of his ships anchoring to engage each of the enemy. As his van steered to the eastward of the island and the shoals and could see the long array of open gun-ports, the French ships appeared well spaced apart: each 160 yards from the next to allow the ship to swing by the single anchor at the bow. With the wind behind him, Nelson could order his captains to anchor, two by two, opposite each enemy ship at the nearer end of their line. Now there was another possibility: perhaps the landward guns of the French were not manned and their port-lids shut. So could the British break through their line and attack it from both sides? Or even outflank it by steering between the leading ship and the shoals? Nelson shouted across to Hood in the *Zealous*, sailing close on his bow: could he take his ship round the end of the enemy line? Hood shouted back that he would try but neither he nor any other captain knew the lie of the shoals; only Foley in the *Goliath* had a recent atlas, published by the French. So the *Zealous* surged ahead, a sailor heaving the lead to take soundings as she approached the long line of half-hidden and invisible shoals on which the sea curled and broke. Nelson now ordered the flagship to fall back and let other ships pass so that he could see and control his fleet more readily. "I wish you success" he shouted after Hood, waving him forward with his hat. Hood waved his hat in return but the wind caught it and whisked it into the sea. "Never mind, Webley," he said to his first lieutenant. "There it goes for luck! Put the helm over and make sail." The *Zealous* turned around the point of the shoals, steering for the bows of the ship at the head of the enemy line. It was six o'clock.

All eyes were upon the magnificent spectacle of the thirteen great ships shining in the glow of the setting sun, *tricolore* flags flying bravely from their mastheads. Then Hood noticed that the *Goliath*, which had been keeping station on his quarter, was beginning to overtake. "This will never do," he told Webley at his side, adding, "Well, never mind, Foley is a fine, gallant fellow. Shorten sail and give him time to take up his berth." The *Goliath* swept past. Foley not only had his chart of the bay but saw that, as the French ships were anchored only by the bow, the ship at the head of the line must have room to swing clear of the shoals. Where there was water for one seventy-four-gun ship to swing, there was water for another to sail past and he ordered his helmsman to steer just ahead of that ship's bowsprit.

Without specific orders from his admiral, Foley had seized the initiative, just as Nelson had at St. Vincent the year before. As he turned around the head of the French line, the frigate *La Sérieuse* attempted to interfere; Foley ordered, "Sink that brute!" and his guns did so. Then, his sailing master recorded: "At 15 minutes past 6, the *Goliath*, being the leading ship, crossed the van of the enemy's line and commenced the action." Passing the blind, shuttered port side of the enemy ship, *Le Guerrier*, Foley left her to Hood, who "commenced such a well-directed fire into her bow, within pistol-shot, a little after 6 that her foremast went by the board in about seven minutes". Following in her wake, the *Theseus* had to brave the French ship's broadside but Ralph Miller, her American captain, "observed their shot sweep just over us and knowing well that at such a moment Frenchmen would not have the coolness to change their elevation, I closed them suddenly and, running under the arch of their shot, reserved my fire, every gun being loaded with two and some with three round-shot". To steer round the head of the French line, he put his helm hard over "until", he said, "I had the *Guerrier*'s masts in a line and her jib-boom about six feet clear of our rigging; we then opened with such effect that a second breath could not be drawn before her main and mizzen mast were also gone." The *Goliath* had anchored abreast the landward side of the second ship, *Le Conquérant*, so, leaving the dismasted hulk of *Le Guerrier* astern, Miller engaged the third ship in the line, *Le Spartiate*, while the *Vanguard* opened fire on her from the other side. "This," Captain Miller noted, "was precisely at sunset."

Darkness fell quickly and the wind dropped but the scene was lit by the flashing of gunfire as two British ships warped themselves into position opposite each of their opponents. Some mistakes were inevitable: Troubridge, in his anxiety to get into action, sailed too close to the rocks and grounded the *Culloden* on the shoals, where she lay stranded and under fire from French guns on the island off Aboukir point; Darby, steering ahead of the anchoring British ships, chose his own opponent only to find that it was Brueys' flagship, the gigantic *l'Orient* of more than twice the size and weight of broadside of his *Bellerophon*. In the mêlée, no other British ship joined him and, in the hour he fought alone, he had two of his masts shot to splinters and nearly two hundred killed or wounded. Crippled, the *Bellerophon* drifted out of the line, her place quickly taken by others, including the little fifty-gun *Leander* which Thompson deftly anchored so that he could rake *l'Orient* and the seventy-four gun *Le Franklin* while outside their field of fire.

After two hours' close action and the surrender of four French ships and seeing his own opponent, *Le Spartiate*, in her final agonies, Nelson decided it was time to demolish the centre and rear of the French line. He was on the quarterdeck of the *Vanguard*, studying a sketch-map of the Aboukir Bay anchorage – taken from a French prize and sent across by Hallowell of the *Swiftsure* – when *Le Spartiate*, in a final spasm, lashed out with a broadside. He staggered and fell, his face masked by blood. A flying fragment had laid open his forehead, blinding him with a tatter of bleeding skin. "I am killed," he gasped to Berry, kneeling beside him. "Remember me to my wife." They carried him down the ladders to the cockpit where the surgeon worked amongst the mangled bodies by the dim light of a lantern, but, as he turned to attend the admiral, Nelson ordered, "No, I will take my turn with my brave fellows." When the surgeon did examine the wound he found it slight but messy, the splinter having slashed his scalp to the skull above his right eye, causing concussion. Kept below to rest, he sent for his secretary to begin dictating a draft of his despatch, but was told that he had been wounded and was too shocked to write; the chaplain also proved incapable when asked to take his place. And so Nelson began trying to write himself until interrupted by a message from Berry that *l'Orient* was on fire.

Up the ladders he clambered to the quarterdeck, a dramatic figure with white face and bandaged head, to see the great ship burn in the moonlight. The blaze, intense when it caught a store of paint, oil and chemicals on her middle deck, glared through the row of square gun-ports and the watchers knew that nothing could prevent the fire from reaching her powder-magazine. "A most grand and awful spectacle," Miller was to recall, watching from the *Theseus*, "such as formerly would have drawn tears down the victors cheeks but now pity was stifled as it rose by the remembrance of the numerous and horrid atrocities their unprincipled and bloodthirsty nation had and were committing." They knew nothing, of course, of Admiral Brueys in the blazing flagship having himself seated in a chair on deck when both his legs were shot away and tourniquets tied around the stumps; facing his tormentors until another shot cut him in two; or of his flag-captain, Casabianca, who refused to save himself, knowing that his wounded son had been taken below to the surgeon and was trapped by the fire. All around the cannonade continued: Hallowell ordered the *Swiftsure*'s guns to be aimed at the heart of the blaze; several British captains cut their cables to get away from the flying sparks and the explosion that was bound to come. But his ship lay so close that he expected the blast and blazing debris would be flung over his mastheads, and ordered the magazine's hatches shut and buckets of water and swabs got ready to douse any fiery fragments that fell.

"At 9, observed *l'Orient* to be on fire," Lieutenant Webley had noted in the *Zealous*, "At 10 *l'Orient* blew into the air!!!" At this moment, Captain Miller confessed "My heart scarcely felt a pang for their fate ... though I endeavoured to stop the momentary cheer of the ship's company." Nelson felt much the same but he had sent away the *Vanguard*'s only surviving boat to pick up survivors. They could be seen struggling in the water when the flash of the explosion lit a scene of shattered ships and wreckage – masts, yards, guns, splintered timber and broken bodies – flung into the night sky.

The stunning detonation silenced the battle and was heard in Alexandria, fifteen miles away. An eruption of fire and fragments, thrown into the sky, imprinted itself on the memories of the thousands who watched. The sparks fell, one of the *Alexander*'s sails caught fire and burned briefly; then all that remained of the shattered hull and splintered masts and yards fell back into the sea, mixing steam with smoke. The van and centre of the French line had been destroyed; now it was the turn of the ships at the rear. The shocked silence that followed the end of *l'Orient* lasted several minutes; then the guns began again. Just before midnight, the *Franklin*, lying next to where the flagship had exploded, struck her colours; the six ships of the rear had slipped their cables to escape the flames of the burning flagship and the British guns and drifted out of the line. By now the British gun-crews were spent, so exhausted by the violence of serving their leaping cannon and the heat of fire and a tropical night, that they fought half-conscious, falling asleep on their feet. Even the silence after the explosion of *l'Orient* offered no rest as Captain Miller reported when he tried to move the *Theseus* into a new position to engage the surviving French ships:

> My people were so extremely jaded that as soon as they had hove our sheet anchor up, they dropped under the capstan-bars and were asleep in a moment in every sort of posture, having been then working at their fullest exertion, or fighting, for near twelve hours, without being able to benefit by the respite that occurred because, while *l'Orient* was on fire, I had the ship completely sluiced as one of our precautionary measures against fire or combustibles falling on board us when she blew up.

All the enemy ships in the van and centre had now surrendered or were trying to do so and attention was now concentrated on the six at the rear. By dawn, the British ships were so shot-shattered that their captains could hardly obey orders to move even if Nelson had been able to give them, for he was half-stunned, in great pain and suffering from shock.

The nearest of the six, the ninety-gun *Le Tonnant*, fought three British ships until battered into silence but she managed to slip her cable and drift out of their range, as did two others, *l'Heureuse* and *Le Mercure*, leaving only three ships of the line – *Le Timoleon*, *Le Guillaume Tell* and *Le Généreux* – fit to fight or make sail. Nelson had earlier ordered all his ships that were not disabled to continue the destruction and go to the help of the *Alexander* and *Majestic* that were then so engaged; only three were fit to do so – the *Zealous*, *Goliath* and *Theseus* – and they did what they could, later joined by the little *Leander*. *L'Heureuse* surrendered to Miller, *Le Tonnant* ran aground and, as *Le Timoléon* tried to make sail, she was shattered by broadsides from the *Theseus* and was run ashore. Two survived – *Le Guillaume Tell* and *Le Généreux* commanded by Rear-Admiral Pierre Villeneuve – and were able to make sail and stand out to sea, accompanied by two frigates; only the *Zealous* being in a fit state to follow. "We hauled to the wind and prepared to engage them," Lieutenant Webley recounted. "But we had not a brace . . . that was not shot away and, before they were spliced, we were recalled."

But for the flying sails, Aboukir Bay was a scene of silent, smoking desolation. "An awful sight it was," remembered a sailor in the *Goliath*. "The whole bay was covered with dead bodies, mangled, wounded and scorched, not a bit of clothes on them but their trousers." Of the thirteen French ships of the line that had lain at anchor the day before, ten had been captured, one had blown up and two escaped. Understanding the consequences of this, Nelson simply said: "Victory is not a name strong enough for such a scene."

The British were again in command of the Mediterranean and Bonaparte's army was marooned ashore in a hostile country without hope of rescue. Now the threat to India was gone and Nelson at once sent a messenger eastward with the news: a Lieutenant Thomas Duval of the *Zealous*, a linguist with some experience of diplomacy, he ordered "to India by way of Alexandretta, Aleppo, Basra and the Persian Gulf," with a letter for the Governor of Bombay. His principal despatch, which he had begun to draft at the height of the battle, he now completed: it began, "Almighty God has blessed His Majesty's Arms in the late Battle by a great Victory over the Fleet of the Enemy, whom I attacked at sunset on the 1st August, off the mouth of the Nile." The French losses he estimated as six times heavier than the British at 1,700 killed, 1,500 wounded and 3,000 taken prisoner; of the seven ships he reported taken, six were fit to be commissioned into the Royal Navy. In this initial report, he mentioned by name only his flag-captain, Berry, and Westcott of the *Majestic*, who was killed. To single out other individuals, he felt, would be invidious; instead, he wrote: "The judgement of the captains, together

with their valour, and that of the officers and men of every description ...
was absolutely irresistible. Could anything from my pen add to the
character of the captains, I could write it with pleasure, but that is
impossible."

Two copies of the despatch were sent: one to St. Vincent with Berry in
the *Leander*, the other to the Admiralty with Captain Capel, who
commanded *La Mutine*. He would make for Naples and there hand over
command to the newly promoted Captain Hoste, who accompanied him,
then give Sir William Hamilton a letter from Nelson before travelling
across the Continent to London. It would be several weeks before the
news could reach England and months before Nelson would hear the
response so, for the time being, he had to be content with the congratulations of his captains. On the day after the battle, he had ordered a break
from swabbing the blood-drenched decks for a service of thanksgiving
and then was told that his "Band of Brothers" were to commission a
presentation sword and a portrait; the latter eventually to be hung in the
premises of the Egyptian Club they now established "in commemoration
of that glorious day". He took satisfaction in the laconic reactions of his
brother-officers, who had not been in the action, as news of it spread
throughout the fleet. "There has been a taut action between Admiral
Nelson and the French," was how Captain Cathcart of the *Alcmene*
reported it to his officers and Cuthbert Collingwood simply described it
as "indeed a charming thing."

Nelson himself was still dazed both by his head-wound – although he
made light of it as his "two black eyes" – and by the scale and scope of his
achievement. Writing to Fanny on 11th August, he repeated his first
reaction to the shambles in Aboukir Bay: "Victory is certainly not a name
strong enough for such a scene as I have passed." Now was not the time
to dwell on future domesticity and he added: "I shall most probably be in
England in November but more of this hereafter." He had decided that
the *Vanguard* needed such drastic repair as only a naval dockyard could
offer and decided to make for Naples, where he could also hope to
strengthen the resolve of King Ferdinand to make a stand against the
French, now that he had crippled their power in the Mediterranean.
There also he could expect to receive replies to his despatch from St.
Vincent and from the Admiralty and also the letters that Fanny and his
family and friends had doubtless been writing to him during the past
three months.

Fanny had been writing regularly from Bath and Roundwood, first
apologising profusely for her inefficient packing when he had left for the
Mediterranean ("You will, I hope, find all your things; I am much
mortified at their being displaced ... Have you stockings enough?";

"Another time I will take more care and hope we shall have proper servants"). She gave him the family gossip, news of naval friends, accounts of their new house and their Suffolk neighbours, not all of whom she considered suitable, finding herself "not at all gratified" on visiting one house "by the indecent ornaments of a gay young man; fine, naked figures and very handsome looking-glasses at the bottoms of the bedsteads – so we left this handsome house . . . not much impressed with favourable sentiments of the owners". The principal decoration of her own house was Lemuel Abbott's newly completed portrait of her husband: "I am now writing opposite to your portrait, the likeness is great . . . It is my companion, my sincere friend in your absence." She told him that engravings of the portrait were popular and that a friend "was told by the bookseller, he had a load of Admiral Nelsons but had sold every one of them, that he had written for another load and one should be saved for her." Moreover, visiting a nursery garden, she had admired a fine carnation and, asking its name, was gratified to be told, "Admiral Nelson – a curious plant."

Fanny still fretted, founding her hopes upon her husband's often-expressed yearning for a life of pastoral simplicity. "As to peace, I most ardently wish for it," she wrote to him, "particularly as you will then be satisfied to live quietly at home. I can't help feeling quite unsettled . . . for, when my spirits are not quiet, you know I am but a poor creature." She was becoming aware that constant reference to her fears might depress a husband on active service and, two days after he had written to her from the shambles of Aboukir Bay, she posted a more cheerful letter from Roundwood: "The weather is very fine; nice clear sky, which helps to cheer us. I was determined to see if I could write without tormenting you with my anxieties, every day produces hopes of hearing from you." But, early in September, rumours – vague but persistent – arrived from the Continent that a great sea battle had been fought in the Mediterranean; all her fears returned and she wrote to him on the 11th: "The newspapers have tormented and almost killed me in regard to the desperate action you have fought with the French fleet. How human faculties can be brought to make others intentionally miserable, I cannot conceive. In my opinion, a newspaper writer, or a fabricator for them, is a despicable creature bearing a human shape."

A week before Fanny wrote in anguish, another letter was written to Nelson by a woman, who had just been told that such a battle had been fought and won. After three months of conflicting reports and rumours of the whereabouts of the French and British fleets, Lady Hamilton had been transfixed by the news that arrived that day. Her attention had constantly been upon the horizon between the cliffs of the Sorrento peninsula and Capri, and between Capri and Ischia, as was that of her English friend Cornelia Knight, who was staying in Naples with her mother, and it was she who described their first intimation of what was to follow. "Our telescope was constantly directed towards the entrance of the beautiful bay, which we so perfectly enjoyed from our windows," she wrote:

At length ... while I was reading to my mother, I happened to turn my eyes towards the sea and thought I discerned a sloop of war in the offing. I consulted the glass and found that I was not mistaken. I also plainly saw that the vessel belonged to the squadron of Sir Horatio Nelson, for blue was also the colour of Lord St. Vincent's flag. My attention was instantly distracted from my book and my dear mother was rather displeased with my evident preoccupation for I did not venture to confess my hopes lest I should raise hers too high and cause her the pain of disappointment.

I forget what I was reading but it was something that peculiarly interested my mother and she began at last to think that I could not be so negligent without a cause of some importance. She rose from her seat and went to the telescope. The sloop was now approaching nearer and nearer to the land. The book was laid aside and we alternately kept an eye at the glass. Presently a boat put off from the shore and pulled out to the ship. Two officers were on deck and drew near to the side. We clearly distinguished a gold epaulet on the shoulder and this was quite sufficient to convince us that one was the commander of the sloop and the other a captain going home with despatches. News of a victory, no doubt. We observed the gestures of the officers while they were conversing with the persons in the boat, Englishmen resident in Naples. We fancied we could see them, with the commotion natural to sailors ... depict by their action the blowing up of some ships and the sinking of others. Our conjectures were soon happily realised. The vessel was the *Mutine* ...

Soon the two officers, Capel and Hoste, were ashore, giving Sir William Hamilton the letter from Nelson. When Lady Hamilton heard the news, Nelson was later told, "the effect was like a shot; she fell apparently dead". But, although bruised and, he was to hear, "seriously ill; first from anxiety and then from joy", she recovered quickly to sweep up the two young officers and, as Hoste said, "made us get into her carriage and parade through the streets till dark; she had a bandeau round her forehead with the words 'Nelson and Victory'. The populace saw and understood what it meant and '*Viva Nelson!*' resounded through the streets."

On her return to the Palazzo Sessa, Emma Hamilton wrote to Nelson:

I am delirious with joy and assure you I have a fever caused by agitation and pleasure. Good God what a victory! Never, never has there been anything half so glorious, half so complete! I fainted when I heard the joyful news and fell on my side and am hurt, but what of that ... I should feel it a glory to die in such a cause. No, I would not like to die until I see and embrace the *Victor of the Nile* ... Sir William is ten years younger since the happy news ... My dress from head to foot is *alla Nelson*. Even my shawl is in blue with gold anchors all over. My earrings are Nelson's anchors; in short, we are all be-Nelsoned ... I wish you could have seen our house, the three nights of illuminations. 'Tis, 'twas covered with your glorious name. There were three thousand lamps and there should have been three million.

This letter was delivered to Nelson, with more of his mail, by Hoste, who had taken over command of the *Mutine* when Capel left Naples for London. The ships met off the volcanic island of Stromboli as the half-crippled *Vanguard* made her slow progress towards Naples. Nelson, who not only suffered from his head-wound – "My head is ready to split and I am always so sick" – and was recovering from a sudden bout of recurrent malaria, now read an invitation from Sir William Hamilton: "A pleasant appartment is ready for you in my house and Emma is looking out for the softest pillows to repose the few wearied limbs you have left." This would only be the beginning of the welcome because a gushing letter from Queen Maria Carolina told him that she had hung his portrait in her room, adding, "*Faites un hip hip hip en mon nom chantez God Saeve die King et puis God Saeve Nelson et marine Britannique*". At the Palazzo Reale, she was in an ecstacy of joy, as Lady Hamilton told Nelson:

She fainted, cried, kissed her husband, her children, walked frantic about the room, cried, kissed and embraced every person near her, exclaiming, 'Oh, brave Nelson; Oh God bless and protect our brave deliverer. Oh, Nelson, Nelson, what do we not owe you! Oh, victor, saviour of Italy. Oh, that my swollen heart could now tell him personally what we owe to him.'

A few days later, the first British ships appeared off the tip of the Sorrento peninsula and were identified as the *Culloden* and the *Alexander*. A procession of boats with King Ferdinand in his barge, the Hamiltons in theirs and musicians of the court orchestra playing in another pulled out to meet them. Hearing that Admiral Nelson was yet to arrive, the King did not go aboard but stood in his boat waving his hat while Sir William called out to the British sailors lining their bulwarks and peering from the gun-ports, "My lads! that is the King whom you have saved with his family and kingdom!" "Very glad of it, sir," came the reply. "Very glad of it."

On 22nd September, the *Vanguard* herself appeared off Capri and a far larger flotilla rowed out with bands playing *Rule Britannia* and *See the Conquering Hero Comes!*, which they had learned for the occasion. On his quarterdeck, Nelson awaited the arrival of the Hamiltons and the King, whom he could recognise as their barge approached. The Hamiltons came aboard first and Nelson described the scene to Fanny:

> Alongside my honoured friends came; the scene in the boat appeared terribly affecting. Up flew her ladyship and exclaiming: *Oh God, is it possible*! fell into my arm more dead than alive. Tears, however, soon put matters to rights, when alongside came the King ... He took me by the hand, calling me his deliverer and preserver with every other expression of kindness ... I hope one day to have the pleasure of introducing you to Lady Hamilton. She is one of the very best women in the world. How few could have made the turn she has. She is an honour to her sex and proof that even reputation may be regained but I own it requires a great soul.

Nelson was writing at the Palazzo Sessa, where he had been given a room from which he could see his ships anchored in the bay. He ended it, as was his custom, with cheering news of Josiah, who had also arrived at Naples in command of a sloop and had joined him ashore, but on this occasion his tact left him. "Her ladyship, if Josiah were to stay, would make something of him and, with all his bluntness, I am sure he likes Lady Hamilton more than any female. She would fashion him in six months inspite of himself."

The curious couple were already taking hold of Nelson's life; persuading him to leave his flagship for the comfort of the Palazzo Sessa; arranging his appointments ashore and now preparing an extravagant party to celebrate his fortieth birthday on 29th September. He had already got to know and admire Sir William through the spasmodic correspondence they had conducted since their first meeting four years before; his wife, met briefly then, had long been the subject of gossip and sexual innuendo, so that he felt as familiar with her as a member of an audience with a celebrated actress. Sir William Hamilton, now aged sixty-seven, was a striking and attractive figure, in conversation ready to switch from contemporary politics to archaeology, arcane Neapolitan customs or the subterranean mysteries of the volcanoes and earthquakes that surrounded Naples and added an edge of danger to its excitements. A man of action as well as a scholar and dilettante, he had been a soldier when young and during his thirty-five years as British representative at the Bourbon court in Naples had made twenty-two ascents of Vesuvius, arousing admiration by his daring in approaching the black rim of the smoking crater.

The son of Lord Archibald Hamilton and grandson of the third Duke of Hamilton, he was well-connected but without a fortune of his own, until he had married Catherine Barlow, the heiress to a Pembrokeshire estate which would produce an income of £8,000 a year. She was a gentle, delicate, loving creature, tolerating his extra-marital escapades with what their rich and eccentric friend William Beckford described as "a pure and uncontaminated mind, at peace with itself and benevolently desirous of diffusing that happy tranquillity around it". On his marrige in 1758, William Hamilton resigned his commission in the Army – although the Seven Years War was in its second year – and was elected to the House of Commons, where he sat as the silent representative for Midhurst in Sussex for four years. In 1763, the post of Envoy Extraordinary to the Bourbon court at Naples became vacant and he applied for it as amusing but undemanding employment that would enable him to indulge his fascination in archaeology – the excavations at Herculaneum and Pompeii had recently been creating a sensation among the dilettanti – in a climate suitable to his wife's health. They arrived at the end of that year and soon their home at the Palazzo Sessa – a great house standing on the bluff behind the Palazzo Reale and commanding what was generally considered the most picturesque view in Europe – became a vortex of cultural activity, visited by the aristocratic and scholarly *cogniscenti* when touring Italy. His diplomatic and social success was recognised, after nine years, with a knighthood.

Ten years later, Catherine Hamilton fell into a decline and as she lay dying that summer, wrote a farewell letter to her husband to express her love and urge him to share her religious beliefs in words that recall Edmund Nelson's strong, simple faith:

> The dissipated life you lead, my dear Hamilton, prevents your attending those great truths in comparison of which all is folly – for God's sake do not reject those truths, nor despise the plain simplicity of a religion upon which our salvation depends and which has been acknowledged by the most sensible and greatest men after their having sustained the contrary ... And now, my dear Hamilton, my husband, my friend, my only attachment to this earth, farewell.

Sir William mourned her but stood by his own creed to "admire the Creator and all His Works, to us incomprehensible; do all the good you can upon earth; and take the chance of Eternity without dismay". But for all his stoicism and wide secular interests, he lived a lonely life in the great house, its dozens of inter-connecting rooms cluttered with marble statuary and Greek vases, its walls hung with massed paintings by Italian, French, Flemish and English masters, its cabinets crammed with Roman coins and curiosities from the excavations on the slopes of Vesuvius. The following year he returned to England with his wife's coffin, to attend her funeral at Selbeck in Wales and then visit his family and his friends in London, amongst them his nephew the Honourable Charles Greville, a dilettante and philanderer after his own heart.

Accustomed to basking in the admiration and envy of visitors to his collection of art and antiquities at the Palazzo Sessa, Sir William found himself envying one of his nephew's possessions: his mistress. At eighteen, Emma Hart was already celebrated for looks familiar in the marble of classical statuary but rarely in the flesh, so that she was sought as a model by the fashionable painters of London, notably George Romney, whose unrequited love for her he expressed in portraits and fantasies in paint. Born Emily Lyon, in 1765, the daughter of a blacksmith in the Wirral district of Cheshire and sent to work as a nursery-maid in London, her looks offered a means of advancement. Her seduction by a naval officer and the birth of a child was only a temporary set-back and she soon found employment as an attendant in "The Temple of Health", a suspect medical establishment in the Adelphi. Promising the restoration of fertility in a "Celestial Bed", this may have been a genteel brothel, although there was no evidence that Emily was a prostitute. Here, probably, she met another lover, the dashing, dissolute Sir Harry Fetherstonehaugh, who swept her off to his country house, Uppark, high on the Sussex downs, to help him entertain his fast-living friends. Usually faithful but generous to a fault, she was pregnant again and possibly not by Sir Harry, who sent her back to Cheshire with just enough money for her fare. Accustomed by now to the comforts and pleasures of the rich, she threw herself on the mercy of one of Sir Harry's more cultivated friends, Charles Greville. After a half-hearted attempt to affect a reconciliation, he took her as his own mistress at Paddington where she was installed as what he jokingly called "the fair tea-maker of Edgware Row". Having already changed her surname to Hart, she now decided to be known as Emma, rather than Emily, while her mother called herself Mrs. Cadogan, after an aristocratic family from the Welsh border country whence she came.

While Emma Hart did not expect Greville to marry her, she loved him deeply and was satisfied with the arrangement, not suspecting that she was becoming an encumbrance since he had begun to look for an heiress of his own social class to marry and had sighted one in a daughter of Lord Middleton in nearby Portman Square. Noting his uncle's eye linger on her, knowing his reputation and realising that he could not be looking forward to his return to the lonely picture-galleries of the Palazzo Sessa, he saw a solution to his own problem. He would present his mistress to Sir William – or, rather, sell her, since he would try to link his gift with a reciprocal promise of an inheritance in his uncle's will – so that she could be removed, far beyond any future embarrassment, to Naples. So he wrote a long letter, making the offer as if presenting a work of art: "Judge then, as you know my satisfaction on looking on a modern piece of *virtu*, if I do not think you a second self in thinking that, by placing her within your reach, I render a necessity, which would otherwise be heartbreaking, tolerable and even comforting."

Sir William accepted with alacrity and, after further negotiations, Emma arrived in Naples early in 1786, accompanied by her mother, imagining that she would only be visiting Sir William to further her education before returning to her lover in Paddington. Her discovery of the truth was agonising but Sir William was gentle and persuasive and she, affectionate as ever, eventually became his mistress. Finally, having made her his hostess at the Palazzo Sessa, he married her while on a visit to London in the autumn of 1791 and she returned with him to Naples as Lady Hamilton. She was now aged twenty-six and he was sixty, which prompted the warning verse by the satirist John Wolcot:

> O Knight of Naples, is it come to pass
> That thou has left the gods of stone and brass,
> To wed a Deity of flesh and blood?
> O lock the temple with thy strongest key,
> For fear thy Deity, a comely She,
> Should one day ramble in a frolic mood.

But to Sir William's delight, she had proved a loyal and stimulating wife, also becoming another beautiful curiosity for him to display. While his first wife had presided over musical evenings at the Palazzo Sessa, herself contributing delicate pieces on the harpsichord, Emma dominated such occasions, singing loudly and performing her "Attitudes", striking poses – an art she may have learned at "The Temple of Health" – within a picture-frame, or between drapes, to represent emotions inspired by Classical mythology, while her husband led the applause. Her flawed morality fitted her well for the worldliness of Neapolitan society; she quickly learned to speak fluent Italian and French and struck up a friendship with the Queen that was useful to both women; the latter seeing Emma as a means of influencing her husband and, through him, the British government; Sir William using his wife in his attempts to persuade the King and Queen to take a stronger stand against the French and for the British.

When Nelson met the Hamiltons for the second time, Emma was aged thirty-three and was as striking as ever. Her face was still beautiful, and although she was growing fat she remained vivacious and bountiful with generosity and humour, combining sexuality with motherliness, both qualities long needed by a naval officer far from home. She displayed an exuberant, original wit that could have reminded Nelson of his father's whimsical humour. She was an enthusiast for friendships, causes and ideas, like her husband, to whose specialised passions for art, archaeology, volcanology and politics she was a foil, illuminating with theatrical intensity whatever person, or pastime caught her fancy. On this occasion it was Rear-Admiral Sir Horatio Nelson.

This bizarre couple at once began arranging lavish celebrations to mark their guest's fortieth birthday on 29th September and a bemused Nelson wrote to Fanny: "The preparations of Lady Hamilton for celebrating my birthday tomorrow are enough to fill me with vanity. Every ribbon, every button has *Nelson*, etc., and the whole service are *'H.N. Glorious 1st August!'*. Songs and sonnets are numerous, beyond what I ever could deserve." The wording of her invitations was irresistible in its enthusiasm, like that to Captain Murray of the *Colossus*, which had arrived off the city: "Tomorrow being the great Nelson's birthday, Lady H. hopes to have the happiness and honour of Captain Murray's company to dinner and as many officers and midshipmen as he can spare for the Ball in the evening as Lady H. loves dearly all seamen but particularly those spoken of so highly as Captain Murray is by our brave Admiral."

Two days later, Nelston wrote again: "On my birthday night, 80 people dined at Sir William's, 1,740 came to a ball, 800 supped, conducted in such a style of elegance as I never saw, or shall again probably. A rostral column is erected under a magnificent canopy, never, Lady Hamilton says, to come down while they remain in Naples ... on the front 'Nelson', on the pedestal *'Veni, Vidi, Vici'*, anchors, inscriptions ... were numerous." This "splendid fête" was also described by Cornelia Knight: "At the extremity of the saloon, where we danced, was a rostral column, on which were inscribed the names of the heroes of the Nile, while a profusion of flowers and a magnificent illumination added to the brilliancy of the entertainment. Nothing could be more gay than Naples ..." Miss Knight, something of an amateur poetess, had composed songs for Emma Hamilton to sing in her loud and soaring voice: one began:

> The British Nelson rivals Caesar's fame,
> Like him, he came, he saw, he overcame.
> In conquest, modest as in action brave,
> To God the glory pious Nelson gave.

Another was to be sung to the tune of the National Anthem, Nelson posted a copy of this to Fanny "as I know you will sing it with pleasure" – enclosing a note from Josiah with another laudatory ballad ("*Brave Nelson fought and scorned the frowns of fate, his tranquil bosom fearless of surprise*") – but adding tactlessly, "Josiah is well but could he be here six months Lady Hamilton would much fashion him, which indeed he wants". This was an oblique reference to a scene at the birthday party, when the young captain – now commanding the sloop *Bonne Citoyenne*, a French prize – drank too much, became obstreperous and had to be taken out by brother-officers. Probably he had been hurt by his stepfather paying little attention to him and too much to their hostess.

It was not only the luxuries of the Palazzo Sessa that were now open to Nelson but a strange and beautiful country of palaces and panoramas. The Bourbons had built *palazzi* or pavilions wherever their pleasures dictated, whether for entertaining, hunting or commanding a remarkable view of green slopes and blue sea dominated by the dark presence of Vesuvius and the volcanic cliffs and crags created by its eruptions. Most remarkable of these was Caserta, built in imitation of Versailles, and there and wherever the royal family might be, the Hamiltons would not be far away. Sometimes they stayed at a rented villa near Caserta, where they could walk in the English Garden laid for the Queen by the landscape gardener, John Graefer, who had been recommended by Sir William. They owned two small houses in the country: the Villa Angelica, near the village of Torre del Greco on the lowest slopes of Vesuvius, from which Hamilton made his expeditions to the crater; and the Villa Emma, so named for his wife, built on the edge of the low cliffs above the sea at Posillipo a few miles north of Naples. At these a variety of entertainment was available: a sail in the bay; a visit to the volcanic craters and springs of hot mud around Pozzuoli; an inspection of the latest finds at Herculaneum or Pompeii; even an ascent of Vesuvius. For a sea-officer accustomed to the rigours and sparse comforts of life at sea and brought up in the simplicities of life in a country parsonage, the prospect was dazzling.

Fanny, meanwhile, was waiting at Roundwood, still agitated by unconfirmed newspaper reports of a battle, writing that she has sent him " . . . 9 small stone jars of cherries in brandy, five of currant jelly and five of apricot. The season was particularly unfavourable for preserving. The torrents of rain bruised the fruit very much." But the husband to whom she wrote was now occupied with more exotic thoughts and no longer dreaming of domestic bliss in East Anglia. He remained the compound of his past: the motherless twelve-year-old sent to "rough it out at sea"; the kinsman of both landowners and tradesmen, whose brother was a failed grocer and two of whose sisters had worked as shop assistants; the son of a family of clergymen, whose own spiritual inspiration had been to revere his King and Country; the naval officer who for so long complained that others had gathered what should have been his own rewards. Now with the fulfilment of his hope for glory, his emotions needed to be earthed in those of others. Fanny was far away but, in any event, her response would be so tempered with anxiety that it would only irritate.

This man, hungry for recognition, applause and affection, had also been affected by the circumstances of his triumph. The tension of the long hunt of the French and the orgasmic release of the eventual battle had left him exhausted. Minor ills – particularly recurrent malaria – had weakened his resistance to the shock of the head-wound. This, although deemed superficial, had caused concussion that might have affected the brain, even impairing some mental faculty, jarring the fine balance of his complex character.[1] All his needs, and more, could now be met by the voluptuous, motherly woman in whose care he rested; whose vitality and vision matched his own; who seemed as ambitious for him as he was for himself. Yet the self-aware parson's son was still part of him and he knew the risk he ran, writing to Lord St. Vincent five days after the birthday party, he concluded his letter: "I am writing opposite Lady Hamilton, therefore you will not be surprised at the glorious jumble of this letter. Were your Lordship in my place, I much doubt if you could write so well; our hearts and hands must be all in a flutter: Naples is a dangerous place and we must keep clear of it."

Naples was also an important place: the capital of the most significant ally in the Mediterranean, for the ramshackle Ottoman Empire and the occasional intrusion of a Russian squadron into its waters added little weight to the strategic balance. All power rested with the King and Queen and their minister, Sir John Acton, and to these the Hamiltons offered immediate access. Whenever he wished, Nelson could be taken by carriage from the courtyard of the Palazzo Sessa, through the noisy, crowded Chaia district to the imposing Palazzo Reale above the habour. Then up the wide marble staircase beneath the sculptured symbols of martial prowess, across gleaming stretches of coloured paving and into great dim rooms, glowing with gilt, glinting with glass; their walls rich with damask, tapestry and gilded picture-frames; their coffered

---

[1] Medical opinion now accepts that damage to the frontal lobes of the brain caused by a heavy blow can have such consequences, sometimes loosening inhibitions and impairing judgement.

ceilings with sensual painting. Here beneath their own portraits he would meet their Serene Majesties the King and Queen of the Two Sicilies.

King Ferdinand, now aged forty-seven, seemed attractive at first sight: robust and forthright, his ugly face creased with jollity. "His features were coarse and harsh," wrote one English visitor, Lady Craven, "yet the general expression of his countenance was rather intelligent, and perhaps even agreeable, although, separately taken, every feature was ugly. His conversation, his deportment, his manners, were from an unpolished simplicity, rude in their nature, though rather pleasing ... He reminded one of a rustic elevated by accident to the crown, but ... not entirely unworthy of such an honour." Queen Maria Carolina could also cut an impressive figure: tall, erect and haughty as befitted a daughter of the Empress Maria Theresa and the sister of Marie Antoinette. Yet there was a coarseness about her, too; the face too long and too heavy in the jaw to be handsome, the blue eyes sometimes bovine, sometimes cunning or wild. She shared with Emma Hamilton a capacity for enthusiasm and generosity that overwhelmed those she made welcome.

The popularity of the King among the mass of his subjects was undisputed because he shared their tastes, their rough sports and their bawdy humour. Not only would he dress as a fisherman to spend the night out in the bay hauling his nets, or a day harpooning, but would sell his catch in the street markets, himself weighing the fish and taking the money. Hunting was his favourite occupation and here his taste was Roman in scale and cruelty, the game being driven into the centre of an extinct volcanic crater where it could be set upon by packs of hounds and speared at leisure by the monarch and his guests. "I was grieved to see in him a disposition to tyrannical cruelty both towards his servants and the animals, which unfortunately fell into his hands," wrote Hamilton, who accompanied the King on these carnivals of slaughter in order to cultivate his trust. "This disposition must prove fatal to his subjects if it should take root."

Yet he was in awe – and, occasionally, fear – of his wife, who had asserted her dominance early in the marriage. Then Ferdinand had described one quarrel in a letter to his father: "She became a fury, she flew at me like a dog and even took my hand in her teeth ... At table she was worse than ever ... screeching like an eagle and in language by no means decent and I ... rose from table and quietly went away." A woman of strong passions – taking lovers as well as bearing seventeen of her husband's children – she was deeply superstitious, so sharing with the Neapolitans their fervid, semi-pagan religion. "The Queen used to be subject to fits of devotion," recorded Cornelia Knight, "at which times she stuck short prayers and pious ejaculations inside her stays and occasionally swallowed them." In her, noted a French diplomatist, "the keenest taste for pleasure has been coupled with a passion for ruling, hence the double depravity of her political intrigues and her private conduct ... The breadth and superiority of her intelligence have been greatly overrated; she will dare anything; that is all her secret."

Nelson, with his reverence for royalty, saw them through other eyes and put their weaknesses down to inexperience, which could be remedied by British advice. His own responsibilities, as laid down by the Admiralty, were for all naval operations east of Corsica and Sardinia and the most pressing of these was the blockading of the French in Alexandria and Malta, for which purposes he had detached small squadrons under Hood and Ball respectively. Hamilton had been urging the King to abandon his precarious neutrality and declare war on France. At the beginning of the year, the French had found a pretext to seize Rome, depose the Pope and establish their own republic there, leaving the Kingdom of the Two Sicilies exposed to their next spasm of aggression. A new alliance between Britain, Austria and Russia was under discussion; if it came about, this could lead to another offensive into northern Italy by the Austrians and renewed pressure from the sea by the British and Russians, so giving King Ferdinand the opportunity to advance from the south and even to capture Rome. Such plans were so advanced that in mid-October an Austrian general, the elderly Baron Karl von Mack, arrived in Naples to take command of the army that was to advance on Rome. With Hamilton's support, Nelson had been urging the King that "the boldest measures are the safest", but the Queen needed no prompting, telling the Austrian: "General, be to us by land what my hero, Nelson, has been by sea." Her hero, who was at the royal dinner table when this compliment was paid him, declared her "truly a daughter of Maria Theresa".

With Hamilton and himself to embolden the King and Queen, Nelson was optimistic but their ministers and courtiers he despised, suddenly longing for the robust simplicities of the naval chain of command. Indeed, he was tiring of social life ashore – always excepting the company of the Hamiltons – and no doubt suffering from an excess of rich food, to which he was unaccustomed, and late nights. "I trust, my Lord, in a week we shall be at sea," he wrote to St. Vincent. "I am very unwell and the miserable conduct of this Court is not likely to cool my irritable temper. It is a country of fiddlers and poets, whores and scoundrels." The *Vanguard* had been repaired and was ready for sea and so, on 14th October, he sailed for Malta to inspect Captain Ball's blockade, telling St. Vincent that the King wanted him back at Naples at the beginning of November for the launching of the offensive towards Rome. "I gave up my plan, which was to have gone to Egypt and attended to the destruction of the French shipping in that quarter," he explained.

There was little he could do at Malta, beyond accepting the surrender of the island of Gozo, for the French garrison was besieged in Valetta by the Maltese and tightly blockaded by Ball's ships, so he arrived back in the Bay of Naples on the last day of October. Now he heard the first reaction from England to the news of his victory – Captain Capel had reached London with his despatch on 2nd October – and of the honours that were to be lavished upon him. The first of these was a barony: a slight disappointment for there had been talk of a viscountcy. Hearing this before Nelson, Emma Hamilton was quick to respond: "Sir William is in a rage with the Ministry for not having made Lord Nelson a viscount," she wrote to Fanny when she heard the news. "Hang them I say!" Then she wrote to Nelson himself, sending the letter to his approaching ship: "If I was King of England I would make you the most noble, puissant Duke Nelson, Marquis Nile, Earl Alexandria, Viscount Pyramid, Baron Crocodile and Prince Victory that posterity might have you in all forms." She also told him that the Sultan of Turkey had presented him with an "order of feather that he took out of his own turban to decorate you". This proved to be the *chelengk*, a plume of artificial diamonds to wear in his hat, described by the giver as "a blaze of brilliants, crowned with vibrating plumage and a radiant star in the middle, turning on its centre by means of watch-work which winds up behind". The theatricality pleased her and she added, " '*Vivo il Turco*', says Emma".

These were only the first tremors of the earthquake of excitement that had shaken England to reach Naples. Captain Capel had travelled safely through Austria and the German states – while Berry had been captured at sea by the French a fortnight after leaving Aboukir Bay in the *Leander* – and he reached London early that October morning. Arriving at the Admiralty he went straight to Lord Spencer and the First Lord at once sent word to the Lord Mayor so that soon after mid-day church bells were ringing and guns firing salutes at the Tower and in Hyde Park. Lady Spencer immediately expressed herself in a letter:

Captain Capel just arrived! Joy, joy, joy to you, brave, gallant, immortalized Nelson! May that great God, whose cause you so valiantly support, protect and bless you to the end of your brilliant career! Such a race surely was never run. My heart is absolutely bursting with different sensations of joy, of gratitude, of pride, of every emotion that ever warmed the bosom of a British woman ... This moment, the guns are firing, illuminations are preparing, your gallant name is echoed from street to street.

Huge crowds had gathered and, she wrote, "London is mad – absolutely mad – Capel was followed by a mob of several thousands from the Admiralty, huzzaring the whole way . . . Joy, joy, joy . . . "

Lord Spencer sent a messenger with the news to the King at Weymouth, and he covered the 130 miles in nine and a half hours, being stopped on the road by a highwayman, who, the newspapers reported, "on being told the contents of the despatches refused to take them" and told the messenger "to proceed with all possible expedition with the good news to his Majesty". When it reached him, King George "read Admiral Nelson's letters aloud four times to different noblemen and gentlemen on the esplanade at Weymouth" while, off-shore, the guardship, the frigate *San Fiorenzo*, prepared to join the "general illuminations" of the town that night with her own display of "variegated lamps".

The news reached Nelson's own county on the same day and set the church bells ringing. At Dereham, a troop of the Norfolk Yeomanry were about to parade, but, as the *Norfolk Chronicle* reported:

> Going into the field they received the glorious news of Admiral Nelson's complete victory . . . It operated as an electric impulse – each man, each horse, seemed more than usually animated; they went through the business of the field with a degree of military accuracy which would have done honour to veteran troops and, on their return to Dereham, were received by a loyal band playing *God Save the King*, *Rule Britannia*, etc., etc., and, after firing three vollies in honour of the day, retired amidst the repeated huzzas of a numerous and admiring concourse of gratified spectators.

Celebrations began immediately in Norwich, Nelson's name being coupled with that of Captain Berry, a native of the city. A ball at the Assembly House, which lasted all night, was enlivened by sixteen toasts such as "May the Wooden Walls of Old England protect the Palace of the Prince and the Cottage of the Peasant" while "the ladies displayed infinite taste in their dresses of anchors, berries, laurel and blue ribbands inscribed with *Nelson, Berry, Victory*." At a concert, a Mr. Sharp added new verses to *Rule Britannia*:

> And see! from Norfolk's favoured site,
> By heav'n uprear'd, a Hero springs,
> Arm'd with the thunder of her might,
> And shielded by her Seraph wings,
>   Rule Britannia, etc.
>
> By NELSON's glorious deeds inspir'd,
> Fresh trophies shall thy children bring,

And with his patriot virtues fir'd,
Protect their County, Laws and King.
Rule Britannia, etc.

The British flag flew above the French from the tower of St. Peter Mancroft and, after dark, more than fifty houses were decorated with coloured transparencies illuminated in their windows: some showing Britannia; one entitled *The Jacobin Club, or Hell upon Earth*, in which the Devil joined Robespierre and the East Anglian radicals Tom Paine and Dr. Priestley; and the transparency in the window of a doctor's house showed a pile of cannon balls above the words: "British pills effectively employed in the case of the French disease." This proved pertinent political comment for the victory extinguished the threat of insurrection in England, assuaging discontent and changing reformist zeal into patriotic fervour for the defences of British liberties.

The news was spread from Norwich by coaches flying flags, coachmen shouting it to wayside inns aroused by the sound of their horns. At the village of Weston Longville, the rector, Thomas Woodforde, wrote in his journal:

> Great rejoicings at Norwich today on Lord Nelson's great and noble victory ... An ox roasted whole in the Market Place, etc. This being a day of general thanksgiving, Mr. Colman read prayers this morning suitable to the occasion. Dinner today, leg of mutton roasted, etc. I gave my servants this evening after supper some strong beer and some punch to drink Admiral Nelson's Health on his late, grand Victory.

The suitable prayers included one suggested by the Bishop of Norwich for use in all services: "O Almightly God, the Sovereign Father of all the World, in whose hand is Power and Might, which none is able to resist; we bless and magnify Thy Great and Glorious Name for the Happy Victory, which Thou hast vouchsafed to the Fleet of Thy Servant, our Sovereign, in distant seas."

The market town of Swaffham, between Hilborough and Burnham Thorpe was, according to the *Norfolk Chronicle*, "in a universal blaze – the Town Hall, the Assembly Rooms, the great west window of the church and several gentlemen's houses were superbly grand, to which were added the ringing of bells and the firing of field-pieces and small arms in a style that pleased everyone and all parties went to bed cheered and delighted." A celebration ball was hastily arranged at the Assembly Rooms, attended by members of both the Nelson and Hoste families. Nelson's niece, Kitty Bolton, told Fanny:

It was as full as could be expected for the neighbourhood . . . They paid Mama the compliment to ask her to begin the Ball but she danced only with Mr. Hoste; it is a dance . . . called the *Vanguard* or the *breaking of the line*. We sent to London for all the songs and we had them and sung . . . Mrs. Hoste's ribbands, which she had from London, were half Navy Blue and half red to signify the Knight of the Bath and the Navy. She gave me a medallion of my Uncle, which I wore round my neck at the Ball. Mrs. Micklethwaite had had a very handsome cap from London inscribed in gold spangles, 'The Hero of the Nile'.

In addition to his new title of Baron Nelson of the Nile and Burnham Thorpe, Nelson was awarded an annual pension of £2,000 and countless honours and presents given by municipalities and institutions that stood to benefit by his victory. He was particularly gratified to hear that his old friend Alexander Davison, whom he had appointed agent to collect the prize-money due for the capture of French ships in the battle, had himself ordered medals commemorating the victory to be struck for all who had taken part: gold for captains, silver for their officers, bronze for the sailors and marines.

Fanny – now Baroness Nelson – was all aflutter at her new home in Suffolk, conscious that she now attracted the attention of the grand county families, which had not been forthcoming when she was only the wife of a knight and a rear-admiral, telling Lord St. Vincent: "Since . . . my husband has gained this victory, I have been honoured with the notice of the great in this neighbourhood – truly I don't thank them: they ought to have found their way to the cottage before." She was piqued, too, at the award of a barony instead of higher rank, as was his brother Maurice, but both were gratified at being the centre of attention; the latter – a self-effacing civil servant – amazed to find himself the guest of honour at a celebration dinner in London at the invitation of Mr. Pitt, the Prime Minister, himself. Indeed, all the family basked in the distant glory, his niece Charlotte writing to him from Hilborough that "there are new songs out every day on the Battle of the Nile, which I learn to play and hope I shall have the pleasure of playing them to you. I am now learning a grand march on your victory and another called Lord Nelson's Fancy . . .".

Lord Nelson's fancy had turned to Emma Hamilton, and this was already attracting comment. When he drove out of Naples to San Germano, where the Neapolitan army was assembling for the march on Rome, he was accompanied by the Hamiltons. There, while the Queen, dressed in a riding habit, inspected the troops from a chariot drawn by four horses, it was recorded that: "Lady Hamilton, who, under pretence of escorting her Majesty, displayed her own beauty in all its magnificence to the camp and paraded her conquest over the victor of Aboukir, who, seated beside her in the same carriage, appeared fascinated and submissive to her charms."

His thoughts were not solely thus occupied for he was becoming increasingly worried by the prospects of the offensive he had been urging. He noted that General von Mack was much concerned with his own comfort and never travelled without a procession of five carriages. His military skill seemed questionable, too, since in the exercises now being held he was out-manoeuvred and surrounded by the soldiers playing the part of the enemy. "I have formed my opinion," he noted, "and heartily hope I may be mistaken." It was planned that von Mack with 30,000 men of what he called "*la plus belle Armée d'Europe*" would advance on Rome, while Nelson landed 4,000 infantry and 600 cavalry from his ships at Leghorn, north of the city, to cut the communications of its French garrison. With Austrian support in the north of Italy, this plan had a chance of success, he felt, but, on the day after the final orders had been agreed, the King received a despatch from Vienna refusing to commit their troops to an offensive unless the French were the aggressors. Nelson, realising that it was too late for second thoughts and that the King's declared intentions would provoke a French counter-attack upon Naples, told him: "Either advance, trusting to God for His blessing on a just cause to die with *l'épée à le main*, or remain quiet and be kicked out of your kingdom."

On 22nd November, King Ferdinand and General von Mack led their army from the camp at San Germano and took the road to Rome, while Nelson sailed with his contingent for Leghorn. Success was immediate and easy: the troops landed at Leghorn without opposition on the 28th and, next day, the King led his army in triumph through the streets of Rome. The French had withdrawn, although a few shut themselves into the castle of Sant' Angelo on the bank of the Tiber and prepared to withstand a siege. Meanwhile, the King installed himself in the Palazzo Farnese and sent an invitation to the exiled Pope to return and, "borne on the wings of the cherubim, descend into the Vatican and purify it with your Holy Presence". His own task complete, Nelson returned to Naples on 5th December and reported to Hamilton the worrying attitudes of many of the Neapolitan officers he had put ashore: they did not seem as eager as their monarch to fight the French.

His own thoughts could now turn homewards. The capture of Rome was a suitably spectacular climax to the remarkable year he had begun in Bath and if his apprehensions were justified he himself would be unable to avert disaster. Despite the attractions of Naples, it would be disappointing to miss the celebration of his fame in England, reports of which were still arriving. Also Fanny had been suggesting that she might join him in the Mediterranean and that was something he wanted to avoid. Probably she was disconcerted by the involvement of her husband with the Hamiltons that was evident from his letters and from his worrying references to her son. He had just written to her: "The improvement made in Josiah by Lady Hamilton is wonderful. She seems the only person he minds and his faults are not omitted to be told him but in such a way as pleases him, and his; your and my obligations are infinite on that score ... His manners are so rough but, God bless him, I love him with all his roughness." This followed a letter from Emma Hamilton herself, telling Fanny: "Josiah is so much improved in every respect ... I love him much and, although we quarrel sometimes, he loves me and does as I would have him." It seemed as though her duties both as a wife and a mother were being usurped.

Therefore as the year ended, Nelson determined to return home to savour the admiration of the King and Country he so revered. Now that the scope for naval operations was so limited, he told Fanny in a letter, "There can be no occasion for a Nelson". He told her that he must now have a house in London, preferably one like the smart new house in Park Street, where he remembered visiting his urbane uncle, Captain Suckling: "If we have the money, a neat house in London near Hyde Park, but on no account on the other side of Portman Square. I detest Baker Street. In short, do as you please; you know my wishes and income. A neat carriage I desire you will order and, if possible, get good servants. You will take care I am not let down."

CHAPTER VIII

Nemesis at Naples
(1798–1800)

"My Lord Thunder..."
– Emma Hamilton's nickname for Horatio Nelson on his becoming
Duke of Bronte; Palermo, 1799

On the black and blowy night of 21st December, 1798, Lord Nelson, wrapped in a boat-cloak, clambered down the side of the *Vanguard* and seated himself at the stern of his barge. This and other boats embarking armed sailors and their officers from the other ships of the squadron, lying at single anchor a mile from shore in the Bay of Naples, began to pull towards the shore. It was a scene to recall the beginning of the disastrous assault from the sea on Tenerife seventeen months before and was the antithesis of his own triumphant arrival here in September to cheering crowds and thumping bands in bright sunshine.

His mission tonight was the rescue of King Ferdinand and Queen Maria Carolina from the invading French and from their own rebellious subjects. Since the King had led his army into Rome the month before, fortunes had been reversed: the French had counter-attacked, routed the Neapolitan troops without having to fight a battle and the King himself had returned to the Palazzo Reale, an hysterical refugee. The pursuing French were now marching on Naples at a steady pace and there would be many to welcome them, including a high proportion of the intelligentsia who longed to replace the vulgar and capricious domination of their monarch with the ideals that had spread the spirit of reform throughout Europe and North America.

The mass of Neapolitans with whom the King sometimes liked to identify himself were, however, eager for a fight, their robust patriotism and superstitious religion rousing them to defend their city against the foreign atheists. To show their loyalty, a mob demonstrated before the Palazzo Reale and, below its windows, lynched a suspected Jacobin spy, who turned out to be one of the royal messengers, caught on his way to Nelson with a letter from the King. But it was obvious that nothing could stop the French and that only flight could save the royal family.

In a brief despatch to Lord Grenville, the Foreign Secretary in London, Hamilton reported:

It is impossible in the hurry that we are in at this moment to enter into any particulars. The fine army of His Sicilian Majesty from treachery and cowardice is fading away ... It needs no great penetration to foresee that in a very short time ... the kingdom is lost. However, fortunately Lord Nelson is here ... which will secure us a retreat.

So royal treasures were packed and taken in covered waggons to the Palazzo Sessa, where they were received by Emma Hamilton, who arranged for them to be smuggled out to Nelson's squadron in the bay. This became a lengthy task when the admiral decided that there was a risk of mutinous Neapolitans seizing the waterfront fortresses of Castel Nuovo and Castel dell'Ovo, and he ordered his captains to move their ships a mile farther out to sea, beyond the range of their guns.

Wild optimism and pessimism alternated in the palace until plans for escape were decided by Nelson insisting that a decision must be taken. On the chosen night, cover for the flight was provided by the Turkish envoy, who had brought the Sultan's gifts to Nelson, holding a reception. Ordering his ship's boats to lie off the quays of the *arsenale* basin beneath the walls of the Palazzo Reale, the admiral joined the Hamiltons and Emma's mother at the party; there, after being seen to be circulating in the crowd, they slipped away. First the Hamiltons were embarked in one of the British boats; then Nelson walked along the quay below the dark bulk of the Palazzo Reale to a doorway in the massive rusticated stone buttresses, where courtiers were waiting and passwords exchanged.

Leaving sailors with drawn cutlasses on guard, he was taken through the stone vaults of the cellars to a hidden door leading to secret passages that riddled the palace; upstairs, the royal family awaited rescue. Then, as Emma Hamilton put it, "Lord N.... got up the dark staircase that goes into the Queen's room and, with a dark lantern, cutlasses, pistols, etc., brought off every soul" and, as the Queen wrote to her mother: "We descended – all our family, ten in number, with the utmost secrecy, in the dark, without our ladies-in-waiting or other attendants. Nelson was our guide." Once on the quay, the fugitives were helped into the boats, orders were given in hoarse whispers and the boats pulled to the open sea, where others waited with manned carronades in their bows to cover their escape. All was silent ashore, no alarms sounded on the ramparts of the castles and the boats rocked under the swell towards the ships anchored in the bay.

The orderly bustle of a ship of the line turned to turmoil on the arrival of the frightened, wet and seasick refugees at midnight. Nelson had given

29 *Above left*: The sophisticated friend. Sir William Hamilton – painted by
C. Grignion around 1794 – was the British minister to the Bourbon court in
Naples and husband of a celebrated beauty and hostess.

30 *Above right*: Emma Hamilton as she liked to see herself. This portrait by
George Romney was to hang in the hall at Merton Place and was eventually
bought by her neighbours, the Penningtons, whose descendants own it still.

31 *Below*: The raffish reputation. When Nelson met the Hamiltons in 1794 and
again in 1798, their reputation was for lavish hospitality and louche living. Lady
Hamilton's past life was widely imagined as here by Thomas Rowlandson.

32 *Above*: The pleasures of Naples included the comforts and splendid views of the Hamiltons' houses: the Palazzo Sessa, the Villa Emma beach-house at Posillipo (shown here in a contemporary drawing); another at Portici within easy reach of Pompeii and Vesuvius; and sometimes a fourth, rented near the royal palace of Caserta.

33 *Below*: The Villa Emma photographed by the author in 1987. The rear of the villa was demolished for the widening of the road through Posillipo but it remains a beach-house despite the loss of its idyllic setting.

34 *Right*: Admiral Nelson when "inactive at a foreign court", as the Admiralty put it. Drawn by an unknown artist at Palermo in 1799, it shows a different face to that recorded by Rigaud and Abbott.

35 *Below*: The Palazzo Sessa at Naples. The British embassy – marked 2 in this keyed engraving and to the right of the dome – still stands above the Piazza dei Martiri, so named in commemoration of the executed revolutionaries of 1799.

1 *The Church of St Mary of Victory.* 2 *Palace of the English Minister.* 3 *Palace of the Imperial Minister.* 4 *Residence of the French Consul.*

36 Ferdinand and Maria Carolina as they saw themselves. The King and Queen of the Two Sicilies take up commanding poses in a contemporary engraving; the reality was less inspiring.

up his own quarters to the royal family and the captain and his officers theirs to the Hamiltons, the Austrian ambassador and his suite, assorted Neapolitan courtiers and royalist nobility. The escape had been arranged by Nelson and the senior Neapolitan naval officer, Commodore Francesco Carraciolo, to coincide with a general evacuation of British citizens (including Cornelia Knight and her mother), French royalist *emigrés*, and associates of King Ferdinand and some two thousand of these were taken out to British and Neapolitan warships and transports. All were under orders to sail at dawn for Palermo, the other capital of the Kingdom of the Two Sicilies.

When the pale sun came up over a wind-whipped sea, it was blowing too hard to leave the bay and too rough to send boats to other ships or the shore. The passengers were unaccustomed to the canvas cots and hammocks hurriedly stitched together by sailmakers and nauseated by the smell of fresh paint and vomit and by the lurching of the ship. But, after a sleepless night, the royal couple were still within sight of their palace. The wind dropped during the following night but, before a decision to sail could be taken, boats were sighted approaching from the shore. They carried deputations from Naples coming to implore the King to change his mind and stay to lead them against the French and one brought the exhausted General von Mack, loyally reporting on the state of his disintegrated army. The Austrian cut a pathetic figure when, after the King had ordered him to make a stand before Naples and, if that failed, to fall back upon Sicily, he returned to duty ashore. "My heart bled for him; he is worn to a shadow," was Nelson's comment.

At last, on the evening of the following day, a Sunday, the *Vanguard* sailed for Palermo, accompanied by Commodore Carraciolo's flagship, the *Sannita*, another Neapolitan warship and about twenty merchantmen. As the ships passed Capri, King Ferdinand stood on deck taking a last look at the capital he had abandoned, and Hamilton approached with a word of comfort. But the King's thoughts were already in Sicily and he remarked cheerfully: "We shall have plenty of woodcocks, *cavaliere*; this wind will bring them – it is just the season. We shall have rare sport; you must get your *cannone* ready!"

The storm that was howling towards them proved to be the most violent Nelson had ever known. It struck the ships on their first morning at sea, squalls of hurricane force flinging them on to their beam-ends and blowing the *Vanguard*'s topsails to tatters. Gangs of sailors braced themselves ready with axes to hack through the shrouds and stays if the masts should snap so that they would not capsize the ship, dragging her over by their rigging. The passengers, dumb with seasickness and fear, clung to whatever would stop them slithering across the canting deck, expecting the ship to capsize at the next roll, pitch and toss. Hamilton staggered to his cabin, where Emma found him wedged into a chair with a loaded pistol in each hand, ready to shoot himself if the ship went over rather than "die with the 'guggle-guggle-guggle' of the salt water in his throat". It was Emma who was the heroine of the storm. As Nelson later reported to St. Vincent: "It is my duty to tell your Lordship the obligations which the Royal Family, as well as myself, are under on this trying occasion to her Ladyship ... Lady Hamilton provided her own beds, linen, etc., and became *their slave* ... nor did her Ladyship enter a bed the whole time they were on board."

The reality was terrifying and exhausting as with courage and devotion Emma Hamilton tended the prostrate Neapolitans, holding the frightened children – one of them an infant of seven weeks – in her arms. The Queen's youngest child, the six-year-old Prince Carlo Alberto, was her particular care and when the storm began to abate that night, he seemed to be recovering and on the morning of Christmas Day was able to eat breakfast. But, soon after, the child went into convulsions which took him beyond the comfort of Emma's nursing and he died in her arms. That afternoon the skull-shaped mass of Monte Pellegrino that stands above Palermo was sighted to the south and the royal standard of the Bourbons was hoisted to the maintop-gallant masthead of the *Vanguard* as she was made ready for entering harbour.

The flagship did not dock until the early hours of Boxing Day and the Queen, distraught with grief, went ashore at once to drive into the capital in a closed carriage while the King made his formal entrance a few hours later, followed by a wagon-train carrying about £2,500,000 in treasure. Ignoring his wife, whom he blamed for urging him to fight the French and thus for their present ignominy, he at once began to prepare for hunting in the park of La Favorita to the west of the city. Rather than live in the vast Palazzo di Normanni in the centre of Palermo, which would be vulnerable to any unrest among the people, he chose as his principal residence the much smaller palace, which included the new Palazzina Cinese built in the Chinese taste, in the Colli district, fashionable for noblemen's summer villas and near his hunting-grounds. For the other refugees, the only available accommodation was in such houses outside the town, which were empty in winter. One of these, the Villa Bastioni near the Flora Reale gardens, was allocated to the Hamiltons; its high-ceilinged rooms were designed for hot weather and it had no fireplaces, so that Sir William, suffering, as he said, "a fever from cold and bile" retired to bed. He had left in Naples "three houses elegantly furnished, all our horses and six or seven carriages" but the best of his pictures and Greek vases he had shipped to England on board several ships. Now he suffered the worst shock of all: news reached Palermo that the *Colossus*, carrying the finest of his vases, had been wrecked off the Scilly Islands and lost. Hearing of this, a friend remarked: "It will go far, I think, to break his heart."

Emma Hamilton's heart was far from broken for her resolution during the storm had finally won the admiration as well as the desire of Nelson. Until now their relationship had been an intense flirtation that heated his infatuation and lust, yet they had probably not become lovers. Now their arrival in Palermo seemed to loosen those inhibitions of formality that had restrained her. In Naples she had lived with the memory of her origins and her early years as a rich man's mistress. Now although she spoke "a *mélange* of Lancashire and Italian", she was his wife, a titled lady, a famous hostess, the confidante of the Queen and the heroine of the storm in which they all might have perished together. She could perform against new and exotic scenery for, even in winter, there was a sultriness about Palermo: the mixture of palm trees, the flamboyant palaces and, here and there, the architecture of the Moors with its suggestions of the seraglio. They would dine with the King and Queen in the Chinese pavilion of the palace, where the frivolous frescoes recalled Venice and Pompeii as much as Peking and where, to ensure privacy, their plates appeared before them through round holes in the circular dining table, hoisted on elevators from the kitchens below. Sir William wilted from the exhaustion of the voyage from Naples, the grief over his collection lost there and at sea and continual digestive troubles; spending much of his time in bed, leaving his wife in the company of their friend.

Nelson was beset by problems. At Palermo he had been greeted with the news that the Admiralty had ordered, over the head of St. Vincent, that the *Levant* should be detached from his command and given to the volatile Captain Sir Sidney Smith, and he took this as a snub and an unacceptable cramping of his style. Then the response to his success that he still needed from his wife and family had dwindled, or so it seemed, for only one letter written by Fanny had reached him since she must have heard the news of his victory. So his letters were brief, sometimes curt, and he became even more blunt in his comments on her son. "I wish I could say much to your and my satisfaction about Josiah but I am sorry to say and with real grief, that he has nothing good about him; he must sooner or later be broke," he wrote. Telling her that the young man had been given command of the frigate *Thalia*, he added, "He has had done for him more than any young man in the service and made, I fear, the worst of his advantage." He recognised that he had perhaps spoiled Josiah with personal attention and accelerated promotion but his heavy drinking and subsequent boorishness was probably in response to his step-father's public dalliance. Even so, Nelson's influence had given him command of the thirty-six-gun frigate *Thalia* in the hope of reform and he had written to his mother: "Josiah is now in full possession of a noble frigate. He has sent to say that he is sensible of his youthful follies and that he shall alter his whole conduct. I sincerely wish he may for his and your sake."

Another of the frayed ties with his past life in the Norfolk parsonage and farm broke early that year when his younger brother Suckling died. He had been at home, having become curate-in-charge at Burnham Norton; an unsuitable priest and a reminder to his brothers of the penalties of failure.

When the Hamiltons moved to more comfortable, warmer quarters in the Palazzo Palagonia in the Piazza della Marina near the harbour, which was more suitable as an embassy, Nelson accompanied them, and it became the admiral's shore headquarters. In the early months of 1799, before spring brought the prospect of expeditions to the country for picnics, hunting and entertainment in the royal parks and gardens, there was little to pass the dark, chill evenings. Emma performed her Attitudes again and took up cards with such enthusiasm that an English visitor to the card-rooms of Palermo remarked: "Her rage is play and Sir William says when he is dead she will be a beggar." Nelson, who had not gambled since he had been a midshipman, sat beside her, drinking more champagne than was his custom, far into the night. Occasionally he seemed to flinch from her extravagances. Once a Turkish messenger, carrying despatches for him from the Tsar Paul of Russia, showed the Hamiltons his scimitar, stained, he boasted, by the blood of French prisoners of war he had himself beheaded. "Her Ladyship's eye beamed with delight," recorded one witness to the scene, "and she said, 'Oh, let me see the sword that did the glorious deed!' It was presented to her; she took it into her fair hand covered with rings, and, looking at the encrusted Jacobin blood, kissed it and handed it to the hero of the Nile! The toad-eaters applauded but many groaned and cried, 'Shame!' loud enough to reach the ears of the Admiral, who turned pale, hung his head and seemed ashamed."

The condition of Nelson in body and mind was poor. As he put it to Lady Parker, once his hostess in Jamaica, in a letter, "My health is such that, without a great alteration, I will venture to say a very short space of time will send me to that bourne from whence none return ... After the action, I had nearly fell into a decline but at Naples my invaluable friends Sir William and Lady Hamilton nursed and set me up again. I am worse than ever: my spirits have received such a shock that I think they cannot recover it. You, who remember me always laughing and gay, would hardly believe the change." He still suffered from headaches, nausea, digestive trouble and recurrent chest spasms, probably induced by stress. But, above all he was depressed and irritable. His bellicose urging of the King in Naples having proved disastrous, he was having to live with the consequences. He had received scant encouragement from his wife in England – albeit through the inevitably slow postal service – and was infatuated with a friend's wife.

This had become more than romantic love, for sexual intimacies had begun. Until now, Nelson had been relatively innocent in such: his early courtships had hardly reached that stage; Fanny was likely to have shown little inclination towards sexual dalliance, particularly in chilly Norfolk; otherwise, his experience had only been with the Italian opera-singer and, possibly, other women met in seaports. But Emma Hamilton had acquired sexual skills among the rakes and courtesans of London and offered her chosen lover new, and probably unexpected, delights. Early in February, 1799, he wrote to her from sea:

> I shall run mad. We have had a gale of wind. That is nothing but I am 20 leagues farther from you than yesterday noon.... Last night I did nothing but dream of you altho' I woke 20 times in the night. In one of my dreams I thought I was at a large table – you was not present – sitting between a Princess, who I detest, and another. They both tried to seduce me and the first wanted to take those liberties with me which no woman in this world but yourself ever did. The consequence was I knocked her down and in the moment of bustle you came in and, taking me to your embrace, whispered, 'I love nothing but you, my Nelson'. I kissed you fervently and we enjoyed the height of love.

In his emotional turmoil, even his allies in the Mediterranean prompted anger. "I hate the Russians," he told Captain Ball. "Their admiral at Corfu, he is a blackguard." He had decided to make Palermo the base for his fleet, knowing that a principal reason for so doing was personal. During that chill January he wondered whether Sicily, too, would rebel and he would have to arrange another rescue, writing to a naval friend in London at the end of the month: "Palermo is detestable and we are all unwell and full of sorrows. I will not venture to say this country will be a Monarchy in six months ... Where is all this to end?"

This weakening of his former single-minded resolution had been caused by ill-health and, perhaps, the concussion he had suffered in Aboukir Bay; his symptoms suggesting damage to the frontal lobes of the brain, resulting in marginal, but important, changes including a loosening of inhibition. Certainly, the portrait painted of him by the Sicilian artist Guzzardi, while in Palermo, shows a very different man from that recorded by Abbott and Rigaud: tired and pale with troubled eyes and a down-turned mouth, the look more stubborn than inspired; his hat pushed back to avoid rubbing the scarred forehead.

The demand for Nelson's services was divided between the Kingdom of the Two Sicilies and the Admiralty. The former looked to him to implement the restoration of Bourbon rule on the mainland, for Naples had fallen to the French at the end of January; a new Jacobin administration, known as the Parthenopean, or Vesuvian, Republic – in honour of Parthenope, the pagan patron-goddess of the city, or the volcano that still threatened it – was led by the liberal aristocracy and intelligentsia. The latter relied upon him to intercept any French fleet entering the Mediterranean to replace that destroyed in Aboukir Bay. To add to his restlessness, the Hamiltons were also talking of returning to England and suggesting that they should make the journey with him in his ship.

A few days after the French columns marched into Naples, King Ferdinand, prompted by Sir John Acton, who was still at his side, appointed a new military commander to replace General von Mack, now a prisoner on his way to Paris. This, surprisingly, was a cleric but Cardinal Fabrizio Ruffo had once been war minister and treasurer to Pope Pius VI in Rome; now a vigorous, middle-aged man, he was loyal to the Bourbons and, as a native of Calabria, could expect to command a following in southern Italy. At the beginning of February he landed there with a staff of only eight and at once proclaimed a holy war to rid the kingdom of the foreign atheists. Recruits, prompted by many motives, crowded to his standard and soon 17,000 fierce, undisciplined irregulars marched northward towards Naples in what he named his Christian Army of the Holy Faith. Their prospects were improved by the Austrians at last declaring war upon the French and the Russians and Turks offering naval support.

Success came as quickly as had disaster. While Italians rose to support Cardinal Ruffo and he swept opposition aside, news arrived of initial success by the Austrians and a Russian army under Marshal Suvorov, and Russian warships in the Adriatic recaptured Brindisi and Bari and blockaded Ancona. Meanwhile Nelson had sent Troubridge to the Bay of Naples to seize the islands and blockade the city with four ships of the line, including his own flagship, the *Vanguard*. He himself lived ashore with the Hamiltons, flying his flag in a small transport moored nearby. From the gilded *salon* of the Palazzo Palagonia he sent his orders to his captains at sea, expecting that it would be they who would take Naples and not Ruffo, whom he dismissed as "a swelled-up priest". His irritability, which had become increasingly noticeable, was apparent in these instructions. Hearing of Troubridge's success, he sent him two hundred Neapolitan soldiers and a judge, telling him: "Send me word some proper heads are taken off, this alone will comfort me." Writing to the Duke of Clarence, and complaining that he was "seriously unwell", he reported that two of King Ferdinand's failed generals were to be court-martialled for cowardice and treachery, adding: "If found guilty . . . they shall be shot or hanged; should this be effected, I shall have some hopes that I have done good. I ever preach that rewards and punishments are the foundation of all good government."

By the end of April, the recapture of Naples seemed imminent. Troubridge had taken the islands of Capri and Ischia, which commanded the seaward approaches, while Hood had taken the coastal town of Salerno to the south and Cardinal Ruffo's mass of irregulars swarmed through the countryside inland. Fearful of being cut off in the city, the bulk of the French troops were withdrawn to the north, leaving only about five hundred men to garrison the castle of Sant' Elmo on the hill behind the city and support the twenty thousand men of the Parthenopean Republic's civil guards.

Then, just when Naples seemed ready for recapture, Nelson received an urgent despatch that brought him back to the wider realities of war. A French fleet of twenty-five sail of the line had escaped from Brest, eluded the fifteen ships with which Vice-Admiral Lord Keith was blockading Cadiz – Lord St. Vincent being ashore and sick at Gibraltar – and entered the Mediterranean. As Keith sailed in pursuit, seventeen Spanish sail of the line left Cadiz and followed their French allies. If the two enemy fleets could combine, their forty-two ships of the line would outnumber whatever force the British collected from the Atlantic and the Mediterranean and could attempt to relieve the French army stranded in Egypt by reinforcing or evacuating it, or bring it westward for an attack on Sicily. Nelson at once ordered ten of his line of battle to steer for Minorca and join the main force but would not accompany them himself, writing to St. Vincent on 12th May: "You may depend upon my exertion and I am only sorry that I cannot move to your help; but this Island appears to hang on my stay. Nothing could console the Queen this night but my promise not to leave them unless the battle was to be fought off Sardinia."

A week later, Nelson did put to sea in the *Vanguard*, which he had recalled to Palermo, but it was only to cruise off Maritimo Island to the west of Sicily. Hearing that the French had passed Minorca and might be sailing eastward, he sent fresh orders to Troubridge and to Ball off Malta, ordering them to join him in the defence of the Bourbon kingdom.

Sailing in the *Vanguard*, and again stimulated by the prospect of action, he prepared to fight the French who might appear at twice his strength. Meanwhile they had arrived at Toulon and the Spanish at Cartagena, while St. Vincent sent reinforcements under Admiral Duckworth to join Nelson and prevent the enemy from reaching their countrymen in Egypt. They met off Palermo, to which the latter had withdrawn on the grounds that its defence took priority over all else. Thereupon Queen Maria Carolina (for whose bellicosity Nelson had high regard) and Emma persuaded him that the time had come to move against Naples from the sea. Accordingly he embarked 1,700 Neapolitan infantry, nominally commanded by the Crown Prince, and on 12th June set sail. They did not travel far; indeed Monte Pellegrino had only just sunk below the southern horizon when sails appeared to the north-west and proved to be two British "seventy-fours" from Lord Keith bringing him news that the French fleet might be bound for Naples. With gun-decks crowded with soldiers, his squadron was in no state to fight so he put back into Palermo to disembark them before sailing to intercept what was reported to be the whole French line of battle. It was a more familiar Nelson who then announced: "I consider the best defence for his Sicilian Majesty's dominions is to place myself alongside the French."

It was while searching for them at sea off Maritimo, that an agitated letter from Hamilton reached him. Events at Naples were coming to a climax, Sir William had written, urging Nelson to play his part. This presented a strategic dilemma: from his present position, he could cover the approaches to Sicily, Malta and Egypt, each a possible destination for the enemy. The alternative was to head for Naples on the chance that the French might have chosen that as their target, and to help extinguish the Parthenopean Republic. His emotional loyalties to Ferdinand and Maria Carolina and to the Hamiltons persuaded him, after much worry, to choose the last option. "I am full of grief and anxiety," he replied to Sir William. "I must go."

The prospect of involvement in Neapolitan intrigue and allying himself with Cardinal Ruffo, whom he distrusted, was particularly daunting without the guidance of Sir William. He wrote to Emma, "It gave me great pain to hear both Sir William and yourself were so unwell. I wrote Sir William yesterday that if you both thought the sea air would do you good, I have plenty of room. I can make you private apartments and give you my honour the sea is so smooth that no glass was ever smoother." He would be going to Naples, he told her, "that their Majesties may settle matters there and *take off* (if necessary the head of) the Cardinal".

But first he would call briefly at Palermo. His squadron did not anchor and he went ashore in his barge for a meeting at the palace. From the clear-cut decisions to be taken at sea, he was back in the louche and labyrinthine politics of the Kingdom of the Two Sicilies. He found Sir William depressed and bilious, still mourning the loss of his collections.

He himself felt guilty at having rejected Fanny's suggestion that she join him in the Mediterranean. He had dismissed the idea in one of his increasingly brief and formal letters to her, saying that if she had decided to visit "a wandering sailor . . . I could, had you come, only have struck my flag and carried you back again for it would have been impossible to set up an establishment either at Naples or Palermo". His links with home were wearing thin and another was broken when he heard of the death of his generous uncle William Suckling. He was losing the comforting proximity of trusted friends, too, and was downcast to learn that Lord St. Vincent was giving up the Mediterranean command and being succeeded by Lord Keith, a stern Scottish nobleman who had reached the rank of vice-admiral and the age of fifty-two with little experience of action. It was symbolic of his sombre mood that a strange gift was presented to him by Captain Ben Hallowell and with perverse pleasure he displayed it in his cabin: made by a ship's carpenter from a baulk of the mainmast of *l'Orient*, found floating in Aboukir Bay, it was a coffin.

In one of the chinoiserie *salons* of the palace, Nelson was told of events in Naples. Cardinal Ruffo's ruffianly Christian Army of the Holy Faith were said to be fighting in the streets of the city while "the Jacobins" had taken refuge in the three huge castles which were under siege. The senior British naval officer in the bay was Captain Edward Foote, commanding the frigate *Seahorse*, having taken over from Troubridge when he had been called away. Now Nelson himself would assume command and he sent a message to Naples with a loyal emissary: "Tell the people on shore when you return that I will batter down their city." From Foote he heard that Bourbon rule had been restored to the Neapolitan islands; and that the triumphant monarchists were taking brutal revenge; three priests, who had supported the rebellion were being sent to Palermo to face trial for treason. He replied: "Your news of the hanging of thirteen Jacobins gave us great pleasure; and the three priests, I hope, return in the *Aurora* to dangle on the tree best adapted to their weight of sins."

In this fierce mood, in which his emotional conflict was compounded by physical stress ("I have not been free from headache, sickness and want of rest, for I know not what sleep is," he complained), Nelson embarked the Hamiltons in his new flagship, the *Foudroyant*, for the voyage to Naples. Sir William would guide him through the political problems ashore, Emma saw herself as "the Queen's deputy" and both would help with interpreting Italian and French. By committing himself and his ships to the restoration of the monarchy in Naples, Nelson was disregarding Lord Keith's strategy of keeping his ships at sea ready to intercept any French attempt to reach one of half a dozen possible destinations in the central and eastern Mediterranean. Instead, he had

been persuaded by the Hamiltons and the Queen that the crushing
of the rebellion in Naples was the key to the stability of the coalition
against the French and this took priority.

The voyage to Naples was in contrast to the fearful passage from the
city six months earlier – "stealing on with light winds", as Sir William
described it – but there was tension on board the flagship for no one
knew what they would find on arrival. It might be the French fleet at
anchor in the bay, for Nelson did not know that that danger had passed
and would not know for many weeks. (They had left Toulon only to land
troops near Genoa to face the advancing Austrians and Russians; then,
realising that more British reinforcements, outward bound from
England, would present unacceptable odds, headed for the Straits of
Gibraltar and, together with the Spanish fleet from Cartagena, escaped
into the Atlantic.)

The most probable forecast was that the fleet would have to assist
Cardinal Ruffo's irregulars in storming the last enemy strongholds by
bombarding the two waterfront castles and perhaps hauling guns up the
hill behind the city to batter the great fortress of San' Elmo, where the
garrison was still French. But such expectations were changed by the
arrival of another despatch from Foote, dated 23rd June, announcing
that a truce had been agreed between Ruffo and the rebels. This was
confirmed when next day the *Foudroyant* led a fleet of seventeen sail of
the line into the bay – leaving a screen of frigates to watch for any
approaching enemy – and anchored before the city.

Captain Foote, as senior British officer in his admiral's absence, was
pleased with the outcome. Cardinal Ruffo, who, he assumed, commanded the King's confidence, had avoided further bloodshed and decided
the issue before any relief force from France could reach the rebels.
Both the rebels and the French in the castles – together with some in
the Palazzo Reale and the monastery of San Martino adjoining San'
Elmo – had agreed to capitulate: the French troops to be shipped to
France and the Neapolitans being given the choice of accompanying
them, or returning to their homes under a general amnesty. But, until
shipping was available for their evacuation, they would remain in the
castles.

Nelson took a different view. Realising that he was already embroiled
in the Neapolitan politics, he had, before his flagship had come to
anchor, drafted his thoughts and decisions on paper. Angered to see
through his telescope that flags of truce were flying not only from the
castles but from Foote's ship, the *Seahorse*, he headed the page:
"Opinion delivered before I saw the treaty of armistice, etc., only from
reports met at sea." He then wrote:

The armistice I take for granted is that if the French and rebels are not relieved by their friends in twenty-one days from the signing of armistice, then that they shall evacuate Naples in this infamous manner to his Sicilian Majesty, and triumphant to them, as stated in the article. All armistices signify that either party may renew hostilities, giving a certain notice fixed upon by the contracting parties. In the present instance, I suppose the Cardinal thought that in twenty-one days he had not the power of driving the French from the Castle of St. Elmo, or the rebels from the lower castles of Ovo and Nuovo.

The French and rebels thought that if they could not be relieved in twenty-one days, they could, when unable to remain any longer, covenant to be removed to a place where they may be in a situation to renew their diabolical schemes against his Sicilian Majesty ... Therefore evidently this agreement implies that both parties are supposed to remain *in statu quo*; but if either party receive relief from their situation, then the compact of course falls to the ground and is of no effect ... And I fancy the question need not be asked whether, if the French fleet arrived this day in the Bay of Naples, whether the French and rebels would adhere one moment to the armistice? 'No!' the French admiral would say, 'I am not here to look on, but to act.' And so says the British admiral ... Therefore the British admiral proposes to the Cardinal to send, in their joint names, to the French and rebels that the arrival of the British fleet has completely destroyed the compact ...

That as to rebels and traitors, no power on earth has a right to stand between their gracious King and them: they must instantly throw themselves on the clemency of their sovereign.

Nor was he mollified when Foote himself came on board with a copy of the agreement and his explanations. These Nelson dismissed as illegal because Ruffo had no authority from the King to agree to any truce and irrelevant because he and his fleet had that authority and the strength to impose an immediate conclusion. He confirmed this in a curt letter to Cardinal Ruffo, stating flatly: "Rear-Admiral Lord Nelson arrived with the British fleet the 24th June in the Bay of Naples and found a treaty entered into with the Rebels which, in his opinion, cannot be carried into execution without the approbation of his Sicilian Majesty." The Cardinal could not agree, for to do so would break his own word, given on behalf of the King and in his absence, and he decided to put his case to the vengeful admiral in person.

Nelson's fleet were anchored in line of battle before the city, their guns able either to bombard it, or to defend it against an attack by the French fleet. The *Foudroyant* was in the van but the admiral planned to shift his flag to the centre ship in the event of an attack from the sea and, remembering how he had outflanked the French line in Aboukir Bay, ordered that his ships should not lie more than two-thirds of a cable (or 133 yards) apart and that either flank should be guarded by Neapolitan gunboats manned by loyal crews. It was a grim array of open gun-ports that faced Ruffo as he was rowed out to the flagship but now they fired only a salute in his honour. On the *Foudroyant*'s quarterdeck, he was greeted by Nelson and his interpreter, Hamilton; the former convinced that "an admiral is no match in talking with a cardinal" and the latter noting that: "Lord Nelson is so accustomed to dealings fair and open that he has no patience with the contrary ... His Eminence is the very quintessence of Italian finesse." There was disagreement from the beginning, freezing into deadlock with Sir William only relieved that "nothing but my phlegm could have prevented an open rupture on the first meeting between Cardinal Ruffo and Admiral Nelson".

Ruffo returned to the city, refusing Nelson's demand that the castles be summoned to surrender unconditionally. He countered by announcing that, if the terms he had agreed were broken, he would withdraw his army and leave the British to capture Naples on their own. A second visit to the *Foudroyant* was equally fruitless and that evening the Cardinal sent word to the rebels that Lord Nelson might be about to break the armistice. Panic followed: neutral Neapolitans struggled to flee the city for fear of being caught amidst more fighting; the monarchists, to whom Nelson had sent a stock of muskets at Emma Hamilton's prompting, set about using them on suspected Jacobins and personal enemies alike; those in the three castles prepared for a renewed siege. In the British ships, shouting and shooting could be heard from the city as darkness fell.

Startling was the surprise when, next morning, Nelson sent a short note to Ruffo saying: "Lord Nelson begs to assure your Eminence that he is resolved to do nothing which might break the armistice, which your Eminence has agreed to the castles of Naples." There were several explanations for this apparent change of mind. One was that Nelson awaited firm instructions from Palermo before taking action which might engulf the city in another bout of civil war. Another was that on reflection he had recognised that Cardinal Ruffo, for all his wily ways, was a man of honour and had acted in what he had considered the best interests of his sovereign. So, that morning, relief was tangible in the streets as refugees returned to their homes and those in the castles hastily prepared to leave, while they could, aboard the ships that were to carry the French troops to Toulon. Meanwhile the Cardinal accepted the service of some 1,500 British marines from the fleet to help keep order.

In the harbour were moored dozens of *polaccas* – small sailing coasters

– that had been commandeered for the evacuation of all who wished to leave rather than trust that the amnesty, to which Ruffo had agreed, would be honoured on the return of the King. Knowing the latter's temper, many decided against taking the risk and all that day families flocked to the jetties with whatever clothing and belongings they could carry while the rebels in the castles joined them without bothering with the ceremonial "honours of war" that Ruffo had granted them. Meanwhile, the Cardinal attended a service of thanksgiving in the dark and ancient church of the Carmina overlooking the Piazza del Mercato – the market-place and usual site of public execution – and sent letters of gratitude to Nelson and Hamilton. As the *polaccas* filled with passengers, one anxiety remained: the vessels had neither bunks nor lavatories and little food. Many of those now aboard were the well-to-do families of the city's intelligentsia, unaccustomed to rough living; they had expected to sail at once for France and there was no explanation for not doing so.

This came two days later in a short letter from Hamilton to Ruffo:

My Lord Nelson desires me to inform your Eminence that in consequence of an order which he has just received from his Sicilian Majesty, who entirely disapproves of the capitulation made with his rebellious subjects in the castles of Ovo and Nouvo, he is about to seize and make sure of those who have left them and are on board the vessels in this port ... and, at the same time, to warn the rebels who have escaped to Naples from the said castles, that they must submit to the clemency of his Sicilian Majesty within the space of twenty-four hours under pain of death.

With that, armed boats from the fleet pulled ashore to escort the *polaccas* out of the harbour, moor them alongside the British warships and put their distraught passengers under armed guard.

The most obvious reason for Nelson's action was a letter that had just reached Emma Hamilton from the Queen in Palermo:

The following conditions ought to form the basis, in the King's opinion and in mind, and we submit them to the excellent judgement and heart of our dear Lord Nelson. The rebel patriots must lay down their arms and surrender at discretion to the pleasure of the King. Then, in my opinion, an example should be made of some of the leaders ... The females who have distinguished themselves in the revolution to be treated the same way and without pity ... This is not pleasure but absolutely necessary for, without it, the King could not for six months peacefully govern his people ... Finally, my dear lady, I recommend Lord Nelson to treat Naples as if it were an Irish town in rebellion similarly placed. France will be none the better for all these thousands of rascals; we shall all be better off without them. They merit being sent to Africa or the Crimea ... They deserve to be branded that others may not be deceived by them. I recommend to you, my dear lady, the greatest firmness, vigour and severity.

A further explanation was being suggested in the city: that Nelson's misleading reassurance of Ruffo had been calculated to produce the result it did. In approving the embarkation of the rebels and their families, he had not given permission for the vessels to sail. Thus he had not only extracted the armed rebels from their defences in the castles but induced those who might have escaped, or not been identified, into delivering themselves into captivity. Perhaps, bewildered by his meetings with the subtle Cardinal Ruffo and suspecting him to be as devious as his fellow politicians, he had attempted to match him with his own cunning, combined with ruthlessness and efficiency. Indeed, there was a saying: "*Inglesi Italianato e diavolo incarnato*": "The Englishman who behaves like an Italian is the devil incarnate."

He then set about making an example of one of the rebels' leaders. Many of those crowded into the *polacces* were known to the Hamiltons, who had met them at court or even entertained them at the Palazzo Sessa. One known to Nelson was Commodore Carraciolo, the nobleman who had commanded the small Neapolitan fleet but, after following the King to Palermo, had deserted to join the Parthenopean Republic. He had been arrested ashore while trying to escape and was brought in irons aboard the *Foudroyant*, where Nelson had hurriedly convened a court martial of loyal Neapolitan officers. The midshipman in command of his escort, George Parsons, described him as "a short, thick-set man of apparent strength, but haggard with misery and want; his clothing in wretched condition but his countenance denoting stern resolution to endure that misery like a man". Knowing himself to be doomed, he defended himself "in a deep, manly tone", accusing the King of being a traitor by deserting his people and fleeing to Palermo. The outcome was inevitable and the president of the court, Count Thurn, put on his cocked hat and announced: "Admiral Prince Carraciolo, you have been unanimously found guilty ... You have repaid the high rank and honours conferred on you by a mild and confiding sovereign with the blackest ingratitude. The sentence of the court is that you shall be hanged by the neck at the yard-arm of your own flagship in two hours' time and may God have mercy on your soul!"

Nelson confirmed the sentence an hour later and the condemned man's plea for a stay of execution to prepare himself, which was supported by Hamilton and Count Thurn, was rejected, as was his request to be shot rather than hoisted to a yard-arm like a mutinous seaman. So Carraciolo was taken across to the Neapolitan frigate *Minerva* and hanged at sunset; the rope then being cut so that the corpse plunged into the sea. While this grisly ceremony was being conducted in full view of the fleet and city, Nelson and the Hamiltons were at dinner in the flagship and heard the report of the signal gun that announced it. Most of the British watched and, as Midshipman Parsons noted: "The seamen of our fleet, who clustered on the rigging like bees, consoled themselves that it was only an Italian prince, and an admiral of Naples, that was hanging – a person of very light estimation compared with the lowest man in a British ship."

Meanwhile other leaders of the revolution were being identified ashore and in the *polaccas* and brought aboard the British ships in manacles. In the city the French in Sant' Elmo had been more cautious than the Jacobins in the waterfront castles and remained within the walls so that the siege began again and the thump of artillery echoed across the bay. The sound of the guns greeted King Ferdinand when he arrived on board the *Foudroyant* two days after the hanging of Carraciolo and took up residence in the admiral's cabin. "The day was passed," recorded Midshipman Parsons, "in administering justice (Italian fashion) to the wretches who fell into the grasp of Cardinal Ruffo's lambs, enlivened by the bombardment of St. Elmo. At noon, dinner was served to the royal party and their guests on the quartedeck, Lady Hamilton's graceful form bending over her harp and her heavenly music gave a gusto to the dessert."

Both she and Nelson were kept busy. He was, as she put it, "here there and everywhere. I never saw such zeal and activity as in this wonderful man"; for, apart from the administration of his fleet there were despatches and letters to be written and a constant flow of reports from, and orders to, the landing parties in the city. There were prisoners to be escorted from the shore to the *polaccas*, order to be kept in the streets and all signs of the revolution eradicated: one "tree of liberty" topped with a red Jacobin cap was burned by Troubridge in front of the Palazzo Reale. For her part, Emma Hamilton was performing what she saw as her duties as the Queen's deputy, even though the King was now present, and it was she who first received anguished pleas for mercy from captured rebels. Writing to Mrs. Cadogan, Nelson assured her that Emma was "perfectly well but has her time much taken up with excuses from rebels, Jacobins and fools that she is every day most heartily tired".

Usually these were letters in which the flowery prose could not hide the fear, but Midshipman Parsons saw many, including women, brought on board the flagship before being taken to the prison-ships, where there were soon fifteen hundred under guard:

> Many, very many, of Italy's beauteous daughters, and those of high rank, have I seen prostrate on our deck, imploring protection ... Their graceful forms bent with misery – their dark eyes and clasped hands raised to the Father of all for mercy – their clear, olive complexion changing to a sickly hue from anguish of mind. How could men, possessing human hearts, refrain from flying to their relief? Yet, I am sorry to say, they were placed (without regard to their feelings) in *polaccas*, under the guidance of young English midshipmen, there to let their afflicted hearts break at leisure ... I grieve to say that wonderful, talented and graceful beauty, Emma Lady Hamilton, did not sympathise in the manner expected from her generous and noble nature.

The prisoners had good reason for fear because, shortly before the return of the King, the first of them had been ferried back to shore for summary trials and the public executions had begun. Some were beheaded but, even more ghastly, were the hangings, when the women suffered with the men before huge crowds in the Piazza del Mercato: one by one, the condemned were strung from a huge gibbet while two executioners swung with them; one clutching their legs, another – often a dwarf – clowning on their shoulders to the cheers and laughter of a drunken mob. Many of these were the most sophisticated of the Neapolitan nobility and intelligentsia. Sir William Hamilton was appalled as he recognised friends in the lists of those executed, writing to his nephew Charles Greville: "The trials of the principal Neapolitan rebels having been carried on without intermission ... many of all classes have suffer'd death by having been beheaded or hang'd; among the latter we have seen with regret the name of Doctor Domenico Grillo, one of the first physicians, botanists and naturalists in Europe." The King's revenge was on a colossal scale as Sir William noted that "the heads of two of the first families of Naples have been sent for life into the subterranean prison in the island of Maritimo off Sicily – a punishment worse than death". There were, he had heard, "more than 8,000 persons confined as Jacobins and Rebels in the Naples prisons".

The roar of the mob in the Piazza del Mercato could be heard in the ships but Nelson's guests in the *Foudroyant* were otherwise isolated from the horrors ashore. Indeed the first anniversary of the Battle of the Nile – as it was now known – was celebrated in a style comparable with his original welcome at Naples. He wrote to Fanny:

In the evening was a general illumination. Amongst others, a large vessel was fitted out like a Roman galley. On the oars were fixed lamps and in the centre was erected a rostral column with my name; at the stern, elevated, were two angels supporting my picture. In short, the beauty of the thing was beyond my power of description. More than the 2,000 variegated lamps were fixed round the vessel, an orchestra was fitted up and filled with the very best musicians and singers. The piece of music was in a great measure of my praises, describing their distress, but Nelson comes, the invincible Nelson, and we are safe and happy again. Thus you must not make you think me vain, so very far from it, and I relate it more from gratitude than vanity.

King Ferdinand, who refused to go ashore, also received a visitation. Early one morning, Midshipman Parsons was woken to be told that the King was already up and on deck and must be waited upon. "I hurried up," recounted Parsons, "and found his Majesty gazing with intense anxiety on some distant object. At once he turned pale and, letting his spyglass fall on deck, uttered an exclamation of horror. My eyes instinctively turned in the same direction and, under our larboard quarter, with his face full upon us, much swollen and discoloured by the water, and his orbs of sight started from their sockets by strangulation, floated the ill-fated prince." The corpse of Carraciolo, weighted by its manacles, floated upright as if about to accuse its executioners. "The priesthood, who were numerous on board, were summoned," continued Parsons, "when one, more adroit than his brethren, told the King that the spirit of his unfortunate admiral could not rest without his forgiveness, which he had risen to implore. This was freely accorded; and on Lord Nelson ... being wakened from his uneasy slumbers by the agitation of the court, he ordered a boat to be sent from the ship to tow the corpse on shore. This unlooked for appearance of the dead did not lessen our appetite for the good things in the King's larder, or our zest for the evening's opera."

Life aboard ship differed from that ashore in other ways. While sentences of death were announced daily in the city, one was passed in the fleet: upon a marine named John Jolly, who had struck an officer when drunk. But Nelson, remembering a similar case at English Harbour many years before, sent an order to the officer responsible for carrying it out: "You will, in obedience to my orders, prepare everything for the execution of the sentence of the Court Martial on John Jolly; but when all the forms, except the last, are gone through, you will acquaint the prisoner that ... I have reason to hope that the sparing of his life will have as beneficial an effect for the discipline of the Service as if he had suffered death." No such mercy was shown in his comment than that the King was dealing with his rebellious subjects "in the most proper manner".

The French garrison of Sant' Elmo finally surrendered after a siege by British marines and a polyglot force, including Russians and Swiss volunteers, and was being shipped back to France. As only those against whom no charge of sedition or treason could be brought were left aboard the *polaccas*, there remained about five hundred still under guard and these were at last allowed to sail for Toulon. On the day after Nelson's anniversary celebrations, the *Foudroyant* also sailed, leaving Captain Troubridge in command at Naples with the temporary rank of commodore. She was bound for Palermo with the King, his courtiers and the Hamiltons on board, although instructions had arrived from the Commander-in-Chief ordering another destination. Three times during July Lord Keith had ordered Nelson that "all, or the greater part of your force should quit Sicily and repair to Minorca", where he feared a French attack was imminent. Although Nelson knew that Keith's fleet would be outnumbered by the French, he refused on the second occasion, writing: "I have no scruple in deciding that it is better to save the Kingdom of Naples and risk Minorca, than to risk the Kingdom of Naples to save Minorca." Only after the third, most strongly-worded order did he send four of his ships of the line, commanded by Duckworth, to Minorca. His disobedience drew a rebuke from the Admiralty in due course – "Their Lordships do not ... see sufficient reason to justify your having disobeyed orders ... or having left Minorca exposed to the risk of being attacked." He dismissed this with a detached arrogance: "My conduct is measured by the Admiralty by the narrow rule of law when I think it should have been done by common sense."

For the six weeks his flagship had lain at anchor in the Bay of Naples, Nelson had behaved in contradiction to his character and training. He had shown a callousness contrary to his usual humanity; he had followed the advice of those who, under other circumstances, he would have disregarded; and on three successive occasions he had disobeyed the orders of his superior officer without the excuse of tactical urgency such as had prompted his action at the Battle of Cape St. Vincent. Yet, outwardly, he appeared confident of having acted correctly. To him, it had been clear that Cardinal Ruffo had no authority to treat with rebels; and he was right. To him, the risk of losing Naples and Palermo to the French was greater than that to Minorca; and, in the event, neither was threatened, the French fleet escaping into the Atlantic and taking refuge in Brest. The only disaster resulting from his actions was accompanied by the creak of the gallows in the Piazza del Mercato.

He had, as he saw it, fought the French and defended an ally and a monarch. That King Ferdinand might be a boor did not lessen his respect for monarchy any more than one dissolute priest would have lessened his reverence for God; against this institution, he set the horrors of the French Revolution, heard at first hand off Marseilles and Toulon. There could be no doubt, too, that southern Italy and Sicily did dominate the central Mediterranean, the Kingdom of the Two Sicilies providing harbours, supplies and a reserve of manpower, albeit of varying quality as fighting men.

So when the *Foudroyant* arrived at Palermo on 8th August to a hero's welcome for the King, who had dared not set foot in his reconquered northern capital, Nelson was confident that he had done his duty and could accept what recognition was now offered with satisfaction. This, in the event, was beyond his expectations: while the titles bestowed upon him by his own monarch had fallen short of his high hopes, that now offered by King Ferdinand exceeded them. For, after the expected gifts, he was given a dukedom. True, there had never before been a Duke of Bronte and few had heard of the estate on the volcanic slopes of Etna, but Nelson eagerly wrote home of its reputed beauty, that it was the finest corn-growing land in Europe and that his tenants would bless the day he became their overlord. The annual income from the estate was said to be some £3,000 and he immediately wrote to his father promising him an income of £500 from this and decided to put aside two years' rent for the improvement of the estate so that "one day it should be called Bronte the Happy". He was not told that the 30,000 acres were mostly strewn with volcanic rocks, or that the principal house, the Castello di Maniace, was a near-ruin and that the only habitable dwelling was a rickety farmhouse appropriately named *La Fragila*. When the King had first offered the title, he had hesitated, cautious about the propriety of accepting without permission from his own sovereign; but, once he had done so, he gloried in a title derived from Bronte, a mythological giant, who had forged Neptune's trident and thunderbolts for Jupiter. Soon he began experimenting with new signatures, trying "Bronte Nelson of the Nile" and finally deciding upon "Nelson and Bronte", while Emma Hamilton half-jokingly called him, "My Lord Thunder".

So it was as a Sicilian nobleman as well as a British admiral that Nelson attended the celebrations of the Bourbons' restoration to Naples in the garlanded streets of Palermo. This was combined with the annual festival of St. Rosalia, whose bones and silver statue were mounted on an ornate, wheeled float, which was dragged through the streets of the city by twenty-eight pairs of mules, while the interior of the cathedral was hung with mirrors to reflect the flames of 20,000 candles. The tinsel and the fireworks that the Sicilians accorded their saint were a foretaste of the carnival with which they would flatter the new Duke of Bronte. This was held in the illuminated gardens of the Colli palace on 3rd September, the anniversary of the arrival of news of Nelson's victory the year before, and culminated in a firework display and the crowning of his statue by the young Crown Prince Leopold. Amongst the British officers invited, Midshipman Parsons entered "the fairy scene presented by the illuminated palace and gardens" and joined the crowds converging on

> a temple erected to the goddess of Fame, who, perched on the dome, was blowing her trumpet above statues of Nelson supported by figure of Sir William Hamilton and his statuesque wife. Then, as a band struck up *Rule Britannia*, Prince Leopold crowned the statue with a laurel wreath inlaid with diamonds and the band played *See the Conquering Hero Comes!*
>
> Lord Nelson's feelings were greatly touched and big tears coursed down his weather-beaten cheeks, as on one knee he received the young prince in his only arm, who, with inimitable grace had embraced him, calling him the guardian angel of his papa and his dominions ... Many a countenance that had looked with unconcern on the battle and the breeze now turned aside, ashamed of their womanly weakness.

The midshipman, who had been eyeing "Italy's nut-brown daughters, their lustrous black eyes and raven tresses, their elegant and voluptuous forms", felt that his admiral's "trusty aide-de-camps could do no less than apply their handkerchiefs" and reached for his own – finding that he had pocketed a rolled white stocking by mistake – and mopped his eyes, admitting that some did so "from a contrary feeling of mirth".

But Palermo was an unhappy place. The hot sirocco was blowing from Africa, unsettling even the most tranquil, while to the rich food that upset the digestions of the British living ashore, were added late nights. When Emma Hamilton was playing cards, after Sir William had stolen off to bed, she expected the Duke of Bronte to keep her company. Late hours in stuffy, painted card-rooms added to Nelson's debility and Lord Elgin, the new ambassador to Constantinople, passing through Palermo, remarked that "he looks very old, has lost his upper teeth, sees ill of one eye and has a film coming over both of them". His naval friends, accustomed to his nocturnal presence on the quarterdeck rather than in salons, worried about him but, when they dared to urge him to caution, were careful to mention only the gossip about gambling. "If you knew what your friends feel for you," wrote Troubridge, "I am sure you would cut out all the nocturnal parties; the gambling of the people at Palermo is talked of everywhere. I beseech your Lordship, leave off. Lady H——'s character will suffer; nothing can prevent people from talking; a Gambling Woman in the eyes of an Englishman is lost."

Even the urbane Hamilton had become irritable When they had returned to Palermo he had written to his nephew: "Lord Nelson and I, with Emma, are the *Tria Juncta in Uno* ... I glory in the hospitality I have had in my power to show Lord Nelson and almost all the Heroes of the Nile." Now, six weeks later, he complained to him of "an expense I can by no means afford as it is now a year that Lord Nelson has lived with us and, of course, the numerous train of officers that come to him on business". He added, "A comely landlady calls more company than I would wish to my house – as they do not, as in other public houses, fatten the landlord." He was "plagued with bilious attacks and diarrhoea continually owing to the heats and damp of this climate" and talked of returning to England, only to dismiss the possibility because it was "impossible to quit Lord Nelson, who doesn't understand any language but his own and fairly said that if we went he could not stay here".

This was not in his power to decide – although it would have seemed so – because he was now Commander-in-Chief in the Mediterranean in all but title. The combined French and Spanish fleets had escaped into the Atlantic, pursued by Lord Keith, in July; the former, under Admiral Bruix, to take refuge in Brest, the latter in Cadiz. So next month, the Admiralty had instructed Nelson to assume command until Keith's return. Thus, although the fulcrum of his responsibilities remained Palermo, they ranged from blockading Cadiz beyond the Straits of Gibraltar and the Levant with squadrons commanded by Duckworth and Sir Sidney Smith respectively. In addition, he had four sail of the line covering Minorca; three supporting a Portuguese squadron off Malta, blockading the French still holding out in Valetta; two smaller detachments off the Italian mainland and whatever ships were on passage, or in harbour; meanwhile at Palermo, he exercised command from the high, fresco'd rooms of the Palazzo Palagonia, where his staff mingled with the household of the Hamiltons. Here he wrote continual orders, letters and despatches and it was here, and not on his quarterdeck, that he met his Russian ally, Vice-Admiral Feodor Ushakov. The two men did not take to each other: the Russian suspected "tricks and turns ... under the cover of politeness"; Nelson thought that "the Russian admiral has a polished outside, but the bear is close to the skin".

Their failure to act as effective allies was not, in the event, of great consequence because the state of embattled Europe was about to change. During the summer of 1799, the French had been expelled from Italy by the Russians under Suvarov; an Anglo-Russian expeditionary force under the Duke of York attacked the French in the Netherlands; and it seemed that the Directory in Paris had at last expended its military energy. Yet the news of these French defeats brought about a funda- mental and, for the allies, catastrophic reversal of fortune. On the coast of the Levant, Sir Sidney Smith had taunted his stranded opponent General Bonaparte by sending him newspapers announcing allied successes and this had had an immediate and unexpected result: realising that the defence of France was of far greater consequence than the conquest of Egypt, Syria or even India, Bonaparte decided to abandon his army and return alone to France. Such had been Nelson's concentration on events ashore that the French frigate, in which he embarked at Alexandria on 23rd August, eluded the few British ships available for the blockade and, after a passage of forty-seven days, landed him at St. Raphael on 9th October. He arrived to news that Marshal Masséna had halted Suvarov at Zurich and, soon after, the Duke of York had surrendered in the Netherlands; allied defeats which led to the withdrawal of Russia from the war. In November, the Directory was overthrown by a *coup d'état* and replaced by three Consuls, one of whom was Bonaparte. A month later, he was established as First Consul, the dictator of France at the age of thirty. Only one man had been able to match his hold on popular imagination, or achieve a crushing, total victory, and that was Horatio Nelson. He was now aged forty-one but his friends had begun to fear that he was maimed in spirit as in body.

This was also suspected by Lord Keith when, leaving the blockade of Brest in other hands, he returned to the Mediterranean at the beginning of 1800. He ordered Nelson to meet him at Leghorn on 20th January and then accompanied him to Palermo, where, as he expected, he found "a scene of fulsome vanity and absurdity". Yet Nelson was to demonstrate that this had not addled the spirit that the British had come to expect.

Impatient for evidence of activity, Lord Keith ordered Nelson to accompany him on a cruise to Malta with the *Foudroyant, Northumberland, Audacious* and the frigate *Success*. South of Sicily on 18th February, a mast-head look-out in the *Foudroyant* sighted unidentified sails and shouted the news to the deck, where Nelson stood. Beside him, Midshipman Parsons heard the dialogue that followed:

"Deck there! The stranger ... is a line-of-battleship, my lord, and going large on the starboard tack."

"Ah! an enemy, Mr. Staines," said Nelson, hoping that it might prove to be one of the two French fugitives from Aboukir Bay, *Le Généreux* or the *Guillaume Tell*. "I pray God it may be *Le Généreux*." Then, turning to his flag captain, Sir Edward Berry: "The signal for a general chase, Sir Ed'ard. Make the *Foudroyant* fly!" As the flagship made sail, the admiral was mortified to see the *Northumberland* gaining on her and snapped,

"This will not do, Sir Ed'ard. She is certainly *Le Généreux* and to my flagship she can alone surrender. Sir Ed'ard, we must and shall beat the *Northumberland*."

As Berry gave orders to use every technical trick to draw the maximum power from the taut sails, he noted a sign of Nelson's mounting tension: the twitching of the stump of his right arm. "The admiral is working his fin," warned Berry. "Do not cross his hawse, I advise you." He was right because Nelson had noticed the quartermaster at the wheel look momentarily inattentive and reprimanded him: "I'll knock you off your perch, you rascal, if you are so inattentive. Sir Ed'ard, send your best quartermaster to the weather wheel." Meanwhile the little *Success* had come up with the enemy and opened fire, only to be crippled by a broadside. "Signal for the *Success* to discontinue the action and come under my stern," ordered Nelson, "She has done well for her size. Try a shot from the lower deck at her, Sir Ed'ard." Both British ships opened fire, Nelson ordering his gunners to aim "coolly and deliberately at her masts and yards". Down came the enemy's spars and sails and, crippled, she surrendered. It was indeed *Le Généreux*, which had been escorting a troop convoy bound for the relief of Malta and triumph was complete when, six weeks later, Berry captured the only other fugitive, the *Guillaume Tell*.

This final prize did not fall to Nelson because he was back in port, flying his flag in a transport, having written to Keith before the Commander-in-Chief sailed for Genoa; "My state of health is such that it is impossible I can remain much longer here ... I must ... request your permission to go to my friends at Palermo"; and this he did. That winter he and Emma conceived a child. This had been inevitable: Sir William would retire to bed after supper, leaving Nelson to escort his wife to the card-tables and to be alone with her in their private apartments in the Palazzo Palagonia. This may have happened immediately before his departure for Malta with Lord Keith, for he was later to write to her; "I did well remember the 12th February ... I shall never be sorry for the consequences." These were, as was to become apparent in the following weeks, that Emma was pregnant. The worldly Sir William may have known, or guessed the truth, but if so, it did not ruffle his stoic urbanity.

When Nelson sailed in the *Foudroyant*, leaving Palermo for Malta on 24th April, he took the Hamiltons with him for "days of ease and nights of pleasure" as Midshipman Parsons put it, in "this Noah's ark". Arriving off the island after dark, the admiral chose an anchorage within sight of the lights of Valetta but supposedly beyond the range of French guns. This he underestimated as Parsons noted: "... the Frenchman waking

... he made us a target for all his sea batteries to practice on. 'All hands up!' 'Anchor ahoy!' resounded fore and aft ... to the music of the shot, some of them going far over us. Lord Nelson was in a towering passion and Lady Hamilton's refusal to quit the quarterdeck did not tend to tranquilize him." Eventually, the ship was warped out of range with a shattered fore-topmast and punctured sails while, according to Parsons, "Lady Hamilton, finding that the French governor would not surrender until he had made a meal of his shoes, influenced Lord Nelson to turn her head for Palermo ... where the balls were not all of iron."

Another voyage was now planned in the *Foudroyant* and that would be homeward bound, for Hamilton had heard that he was to be replaced as ambassador. As for Nelson, he was committed to supporting the Kingdom of the Two Sicilies but could not do so without the Hamiltons to advise, persuade and interpret. His own inclination to accompany them home was reinforced by a brusque letter from the First Lord of the Admiralty, who had heard the gossip from Naples and Palermo with increasing disquiet. Lord Spencer wrote:

> It is by no means my wish to call you away from service, but having observed that you have been under the necessity of quitting your station off Malta, on account of the state of your health, which I am persuaded you could not have thought of doing without much necessity, it appeared to me much more advisable for you to come home at once than to be obliged to remain inactive at Palermo ... you will be more likely to recover your health and strength in England than in an inactive situation at a foreign Court, however pleasing the respect and gratitude shown to you for your services may be.

England seemed as far away in time as in distance. His wife, whom he had not seen for more than two years, wrote him dutiful letters about nursing his father after an illness and finding a suitable school in Chelsea for his niece Charlotte, whose father William was avid for promotion from a Norfolk parish in recognition of his brother's fame. She had tried to please by offering to send "Lady Hamilton a cap and a kerchief such as are worn this cold weather", for Christmas and reminded him of her own suffering that winter: "I am clothed in two suits of flannel and I shall be better for it." She constantly asked for news of Josiah but Nelson's brief replies seldom mentioned him beyond writing, "I trust for his sake that he has seen his follies". He did not confide to her, as he did to Admiral Duckworth, that a particular worry was that there were two women on board Josiah's ship "who do no good and I wish were out of her". She was, however, pleased that a naval storeship had been named the *Lady Nelson*. The only reminder of Nelson's domestic past and his Norfolk roots was the constant presence of his servant, Tom Allen, who had followed him to sea in the *Agamemnon* from Burnham Thorpe and had never lost his Norfolk accent or blunt manner; once when King Ferdinand came on board the *Foudroyant* and extended a hand to be kissed, he shook it, saying, "How do you do, Mr. King."

Tom Allen and the officers and ratings of the fleet felt only anxiety when they heard that Nelson was preparing to return home; the relief was confided to those who shared his evenings ashore, or were privy to the orders from Lord Keith that he had chosen to disregard. As a seaman and a commander he still commanded their love and respect. The crew of the *Foudroyant*'s barge wrote to him, asking him to pardon "the rude style of seamen" to "most humbly beg of your Lordship to permit us to go to England as your boat's crew". Captain Berry, writing to him the day after his capture of the *Guillaume Tell*, confessed: "How very often I went into your cabin last night to ask you if we were doing right; for I had nothing to act upon!"

For their return, Nelson planned to hoist his flag in the *Foudroyant*, he and Berry giving up their cabins to the Queen and the Hamiltons and their retinues; the former bound for Vienna with some of her children and the latter travelling on to England. They would only sail to the mainland of Italy, Lord Keith having refused to allow the *Foudroyant* to return home as his flagship. With his guests on board, he left Palermo on 10th June, 1800, bound for Leghorn, from whence they could travel overland, or by other ships. It was a rough passage and the pregnant Emma Hamilton could not repeat her brave performance on the voyage from Naples: one of the princesses reported that, while Nelson was trying to reassure the passengers, the ship pitched so wildly that he "went white as a sheet" and hurried on deck "while Emma began to wail and roll about".

Arriving at Leghorn at night, they decided to complete their journeys overland as far as possible, although the Adriatic and the North Sea would both have to be crossed; the former because Bonaparte was again invading Italy and on that very day defeated the Austrians at Marengo. Indeed there was doubt as to the safety of the road across Italy to Ancona, where they would embark for Trieste, and, after flustered hesitation by the Queen, a cavalcade of fourteen coaches and four baggage-wagons was assembled. The Queen's party left Leghorn for Florence on 12th July; Nelson and the Hamiltons – accompanied by old Mrs. Cadogan and Cornelia Knight, who had been living with them since the death of her mother in Palermo – the following day. It was an uncomfortable, dangerous journey: the windows of the lurching carriages shut tight against the billowing dust, despite the July heat; at one point the road passed within a mile of French patrols.

After twenty-six hours of this, they spent two days in comfort at Florence, then pressed on into the Apennines. The Queen's column had driven ahead for fear of the French, but the British were delayed by the over-turning of the Hamiltons' coach, in which Nelson was riding, and it broke down again at Arezzo. There it was decided that it would be better to risk the capture of lesser members of the party and the three transferred to the coach carrying Mrs. Cadogan and Miss Knight, who were left at the inn to follow when, and if, they could. In the event, the coach was repaired in three days and the two women travelled day and night along mountain roads often crowded with Neapolitan troops retreating south. On arrival at Ancona, they found that the Queen had refused to sail in an Austrian frigate, which had been fitted as a royal yacht, because there had recently been a mutiny on board. So the combined parties embarked in Russian frigates, while Nelson muttered that they would have been much more comfortable and safer in the *Foudroyant*.

On 1st August, the travellers arrived at Trieste to find its waterfront illuminated in celebration of the second anniversary of the Battle of the Nile. The Queen and Sir William both had colds and all were tired, but the festivities and lionizing began with "many *Viva Nelsons!*" shouted by the crowds gathered to see the only man who had been able to defeat Bonaparte. The road northward lay through Laibach in Slovenia, where the philharmonic orchestra performed a specially composed work, *La Virtu Britannica*, then through the mountain passes to Klagenfurt and Graz in Austria and finally to Vienna. The British ambassador to the Imperial Court was Nelson's old friend, Lord Minto (the former Sir Gilbert Elliot) and there was a happy reunion when the travellers arrived in the centre of the city for a stay of six weeks. Lady Minto was delighted to declare: "He is just the same with us as ever he was." He had "the same honest, simple manners; but he is devoted to Emma; he thinks her quite an *angel* and talks of her as such to her face and behind her back and she leads him about like a keeper with a bear." Others were less approving and a Franz Collenbach noted: "Lady Hamilton never stopped talking, singing, laughing, gesticulating and mimicking, while the favoured son of Neptune appeared to leave her no more than did her shadow, trying to meet with his own small eyes, the great orbs of his beloved and, withal, as motionless and silent as a monument, embarrassed by his poor figure and by all the emblems, cord and crosses with which he was bedecked." There were late nights of card-playing and Tom Allen was heard to warn his master against drinking too much champagne: "You will be ill if you take any more."

After an emotional farewell to Queen Maria Carolina, they set out for

Prague and more receptions, banquets and flattery. After celebrating Nelson's forty-second birthday, the party left for Dresden, embarking on barges so that the last stage of the journey was on the Elbe when the admiral was "much amused by this fresh-water voyage". There, too, they were watched by sharp, unbedazzled eyes, one German describing Nelson as "one of the most insignificant figures I ever saw in my life . . . a more miserable collection of bones and wizened frame I have yet to come across. His bold nose, the steady eye and the solid worth revealed in his whole face betray in some measure the great conqueror. He speaks little, and then only English, and he hardly ever smiles . . . Lady Hamilton behaved like a loving sister towards him; led him; often took hold of his hand, whispered something into his ear, and he twisted his mouth into the faintest resemblance of a smile." An Englishwoman in Dresden, a Mrs. St. George, wrote in her journal that: "It is plain that Lord Nelson thinks of nothing but Lady Hamilton . . . She puffs the incense full in his face; but he receives it with pleasure and snuffs it up very cordially."

The tour continued by barge down the Elbe – stopping at Dessau where yet another German princeling, Prinz Franz Von Anhalt-Dessau, entertained them ashore and commemorated their visit by naming a conical mound the Nelsonburg – to a fulsome welcome at Magdeburg. There the crowds were so curious that at the *König von Preussen* inn, where they stayed, Nelson "dined with open doors and had wine and refreshments handed out to the crowd of onlookers of every standing". Amongst these were several Englishmen, and, noted a Saxon officer: "He busied himself a good deal with them, assuring them that he was nothing less than a great man; they must be loyal and industrious, then they would do equally well; but above all he urged upon them an eternal hatred of the French." He added that "*Die Hamilton*", who helped him to his food at table, was "a woman full of fire, in whom one can still clearly see the beauty of youth; she is somewhat stout". They departed by water, Nelson standing alone in the barge, doffing his hat to the crowds ashore and in boats, one of which, approaching too close, was rammed and capsized, the admiral directing the rescue of those aboard. The journey down the Elbe lasted eleven days, stopping every night and not always in comfort; the party's quartermaster had not ordered sufficient food and wine, or, at least, it failed to reach their table and they nicknamed him "The Jackal".

On arrival at Hamburg they had expected to be met by a British frigate to carry them home across the North Sea, but none was there. Nelson wrote to the Admiralty asking for a ship and they settled down to wait with more feasting and jollities. When no Royal Navy ship arrived, they decided to make their own way and, on the last day of October, boarded the mail-packet *King George* bound for Great Yarmouth. Just before embarking, Cornelia Knight accompanied Nelson to the shops to buy, on her advice, some lace trimmings for a court dress as a present for Fanny.

She meanwhile, together with her father-in-law, awaited her husband's return to London, staying at Nerot's Hotel in King Street, St. James's, while the house that Alexander Davison had rented for them in Dover Street was made ready. There they read in the newspapers that Lord Nelson, accompanied by the Hamiltons, had landed at Great Yarmouth on 6th November, 1800, in stormy weather. Two days later, Captain Thomas Hardy, Nelson's former flag captain who was also staying in London, wrote:

Notwithstanding all the newspapers, his Lordship is not arrived in town and when he will God only knows. His father has lost all patience, her Ladyship bears up very well as yet but I much fear she also will soon despond. He certainly arrived at Yarmouth on Thursday last and there has been no letter received by anybody. Should he not arrive tomorrow, I think I shall set off for Yarmouth *as I know too well the cause of his not coming.*

CHAPTER IX

To the Baltic
(1800–1)

"I felt all my conception of what constituted a grammar-school hero
utterly discomforted."
– a witness of Nelson's arrival at Salisbury; 20th December, 1800

Thunderclouds had drenched London, a gale had torn up trees in
Kensington Gardens, and the streets were wet, windy and dark as the
carriage carrying Lord Nelson and the Hamiltons rattled past St. Paul's
Cathedral on the afternoon of Sunday, 9th November, 1800, to the
reunion that he and his wife had awaited for nearly three years.

Since their arrival at Yarmouth on Thursday, the return had been all
jollity and muddle. The town clerk of the seaport had, when Nelson was
being sworn as a freeman of the borough, asked him to place his hand on
the Bible and, when he did so, said, "Your *right* hand, my Lord". That
had been a moment for laughter as when the landlady of The Wrestlers
inn had asked if she might rename it the Nelson Arms and he had
quipped: "That would be absurd seeing I have but one". There had been
much jollity, too, when he told the welcoming crowd, waiting in the rain,
"I am a Norfolk man and glory in being so" and when he entered a
Norfolk church again after so many years – no painted, plaster saints,
incense or guttering candles here – while the organ wheezed *See the
Conquering Hero Comes!* There had also been an invitation from Fanny to
bring his friends to join her at Roundwood, their new house near Ipswich.

Cavalry from the Norfolk Volunteers had escorted the carriage to the
Suffolk border next day and at Ipswich, the crowds had taken the horses
from the traces and dragged the carriage round the town and followed it
to Roundwood to cheer the reunion. Up the gravel drive they swept,
braced for the meeting, but there was no Lady Nelson waiting on the
doorstep to greet them; the house was empty; once again, Fanny seemed
to have muddled simple arrangements.

She had, in fact, decided that it would be more appropriate to await her
husband in London rather than delay his attendance on the First Lord of
the Admiralty. She did not know that he had already written to the

Admiralty from Yarmouth asking for an immediate return to active duty because he foresaw the crisis that awaited him when he introduced his pregnant mistress to his wife. This he did on arrival at Nerot's Hotel with formality stretched taut by what Emma described as Fanny's "antipathy not to be described" and her tightly controlled horror at seeing the ugly rumours of the past years made voluptuous flesh. At dinner, the presence of the benign old Edmund Nelson eased the tension and the meal had to be curtailed so that Nelson could call at the Admiralty and the Hamiltons move to the house in Grosvenor Square lent by their friend William Beckford, the rich dilettante. Meanwhile Mrs. Cadogan and Cornelia Knight had settled into an hotel in Albemarle Street and there the latter had a visitor, last seen at Palermo; Captain Troubridge had called to urge her privately to drop her friendship with the *Tria Juncta in Uno* if she wished to take her appropriate place in London society. After dining in their company at Grosvenor Square – the presence of Emma's former lover Charles Greville giving added sexual piquance to the occasion – she finally saw them through the eyes of a quietly ambitious lady of quality and decided to do so. For this, Nelson swore "What a ———— Miss Knight is!"

As the thunder rolled away, the Hamiltons clattered off in their carriage to 22 Grosvenor Square, a mile distant, while the Nelsons remained at the hotel because the house they were renting – 17 Dover Street – was not ready: Fanny, having failed to welcome the party at Roundwood, had failed even to provide a temporary home for her husband and his friends. The next day was busy with official engagements: Hamilton reported to Lord Grenville at the Foreign Office and Nelson to the Admiralty and then the Navy Office off the Strand. He was recognised and surrounded by a crowd, from which he was extracted by his agent, Alexander Davison, before the first of the festivities for he was to be guest of honour: the banquet following the Lord Mayor's procession on the day of his accession. Again the horses of his carriage were replaced by cheering crowds who dragged him up Ludgate Hill to the Guildhall, where he was presented with an engraved sword by the City of London. Next day he was invited to a levee at St. James's Palace, where he would be presented to the King. It was not a success. Nelson was piqued because no invitation had been sent to the Hamiltons, although a returned ambassador could have expected one. The King was not pleased to see the admiral festooned with Neapolitan decorations and a spray of Turkish artificial diamonds pinned to his hat; who called himself a Sicilian duke and was the butt of London gossip. When he arrived at court, his reception "was not very flattering, having been the admiration of that of Naples", his loyal friend Cuthbert Collingwood recorded after Nelson had told him about it: "His Majesty merely asked him if he had recovered his health; then turned to General ———— and talked to him near half an hour in great good humour. It could not have been about his success."

The First Lord of the Admiralty and Lady Spencer were entertaining the Nelsons to dinner that same evening amongst the painted sea-battles and the gilded furniture of Admiralty House. Their hostess, who remembered the couple's devotion on the last such occasion three years before noted that "he treated her with every mark of dislike and even of contempt ... Such a contrast I never beheld!" The admiral, tense from his rebuff at the levee, sat silent at table while Fanny, remembering the little attentions necessary to a one-armed man, peeled some walnuts for him and pushed them across the cloth towards him in a wine-glass. He pushed it aside so roughly that it hit a dish, shattered and Fanny burst into tears. Later, while the men sat over their wine and conversation, she followed Lady Spencer into the drawing-room where, as the latter put it, "she told me how she was situated".

Although the King had turned his back upon the nation's hero, the Prince of Wales appeared at a dinner given by Alexander Davison at his grand house in St. James's Square and, Nelson noticed, cast a lustful eye at Emma Hamilton. But five Cabinet ministers, including the Prime Minister, William Pitt, also attended and this was an agreeable introduction to national politics since on 20th November, 1800, he took his seat in the House of Lords, introduced by Lord Romney and Lord Grenville, the Foreign Secretary. Mr. Pitt and the Duke of York, the Commander-in-Chief of the army lately extricated from the Netherlands, were also present at a dinner given for him by the East India Company at the London Tavern on Ludgate Hill, when large, coloured transparencies were displayed of scenes in Aboukir Bay which had saved India from possible French invasion. Lady Nelson had not accompanied her husband to either dinner. Still hoping that he could be changed back into the affectionate, dutiful husband she remembered, she accompanied him and the Hamiltons to the theatre, where the audience noted her severe elegance (white dress and violet satin turban) in contrast with Emma's blowsy flamboyance (bright blue satin dress and many feathers). Tributes to the nation's hero – songs, ballads and cheers – were part of these performances and brought the admiral to his feet in the party's box. On one occasion Emma Hamilton – now in an advanced stage of pregnancy, her condition concealed by her natural bulk and her voluminous dresses – felt faint at the theatre and had to be helped from the box for some remedial fresh air by Fanny, who may then have guessed the biological truth for the first time. On another, while watching the play

Pizarro, it was Fanny who fainted, on hearing the words spoken on stage: "How a woman can love, Pizarro, thou hast known ... how she can hate, thou hast yet to learn ... wave thy glittering sword, meet and survive – an injured woman's fury." Soon afterwards when the Nelsons invited the Hamiltons to dine at Dover Street, Emma left the table, saying that she felt unwell; Fanny, chided by her husband for not being more attentive to her guest, followed to find her being sick.

That night, it has been said, when the guests had gone, Nelson, unable to stand the tension of sharing a bed with the wife he had betrayed, left the house to walk the streets. Through the dark and sleeping city, lit by the glimmer of oil lamps, he paced; along the Strand, past his old lodgings in more innocent days, down Fleet Street to where the great bulk of St. Paul's blotted out the sky; he turned, walking back through Holborn and Soho to Grosvenor Square, to knock on the door of No. 22 and find sanctuary with the startled Sir William.

Nothing Fanny could have said or done could have held him now. She had never understood the emotions and ambition that drove her husband: the small boy searching for a lost mother; the unemployed officer, related closely to poor shopkeepers and distantly rich land-owners; the mystical experience that had inspired a driving self-confidence; the mixture of courage and humanity that inspired those he led; the sometimes urgent libido; the constant need for encouragement, praise, even flattery. Fanny could offer only love and a genteel back-ground to a naval officer's life, often worrying and becoming stupidly ineffective in organising the practicalities of everyday living for an obsessively orderly husband.

Of the other women he had known, only Mary Moutray might have succeeded: had her elderly husband died a few months earlier and in Antigua, instead of Bath; had she and Nelson married, her warmth, wit and perception – together with her background of smart London society – might have held him and left him immune to Emma Hamilton.

"This place of London but ill suits my disposition," wrote Nelson to Hercules Ross, in reply to a letter of welcome. He had again asked the Admiralty for employment but meanwhile it was important to avoid the stare of the public and the press. So it was fortunate that an invitation arrived from William Beckford suggesting that he, accompanied by the Hamiltons and Mrs. Cadogan – but not by his wife, since the withering of the marriage was already the talk of the capital – should spend Christmas with him at his mansion, Fonthill Splendens. Leaving Fanny with his father and his elder brother William and his wife, who had arrived in London in the hope that his reflected fame might prove useful in winning ecclesiastical promotion, he and the Grosvenor Square party took a coach for Wiltshire on 19th December.

There was another civic reception at Salisbury with an escort of volunteer cavalry, bands playing patriotic tunes, the freedom of the municipality to be bestowed, speeches to be made and everywhere cheering crowds, amongst them a few old shipmates to be greeted and an occasional diarist to record immediate reactions: "As he alighted from his carriage, I could not help asking myself if that one-armed, one-eyed man could really have scattered destruction among the fleets of France. I felt all my conception of what constituted a grammar-school hero utterly discomforted."

Their final destination was a return to the fantasies of the courts of Naples and Palermo. William Beckford was *nouveau riche* with a West Indian fortune and widely known to be bisexual and eccentric. In addition to Fonthill Splendens, his Palladian mansion that recalled the style of Holkham Hall, he was building a gigantic Gothic folly "in the monastic taste", Fonthill Abbey, above which a pinnacled, octagonal tower was rising to a height of 278 feet.

As Nelson was beginning to find himself ostracized by the upper reaches of polite society in London, so the "county families" of Wiltshire kept clear of Fonthill. Amongst the guests this Christmas were successful near-bohemians: James Wyatt, the architect of the folly: Benjamin West, the President of the Royal Academy; Madame Banti, an Italian opera-singer who had known the Hamiltons in Naples and Dr. John Walcot, who had written satirical verse about them under a pen-name. Their host, too, was prone to a little mockery behind their backs, talking of "Lord Nelson's Lady Hamilton, or anybody else's Lady Hamilton".

Most of the entertainment was much as would have been arranged by any ostentatious landowner in his mansion: dining and wining; tours of the gardens and rides in the park. It was nearly a decade since Nelson had enjoyed English country life and the loss of an arm and poor eyesight left him nervous at its resumption. When Beckford took him on a drive round his plantations in a four-horse phaeton, the speed and motion combined with his own lack of balance alarmed him so that he said, "This is too much for me – you must set me down" and he walked back to the house. The climax of the holiday was an elaborate "monastic fête" that Beckford had planned to "steal upon the senses, to dazzle the eye and to bewilder the fancy" and echo festivals of Naples and Palermo. It was, of course, to be held in the gaunt folly that was rising on the skyline.

When night had fallen, a procession of carriages escorted by cavalry of his own volunteer regiment, swept the guests from Fonthill Splendens and through woods lit by flambeaux and where hidden musicians played, some more distant than others to simulate echoes. Reaching the tower and turrets of "the Abbey", they were conducted into the hall and gallery, hung with rich, dark drapery, the vaulted roof lost in gloom. Then up stone stairs lighted by "certain mysterious living figures ... dressed in hooded gowns and standing with wax torches in their hands" to a medieval banquet and a performance by Emma Hamilton of her Attitudes. Finally they returned to the mansion for supper, looking back on the evening's entertainment with a *frisson*, for, as one put it: "On leaving this strange nocturnal scene of vast buildings and extensive forests, now rendered dimly and partially visible by the declining lights of lamps and torches, and the twinkling of a few scattered stars in a clouded sky, the company seemed ... as if waking from a dream, or just freed from the influence of some magic spell."

The party broke up on Boxing Day, Nelson and the Hamiltons returning, respectively, to Dover Street and Grosvenor Square. There Fanny was waiting, now almost resigned to the inevitable. The position of both under the same roof was intolerable and a climax to their incompatibility was inevitable. This came at breakfast one morning and was witnessed by Nelson's solicitor, William Haslewood. Once again Nelson had spoken of Emma Hamilton and Fanny stood up and said: "I am sick of hearing of dear Lady Hamilton and am resolved that you shall give up either her or me!" To this, according to Haslewood, he replied: "Take care, Fanny, what you say. I love you sincerely but I cannot forget my obligations to Lady Hamilton or speak of her otherwise than with affection and admiration." Lady Nelson left the room, saying something about her mind being made up, and soon afterwards her husband left, never to spend another night in that house. He did, it was said, return once, going to her room where she lay in bed one morning. Holding out a hand to him, she asked whether she had ever given him cause for complaint or suspicion; he replied that she had not. With that they parted, Nelson finally deserting all but the legal formality of his marriage.

The Admiralty had cut short the agony, by appointing him second-in-command of the Channel Fleet with the rank of vice-admiral, a promotion dating from the first day of 1801. So, leaving the house in Dover Street on his parting from Fanny, he travelled south-west, arriving at Southampton, on his way to Plymouth, that night. There he would join his new flagship, the *San Josef*, which he had taken by boarding off Cape St. Vincent nearly four years before. He was making his escape to sea only just in time for the scandal of his entanglement was now wholly public and the caricaturists were using their pens with cruelty and lewd wit. Now there might as easily be laughter as cheers when he made public appearances with the Hamiltons.

It was not only Fanny who was fading from his life. His father, her companion and confidant during his long absence, was shocked and grieved at their parting. His uncle, William Suckling, had been dead a year, and his mentor, William Locker, had died at the end of December. Friendships were under stress, too. His friend, contemporary and subordinate, Tom Troubridge, had, although still a captain, been appointed a Lord Commissioner of the Admiralty and could be expected to keep a sharply critical eye on his private life ashore. There was even strain in his relations with Lord St. Vincent, who, as the Commander-in-Chief of the Channel Fleet was again his superior.

Nelson and St. Vincent were engaged in litigation over prize-money. The latter had claimed his share of that due from captures during the four months of 1799 when he had been absent from the Mediterranean and Nelson had taken temporary command. His view was that, whether he was present or not, the burden of responsibility over the whole period of his appointment had earned him whatever was legally due. Nelson, on the other hand, felt that, as Commander-in-Chief in all but title, he himself should not be deprived of the rewards of the fleet's activity under his direction and he estimated this was "my undoubted property" and worth £20,000. The lawyers of both were preparing their cases, which were to be heard in the spring or early summer but when the two friends met at Plymouth, the dispute was not mentioned. However, Nelson was, as ever, unable to hide his feelings and St. Vincent wrote to Evan Nepean, the Secretary of the Admiralty: "Nelson was very low when he came here ... appeared and acted as if he had done me an injury and felt apprehensive that I was acquainted with it." As usual, he tried to hide his worries behind a showy but ill-fitting mask. "Poor fellow!" continued St. Vincent. "He is devoured by vanity, weakness and folly; was strung with ribbons, medals, etc., and yet pretended that he wished to avoid the honour and ceremonies he everywhere met with on the road."

These were signs of the turmoil within: guilt and passion dictating alternating moods of irritation, lust, piety and jealousy. Once again his trunks had been carelessly packed and, almost by force of habit, he blamed Fanny, writing to her of his complaints: lost keys, clothes missing and table services incomplete. "In short I find myself without anything comfortable or convenient ... It is now too late to send half my wardrobe, as I know not what is to become of me, nor do I care." In contrast, he had become wildly jealous of Emma – heavily pregnant as she was – since he had heard that the Prince of Wales had remarked that she had "hit his fancy" at the dinner party in St. James's Square. Knowing him as a libertine and fearing what might happen if Sir William invited him to the house they had taken in Piccadilly, he wrote to her: "I own I wonder that

Sir Wm. should have a wish for the Prince of Wales to come under your
roof ... Even one visit will stamp you as his *chère amie*, and we know he is
dotingly fond of such women as yourself ... But, my dear friend, I know
you too well not to be convinced you cannot be seduced by any prince in
Europe. You are, in my opinion, the pattern of perfection." His dreams of
bliss in a Norfolk cottage had been supplanted by one of taking Emma
away from the gossips to Bronte and he wrote to her: "I long to get to
Bronte, for, believe me, this England is a shocking place; a walk under the
chestnut trees, although you may be shot by a banditti, is better than to
have our reputations stabbed in this country."

It was agonising to leave her a prey to scandal and his suspicions,
particularly as the birth of their child was imminent; Sir William probably
knew, as did her mother, for they were living together at 23 Piccadilly and
the secret would have been almost impossible to keep in such confines.
Nelson trusted only one emissary, James Oliver, Sir William's confiden-
tial secretary, to carry intimate letters between his flagship and the house
in London. Otherwise he invented a simple fiction under which they
could correspond: he would write to her about one of his sailors, named
Thompson, whose lover was being befriended by Lady Hamilton but
whose marriage was being prevented by an uncle. "Poor man!" he wrote
towards the end of January 1801. "He is very anxious and begs you will, if
she is not able, write a line just to comfort him." Although supposedly
unmarried, he wrote of the lovers as if they were, writing to Emma, "Mrs.
Thompson's friend is this moment come into my room ... He appears
almost as miserable as myself." As for their own relationship, his letters
trusted to the post, could go no farther than declare that "where
friendship is of so strong a cast as ours, it is no easy matter to shake it –
mine is as fixed as Mount Etna and as warm on the inside as that
mountainside". But even though he was again in his own flagship with the
prospect of active service before him, he repeated, "I wish I was just
setting off for Bronte. I should then be happy".

On 1st February, the *San Josef* anchored in Torbay and Nelson went
ashore to pay his respects to Lord St. Vincent. He was told that
operations in the Baltic were being planned to pre-empt the formation of
an active alliance between the French, the Scandinavians and Russia. A
fleet was being prepared for northern service under the elderly Vice-
Admiral Sir Hyde Parker with Nelson as his second-in-command. He
would therefore shift his flag to the seventy-four gun *St. George*, which
drew less water than the *San Josef*, essential for the shallow waters of the
Baltic.

It was then that he received a cryptically worded letter from London,
which he immediately burned (but for two lines that he cut out to keep) for

it told him that Emma had been delivered of a baby daughter. "I believe poor dear Mrs. Thompson's friend will go mad with joy," he wrote to her at once. "He cries, prays and performs all tricks, yet dare not show all or any of his feelings but he has only me to consult with. He swears he will drink your health this day in a bumper and damn me if I don't join him ... I cannot write I am so agitated by this young man at my elbow. I believe he is foolish; he does nothing but rave about you and her. I own I participate of this joy and cannot write anything." He then wrote to "Mrs. Thompson" as from the sailor to "his only, *only* love" that "he swears before heaven that he will marry you as soon as it is possible ... He charges me to say how dear you are to him and that you must, every opportunity, kiss and bless for him his dear litle girl, which he wishes to be called Emma out of gratitude to our dear, good Lady Hamilton."

In his paroxysms of joy, Nelson only wanted to think of idylls ahead with no thought for the practical problems facing Emma in London. At the end of January, after a few days' indisposition – assumed, no doubt, to be a winter cold by her acquaintances – the child had been born at 23 Piccadilly; soon after to be taken in a closed carriage to be put in the care of a nurse, a Mrs. Gibson of Little Titchfield Street just to the north of Oxford Street. The infant may have been a twin and there is some evidence that this was so; that the second baby was given to the Foundlings' Hospital while Nelson was told that it had died. Silence had concealed an earlier birth that Emma had kept from her lover: the child born after her stay at Uppark was now a young woman of twenty named Emma Carew, who occasionally wrote to her mother and even visited her, when she was said to be a distant relation.

Motherhood had not softened the passion; or, if Emma feared that it might, she played upon Nelson's jealousy of the Prince of Wales. Alone in his cabin as his flagship heaved and tugged at her moorings, he stared at her portrait in the dim lantern-light and his imagination broke loose, even imagining her husband to be bent on procuring the Prince as her lover. Writing to her as "Mrs. Thompson" with Sir William cast as her wicked uncle, he declared: "If the beast turns you out of his house because you will not submit to be thought a w——e, you know then what will happen ..." He even wished him dead, writing of himself in the third person: "He wishes there was peace, or that if your uncle would die, he would instantly then come and marry you, for he dotes on nothing but you and your child."

He was not only distracted by jealousy but queasy from sea-sickness and worried about his sighted eye which was weakening to the point where the Physician to the Fleet suggested an operation, the wearing of a green eye-shade and an end to letter-writing. Instead of being able to lose himself in professional duties he was now faced with becoming second-in-command to an elderly admiral and having to move into what he considered an unworthy flagship. He wrote to Emma on 10th February:

> The *St. George* is just arrived, but it blows so strong and such a very heavy sea that my things cannot be moved ... You cannot think how dirty the *St. George* compared to my own *San Josef* and probably her inside is worse than her outside appearance. The ship is now fitted for a flag, her decks leaking and is truly uncomfortable but it suits exactly my present feelings, which are miserable in the extreme. I have not closed my eyes all night and am almost blind and far from well.

Strangely, his only comfort was religion. Brought up in a strict, almost puritan, family and having formerly shown himself to be a man of principle, he was – however his inhibitions may have been loosened – well aware of his transgressions of Christian morality. His defence against his own conscience was to rationalize and this was made easier by the sense that he enjoyed a privileged communion with the deity. So he was able to persuade himself that his liaison was, despite the legal and social obstacles, a spiritual marriage. In a letter delivered to Emma by the hand of James Oliver and therefore unfettered by caution, he addressed her as "my own dear wife, for such you are in my eyes and in the face of heaven".

This belief was matched by the formalities of prayer that he had learned in the church at Burnham Thorpe and he not only composed a prayer late one night in the *San Josef* but enclosed it with a letter to Emma complaining about the state of his new flagship. He wrote:

> O God, who knowst the purity of my thoughts and the uprightness of my conduct, look down, I beseech Thee, on me; one, I own, of the most unworthy of Thy servants, help and support me, for Thou, O Lord, art my only comfort and to Thy infinite mercy alone do I look for support to bear me through this transitory life, and I beseech Thee, O most merciful God, that in Thy good time Thou will take me to Thyself and remove me from this world, where I have no friends to comfort or relieve me even on the bed of sickness. Relieve me, O Lord, from the miseries of this world speedily, speedily, speedily. Amen, amen, amen. Nelson and Bronte. Ten o'clock Monday night.

Pleas for divine mercy had, of course, to be matched with good works as life in a parsonage had demonstrated and he wrote to the secretary of the Society for the Promotion of Christian Knowledge asking for a consignment of Bibles to be sent for his ship's company. "I trust that the conduct of the *Agamemnon* and *Vanguard* has been such as to induce a belief that good to our King and Country may have arisen from the seamen and marines having been taught to respect the established religion ... I therefore hope that the Society will again make a present of Books to the crew of the *San Josef* – the number near 900 – and that she may be as successful as the former ships you gave them to."

His longing for domestic bliss was accentuated by meeting Cuthbert Collingwood with his wife and their adored daughter Sarah ashore in Plymouth and seeing their contentment. Ironically, Collingwood described the occasion in a letter to Mary Moutray, who had also shown him the happiness of family life. "How surprised you would have been to have popped in to the Fountain Inn," he told her, "and see Lord Nelson, my wife and myself sitting by the fire cosing and little Sarah teaching Phyllis, her dog, how to dance."

Now there was a chance that Nelson might be able to see his daughter. Once he had moved to the *St. George*, he would sail for Spithead to put himself under the command of Sir Hyde Parker and there would be hope of a few days' leave in London. Before leaving Torbay, he bid farewell to St. Vincent, who was also going there to take up his appointment as First Lord of the Admiralty, and it was a sign of his rising spirits that he asked if he could engage nearly half of the twenty-six Italian and Maltese musicians of the earl's orchestra for his own flagship: "If your Lordship do not take your musicians on shore, I shall be very happy to have ten or twelve of them and will with pleasure pay them the same as you do."

On 22nd February, he arrived at Spithead where loving letters from Emma awaited, telling him that their child was to be named Horatia. "You win my heart for ever," he replied "I am all soul and sensibility." It was agonising to be only a day's journey from Emma and he refused all invitations to dine ashore in Portsmouth, whether from the admiral "an old man with an old wife dressed old ewe lamb fashion", or an old friend from his time as a midshipman with a wife who "likes a drop and looks like a cook-maid". Writing this to Emma, he added: "I will dine nowhere without your consent although with my present feelings I might be trusted with fifty virgins naked in a dark room." That letter was sent by a secure hand but, when another had to be sent by mail-coach, he used their simple code. "Poor Thompson seems to have forgotten all his ill health and all his mortifications and sorrows in the thought that he will soon bury them in your dear, dear bosom," he exulted. "I dare say twins will again be the fruit of your and his meeting. The thought is too much to bear. Have the dear thatched cottage ready to receive him and I will answer that he would not give it up for a queen and a palace. Kiss dear H. for me."

At last the Admiralty sent a signal to Portsmouth down the line of hill-top semaphore stations granting him three days' leave and he took the overnight coach to London, arriving in the grey light before sunrise and breakfasting at Lothian's Hotel. Fanny, he knew, was staying in Brighton and fearing that, hearing of his arrival in London, she might try to see him, he wrote to her: "I am sent for to town on very particular business for a day or two. I would not on any account have you come to London but rest quiet where you are. Nor would I have you come to Portsmouth for I never come on shore." So the triumphant Emma had Nelson to herself, taking him on a visit to 9 Little Titchfield Street to kiss his infant daughter. She had no mercy for her crushed rival, writing to Sarah, the wife of William Nelson, "O what real pleasure Sir W. and I have in seeing this our great, good, victorious Nelson. His eye is better." Then using the nickname she had invented for the shy, bird-like Fanny, she continued: "Tom Tit does not come to town; she offered to go down but was refused. She only wanted to do mischief to all the *great Jove's* relations. 'Tis now shown, all her ill-treatment and bad heart – *Jove* has found it out."

Their parting was as deliciously anguished as their reunion had been ecstatic. "My heart is full to burst – oh, what pain, God only knows!" gushed Emma to Sarah, now her confidante. "I shall go mad with grief. Oh, God only knows what it is to part with such a friend – *such a one.* We were truly called the *Tria Juncta in Uno* for Sir W., *he* and I have but one heart *in three bodies.*" Nelson felt likewise: "Parting from such a friend is literally tearing one's own flesh."

Although the reunion had stilled his jealousy, it had sharpened his infatuation so that when, on his return to the *St. George*, Oliver came aboard with more private letters from London he immediately imagined some disaster and, as he wrote to her: "So much anxiety for your safety rushed into my mind that a pain immediately seized my heart, which kept increasing for half an hour, that, turning cold, hot, cold, etc., I was obliged to send for the surgeon, who gave me something to warm me, for it was a deadly chill."

Now knowing that he was bound for the Baltic and operations against the threatened alliance and embargo on trade with Britain, and conjuring up his usual visions of a glorious death in battle, he replied in another private letter that reflected both his heightened love and lust.

You know, my dearest Emma, that there is nothing in this world that I would not do for us to live together and have our little child with us. I firmly believe that this campaign will give us peace and then we will set off for Bronte. . . . We must manage till we can quit this country or your 'uncle' dies ... You, my beloved Emma, and my Country are the two dearest objects of my fond heart – a *heart susceptible and true.*

A heart so susceptible that, warming to his theme, he added: "My longing for you, both person and conversation, you may readily imagine. What must be my sensations at the idea of sleeping with you! It sets me on fire, even the thoughts, much more would the reality. I am sure all my love and desires are all to you, and if any woman naked were to come to me, even as I am from thinking of you, I hope it might rot off if I would touch her even with my hand. No, my heart, person and mind is in perfect union of love towards my own, dear beloved Emma."

Fanny stood no chance of survival against this torrent of emotion and at the beginning of March she received what she described as "my Lord Nelson's letter of dismissal". Beginning by assuring her that he had tried to arrange another command for Josiah, he added:

I have done *all* for him and he may again, as he has often done before, wish me to break my neck and be abetted in it by his friends, who are likewise my enemies. But I have done my duty as an honest, generous man, and I neither want or wish for anybody to care what becomes of me, whether I return, or am left in the Baltic. Living, I have done all in my power for you and, if dead, you will find I have done the same; therefore my only wish is to be left to myself; and wishing you every happiness, believe me that I am, your affectionate Nelson and Bronte.

He now turned his attention to war, or at least to the naval operations that would be necessary to keep British trade moving to and from the Baltic ports. It seemed certain that a major show of force would be necessary to demonstrate to the Danes and their subject Norwegians, the Swedes and the Prussians how unwise they would be to follow the Russian lead in forming the Armed Neutrality of the North in alliance with France. They had much to lose, for their export of raw materials essential to a maritime nation – timber, hemp, canvas, pitch, tar, copper and iron – were traded with Britain for manufactured goods, coal, salt and cargoes that passed through British ports such as sugar, tobacco and tea. The unstable Tsar Paul of Russia, so recently allied to the British with his ships active against the French in the Mediterranean, had been prompted to change sides by the British refusal to allow him to share in the final capture of Malta, while Bonaparte had cunningly offered to surrender Valetta to him. As for the Baltic states, their pragmatism had been overcome by irritation at the British searching of their ships trading with French ports, and sometimes the seizure of their cargoes. Neither the Northern Powers, nor Britain, had declared war, so that the fleet assembling off

Yarmouth under Sir Hyde Parker was being prepared for the possibility of a pre-emptive attack.

Before sailing from Spithead, the *St. George* embarked a detachment of infantry to reinforce her marines and their senior officer was a Lieutenant-Colonel the Honourable William Stewart, who, fascinated by the admiral, recorded his behaviour. Thus, shortly after leaving the shelter of the Isle of Wight, he noted how Nelson, again fussing over detail, would involve himself with the handling of the ship and the responsibilities of her captain, his friend Thomas Hardy. "His Lordship was rather too apt to interfere with the working of the ship," he wrote in his journal, "and not always with the best judgement. The wind, when off Dungeness, was scanty and the ship was to be put about; Lord Nelson *would* give the orders and caused her to miss stays," so failing to tack at the right moment.

> Upon this, he said rather peevishly to the master, or officer of the watch, 'Well now, see what we have done. Well, sir, what do you mean to do?' The officer saying with hesitation, 'I don't exactly know, my Lord. I fear she won't do.' Lord Nelson turned sharply towards the cabin and replied, 'Well, I am sure if you don't know what to do, nor more do I either.' He then went in, leaving the officer to work the ship as he liked.

Perhaps his long spells ashore had blunted his seaman's instinct, or his skills, first acquired in the creeks and among the sandbanks of the Norfolk coast, were more attuned to inshore navigation and ship-handling; if so, he was about to sail for shallow waters where they could be put to practical use.

On arrival off Yarmouth on 6th March, he was surprised and annoyed to find that the Commander-in-Chief was living ashore. Admiral Parker belonged to a renowned naval family but had seen little active service and, a rich man, had grown portly and florid with good living; also, at the age of sixty-one he had just married a girl of eighteen, pleasing but plump and nicknamed "the batter pudding". This prompted Nelson to remark: "Consider how nice it must be laying in bed with a young wife, compared to a damned cold, raw wind." Moreover young Lady Parker was directing her husband's attention to an elaborate ball she had arranged in the town for the following week. To remind the Commander-in-Chief of his professional duties, Nelson proposed to make his first official call on him next morning at The Wrestlers inn, where he and the Hamiltons had stayed when they had landed four months before, at an hour that would summon him from that bed. "We breakfasted that morning, as usual, soon after six o'clock, for we were always up by daylight," Colonel

Stewart recorded. "We went on shore, so as to be at Sir Hyde's door by eight o'clock, Lord Nelson choosing to be amusingly exact to that hour, which he considered as a very late one for business." Sir Hyde received them downstairs with formal courtesy then, without having mentioned the coming expedition or giving any orders to his second-in-command, turned and climbed the stairs to his bedroom.

Nelson, whose cardinal principle it was to keep his subordinates fully informed and ready for his next orders, was appalled and wrote to Troubridge at the Admiralty – knowing that his letter would be shown to St. Vincent – pleading for sailing-orders: "Get rid of us, dear friend, and we shall not be tempted to lie abed till 11 o'clock ... " The frustrations revived his worst fantasies of Emma disporting herself with the Prince of Wales – imaginings that she played upon to excite his jealousy – and he wrote distracted letters: "My senses are almost gone tonight; I feel as I never felt before. My head! My head! but I will lay down and try to compose my spirits, miserable wretch that I am ... No, I will never believe anything against my friend's honour and faith to me. Goodnight, I am more dead than alive, but all yours till death – no, the thought of Horatia cheers me up. We will be yet happy ... " He was calmer for two or three days, then the fantasies flooded back: "I see clearly, my dearest friend, that you are on SALE. I am almost mad to think of the iniquity of wanting you to associate with a set of whores, bawds and unprincipled liars. Can this be the great Sir William Hamilton? I blush for him ... "

His letter to Troubridge had, however, taken effect and St. Vincent had written a sharp reminder to Parker:

> I have heard by a side wind that you have intention of continuing at Yarmouth until Friday on account of some trifling circumstance. I really know not what they are, nor did I give myself the trouble of inquiring into them, supposing it impossible ... that there could be the smallest foundation of this report. I have, however, upon consideration of the effect of your continuance at Yarmouth an hour after the wind would admit of your sailing ... sent down a messenger purposely to convey to you my opinion, as a private friend, that any delay in your sailing would do you irreparable injury...

The trifling circumstance was, in fact, Lady Parker's ball and this was cancelled; she was sent home to London and Sir Hyde at last embarked on his flagship, which had arrived the day before, the *London*. Thereupon, a gleeful Nelson wrote a mordant letter to Troubridge: "Now we can have no desire for staying, for her Ladyship is gone and the ball for Friday knocked up by you and the Earl's unpoliteness to send gentlemen to sea instead of dancing with nice white gloves." Then he added sharply,

"I will only say that I know not that we are even going to the Baltic except from newspapers ..."

Although Parker had been at Yarmouth for nearly a fortnight and had known the names of the ships he would command for almost a month, he had issued no orders. He now began to do so and ordered the fleet to be ready to sail by midnight, creating chaos ashore as his captains, lulled by his lethargy, hurried to embark men and stores, prompting an amused midshipman to record: "The scene upon Yarmouth jetty this evening was highly interesting and in the hand of Hogarth might have made a good companion to *The March to Finchley*, but that the importance of the event left no room in mind for levity or ridicule."

At last, Sir Hyde Parker sailed on 12th March, with a powerful fleet of fifteen ships of the line, two fifty-gun ships, frigates and brigs with nearly a thousand troops embarked; later to be reinforced by three more sail of the line (four should have joined off the Danish coast but one, the *Invincible*, ran aground off the Norfolk coast, where she was pounded to pieces by heavy seas and lost with almost all hands within sight of shore). A strong fleet would be necessary because, should the Northern Powers be able to concentrate their squadrons, Parker might face a line of battle composed of as many as twenty-three Danish ships, eighteen Swedish and eighty-two Russian, although many would be poorly manned, ill-equipped and it was doubtful whether any two of their fleets could work together at sea. Yet, even now, Sir Hyde refused to take Nelson into his confidence, so nervous was he of his subordinate's unsettling reputation for originality and dash, and probably jealous of it. Even when orders from the Admiralty reached him by despatch-boat, he kept to himself their instructions to appear off Copenhagen and demand that Denmark withdraw from the Armed Neutrality, enforcing this either by "amicable arrangement or by actual hostilities". Then he was to continue north-eastward to make "an immediate and vigorous attack" on the Russians off Reval and again off their lair at Kronstadt deep in the gulf leading to St. Petersburg.

It took a spontaneous, generous gesture by Nelson to crack Parker's shell. Somewhere over the Dogger Bank, a lieutenant in the *St. George* caught a fine turbot and Nelson, knowing his admiral's fondness for good living, sent it across to the flagship with a graceful note. So, when the fleet had rounded the Skaw – the northerly point of Jutland – and turned south down the broad channel of the Kattegat, Parker ordered his captains to anchor and invited Nelson on board.

"Now we are sure of fighting," he wrote to Emma, "I am sent for. When it was a joke I was kept in the background." But the conference in Parker's cabin was not in Nelson's style, for the agenda kept all options open, including the most cautious. The officers listened to a British diplomat, Nicholas Vansittart, who had just returned from Copenhagen, saying that the ulitmatum had already been rejected and that vigorous preparations were being made for the defence of the city. Parker seemed to favour the easiest, most cautious alternative of remaining at anchor where the fleet now lay and imposing a blockade of the Baltic; then await reactions, so giving the Northern Alliance time to concentrate their fleets and attack. "If a man consults whether he is to fight, when he has the power in his own hands, it is certain that his opinion is against fighting," Nelson considered and he boldly spoke up for his favoured option, which was to sail past Copenhagen, leaving a small squadron to blockade it, make straight for the Russian fleet and destroy it. Parker shied at the idea, unable to think farther ahead than the Danish capital.

On his return to the *St. George*, Nelson wrote to Troubridge that when he had been summoned to the conference, "little did I think it was to converse on not fighting. I feel happy that I had so much command of myself, for I should have let out what you might have been sorry to see, especially fancying I had been, to say no worse, very unkindly treated by Sir Hyde; that is, with a degree of haughtiness which my spirit could not bear." He then composed a memorandum to Parker stating baldly that "the more I have reflected the more I am confirmed in opinion that not a moment should be lost in attacking the enemy: they will every day and every hour be stronger ... I am of opinion the boldest measures are the safest." Perhaps his stress on safety appealed to Sir Hyde, because he now prepared to take the fleet through the narrows between Kronborg castle on the Danish shore and the batteries on the Swedish coast. Nelson was to shift his flag into the shallower-draught *Elephant* and take command of about half the fleet – ten sail of the line with shallow draught and twenty-seven smaller ships, including frigates, bomb-ketches and fire-ships – for a direct attack upon the city, perhaps to be followed by the landing of troops. So on 30th March, 1801, the whole fleet sailed in two divisions and safely passed the narrows, keeping towards the Swedish shore, where the batteries remained silent, while the Danish fortress erupted in the smoke and flame of an ineffective cannonade at extreme range.

Now that Copenhagen was in sight, Sir Hyde accompanied Nelson on a reconnaissance in a schooner and they were able to see the formidable defences – some of them natural – that they faced. The capital lay within its batteries, walls and moat on the eastern shore of the island of Zeeland and could only be approached by two channels to either side of a large shoal known as the Middle Ground. The inner, narrower passage, known as the King's Channel, was heavily defended by shore batteries – notably the great Trekroner fortress, so named after the three crowns of Denmark, Norway and Sweden – and, running southward from this, a line of nineteen moored ships, hulks and floating batteries. The guns of the Trekroner were the keystone of the defence and any approach from the north had first to pass through their arcs of fire. The alternative was to pass the city to the east of the Middle Ground along the wide Outer Deep channel, turn and attack from the south, so avoiding the fearsome fortress: a northerly wind would be needed for the first move and a southerly wind for the second. An added advantage of this approach was that a squadron lying to the south of the city would cut it off from reinforcement by the Russians or Swedes. This was the option that Nelson chose, telling Emma in a letter: "I have just been reconnoitering the Danish line of defence. It looks formidable to those who are children at war but, to my judgement, with ten sail of the line I think I can annihilate them; at all events I hope to be allowed to try."

Sir Hyde, happy to leave the risk-taking to one who sought risks, approved and remained to the north of the city with his heavy ships. Nelson was unperturbed by the prospect of shoals, shallows and the caprice of the wind for these had become familiar hazards in Norfolk creeks, the Thames, the Mosquito Shore and Aboukir Bay; as he was to say in another context: "I own myself one of those who do not fear the shore, for hardly any great things are done in a small ship by a man that is." There was a final council of war at which Parker allocated two more ships of the line to Nelson. Then, on 1st April, he took advantage of a northerly wind, safely sailed through the Outer Deep and anchored to the south, deciding: "I fight them the moment I have a fair wind." His aim was not to devastate the magnificent city, whose copper-green spires could be seen above its steep-pitched roofs, but to destroy its defences so that capitulation or compliance would be the only alternative to destruction.

Nelson made his plan of attack on 1st April. It recalled Aboukir Bay in the pale northern light: the shoals and shallows and the enemy at anchor close inshore. His flag captain in the *Elephant* was Thomas Foley, who then had led the way round the head of the French line; but that could not be repeated here because of the shore batteries which commanded the half-mile of shallow water between ships and shore. But he could again concentrate overwhelming gunfire upon each moored enemy in turn and so move up their line, destroying it piecemeal. So after dining with his captains in his flagship and drinking a toast to success, he sent them back to their ships and, with Foley and Captain Riou of the frigate *Amazon*, a superb seaman, who sounded and buoyed a channel for the approach, he began to draft and dictate his orders. So exhausted by the late hours and nervous tension of the past few days was Nelson that his servant Tom Allen laid his cot on the deck of the cabin and he lay in it, continuing to dictate; in the next cabin six clerks began transcribing his instructions into thirty sets which would be required for the different ships. He was up and dressed by the time they had finished at six and the written orders were with his captains by eight. During the night the wind had swung through a hundred and eighty degrees and now blew from the south. The attack could begin.

Without Nelson to inspire the British fleet, the preparations for battle off Copenhagen would have seemed particularly dreadful and cold-blooded. There was no hatred of the enemy as there had been at Aboukir Bay and would be no test of tactics and seamanship as there had been at St. Vincent. The British liked and admired the Danes, who manned their hulks and floating batteries and crowded on the quays and rooftops of their capital. The British ships had already cleared for action; bulkheads removed to clear the gun-decks from stem to stern and all furniture struck down into the hold. The lids of the gun-ports were swung upward along the lengths of ships painted yellow with a broad black band between the tiers of square openings, through which the gun-muzzles were run out. The six-man crews stood to each gun, the powder-boys crouched behind, ready to scamper with fresh canvas cartridge-cases; marines guarding the hatchways and lining the upper deck behind barricades of tightly-rolled hammocks stowed in netting along each bulwark, ready to fire muskets or haul ropes; on the orlop deck below the waterline, the surgeons and their mates, laying out surgical instruments and bandages; on the quarterdeck, the captains and their officers, standing alert but with assumed nonchalance. All on deck watched as, at half-past nine, the first signals flew up the *Elephant*'s halyards: first, to weigh anchor and make sail; each captain knew where his position should be.

Under topsails, the British ships glided towards the long line of moored enemies and the hump-backed earthworks of the Trekroner fortress. Their gun-crews might be superbly trained; their rate of fire second to none with a broadside every forty seconds; but they faced batteries of heavy guns, often heavier than their own – many Danish cannon fired shot weighing nearly forty pounds – manned by determined patriots. The British were to anchor opposite their allotted opponent and, when that had been battered into submission, move along the line, passing the disengaged sides of their own ships, to attack another. Meanwhile seven bomb-ketches were to anchor to the east of the British line and throw their bombs over it. Finally, when the Trekroner batteries were silenced, they were to be stormed by landing parties of infantry, marines and sailors. Sir Hyde Parker and his heavy ships would await the outcome, at anchor six miles to the north (see plan, page xv).

The first broadsides were crucial as they might be the last to be co-ordinated and aimed with any precision for gun-smoke would blow back into the ships, billow and drift around them and the noise would drown all shouted orders. So when the first British ships anchored some two hundred yards from their enemies' guns and their first broadsides thundered, the battle became a series of half-blinded, deafened duels between batteries of cannon at point-blank range.

Each ship presented sudden scenes of horror as the heavy shot punched through the thick wooden sides in a shower of splinters: a midshipman in the *Monarch*, sent below on an errand to the magazine, stumbled down the ladder and reported: "When I arrived on the maindeck, along which I had to pass, there was not a single man standing the whole way from the mainmast forward, a district containing eight guns, some of which were run out ready for firing; others lay dismounted; the others remained as they were after recoiling ... I hastened down the fore ladder to the lower deck and felt really relieved to find someone alive." On the quarterdeck of the *Elephant*, Nelson stood with his officers in the smoke with shot howling and snapping overhead. "It is warm work," he remarked to Colonel Stewart at his side, "and this day may be the last to us at any moment. But, mark you, I would not be elsewhere for thousands!"

Watching from the north, Admiral Parker had seen the long lines of ships almost disappear in smoke stabbed with gun-flashes and after nearly two hours, when his watch showed one o'clock, the rumble and thunder of gunfire continued, heavy as ever. He also saw that two of Nelson's ships were flying distress signals and that another appeared to have run aground. It was often said that ships could not stand and fight against fortifications: here, as well as shore batteries, the British ships faced strongly built, low-lying floating batteries. Fearing that Nelson was being fought to a standstill but unwilling to withdraw without orders, Parker told his flag captain: "I will make the signal of recall for Nelson's sake. If he is in condition to continue the action, he will disregard it; if he is not, it will be an excuse for his retreat ... "

On the quarterdeck of the *Elephant*, Lieutenant Langford, turning his telescope on the distant flagship, saw the signal through the smoke, and called to Nelson that she was flying the signal to discontinue action. The admiral appeared not to have heard and when the lieutenant shouted again, called back irritably: "Mr. Langford, I told you to look out on the Danish commodore and let me know when he surrendered; keep your eye fixed on him." At this, the dutiful Langford asked a question that could not be ignored: should he repeat the Commander-in-Chief's signal to the other ships? "No, acknowledge it," snapped Nelson, then asked whether his own signal for close action was still hoisted. Being told that it was he ordered: "Mind you keep it so." Then, walking to and fro nervously working the stump of his right arm, he stopped by Colonel Stewart and said, "Do you know what's shown on board of the Commander-in-Chief? No. 39!" Asked what that meant, he replied, "Why, to leave off action! Now damn me if I do!" Then he turned to Foley and, as Stewart reported, said: "You know, Foley, I have only one eye – I have a right to be blind sometimes" and then, with the archness peculiar to his character, putting the glass to his blind eye, he exclaimed, "I really do not see the signal!"

Another soldier on board the *Elephant*, Captain Thomas Beckwith, added that, when Nelson ignored the signal, he remarked that "the enemy were gallant fellows, but if he could not beat them in two hours he must take three, or if that would not do, he must take four hours to do it."

The battle blundered on for another hour, when the cannonade slackened, for most of the Danish ships and batteries were smoking wrecks and the British, too, battered and bloody. But there was no sign of general capitulation and Nelson decided to try to bring the slaughter to a halt. Just then, British boats pulling towards Danish ships that had been battered into silence and were thought to have surrendered, were fired upon. Angrily Nelson determined to impose a conclusive end with a ruthlessness that recalled his mood at Naples two years before. Sending for paper, pen and ink and spreading them on the wooden casing over the rudderhead, he wrote: "To the Brothers of Englishmen, the Danes – Lord Nelson has directions to spare Denmark, when no longer resisting; but if the firing is continued on the part of Denmark, Lord Nelson will be obliged to set on fire all the floating batteries he has taken without having the power of saving the brave Danes who have defended them." This he sealed carefully with wax and his own heraldic seal so that, as one of his officers explained, the enemy would not think that it had been written and sent in a hurry.

The message was sent ashore with a Danish-speaking officer, who landed under a flag of truce at the sally-port in the seaward walls of the city and delivered it to Crown Prince Frederick, who was there with his staff. Startled by Nelson's threat, he sent an aide-de-camp, Captain Hans Lindholm, across to the flagship to question it. On the quarterdeck Nelson received him, was impressed by his manner and asked him to put his question in writing. This he did in English, winning the approval of the British officers around him with a brave little joke: "If your guns are not better pointed than your pens, you will make little impression on

Copenhagen." To this, Nelson responded with a cool-headed, even amiable reply, also in writing:

> Lord Nelson's object in sending on shore a flag of truce is humanity: he therefore consents that hostilities shall cease till Lord Nelson can take his prisoners out of the prizes and he consents to land all the wounded Danes and to burn or remove his prizes. Lord Nelson, with humble duty to his Royal Highness, begs leave to say that he will ever esteem it the greatest victory he ever gained if this flag of truce may be the happy forerunner of a lasting and happy union between my most gracious Sovereign and his Majesty the King of Denmark.

Both sides needed the cease-fire since they had suffered heavily: the British losing about a thousand killed and wounded, a third of them dead or dying; the Danes, a hundred or so more than that. Six of the British ships were aground, others so damaged aloft that they would be difficult to handle and the only way out of the narrow channel was to wait for another change of wind, or try to sail northward past the still unsubdued batteries of the Trekroner. The *Elephant*, too, was aground so that evening, a twenty-four-hour cease-fire having been agreed, Nelson took a boat past the silent Danish batteries to the *London*, which had now approached to about three miles of the smoke that still rose from the smouldering wrecks. "I have fought contrary to orders and I shall perhaps be hanged," he quipped. "Never mind, let them." But Parker was almost as grateful as Jervis had been after St. Vincent; indeed so admiring of his second-in-command that he asked him to go ashore next morning and conduct negotiations with the Crown Prince for a further term of truce. Nelson was exhausted and, rather than return to the *Elephant* which was still cleared for action and noisy with the hammering of repair-parties, he crossed to the *St. George* to sleep.

Next morning he first visited his own ships, which were already looking orderly: wreckage cut away, severed rigging and tattered sails replaced, blood washed away and decks scrubbed with vinegar. His principal task was ashore, and, accompanied by Hardy, he landed from his barge at a quay in the dockyard where thousands of Danes were waiting for news of their losses in the battle. His meeting with the Crown Prince was to be in the Amalienborg Palace and a carriage with a strong military escort awaited, but he chose to walk through the crowds along the wide, handsome Amaliegade. The shock of the battle had, said Colonel Stewart, "plunged the whole town into a state of terror, astonishment and mourning; the oldest inhabitant had never seen a shot fired in anger at his native country." But, although the crowds were expected to show "rage mixed with admiration" at their conqueror walking amongst them, he met with "a mixture of admiration, curiosity and displeasure". The contrast to his expectations led him to exaggerate when later telling his friend Troubridge that: "My reception was too flattering and landing at Portsmouth or Yarmouth could not have exceeded the blessings of the people ..."

In the rococo audience chamber of the palace, Nelson, Hardy and their interpreter, Captain Thesiger, were received with courtesy by the Crown Prince and his ministers while Nelson began an unaccustomed rôle for, as he said in a letter to St. Vincent: "A negotiator is certainly out of my line, but, being thrown into it, I have endeavoured to acquit myself as well as I was able." This he did by never losing sight of the essential aim, which was to detach Denmark from the alliance with Russia and that the final arbiter would be the weight of broadsides he could bring to bear on the city. "The more I see of his Lordship, the more I admire his great character," remarked Hardy, "for I think on this occasion his political management was *if possible* greater than his bravery." In two hours' conversation, he attempted to allay Danish fears of Russia, which he rightly took to be the motivation of their alliance, by stressing British goodwill and the protection that a British fleet in the Baltic could afford. He did not expect a lasting settlement but he did manage to extend the cease-fire into an indefinite armistice. Then he left the Crown Prince with the demand that Denmark withdraw from the Armed Neutrality of the North and with time to consider the alternative implied by the long array of British masts and yards visible above the rooftops to the east.

For five days, negotiations between the palace and the two British flagships continued by letter with Nelson reporting progress both to the First Lord of the Admiralty and to the Prime Minister, Henry Addington, who had succeeded William Pitt. On 8th April, he again went ashore, with a larger suite including Colonel Stewart, to present a formal armistice agreement. The first six articles were agreed but the Danes objected to the seventh, which stipulated that the armistice should last for sixteen weeks. At this Nelson explained that the time-span was to allow time for naval operations and, reported Stewart, "assured them, with a candour not quite customary in diplomacy, that his reason for requiring so long a term as sixteen weeks was that he might have time to act against the Russian fleet and then return to them". At this one of the Danes turned to another and said in French – assuming that the British would not understand – that disagreement might mean the renewal of hostilities. "Renew hostilities!" repeated Nelson in English to their surprise; then, turning to his interpreter, said, "Tell him that we are ready at a moment; ready to bombard this very night!" There was a flurry of embarrassed apologies and the tension passed for the Danes knew that over the past week the British ships' moorings had been adjusted to bring their broadsides – and, particularly, the heavy mortars of the bomb-ketches – to bear on their chosen targets. Thereafter Nelson kept his manner balanced between amiability, and even flattery, and the threat of force. When the talks were interrupted for dinner and the party was ascending the great staircase to the dining-room, Nelson looked around him and remarked to Stewart, "Though I have only one eye, I see all this will burn very well." At table, there was much affability and when Nelson remarked that the bravery of one young Danish officer in the battle made him worthy to be an admiral, the Crown Prince replied: "If I were to make all my heroes admirals, there would be no lieutenants or captains left!" But Stewart could see that the badinage masked a determination in Nelson: "He even then was thinking more about the bombardment than about dinner."

Later that evening the negotiations were resumed and an armistice agreed although, as a sop to the Danes, Nelson allowed a term of fourteen, rather than sixteen, weeks. During the final hour of the meeting, it was said, Captain Lindholm entered the room and whispered in the Crown Prince's ear. What news he brought was not then declared but it was later thought that it made not only the present diplomacy but the recent battle itself unncecessary. It was not for several days that Nelson and Parker heard that Lindholm had told the Crown Prince that, on 24th March, more than a week before the battle, a group of dissident Russian officers had assassinated Tsar Paul.

Before this was known by the British, the armistice was signed and next day, 10th April, Colonel Stewart sailed for England with a copy for the British Government. As a professional, Nelson was well satisfied with the performance of his ships but he turned his attention to his public image that had assumed new importance since he had been subjected to scurrilous gossip and the disapproval of polite society. Thus the ruthless-ness he had been ready – perhaps eager – to display was now muted and he wrote to Emma of his reception by the Danes: "I received as a warrior all the praises which could gratify the ambitions of the vainest man and the thanks of the nation ... for my humanity in saving the town from destruction. Nelson is a warrior, but will not be a butcher. I am sure, could you have seen the adoration and respect, you would have cried for joy; there are no honours can be conferred equal to this." Ashore in the city he began living up to his self-regard and a Captain Sneedorff, the commandant of the Danish Naval Academy, was astonished to receive a present from him of a gold medal commemorating the Battle of the Nile with a covering letter that concluded: "I send you also a short account of my life; it cannot do harm to youth and may do good as it will show that perseverance and good conduct will raise a person to the very highest honours and rewards."

Now that there would be no interference by the Danes for at least three months, Parker felt able to leave the remains of their fleet astride his communications and sail into the Baltic to deal with the other members of the Armed Neutrality, Sweden and perhaps Russia, for it was not yet clear what the new Tsar Alexander's policy towards France and Britain would be. On 12th April, he sailed into the Baltic with seventeen sail of the line and was soon greeted with the news that a Swedish squadron was at sea. The Swedes, hearing of the British approach, wisely turned back for Karlskrona while Parker anchored off the port and sent in a boat with an account of the Danish armistice and a request that Sweden would follow their example, which drew a cautious, courteous reply but no commitment.

Nelson had been astern of the main fleet, becalmed in the *St. George*, and, hearing that action might be imminent, boarded a six-oared boat to catch up, spending five hours exposed to the chill night without a cloak. "A cold struck me to the heart," he later told Emma. "I had one of my terrible spasms of heart-stroke", followed by fits of retching so that "I brought up what everyone thought was my lungs and I was emaciated more than you can conceive". Sick as he was, Nelson fretted with frustration when Parker refused to sail for the eastern Baltic to carry out his orders to confront the Russians at Reval before the thaw enabled the ships at Kronstadt to join them. Instead, for fear of the weak Swedish squadron which such a move would leave in his rear, he returned to Copenhagen; there he was met with a message from the Admiralty ordering him to hand over command to Nelson and return home. Word of Parker's timidity – particularly during the action off Copenhagen – had reached St. Vincent, who had ordered his recall to certain retirement and possible court-martial. Nelson was ambivalent towards him, however: "They are not Sir Hyde Parker's real friends who wish for an enquiry. His friends in the fleet wish everything to be forgot, for we all respect and love Sir Hyde; but the dearer his friends, the more uneasy they have been at his *idleness*."

For the first time, on 6th May, 1801, Nelson hoisted his flag as an official commander-in-chief and at once took positive action, sailing for Reval while leaving a small squadron to watch the Swedes. He arrived off the Russian base on 14th May to find that the ice had cleared in the gulf so enabling the Russian ships to withdraw to Kronstadt and combine with their main fleet. The Tsar might be ready to end the Armed Neutrality but had no wish to appear to be acting under duress and he sent a sharp note to Nelson stating that negotiations could not be considered while

British warships lay in sight of Russian ports. Controlling his impulse to present another ultimatum, Nelson became the diplomatist and composed a silky response, maintaining that the presence of his ships was prompted solely by "my desire to pay marked attention to his Imperial Majesty" and had been "entirely misunderstood. That being the case, I shall sail immediately into the Baltic." His restraint was justified when, three days after he had sailed, the Armed Neutrality was disbanded.

His reward was not only the success of the mission for which the fleet had originally been sent to the Baltic. There might be more trouble hereabouts – the Russians were mercurial and the Danes were already showing their predilection for an alliance with France – but there was now no immediate threat to British trade.

Nelson was fretting both for activity and for Emma and his hopes rose when an Admiralty despatch-vessel sailed into Copenhagen roads on the evening of 12th June. She brought the news that he had been created a viscount and, better still, that as soon as his successor, Admiral Pole, arrived to relieve him, he could return home. A week later the new Commander-in-Chief arrived, Nelson sailed in a brig – reluctant to deprive the Baltic fleet of a useful fighting ship – and on 1st July, again landed at Yarmouth. His first act was to visit the naval hospital, which was crowded with sailors wounded in action at Copenhagen. A doctor, who greeted him, described how "I went round the wards with him and was much interested in observing his demeanour to the sailors: he stopped at every bed and to every man he had something kind and cheery to say. At length he stopped opposite a bed on which a sailor was lying, who had lost his right arm close to the shoulder-joint, and the following short dialogue passed between them:

Nelson: 'Well, Jack, what's the matter with you?'
Sailor: 'Lost my arm, your honour.'
Nelson paused, looked down at his own empty sleeve, then at the sailor, and said playfully, 'Well, Jack, then you and I are spoiled for fishermen.'

After giving a guinea to each nurse, he set out for London in a fast post-chaise, its postillions dressed as sailors. After nearly four months in his natural environment, he was about to immerse himself again in emotional turmoil. As so often on his return, he was without another pillar of his former stability; this time it was his brother Maurice, who had died suddenly of "a brain fever" in April on the eve of his promotion – thanks to his brother's renown – to be a Commissioner of the Customs and Excise and then to fill the next civilian vacancy on the Navy Board.

He and Horatio had helped each other over debts and he had proved loyal and discreet, particularly when both brothers were living irregular private lives. Maurice had left his middle-aged mistress, Mrs. Sarah Ford, alone, poor and almost blind, so his brother at once instructed his agent to provide a modest income for "Poor Blindy". Now only Horatio and William survived out of the eight sons Catherine Nelson had borne.

Arriving in London, Nelson again lodged at Lothian's Hotel, close to the Hamiltons' house in Piccadilly, where the welcome was all he had imagined. On hearing the news of his victory at a dinner party for a few friends, including the actor Kemble, Emma had danced an impromptu tarantella of triumph; first with Sir William as her partner, then, when he was exhausted, the others and finally the servants, including her Nubian maid Fatima. "It was certainly not of a nature to be performed except before a select company," thought one of the guests, "as the screams, attitudes, starts and embraces with which it was intermingled gave it a peculiar character".

Among naval officers Nelson's reputation was now secure for the Baltic campaign had added strategic and political insight to the impulsive brilliance that had been displayed at Cape St. Vincent and in Aboukir Bay. "Lord Nelson is an incomparable man," wrote Cuthbert Collingwood, who knew him so well, in summing up his qualities at this time: "Without much previous preparation of plan, he has the faculty of discovering advantages as they arise and the good judgement to turn them to his use. An enemy that commits a false step in his view is ruined."

There were unwelcome congratulations in a letter from Bath, where Fanny had been staying with his father and she now wrote: "I cannot be silent in the general joy throughout the kingdom. What my feelings are, your own good heart will tell you. Let me beg, nay, entreat you to believe no wife ever felt greater affection for a husband than I do, and, to the best of my knowledge, I have invariably done everything you desire. If I have omitted anything I am sorry for it ..." He did not reply. Formal congratulations came from St. Vincent but were not echoed in the streets for the British had not regarded the Danes as enemies for almost a thousand years. This was reflected at court, where it combined with royal displeasure at the national hero resuming his scandalous association with the Hamiltons. When Nelson called at St. James's Palace to pay his respects, King George simply asked: "Lord Nelson, do you get out?" Recounting this, Nelson remarked: "I was tempted to say, 'Sir, I have been out and come in again. Your Majesty has perhaps not heard of the Battle of Copenhagen?'"

CHAPTER X

Paradise Merton
(1801–2)

"I am quite Nelson mad for him again as an orator . . . in this his new
career . . . in the British Senate."
– Emma Hamilton to Sarah Nelson, in a letter written from Merton
Place, 4th November, 1801

"The gallant Lord Nelson, the terror of the French, the Spaniards and
the Danes, is now amusing himself with Sir William and Lady Hamilton
by *catching gudgeons* at Shepperton," reported *The Oracle* with a touch of
the mockery with which the press and the caricaturists greeted the hero
they were as ready to applaud. London was not a comfortable place for
the *Tria Juncta in Uno* in July, 1801, and they had left its hot streets and
gossip for the English countryside and the simple comfort of its inns:
first, for a few days at the Fox and Hounds at the foot of Box Hill in
Surrey, then moving to The Bush at Staines, where Sir William could
fish in the clear water of the Thames.

Even there they were unable to escape the pressures. Fanny had
written another loving letter, thanking her husband for "your very
handsome quarterly allowance . . . Accept my warmest, most affectionate
and grateful thanks. I could say more but my heart is too full . . ." His
father visited him on his way from Bath to Burnham Thorpe and it was
clear that he disapproved of his son's conduct and intended to maintain
his close relationship with Fanny.

At Staines, they were joined by his brother William and his family
with repeated hints that he use his influence to effect his promotion. A
friend of the party, Lord William Gordon, wrote a satirical ballad about
each one of them and the verse devoted to the Reverend William Nelson
ran:

> But, to return to this same worthy Vicar,
> Who loves, you say, good eating and good liquor,
> Know, lady, that it is our earnest wish,
> That we, ere long, may greet him – Lord Archbish . . .

Nelson was missing his solemn brother Maurice, in whom he could confide, and visited his widow "Blindy", at the neighbouring village of Laleham to make sure she was not in need. He had sent her £100 the day after landing at Yarmouth and written suggesting she stay at Maurice's house "with horse, whisky and keep every convenience to make your stay comfortable . . . Nothing, be assured shall be wanting to make your life as comfortable and cheerful as possible." The visit to his brother's house in Emma's company gave him a sudden vision of the domesticity he had missed and of what still might be; his dream of love in a Norfolk cottage or a sunlit retirement at Bronte were now replaced by pastoral bliss by the Thames. "Would to God I was with you at Laleham," he wrote to Emma later. "I shall never forget our happiness at that place." It had prompted a new ambition and he began to talk of buying a house, which would be his property but shared with Emma and her husband, for he was imagining her as the wifely home-maker that she was not and Fanny longed to be.

The one reminder of professional realities was the presence in the fishing party of an intelligent and lively naval officer, Captain Edward Parker, to whom Nelson had taken a liking in the Baltic and who had been granted leave from the command of a sloop to accompany him as aide-de-camp. The successor to his first favourite, William Hoste, in the rôle of the son he had never had, Parker, aged twenty-three, was also warm in his response declaring that "to call me a Nelsonite is more to me than making me a duke". So when, on 20th July, the holiday was interrupted by a summons from the Admiralty to report for orders, the two returned to London together and Nelson determined that, whatever duties now transpired, young Parker would accompany him.

London was gripped by a new alarm, fed by reports of troop-movements on the Continent. Since France had made peace with Austria by the Treaty of Lunéville in February and the Armed Neutrality of the North had broken up with the British foray into the Baltic and the assassination of Tsar Paul, Bonaparte could turn his full attention to his most implacable enemy, Great Britain. Now he was reported to be massing troops and landing-barges on the Channel coast for an invasion. Even if the French troop movements in the Pas de Calais and the Low Countries were only a threat they had the intended effect in England, where a typical newspaper report announced that the Lord Mayor of London had been told: "His Majesty's Ministers FULLY EXPECTED the French would attempt an IMMEDIATE DESCENT on this island." To appoint Nelson to command the hastily assembled counter-invasion forces was both a prudent act of public relations and a deterrent, for, as Lord St. Vincent told him, "how very important it is that the enemy should know that *you* are constantly opposed to him." It was as important to the British public to know that their hero, sword in hand, would be defending them not only against invasion but bloody revolutionaries and the guillotine. Yet, as a realist, the First Lord knew that, even without Nelson to oppose them, a successful invasion was unlikely and he concluded memorably: "I do not say that the French cannot come. I only say they cannot come by sea."

Other admirals would be involved: Graeme commanding at the Nore and Lutwidge, the boy Horatio's captain in the expedition to the Arctic twenty-eight years before, at the Downs roadstead off Deal. His own duty would be to command a sea-going Squadron on a Particular Service of frigates, brigs, bomb-ketches, floating batteries and an armada of small craft, and also to supervise the preparation of defences along the coast from Orfordness around the North Foreland to Beachy Head; this to include the mobilisation of the locally raised Sea Fencibles naval volunteers. Across the sea, he would be faced by one of the most able French commanders, Rear-Admiral Louis de la Touche-Tréville, charged, it was believed, with delivering those vast and invincible armies on to English beaches aboard hundreds of sloops, gunboats and barges assembled at ports from Flushing to Cherbourg. For Nelson the prospect was stimulating.

Attended by Captain Parker, Nelson returned to a nervous London where the worst forebodings had been confirmed by the reviewing of volunteer militia by the Prince of Wales in Hyde Park. After receiving his orders and meeting the Prime Minister, Henry Addington, before leaving to take up his command at Sheerness, he put his ideas on paper in a long memorandum written at his desk in London and entitled *Observations on the Defence of the Thames*:

Supposing London the object of surprise I am of opinion that the enemy's object *ought* to be the getting on shore as speedily as possible, for the dangers of a navigation of 48 hours appear to me an insurmountable objection to the rowing from Boulogne to the coast of Essex. It is therefore most probable ... that from Boulogne, Calais and even Havre, the enemy will try and land in Sussex, or the lower part of Kent; and from Dunkirk, Ostend and the other ports of Flanders to land on the coast of Essex or Suffolk ... I will suppose that 40,000 men are destined for this attack, or rather surprise, of London; 20,000 will land on the west side of Dover, 60 or 70 miles from London, and the same number on the east side: they are too knowing to let us have but one point of alarm for London. In very calm weather, they might row over in 12 hours ... If it is calm when the enemy row out, all our vessels and boats appointed to watch them must ... meet them as soon as possible ... If a breeze springs up, our ships are to deal *destruction*; no delicacy can be observed on this great occasion.

He speculated on covering operations by the enemy fleets and outlined possible dispositions for his own forces, concluding: "I feel confident that the fleets of the enemy will meet the same fate which has always attended them." That was what the Government, the Lords of the Admiralty and the crowds in the London streets wanted to be told, for the man they had mocked had become the focus of their national identity and their will to prevail.

On 27th July, Nelson hoisted his flag in the *Unité* – a frigate captured from the French – at Sheerness and at once, noted Parker, "He gave orders for 30 of the ships under his command, made everyone pleased, filled them with emulation and set them all on the *qui vive*". Almost immediately he sailed for the great anchorage of the Downs between the Goodwin Sands and the Kentish coast and shifted his flag to another frigate, the *Medusa*. He was in a state of excitement at the prospect of action, the thought of Emma being so tantalizingly close and from the volume of correspondence which reached him each day, including many in her exuberant scrawl and the newspapers she sent him. "I have receiv'd, I believe, every letter and paper," he wrote to her. "Never ask the question, do they bore me? *All* others do most damnably. Yesterday I receiv'd more than one hundred ... " He replied to these punctiliously in his crabbed left-handed writing until, he said: "My hand aches before night comes." His attitude to public acclaim was ambivalent, as Lord St. Vincent had noted, and he wrote from his ship: "Fifty boats, I am told, are rowing about her this moment to have a look at the one-armed man" and declared "Oh! how I hate to be stared at."

When there was an enemy within reach, he could not rest at anchor and on 1st August, the third anniversary of the Battle of the Nile, he made sail for the French coast to "look into Boulogne". Nor was it only a look at the line of 24 brigs, luggers and gunboats anchored across the harbour mouth, the thickets of masts within and the coastal batteries being built; he sent his bomb-ketches close inshore to lob a dozen shells at them before a falling wind obliged him to call them off for fear of being becalmed. Again he was exulting in activity and, while still lying off the town, wrote brief reports to St. Vincent and Admiral Lutwidge, telling them both: "Boulogne is certainly not a very pleasant place this morning."

Despite this brush with the enemy and the prospect of further action, he was missing Emma desperately and on this anniversary wrote to her, "So many things rush into my mind that I am really this day very low indeed. Even Parker could not help noticing it by saying, 'On this day you should be cheerful'. But who can tell what passes in my mind? Yes, you can; for I believe you are feeling as I do. When I was in the battle perhaps I did not feel so strongly our separation, or whether being at sea makes it appear more terrible, for terrible it is. My heart is ready to flow out of my eyes ... " Then he grew calmer and could sign: " 'Tis but a life of sorrow and sadness. But, *patienza per forza*!" Becoming practical, he urged Emma to take lodgings at Dover, Deal or Margate so that they could meet and he was also looking forward to the house he hoped to buy. Emma had been looking at properties suitable for a gentleman of means and had suggested one at Turnham Green near Chiswick. "I hope you will get the house," he told her. "If I buy, no person can say – this shall or not be altered; and you shall have the whole arrangement."

He had planned a reconnaissance of Flushing but contrary winds and a directive from the Admiralty brought him back across the Channel to Margate to put some order and enthusiasm into the Sea Fencibles. These volunteers were terrified of being pressed into sea service on board warships and of the 2,600 who had enrolled along the stretches of coast under Nelson's command, only 285 had agreed to service at sea, even in coastal waters. So he had to assure their commanding officers that they "shall not be sent off the Coast of the Kingdom, shall be kept as near their own homes as the nature of the service will admit and that the moment the alarm of the threatened invasion is over, that every man shall be returned to their own homes". This was not the spirit to which he was accustomed and he added sharply: "I flatter myself that at a moment when all the volunteer corps in the Kingdom are come forward to defend our land, the seamen of Great Britain will not be slow to defend their own proper element and maintain as pure as our glorious ancestors have transmitted it to us, our undoubted right to the Sovereignty of the Narrow Seas, on which no Frenchman has yet *dared* to sail with impunity."

Even if the longshoremen and fishermen were wary, he was not going to disappoint the nation and he drew up plans for something far more dramatic than a bombardment. Believing that the main invasion force would be more likely to sail from Flushing he proposed an amphibious attack on the port which he would assault with 5,000 troops. When St. Vincent decided that the currents and sandbanks of the Scheldt estuary were too dangerous, he proposed another attack on Boulogne with the aim of "cutting out" the French ships moored off-shore "until the whole flotilla be either taken, or totally annihilated". His plan was for a night attack as at Tenerife. Then there had been no need for a rear-admiral to lead the landing-parties; now his instinct would put him at the head of his men, sword in hand, but for thoughts of Emma, whose worries for his safety influenced him more than Fanny's once had. Two days before he planned to attack, he wrote to her: "Your dear friend Nelson cannot but cheer up Fair Emma, Good Emma, Great Emma, Virtuous Emma and my own dear friend Emma cheer up. The services on this coast are not necessary for the personal exertions of a vice-admiral; therefore I hope that will make your dear, good, friendly heart easy. You would naturally *hate* me if I kept back when I ought to go forward. Never fear, that shall not be said of me."

His plan now was that fifty-seven boats – big, lugger-rigged flat-boats armed with howitzers or carronades and boats from the ships of his squadron – would be formed into four divisions each under the command of a captain, one of them Edward Parker. The main force was to launch a surprise frontal attack on the moored ships – the sailors boarding with cutlasses, pikes and tomahawks; the marines with musket and bayonet – while two boats from each division pulled through the enemy line to cut their cables. Any prizes that could not be brought out to sea were to be burned. The password amongst the boats was to be "Nelson"; the answer, "Bronte".

The attack was planned for the night of 15th August but that day, as the *Medusa* led the flotilla down-Channel towards Boulogne, Nelson's concentration strayed and he wrote to Emma:

> From my heart I wish you could find me out a good comfortable house, I should hope to be able to purchase it. At this moment, I can command only £3,000; as to asking Sir William, I could not do it; I would sooner beg. Is the house at Chiswick furnished? If not, you may fairly calculate £2,000 for furniture ... As you may believe, my dear Emma, my mind feels at which is going forward this night; it is one thing to order and arrange an attack and another to execute it. But, I assure you, I have taken much more precaution for others, than if I was to go myself ... After they have fired their guns, if one half of the French do not jump overboard and swim on shore, I will venture to be hanged ... If our people behave as I expect, our loss cannot be much. My fingers itch to be at them. What place would you like to come to, Margate or Deal?

Amidst such diversions, he under-estimated both his opponent and the problems of the narrows, where the tides ran strong. At Boulogne, La Touche-Tréville knew that such an attack was almost inevitable, a supposition supported by reports from the spies, smugglers and fishermen who traded in scraps of intelligence along both shores of the Channel. He left his line of twenty-four ships moored across the mouth of the harbour and, so that they could not be boarded, ordered that heavy nets be hoisted from their bulwarks to their yard-arms after dark and, so that they could not be moved, moored with cables of chain instead of hemp which could be cut by boarding-parties' axes and each craft fastened to the next with chains. Finally, he put aboard several hundred soldiers as well as sailors and guns' crews, so that each was defended with both musketry and grapeshot.

The British boats were manned at half-past ten that night. Half an hour later, when the four divisions were ranged astern of their commanders' boats, each loosely roped to the next, Nelson ordered six lanterns to be hung over the side of the *Medusa* as the signal to pull for shore. Swallowed by the darkness, the boats were swept towards their enemies by the set of the current which bore some more swiftly than others. As at Tenerife, the assault force was dispersed, lost contact and any hope of co-ordination. Of the four divisions, Parker's found the enemy first when an anchored brig, flying a commodore's pendant and veiled in netting, appeared in the gloom. Ordering the nearest boats to follow, Parker made for her; himself standing in the bows, sword drawn, at the head of his men. A blast of grapeshot and musketry cut through them and the survivors scrambled up the ship's sides to be enmeshed in the netting. The decks were crowded with soldiers and the British struggling at the nets were thrust back by bayonets.

While Parker's own boats drifted away, full of dead and wounded, the rest of his division ran alongside another brig moored nearby and they, too, were beaten off; but they managed to board and take a lugger, only to find that she was moored by chains and could not be towed away. Another division attacked farther along the French line and was beaten back; a third, swept past Boulogne by the tide, could not attack for another three hours; then took a brig, found that she was immovable, and, when daylight came, was driven off by gunfire from other French ships and the shore. The last division was carried so far past its objective that it never went into action and eventually returned to Nelson's squadron waiting out at sea.

It was a decisive defeat. Nothing had been accomplished and the cost was heavy with forty-four killed and 126 wounded in the boats. When what was euphemistically described as "boat-work" or "service hand-to-hand" miscarried, as it had at Tenerife and now off Boulogne, the cost was likely to be high in young officers of zeal and promise. As the boats came alongside the *Medusa*, it was learned that eighteen had been killed or wounded – among the latter, Captain Parker – as well as 172 seamen and marines.

There were no excuses to be made and the admiral at once sat down by the curved row of windows in his cabin across the stern of the frigate and wrote to the First Lord of the Admiralty: "I am sorry to tell you that I have not succeeded in bringing out or destroying the enemy's flotilla moored in the mouth of the harbour of Boulogne. The most astonishing bravery was evinced by many of our officers and men ... We have lost upwards of 100 killed and wounded ... Dear little Parker, his thigh very much shattered; I have fears for his life."

That night the British ships anchored off Deal and the wounded were sent ashore to hospital, the less serious cases to lodging-houses. For his own two particular friends, Parker and Lieutenant Frederick Langford, his flag lieutenant in the *Medusa*, Nelson rented rooms in a little three-storey house in Middle Street which could be reached quickly through an alley between the sea-front houses from the beach, where the squadron's boats put them ashore. "How is it possible for me ever to be sufficiently thankful for all his attentions!" wrote young Parker to Emma Hamilton. "He is now attending me with the most parental kindness; comes to me at six in the morning and ten at night; both late and early his kindness is alike ... I would lose a dozen limbs to serve him." Both young officers, resting in rooms to either side of the hall of the little house and so able to converse and share visitors, seemed likely to recover. The funerals of other young officers killed in the attack had been held at Deal watched by crowds assembled to watch the nation's hero following the coffins with tears on his lined cheeks.

Nelson was frustrated by his realisation that an attack on Flushing was impracticable when he crossed the North Sea to assess the problems for himself ("I long to pay them for their tricks t'other day, the debt of a drubbing, which surely I'll pay," he wrote to Emma, "but *when, where* or *how* it is impossible ... for me, or mortal man, to say.") His lover's absence was also frustrating and, for that, he blamed St. Vincent and Troubridge, believing that his appointment to a sea command had been a means of keeping him away from the Hamiltons. To a degree, he could accept the First Lord's reasoning that "the public mind is so very much tranquillis'd by your being at your post, it is extremely desirable that you should continue there ... Let me entreat your Lordship to ... give up, at least for the present, your intention of returning to town." So the brunt of the blame was borne by his old friend and former subordinate, Troubridge: "It is all his doing, my not coming to London."

So he continued to plead with Emma to visit him at Deal: "The Three Kings, I am told, is the best house (it stands on the beach) if the noise of constant surf does not disturb you ... Your interest with Sir William is requested to come and see a poor forlorn sailor." It would, he wrote, invoking the plight of the wounded, "be a charity to me and Parker and Langford and I hope you would benefit by the jaunt. You can bathe in the sea that will make you strong and well ... I hate the Downs but if my friends come it will be a paradise."

He had put a brave face on the disaster at Boulogne but there was criticism about and even a clumsy attempt at blackmail when a letter from a stranger arrived threatening to publish an exposure of his misman-agement of the attack unless he paid the writer £100. This brought the sharp retort: "Very likely I am unfit for my present command ... but you will, I trust, be punished for threatening my character. But I have not been brought up in the school of fear and therefore care not what you do. I defy you and your malice." There were jokes told in the wardrooms of the fleet, some of them double-edged, and one was printed in the *Naval Chronicle*, his favourite reading, about two Greenwich naval pensioners discussing the failure at Boulogne. "I say, Ben," one was supposed to have said, "do you know who this Bronte is that Nelson has got hold on?" "No, I don't; all I can say is that he is a d——d fool, begging his pardon, for *taking a partner*, for, depend on it, nobody will ever do so well as Nelson himself." There was also blame implied that he had not himself accompanied the boats and a pensioner was quoted as saying, "You see this last business; tho' I daresay everything was done that could be done without him – had he gone in, the boats, the chains and all would have come out along with him." Instead of the customary anthem of praise, the *Naval Chronicle* had printed a single verse:

> Exult not, France, that NELSON's vengeful blow,
> Has not, as usual, thy destruction gain'd;
> Say what you will, this truth the world must know,
> Altho' unconquer'd, you were left enchain'd.

Relief came with the realisation of a dream: Emma had found him a house. It was at Merton, a village to the south-west of London, and although it was not near the Thames, the river Wandle ran past its garden; it was only an hour's ride from the Admiralty and convenient for the Portsmouth road. Trusting her judgement, he agreed to buy without asking for more information than the price, which was £9,000. "I approve of the house at Merton," he wrote to her on 20th August, "and as the Admiralty are so cruel ... as Troubridge and the Earl are so cruel as to object to my coming to London to manage my own matters, I must beg and entreat you to work hard for me." A week later, on his return from the reconnaissance of the approaches to Flushing, he was back at Deal and writing to his lawyer William Haslewood about payment for the house: he could afford £3,000 at once, the rest payable in two instalments within three years. Above all, he insisted on paying the asking price to avoid risk of another snatching his prize. "The place I wish much to have

37 *Above*: The victor of Copenhagen. A confident Lord Nelson shown holding a letter to Rear-Admiral Thomas Graves, his second-in-command, painted in 1823 by James Northcote.

38 *Below*: The battle with "the brothers of Englishmen, the Danes", as Nelson wrote. The Battle of Copenhagen painted from eye-witness accounts by Nicholas Pocock, himself a former sea-captain and war artist.

39 *Above left*: The Earl St. Vincent – formerly Admiral Sir John Jervis – was both warm-hearted friend and stern superior officer at sea and at the Admiralty, and came to trust Nelson's mercurial flair.

40 *Above right*: Captain William Hoste was Nelson's first and favourite protégé and served on board his ship until the Battle of the Nile. He was sent on a diplomatic mission just before Trafalgar.

41 *Below left*: Vice-Admiral Cuthbert Collingwood was Nelson's most intimate naval friend, following him in command of ships from their first meeting in the Caribbean as young captains until he succeeded Nelson in command of the fleet after Trafalgar; here painted by Henry Howard.

42 *Below right*: Captain Thomas Hardy, later First Sea Lord, was Nelson's flag-captain for most of the time from the Battle of the Nile to Trafalgar, when he was with him in the final hours; painted in 1809 by Domenico Pellegrini.

43 *Above left*: The Earl of Minto – formerly Sir Gilbert Elliot – was typical of Nelson's civilian friends: shrewd, generous and amusing; they had met in the Mediterranean. Here painted by Sir Thomas Lawrence.

44 *Above right*: Alexander Davison was Nelson's close adviser ashore, persuading him to abandon his hopeless courtship in Quebec; finally becoming his prize-agent. This engraving is after a portrait by Lemuel Abbott.

45 *Below left*: Abraham Goldsmid, a rich and generous Jewish financier, was Nelson's neighbour at Merton Place from 1801. Detail from a portrait by Robert Dighton. A loyal friend, Goldsmid helped support Emma Hamilton after Trafalgar; he committed suicide after a financial disaster in 1810.

46 *Below right*: James Perry, editor of the *Morning Chronicle*, was another neighbour at Merton and was tactful in reporting Nelson's relationship with the Hamiltons; an engraving from a portrait by Abraham Wivell.

47 *Above*: Paradise attained. Merton Place, the country house that Emma Hamilton found for Nelson in Surrey and converted into the home for which he had longed, combined the farm of his fantasies with a shrine to his achievements. It was demolished in 1846 and now nothing remains.

48 *Below*: Paradise unattained. The Castello di Maniace at Bronte, Sicily, presented to Nelson by the grateful King Ferdinand in 1799. Nelson had seeds and garden tools taken to Sicily by Captain Hoste and the garden laid out by John Graefer, who had planned the English Garden at Caserta. He hoped to retire there with Emma and Horatia, their daughter.

and, sailor-like, a few pounds more or less is no object," he wrote. "I never knew much got by hard bargains. I trust to you doing the needful and quickly. I approve of the gentleman's plan that went to see an estate, bought it as it stood, dinner on table; the former owner sat as his guest." Unable to resist involving himself in the detail of creating reality out of his fantasy, he was writing to a London removals and storage contractor, recommended by Alexander Davison, called Dodds of Brewer Street in Soho, making preliminary arrangements and adding "I shall probably employ you very soon".

The sea was rough, even in the Downs, and Nelson was complaining, "I am so dreadfully seasick that I cannot hold up my head!"; and "How I hate going to sea ... I am damned sick of the sea." But further relief was to hand because the Hamiltons had decided to visit Deal, as he had hoped, and bring with them Sarah Nelson, wife of his brother William. She had become a willing confidante for Emma's monologues, declarations of adoration for their hero and railings against poor Fanny and Josiah Nisbet, whom they had nicknamed "Tom Tit" and "the Cub".

Emma had usurped Fanny's responsibilities for the parson's school-age children: Horatio, who was at Eton, and Charlotte, whose education had been supervised by Fanny at Whitelands House in Chelsea, where, her father was gratified to find, "the attention paid to the health and *morals* of the young ladies *unequalled* by any other school in or near London". She further strengthened her hold on the family by declaring a passionate interest in William's future prospects; "Hang the Ministers – *shame to them* – for letting Lord Nelson's brother be a slave in a little country parsonage house, when at least he ought to be in the palace of Lambeth for to pay Lord Nelson and his family for the great and important services he has rendered his country. He ought to be a duke greater than Marlborough, you an archbishop, his father with a title ... your children both in the title and all his sisters and their children's children for ever-lasting provided for ..." Flattered by such attention, Sarah Nelson was delighted to accompany the Hamiltons to the Three Kings inn, where Nelson had reserved three rooms linked by a gallery. "Sir William, Mrs. Nelson and I are going down to Deal to see Milord and our dear, glorious friends Parker and Langford also," Emma told William. "Could you not come to Deal with us? Lord, that would be nice, as the children say ... Tom Tit has been in town, I heard, and Mrs. Nelson a few days ago saw, *met* the Cub, but he looked as if he was going to be hanged, but did not speak to her. The precious couple are fit for each other."

When Nelson returned from sea at the end of August, he found the Hamiltons and Sarah waiting for him. Much as Emma disliked "this dreary place" where the North Sea gales howled through the narrow alleys and rattled the windows, she rose to the occasion when Nelson came ashore, relieved to see that, despite his customary protestations of ill-health, "he is grown so fat and looks so well since he drinks porter". Having taken possession again, she was determined to keep him from danger and wrote to William: "I can only say we are as happy as possible with our dear, invaluable Nelson. He will go soon again on the coast of France but I *hope* and *believe* not to fight for I tremble for him, but I think Sir William has made an impression on him not to risk his dear, precious life without *greatest* necessity."

Meanwhile Sarah Nelson was happily engaged in the tasks of a lady-in-waiting. "My lady call'd me this morning soon after six to go to bathe and a very fine dip we had; our maids do the same," she recorded. "I am now just come from making breakfast." Both ladies had begun visiting the wounded Edward Parker and Frederick Langford at their lodgings and Sarah wrote brightly: "We went yesterday to drink tea with poor Parker and Langford. They are both in good spirits and Langford will soon be well but God knows when poor Parker will. All we can do is pray for him; at present he does not suffer much pain." But the young man's thigh-bone had been shattered, and gangrene was suspected and amputation of the leg might be necessary.

The party at the Three Kings became frequent visitors, usually twice a day, chatting over cups of tea, suggesting suitable diets – port wine and jelly was ordered – and Emma arranged for a sofa to be moved into the little house for the time when they could leave their beds. Nelson often accompanied them and young Parker was overcome by such attention describing him to Emma as "my friend, my nurse, my attendant, my patron, my protector". The visits could leave him exhausted but he wrote gallantly in a letter to Sarah Nelson's son Horatio at school:

> The medical attendants are angry with me at my having so much company and say it does me harm. But I think it contributes to do me good for I am sure that if they were not to come, and that very often, and I knew they were here, I should pine myself to death. This is the longest letter I have written for writing is rather tiresome to me, which you will believe when I tell you that I lie upon my back the whole time.

Soon after, it was decided that the only hope of saving his life was to amputate the gangrenous leg close to the hip and early in September Emma wrote to William Nelson: "Poor dear little Parker had his thigh taken off and what he suffered is not to be described ... The operation was long, painful and difficult ... his groans were heard far off. If Nelson had been his father, he could not have suffered more ... the leg and thigh was buried in the grave with Gore and Bristow, the two mids. that died on the glorious and brave attack."

On 20th September, the Hamiltons and Mrs. Nelson departed for London, the journey making it seem more distant than it was because of bad roads that sometimes slowed the coach to walking-pace. Nelson was left aboard his new flagship, the frigate *Amazon*, anchored off-shore, miserable at her departure and the sharp deterioration of Edward Parker's condition since the amputation. He wrote:

> Although I ought to feel grateful for Sir William, you and Mrs. Nelson's goodness in coming to see a poor forlorn creature at Deal, yet I feel at this moment only the pain of your leaving me, to which is added the miserable situation of our dear excellent little Parker. It can hardly be said that he lives at this moment and before night will probably be out of this world, and, if real worth and honour have a claim to Divine favour, surely he stands a fair chance of happiness in that which is to come.

Throughout the following week, as hopes and fears for Parker alternated, Nelson refused to take his ship to sea and wrote frequent bulletins for Emma. On the 27th, he wrote to her:

> I had intended to have gone on shore this morning to have seen dear Parker but the accounts of him are so very bad that the sight of his misery, poor fellow, would have so much affected me and, if he had been in his senses, must have given him pain that I have given up the idea unless he feels better and expresses a wish to see me ... I slept not a wink all night and am today very low and miserable ... but he will soon be at a place of rest, free from all the folly of this world.

At this point Nelson was interrupted in his writing by a boat from shore coming alongside and his flag-captain, Samuel Sutton, entering the cabin. When they had spoken, he continued writing; "Sutton is returned. Dear Parker left this world for a better at 9 o'clock; I believe we ought to thank God. He suffered much and can suffer no more." He finished the letter and added a postscript: "My heart is almost broke and I see I have wrote nonsense; I know not what I am doing." The funeral was held next day, beginning at noon when minute-guns began to thud from the *Amazon* and the shore battery and muffled drums, swagged with crape, began to beat. The procession, led by two hundred men of the Derbyshire Regiment, marching with reversed arms, moved down the straight street to the red brick church of St. George. Six captains bore the coffin on their shoulders and Admiral Nelson followed, weeping. At the graveside, he steadied himself with his hand on a tree-trunk in an

attitude of grief that remained in the memories of the mourners. He had
kept a lock of "dear Parker's hair, which I value more than if he had left
me a bulse of diamonds". A basket of fruit sent to the young man by
Emma was given to Langford.

All had turned to ashes, it seemed. The Admiralty refused to pay for
Parker's lodgings or his funeral; "he might have stunk above ground, or
been thrown in a ditch" wrote Nelson to Emma, telling her that he had
paid these bills – amounting to nearly £200 – himself. The young man's
father had arrived at Deal but proved a grotesque opposite to his son,
cadging money and prompting Nelson's comment that he was "a very
different person from his son. He has £72 more in his pocket than when
he came to Deal. I wish for his own sake that his conduct had been more
open and generous, like mine to him; but never mind."

There was only the consolation that he had ensured Edward Parker –
unlike so many young officers – remembrance in the reflection of his
patron's fame. A whole page of verse was accorded him in the *Naval
Chronicle*:

> Why does the voice of public sorrow swell;
> Why pours the gallant breast that manly sigh;
> Why does the tear of gen'rous anguish dwell
> On NELSON's cheek and dim his ardent eye?
>
> One simple word the mighty grief will speak,
> 'Tis PARKER's death that breathes the gen'ral gloom,
> That strikes the living glow from Beauty's cheek,
> The flow'r of valour wither'd in its bloom.

There would be other young officers for Nelson to cherish like sons and,
even as he mourned, he wrote to a Mr. Derse, who supplied him with
telescopes: "Send me down directly a two-foot glass covered with black
leather. It is a present for the signal midshipman of this ship."

There were also worries about Merton as he was anguished at having
to leave the problems to Emma, Davison and Haslewood while he paced a
gale-blown deck off the coast of Kent. One problem was an appalling
surveyor's report on the house, which was described as "an old paltry,
small dwelling of low storeys and very slightly built"; it was in a poor state
of repair and the garden and grounds "worn and out of condition"; it
possessed "not the least privacy as a place for pleasure" and, the surveyor
concluded, "it is altogether the worst place, under all circumstances, that
I ever saw pretending to suit a gentleman's family". Moreover the price
and the cost of furnishing would swallow all of his £10,000 capital and,
even if Sir William shared the running costs, he would be living beyond

his means. Yet there was no going back now and no alternative to the dream so nearly within his grasp and he wrote to Davison: "I am after buying a little farm at Merton ... if I cannot, after all my labour for the Country, get such a place as this, I am resolved to give it all up and retire for life."

Yet the romantic dream of life with Emma in his own house had become his one hope of happiness. There were sudden panics that the Prince of Wales might descend upon Merton before his arrival and seduce Emma; or that he would be cheated over the furnishings he had agreed to buy; then would come thoughts of escape to Bronte, beyond reach of gossip or treachery. "I am sure you will not let any of Royal blood into your house; they have the impudence of the devil," he wrote to her. "Let us turn our thoughts to the dear farm ... Take care I am not cheated ... *poco poco* we can get rid of bad furniture and buy others; and all will probably go to Bronte one of these days. I shall certainly go there whenever we get peace." Indeed Captain Hoste was under orders to take his frigate to Sicily, as he told his family, with a cargo of "ploughs, harrows and garden stuff for my ever-respected patron Lord Nelson".

Guilt over his desertion of Fanny had been joined by that for the death of young Parker for he was still conscious of whispering behind his back and at the end of September he wrote frankly to Evan Nepean, the Secretary of the Admiralty:

A diabolical spirit is still at work. Every means, even to posting up papers in the streets of Deal, has been used to set the seamen against being sent by Lord Nelson to be butchered, and that at Margate it was the same thing, whenever any boats went on shore, '*What*, are you going to be slaughtered again?' Even this might be got over, but the subject has been fully discussed in the wardrooms, midshipmen's berths, etc ... as I must probably be, from all the circumstances I have stated, not much liked by either officers or men, I really think it would be better to take me from this Command.

The Admiralty realised, however, that, despite this setback, Nelson remained a deterrent to the French and a reassurance to the British, so in the narrow seas he would remain. But the war seemed to be petering out: France had made peace with Austria in February; the British had landed in Egypt in March and destroyed the French army on the shores of Aboukir Bay, where Nelson's victory had marooned it; Nelson's success at Copenhagen in April had hastened the collapse of the Armed Neutrality of the North; now, at the beginning of October, negotiations for a settlement between France and Britain were being discussed. Nelson felt that he had been deliberately isolated in his sea-tossed frigate, banished from the pleasures that were now his due. For this he still blamed Troubridge. "He ought to have recollected that I got him the medal of the Nile," he wrote to her. "Who brought his character into notice? Nelson, that he now lords it over. So much for gratitude. I forgive him but, by God, I shall not forget it ... I have been so rebuffed that my spirits are gone and the Great Troubridge has what we called cowed the Spirits of Nelson."

He was comforted by a word of support from his own hero, William Pitt, who had resigned as Prime Minister in March over the King's opposition to his plans for Roman Catholic emancipation in Ireland and had been succeeded by Addington; now he was staying nearby at Walmer Castle. The two exchanged calls and admiration was mutual: Nelson describing "Billy", who was a year his junior, with some awe as "that great man"; Pitt supporting his grievance against the Admiralty ("He thinks it very hard to keep me now all is over"). As to the new administration's agreement to terms for peace with France, Nelson was aghast: Britain was to return all conquered territories to France, Spain and Holland, except Ceylon and Trinidad, and Malta to the Knights of St. John; France was to do little more than accept the resumption of Ottoman rule in Egypt and withdraw from Naples and the Papal States. He put his own view bluntly: "Although it is peace, I wish all Frenchmen to the devil." Emma saw it as a missed opportunity, telling Sarah Nelson: "You have not an idea what a sensation the peace has been. If we could have had an idea, we might have made £30,000 by stock-jobbing."

At last a date for an official end of hostilities was announced and Nelson was told that, although he must leave his flag flying in the Downs, he could go ashore on 22nd October. In a high state of anticipation and still fussing about his health ("My cold is still very troublesome; I cannot get my bowels in order; in the night I had a little fever," he wrote to Emma), he was overwhelmed with relief. Delight followed when a letter arrived from Sir William, who together with Emma and her mother, had, on his instructions, taken up residence at Merton Place. He wrote:

We have now inhabited Your Lordship's premises some days and I can now speak with some certainty. I have lived with our dear Emma several years. I know her merits, have a great opinion of the head and heart that God Almighty has been pleased to give her; but a seaman alone could have given a fine woman full power to choose and fit up a residence for him without seeing it himself. You are in luck, for, in my conscience, I verily believe that a place so suitable to your views could not have been found ... You have nothing but to come and enjoy immediately. You have a good mile of pleasant dry walk around your farm. It would make you laugh to see Emma and her mother fitting up pig-sties and hen-coops and already the canal is enlivened with ducks and the cock is strutting with his hens about the walks. Your Lordship's plan as to stocking the canal with fish is exactly mine. I will answer for it, that in a few months you may command a good dish of fish at a moment's warning.

Nelson was impatient to start strutting about the walks himself but there were a few more days to wait. His imagination was ahead of him and in his daily letters to Emma he wrote a succession of instructions, questions and exhortations. "You are to be, recollect, Lady Paramount of all the territories and waters of Merton and we are all to be your guests and to obey all lawful commands," he declared, then switching to practicalities: "I admire the pigs and poultry. Sheep are certainly most beneficial to eat off the grass ... I intend to have a farming book. I am glad to hear you get fish; not very good ones, I fancy. It is, thank God, only six days before I shall be with you and to be shown all the beauties of Merton"; "Have we a nice church at Merton? We will set an example of goodness to the under-parish"; "We will eat plain, but will have good wine, good fires and a hearty welcome for all our friends, but none of the great shall enter our peaceful abode. I hate them all."

It was to be a private world, set apart even from present loyalties for, he wrote, "The Peace seems to make no impression of joy on our seamen; rather the contrary, they appear to reflect that they will go from plenty to poverty. We must take care not to be beset by them at Merton, for every beggar will find out your soft heart and get into your house." His home would be a pastoral and aquatic paradise for Emma had jokingly talked of the ornamental canal as The Nile and they would have a boat upon it and he delighted in the idea: "How I should laugh to see you, my dear friend, rowing in a boat: the beautiful Emma rowing a one-armed Admiral in a boat! It will certainly be caricatured. Well done, farmer's wife!" The last letter was written on 21st October, as full of enthusiasm as a schoolboy's on the last day of term.

He had ordered one of the long, narrow Deal galleys, with a high freeboard needed to run on to the beach through surf, to take him ashore next morning in preference to his own barge; if the surf was too heavy he would land at Ramsgate pier. He almost relished his last day of misery: "This place is the devil's for dreadful colds and I don't believe I should get well all the winter, for both cough and bowels are very much out of order ... You are now writing your last letter for Deal; so am I, for Merton, from Deal: at least, I hope so ... I shall never get warm again, I believe. I cannot feel the pen." Another touch of pastoral sentimentality followed: "I expect that all animals will increase where you are, for I never

expect you will suffer any to be killed." Then, despite his professed
contempt for politicians and the powerful, he looked forward to his return
to the House of Lords as a viscount, who had at last been granted royal
sanction to use the title Duke of Bronte: "Has Mrs. Cadogan got my
Peer's robe? for I must ... have it altered to a Viscount's." Next morning,
he jumped from the bow of a Deal galley on to the shingle at Deal and
boarded a coach for London and Merton.

In Surrey, the curious *ménage* that was about to envelop him waited
with eager anticipation: the Hamiltons, Mrs. Cadogan and his fourteen-
year-old niece, Charlotte, who was on holiday from the school in Chelsea,
which Fanny had chosen for her but who had now, like her parents,
William and Sarah, transferred her affection to Emma. The allure of
their welcome drew him through London without lingering; past St.
Paul's, vast on the skyline of rooftops; through empty streets lit by
wavering oil-lamps, across the river by Westminster Bridge and through
the prosperous suburb of Lambeth. Then, as the sky lightened, past new
flat-fronted brick terraces and comfortable houses standing with their
stables amongst market-gardens and dairyfarms. Then the carriage
bowled along the country road, through the villages of Balham and
Tooting; past inns and an occasional church tower rising above a clump
of trees. He was heading south-west, as if for the Portsmouth road,
leaving the low plateau on which Wimbledon stood and its common
spread, until he reached a village of some hundred and fifty houses and
cottages and eight hundred people. This was Merton but when the
coachman asked him the way to his house he did not know. He had
arrived earlier than expected and there was no crowd to greet him, and,
on this occasion, show him the way home.

At Merton Place, the household was up early and, as Charlotte Nelson
told her mother in Norfolk, was taken by surprise. "My dear uncle
arrived safe here this morning at eight o'clock," she wrote. "He looks
very well and is much pleased with Merton. The Volunteers we expect
every moment. We have had some people firing and they came in and saw
my uncle; he spoke to them and they seemed so happy to see him. The
horses were to have been taken out of his carriage and the people to have
dragged him to Merton but they were all disappointed as my uncle came
before they expected him ... " A postscript was added by an exultant
Emma: "He was here by eight o'clock and travelled all night and only
came on shore yesterday ... He is better than I expected in looks ... We
are all so joyous today, we do not know what to do. Believe me, my heart is
all convulsed seeing him again *safe on shore*, safely *moored with me* – I must
not say *me*."

He was at once conducted on a tour of the house and grounds. Merton

Place was a small, dignified residence with a façade and pediment in the Palladian taste standing on the eastern outskirts of the village and facing the road which divided its garden from more land lying on the north side. Emma had worked hard at creating both a comfortable, cheerful house and an approximation to "the farm" of his dreams: "There are cows now and greenhouse plants," she had noted. Although small by the standards of gentlemen's residences around the more fashionable villages of Richmond, Twickenham and Wimbledon, the rooms were spacious and Emma planned to make them seem more so with glass doors opening on to the garden and doors faced with mirror-glass into the reception rooms. Outside, the principal feature of the garden was "the Nile", the ornamental canal spanned by a bridge leading the drive to the north front; otherwise there were lawns, ornamental trees and some statuary which Nelson and Sir William decided were not up to their Classical standards and should be removed. On the far side of the road – and to be linked with a brick-built subway – were the stables, shrubberies and an artificial mound commanding a view over the flat countryside to either side of the little river Wandle and a distant prospect of low Surrey hills. As one delight after another was shown, he could only exclaim, "Is this, too, mine?"

At last the tour was over, the welcoming worthies gone and Emma could write contentedly: "Lord Nelson is delighted with Merton ... It was quite affecting to see the manner our Hero was received ... Now we are got quiet and comfortable." The new owner of Merton Place quickly settled into a household that was reminiscent of both the Parsonage at Burnham Thorpe and the Palazzo Sessa. There were more celebrations and Charlotte admired "some very fine fireworks, which, falling into the water, had a very beautiful effect". On Sunday they all drove to the little Norman church of St. Mary, almost a mile away on the far side of the village, where Nelson was gratified by his niece's attentions, turning the pages of his prayer-book for him and helping him with his top-coat. She gloried in the romantic household and wrote excited commentaries to her mother, sometimes with footnotes added by her uncle or Emma. "Lady and Sir William Hamilton, Lord Nelson, Mrs. Cadogan and myself are just returned from church," she wrote on Sunday. "I had been fishing with Sir William and caught some carp"; to this Nelson added, "For carp read pike. We caught three very fine fish". On another day she described a singing lesson she had been given by an Italian music-master and continued: "Lady Hamilton is now singing. My uncle was so very good as to give me a diamond ring. It is so beautiful. Indeed I am so proud of it that I am always looking at it. Lady Hamilton was so good as to choose it for me." To this, Emma had added the postscript, "You must not think

Charlotte's diamond ring much but it is pretty ... It is a little, single diamond and well set."

Nelson found Charlotte "very much improved ... in every respect a very charming girl". He had further endeared himself to her before the end of the school term by asking the headmistress of the Chelsea school, Miss Veitch, to give the girls a day's holiday. Charlotte had written to her mother, "Miss Veitch gave us apple pies, also custard and then negus to drink my uncle's health. Miss Veitch gave us the toast, it was, 'Lord Nelson – may his future years be as happy as his past have been glorious.' How proud I am to have the approbation of my most glorious, victorious, virtuous uncle ... "

There were, however, worries about her brother, who was being bullied at Eton presumably because his name was also Horatio Nelson and the affair of his uncle and Lady Hamilton was again the butt of adolescent humour and also because as his uncle's male heir he might one day become Duke of Bronte. "It would be worse for him now than ever for the great boys would take more liberty with him, knowing what he would one day have," wrote Nelson and asked his brother to move him to lodgings so that he could attend as a day-boy, the excuse being that he could then take outside tuition in foreign languages: "As it is very necessary that my nephew Horatio Nelson should learn French and Italian and for his future prospects in life, I have to request that you will do me the favour to remove him from the foundation of the school to be an Oppidan and you will much oblige me."

His two closest blood-relations were, however, missing. The infant Horatia was still with her nurse in London and his father was also absent. This, together with a correspondence that had begun while his son was still at sea, could cast a cold shadow over the glow of happiness and self-regard at Merton. The problem was Fanny: she and Edmund Nelson had always been close, despite his occasional irritation with her fussiness and he still treated her as his daughter-in-law. Edmund had long believed "not that it is the province of a father to be the censor of his children when their mature age claim a perfect freedom to act from circumstances" but, as his son knew, he was shocked and saddened by his treatment of Fanny. In a long letter, written from Burnham Thorpe shortly before his son had left for Merton, he had told him:

As a public character, I could be acquainted only with what was made public respecting you. Now, in a private station, possibly you may tell me where it is likely your general place of residence may be so that sometimes we may have mutual happiness in each other ... If Lady Nelson is in a hired house and by herself, gratitude requires that I should sometimes be with her if it is likely to be of any comfort to *her* ... At present I am in the Parsonage; it is warm and comfortable. I am quite by myself, except the gentleman who takes care of the churches ... But, my dearest son, here is still room enough to give you a warm, joyful and affectionate reception if you could find an inclination to look once more at me in Burnham Parsonage.

This letter, gentle as it was, undermined Nelson's elaborate self-justification of divine dispensation, and a marriage-in-the-sight-of-God, because his father's saintliness had been the foundation of his own religious instinct. He told Emma that the letter "has hurt me" but she was enraged, seeing old Edmund as the ally of the woman she and her lover had defeated but whom she still regarded as a threat. She wrote to Sarah Nelson:

His poor father is unknowing and taken in by a very wicked, artful woman acting a bad part. He would, if this designing woman had had her way, have put you all aside. *Your* father, Nelson's father, protects this woman and gives a mortal blow to his son. The old man could never bear her until now and now he conspires *against the saviour* of his Country and his darling, who has risen to such a height of fame and for whom a *wicked, false, malicious* wretch, who rendered his days wretched and his nights miserable. And the father of Nelson says, 'I will stab my son to the heart.' But indeed *he* says, 'My poor father is old now – he does not know what he does.' But oh how cruel, shocking it is.

Conscious that both Nelson's sisters were trying to remain neutral and maintain something of a friendship with Fanny, Emma told Sarah: "I am afraid the Boltons are not without their share of guilt in the matter. Jealous of you all, they have, with the Matchams, pushed the poor dear old gentleman to act this bad and horrible part to support a false, proud, bad woman ... But let her own wickedness be her punishment; her sins be on her head ... 'Tis a bad bird that befowls its own nest ... What do you think, my dearest friend, of her impudence? Tom Tit is despised and hated by even those that pretend to protect her ... My adored Nelson ... is, if it is possible, more kind, more tender than ever."

The reality was a sad, fond correspondence between Fanny and her father-in-law, which he had begun at the beginning of the year by offering her his company and help in finding a house in London and later offered to stay there with her. In August, he had written: "Whenever you have a house likely to be your residence, which is convenient for receiving me, I will be ready if you think you shall add any comfort to yourself from my being with you." Instead, she proposed a visit to him at Burnham

Thorpe in September, insisting: "Do not incommode yourself in the least to receive me – as there is a good inn at Holkham, or the accommodation will do quite well enough at Burnham Market for two nights and the days I can spend at the Parsonage." She went but on her return to London wrote to him:

> My visit to Burnham was one of duty rather than of pleasure. I assure you it called forth all my feelings. The impression your situation has left on my mind is so strong that I cannot delay any longer in offering my opinion on the subject of your living with me, which from your conversation makes it *impracticable*; the deprivation of seeing your children is so cruel even in thought that it is impossible you can any longer indulge the desire. I am not surprised for I knew Lord Nelson's friends would not like it; even supposing his Lordship resided in Italy the offence would be just the same and, in my opinion, greater. I told Mrs. M. [Matcham] at Bath that Lord Nelson would not like your living with me. 'Oh! my dear Lady N., my brother will thank you in his heart for he knows no one can attend to my father as you do.' I had seen the wonderful change, past belief. She had not.

But the old man was not to be dissuaded and he wrote to her again a few days before Nelson arrived at Merton:

> Be assured I still hold fast my integrity and am ready to join you whenever you have your servants in the London house ... The opinion of others must rest with themselves and not make any alteration with us. I have not offended any man and do rely upon my children's affection that, notwithstanding all that has been said, they will not in my old age foresake me.

He then told her that he would be leaving Norfolk at the beginning of November for London and then Bath. He had been invited to stay with his son at Merton and accepted, adding that he first had to attend to "some necessary business in town" rather than admit that he would be staying with Fanny at her rented house in Somerset Street near Portman Square. "If he remains at Burnham he will die," Nelson had told Emma, adding, "I am sure he will not stay in that damned Somerset Street." But he was not so sure and continued: "If he ever mentions her name I shall stop that directly, I shall never go there to see him. Pray let him come to your care at Merton. Your kindness will keep him alive for you have a kind soul. She has none."

Fanny had also been in Norfolk again, staying with the Walpoles at Wolterton and her arrival in London was noted in newspapers that reached Merton, prompting Emma to dash off a note to Sarah: "I wonder where Tom Tit goes? I dare say I find by today's papers that she is arrived in town. She must give five shillings to put in the papers such insipid stuff." Old Edmund arrived on 18th November, full of affection and gratitude, yet Emma was wary, fearing him to be the emissary of "that vile Tom Tit ... her squinting brat and ... her dirty tribe". Again she wrote to Sarah: "Psha! I am got out of bed the wrong side you will say ... The old gentleman is tolerably well content, contradicts *a little* every now and then. I find him *very feeble* indeed and inclined to sleep." She was happiest when he was out of the house, as when she wrote to Sarah: "Mr. N. is gone to church, Lord Nelson and your Humble Servant are writing, Sir William gone fishing; so we are all doing what we like ... We have got for dinner today a turtle dress'd and a haunch of venison. Don't your mouth water?"

When Edmund continued his journey to Bath early in December, Fanny realised that her last chance of a reconciliation was to take advantage of any influence he might have had over her husband. She did not know that Edmund, accepting there was now no hope for the marriage, had written to his son to thank him for his hospitality and told him: "I now rejoice to see so few impediments to as much felicity as falls to the share of mortals." As ladylike in her manners as ever, she decided not to write to her husband at Merton but at Alexander Davison's house in St. James's Square.

"It is some time since I have written to you," she began, writing from 16 Somerset Street on 18th December:

> The silence you have imposed is more than my affections will allow me and in this instance I hope you will forgive me in not obeying you. One thing I omitted in my letter of July which I have now to offer for your accommodation is a comfortable, warm house. Do, my dear husband, let us live together. I can never be happy until such an event takes place. I assure you again I have but one wish in the world, to please you. Let everything be buried in oblivion, it will pass away like a dream. I can now only entreat you to believe I am most sincerely and affectionately your wife, Frances M. Nelson.

The letter was forwarded to Merton and then returned to Fanny, sealed again and bearing the words, signed by Davison: "Opened by mistake by Lord Nelson, but not read." This, she accepted, was the end.

There was now a new interest to enhance Nelson's joy and sublimate his guilt: politics. He had never held a consistent political view: his immediate family had usually supported the Tory faction; his rich, landowning cousins, the Whigs; he himself had followed his instinct as a patriot and an ambitious and acquisitive officer. He had toyed with the idea of standing for Parliament when in London on leave in 1784. When unemployed in Norfolk, a few years later, he had disagreed with his neighbour Thomas Coke's Whig sympathy for the radical movements in America and France but, when patriotism was no longer in doubt, had been influenced by his Walpole cousins, also Whigs. So subsequently he had written to his uncle William Suckling: "I will not attempt to come into Parliament but in support of the real Whig interest." But he still saw politics in robust, sailor-like terms: "If that part of my country, who may honour me with their confidence in Parliament, think me an eligible person to serve them in the House of Commons, the same zeal shall manifest itself there as it has so repeatedly in their service against the French." Since his victories, he had met both William Pitt and Henry Addington, who had succeeded him as Prime Minister, and sniffed the strong scent of political power. He had taken his seat in the House of Lords as a viscount on 29th October accompanied by his old commanding officer, Lord Hood (now nicknamed "Lord Nosey" by Emma because of his profile) and could himself taste, and even exercise power. Content in seclusion at Merton, he nursed two immediate, if modest, aims: one was more public recognition of his success at Copenhagen; the other, promotion for his brother William.

Nelson delivered his maiden speech on the day following his arrival, seconding Lord St. Vincent's motion of thanks to Admiral Saumarez for his successful action off Algeciras during the summer. He was warmly applauded and took the opportunity to please both Hood and St. Vincent by declaring that they had been the masters of the school in which Saumarez had been so well educated. On 3rd November, he had again addressed the House, this time at the request of the Prime Minister, and was less successful. Aware of widespread criticism of the terms for peace with France, which were yet to be formulated in a treaty, and aware also that most of the British concessions were in relinquishing the fruits of naval success, Addington wanted his government's case supported by two naval heroes: St. Vincent and Nelson. The former confined himself to denying that the terms were humiliating and stressing the value of Ceylon and Trinidad, which had been gained. Nelson, however, surprised his listeners by his belittling of the value of Minorca, Malta and the Cape of Good Hope, which Britain stood to lose. Speaking with more experience of his subject than most, he announced Minorca was too far from Toulon to provide a base for a blockading fleet; Malta might offer a most commodious harbour, but its occupation by anybody, except the French, was immaterial; as for the Cape, it had once been useful for the refitting of East Indiamen but, now that these had coppered bottoms and were swifter sailers, they did not need to stop there; he himself regarded it as merely a tavern to visit on the voyage and an expensive one at that; expensive to maintain and more useful as the free port it was now to become.

His words did not carry the weight of his own conviction and he was aware that they were the repayment of a debt for past, and perhaps future favours. Writing to Captain Sutton, aboard the frigate *Amazon*, which was still flying his vice-admiral's flag while he was on indefinite leave, he admitted as much: "You will see my maiden speech – bad enough, but well meant – anything better than ingratitude. I may be a coward and good for nothing, but never ungrateful for favours done me."

Others expressed surprise and disappointment privately. William Huskisson, the former Under-Secretary for War, writing to Lord Dundas, the War Minister who had devised the campaign for the expulsion of the French from Egypt, declared:

> I was obliged to Lord Nelson for giving me anything that could create a smile on such a grave and awful subject. His Lordship's experience might have convinced him that a seaman could find a tavern nearer home than the Cape of Good Hope, and if Malta is not to be considered of importance because it does not serve to blockade Toulon, we must be obliged to conclude that no station in the Mediterranean is a good one. How can Ministers allow such a fool to speak in their defence?

Even his admirer, Captain Hardy, expressed his bluff regret: "I see almost by every paper that Lord Nelson has been speaking in the House; I am sorry for it and I am fully convinced that sailors should not talk too much."

A week later, he was on his feet again: first, seconding a vote of thanks to Lord Keith for the successful landings in Aboukir Bay earlier in the year and, next day, at the opening of the new Parliamentary session, he spoke in support of the new accommodation with the Baltic powers – particularly Russia – that had been the outcome of his own campaign in the Baltic. Describing this as peace with honour, he told the House: "I, my Lords, have, in different countries, seen much of the miseries of war. I am therefore, in my inmost soul, a man of peace. Yet I would not, for the sake of any peace, however fortunate, consent to sacrifice one jot of England's honour. Our honour is inseparably combined with our genuine interest." He was getting into his stride as an orator, expressing the simple philosophy of honour and decency, which he himself had set aside in his personal life, in the rolling phrases of the politician. "My professional education will plead my excuse for the imperfect manner in which I deliver my sentiments," he concluded, "but I should not have done my duty if I had not, even in this plain seamanlike manner, seconded this present address."

Attendance at the House of Lords added a new dimension to his life, allowing him to live privately at Merton and publicly in London. As he wrote to Captain Sutton, still aboard the *Amazon*, in mid-November, "Yesterday was a fagging day: 150 dined at the London Tavern and I, being cock of the company, was obliged to drink more than I liked but we got home to supper ... Yesterday was a busy day, between gardening, attending the House and eating, drinking and hurra-ing." But while Parliament provided an outlet for his energy and ambition, to Emma it began to present the possibility of a new life for them both: for him as a politician; for her, as his hostess.

"Our dear Nelson came home at six o'clock, the House broke up at five," she noted in November, he having "made a famous good speech". This was the opinion of others, she wrote to Sarah Nelson: "I have seen several gentlemen who heard him speak and they tell me he spoke firm, well, distinct and audible. Indeed, he succeeds in all he does." As ever, her imagination raced ahead and she continued:

> I am quite Nelson mad again for him as an orator ... I think this is my Hero's second speech. I have been making him say it to me as he said it to the House. I could hear him talk for ever and am just as anxious that he should be admired in this his new career as I was when he went out to battle, but I fret and weep that I cannot go and hear him in the British Senate. How my heart would throb and beat high, how should I exult to see him standing up with his manly look and honest, dear, innocent, energetic-looking face, speaking truth to people who hardly speak it and then his glorious limbs and blood that he has lost for his Country ... showing them perpetually that he has been their saviour and still is and will be altho' not rewarded a quarter part he deserves. *Shame on them all* ... If another Blenheim were built five times as large with five times the income, it would be only right; it would be no favour.

At this moment she stopped writing as Nelson entered the room and then she scrawled a final line: "Nelson comes reading my letter. I tell him to read – 'tis all true."

Amongst the unpleasant realities that were to be excluded from Merton was the risk of snubbing and Nelson announced that he would not accept invitations to dine with neighbours so as to avoid worrying about who had invited them and who had not. They would be socially self-sufficient, entertaining their own family and chosen friends, many of them naval. There were, however, a few exceptions for it was not a fashionable district and their immediate neighbours offered no threat of ostracisation. At Morden Hall, for example, lived Abraham Goldsmid, the banker, who was said to be involved with government finance and certainly was a friend of William Pitt; he was also an admirer of Nelson and had given a feast to celebrate the Battle of the Nile. Now he became a welcoming neighbour, who "beamed with genial kindness" although the Nelson party did not care for his kosher food and found the furnishing of his large house too gaudy for their taste. At Wandle Bank House, lived James Perry, an acquaintance of Emma's early days in London, who was now editor of the *Morning Chronicle*, which never sneered at the couple; indeed, earlier in the year Nelson had noted the newspaper's reporting of his activities and told Emma, "I *like* the *Morning Chronicle*". He was generous, too, and had invited Sir William to fish for pike in his water.

Another neighbour was John Pennington at Southside House on the edge of Wimbledon Common. A cotton merchant and manufacturer of fustian cloth, he was more interesting than first appeared for he had been in Paris during the Revolution and had strange tales to tell. At the behest of the British ambassador's wife and her friend Josephine Beauharnais, he had, he said, helped fugitives from "The Terror" escape to England. Piquancy was added to these escapades since Madame Beauharnais had subsequently married General Bonaparte. Now, together with the Hamiltons, Nelson would visit the Penningtons to play cards and for musical evenings when a low dais was set between fluted pillars in the music-room for the performance of Emma's Attitudes.

As Christmas approached, guests began to gather at Merton. They were few because neither the Boltons nor the Matchams could come for several reasons, including their unease over the question of Fanny and Emma. But William Nelson and his wife arrived to join their children and old Edmund sent his greetings from Bath with a touch of wistful whimsy: "Even the severity of the season, which makes many a poor creature, such as myself, to shake, gives much pleasure to the skating parties, so that I hope all in their turns have their hours of enjoyment at a season when all the Christian world do celebrate with songs of praise the return of Christmas". He looked with the apprehension of the old and infirm to the worst of winter and the snow he had once described so lyrically at Burnham Thorpe: "The white robe which January wears, bespangled with ice, is handsome to look at; but we must not approach too near."

There was no such risk at Merton Place, where all was jollity, that continued long after Christmas, when more guests arrived, including a Miss Furse, a school-friend of Charlotte's, and young Sam Hood, the grandson of Lord Hood. The end of the holidays was celebrated with a splendid dinner party at which, Emma reported to the girl's mother, now returned to Norfolk, she excelled herself. "Sam Hood is quite delighted with Charlotte," she wrote. "He seemed to devour her with his eyes. *That would* be a *good match* ... [1] Lord N., speaking of you at table, said, 'Charlotte, your mother was a fortune of £100,000 to my brother and I am prouder to have her for my sister than any woman in the kingdom.' Charlotte became quite red and the tears in her eyes and she said she would not thank her dear uncle for his kind speech about the best of mothers – her heart felt it but her feelings would not let her speak – was it not pretty?"

Another guest, Lord Minto, their old friend from the Mediterranean was also "charmed with Charlotte" but less so with her young friend. "Miss Furse ate so much that in the evening she vomited before us all," Emma reported. "Charlotte covered her *retraite* and got her out. She came in again and played at cards ... Lord Minto played. Mrs. Tyson was drunk and, when she talked nonsense, her husband tipped her the wink and she held her tongue." When the eating and drinking parties were over and the guests departed, Charlotte was sent back to school "much better for the discipline of physic she has undergone", as Emma told her mother.

Lord Minto returned to London and wrote sadly to his wife:

I went to Lord Nelson's on Saturday to dinner and returned today in the forenoon. The whole establishment and way of life is such to make me angry as well as melancholy; but I cannot alter it and I do not think myself obliged or at liberty to quarrel with him for his weakness, though nothing shall ever induce me to give the smallest countenance to Lady Hamilton. She looks ultimately to the chance of marriage, as Sir W. will not be long in her way and she probably indulges a hope that she may survive Lady Nelson; in the meanwhile she and Sir William and the whole set of them are living with him at his expense. She is in high looks, but more immense than ever. She goes on cramming Nelson with trowelfuls of flattery, which he goes on taking as quietly as a child does pap. The love she makes to him is not only ridiculous but disgusting: not only the rooms, but the whole house, staircase and all, are covered with nothing but pictures of her and him, of all sizes and sorts, and representations of his naval actions, coats of arms, pieces of plate in his honour, the flagstaff of *l'Orient*, etc. – an excess of vanity which counteracts its purpose. If it was Lady H.'s house there might be a pretence for it; to make his own a mere looking-glass to view himself all day is bad taste.

---

[1] Charlotte Nelson married Samuel Hood, Baron Bridport, on 3rd July, 1810.

Privately, such thoughts were shared by Sir William Hamilton, who found himself living amongst this collection of *objets d'art* glorifying his wife's lover. That fate he might have accepted with a world-weary shrug but he also found himself deprived of his expectations of a contented retirement. From the house in Piccadilly, which he still maintained, he could pursue his principal recreations: visiting the British Museum and Mr. Christie's saleroom and attending meetings of the Royal Society, but all these were now an hour away at the least. At Merton, he could go pike-fishing but this seemed increasingly an escape from the house where his wife devoted her energies to entertaining their friend and his family. He was also in debt, his contributions to the running costs of Merton Place now added to the expense of keeping his house in London and compounded by the government's failure to pay the expenses he had incurred while its representative in Naples and Palermo. At Merton, he kept this discontent to himself, but he did confide to his nephew Charles Greville in a letter written on 24th January, 1802, that he felt "that it is reasonable, after having fagged all my life, that my last days should pass off comfortably and quietly. Nothing at present disturbs me but my debt and the nonsense I am obliged to submit to here to avoid coming to an explosion, which would be attended with many disagreeable effects and would totally destroy the comfort of the best man and the best friend I have in the world."

Another prudently silent critic – one of whom Nelson was well aware – was Edmund Nelson, returned again to lodgings at 10 New King Street in Bath. Although he had never criticised his son's behaviour openly, there had been oblique hints that could have referred to nothing else. Even had he remained totally silent Nelson would have felt reproved for his father was the embodiment of the Christian ethics with which he had been indoctrinated in youth. He loved the father who had been the most profound influence on him for the first forty years of his life; the aberration having taken hold over the past three. But now he was beginning to fade.

On 20th April, Edmund Nelson wrote a letter in a wavering hand to Fanny at her London house, telling her that his youngest daughter, Kitty Matcham, had been delivered of an infant daughter while staying at Bath, and that, having heard she planned another move, "Rest assured that in all places I wish for your happiness". Soon after, both she and her estranged husband received urgent letters from George Matcham, telling them that Edmund was ill and not expected to live. Fanny at once left for Bath and Nelson wrote to his brother-in-law: "I have no hopes that he can recover. God's will be done. Had my father expressed a wish to see me, unwell as I am, I should have flown to Bath, but I believe it would be too late. However, should it be otherwise and he wishes to see me, no consideration shall detain me a moment . . . I shall therefore only say that he is to be buried at Burnham." It was already too late for on 26th April, 1802, the day on which Nelson wrote, his father died.

William Nelson, piqued when he was told of his father's illness by his younger brother and not informed first, hurried to Bath; Fanny, duty done, again faded away. Yet on her return to London she received a letter from her sister-in-law Susannah Bolton, both of gratitude and dismissal. "Your going to Bath, my dear Lady Nelson, was all of a piece with your conduct to my beloved Father . . . I am going to London in about a fortnight but, my dear Lady N., we cannot meet as I wished for everybody is known who visit you . . . but be assured I always have and always shall be your sincere friend S. Bolton."

Nelson's own protestations of indisposition were not unwarranted, for life at Merton had not yet restored him to healthfull but they were prompted primarily by his fear of meeting Fanny at his father's bedside and now he made the same excuse to avoid attending the funeral at Burnham Thorpe. With his customary attention to detail, he wrote to George Matcham, who was making the arrangements with the undertakers at Bath and would be travelling with the coffin to Norfolk:

> My brother tells me that great care must be taken to have the leaden coffin well soldered, for Mr. Coke was so offensive owing to this neglect that it was almost impossible to attend the funeral, and he wants to know the exact size of the coffin as the grave will be bricked . . . let me know when the body sets out from Bath and when, by the undertaker's calculation, it will arrive at Burnham. I am still very much indisposed.

So Edmund Nelson's body made the long journey across England and into Norfolk to be buried before the altar of his church. His son-in-law, Thomas Bolton, was there and his wife recorded: "The church was crowded, everyone lamenting the loss of a friend . . . Six clergymen attended as bearers . . . the farmers in the three parishes followed."

Despite his own absence from the funeral, Nelson was annoyed that his sister-in-law had not accompanied her husband to join the mourning at Merton. He made sure that she knew of this and her daughter Charlotte wrote to her:

> My uncle is very much hurt at your not being here this morning and he begs me to say it would be indecent for me to be at school and has ordered Lady Hamilton to write to Miss Veitch the reason for my not coming. We are all going into deep mourning as my uncle is very particular that all possible respect should be paid to my dear Grandpa-

pa's memory. He would not let Horatio go a-fishing . . . this morning, nor do we see anybody. A written paper is shown at the gate to everyone that comes . . . My spirits are worn out seeing my good uncle's suffering.

Nelson's father no longer stood in his path but he was not forgotten. Two years later, when replying to a letter from a Norfolk friend, he wrote: "I have a satisfaction in thinking that my bones will probably be laid with my Father's in the village that gave me birth . . . The thought of former days brings all my Mother to my heart, which shows itself in my eyes."

CHAPTER XI

The Long Watch
(1802–5)

"Either the distances between the distant quarters of the globe are diminished, or you have extended the powers of human action."
– Hugh Elliot in a letter to Vice-Admiral Viscount Nelson,
August, 1805

At the beginning of 1802, Lord Nelson increased his regular order for newspapers and journals to Mr. Smart the newsagent at Merton, adding to the list the *Monthly Review*, the *European Magazine* and the *Naval Chronicle*. The first would be of particular interest to Sir William Hamilton since its January issue included reviews of two new books, *The Natural History of Volcanoes* and *Travels in Greece and Turkey*, which he would doubtless want to read. The second would serve to keep them both in closer touch with current affairs. The third was his own favourite reading: a monthly journal of naval news and comment, describing recent actions, publishing relevant extracts from state papers, reporting courts martial, giving news of appointments and deaths, airing views in its correspondence pages, reviewing books about maritime topics and flattering its readers with pages headed "Naval Poetry". Nelson had often found his name in the latter and, even in January, it was there in capital letters; this time in a long ballad about events in the Baltic the year before:

> Ah! no, what breast could feel or cherish fear?
> When NELSON hoists his flag, a triumph's near.

Such effusions had become familiar since Cornelia Knight's first compositions more than three years ago and it was not only in songs, broadsheet ballads and declamatory verse that he was constantly proclaimed. All the media of popular communication had concentrated upon him: the newspapers and periodicals, of course; engravers and caricaturists; the manufacturers of commemorative pottery and painters and sculptors whose works would go on public exhibition. Even now engravers and print-publishers found his earlier victories a profitable subject and Nelson replied to one of them, James Fittler of Upper Charlotte Street, thanking him for a proof: "I have receiv'd your most beautiful print of the Battle of the Nile and if you will be so good as to let me know the price of the print, I will try to get some of them sold, but I fear the time for such events being interesting is past." He was wrong.

This publicity could be as mocking as flattering and he could see, displayed in the windows of London print-shops, the bright colours of insulting caricatures alongside the dignified monochromes of his engraved victories. Before his return from the Mediterranean, the caricatures sent to him from home had all been complimentary: Nelson belabouring French crocodiles at the Nile, or serving John Bull with a dish of broken French ships as *Fricassée à la Nelson*. The mockery had begun on his return; most of it directed at the whole *Tria Juncta in Uno*. First, when he had sailed for the Baltic, there had been a gross Emma as "Dido in Despair", bewailing the loss of her Aeneas, but this had been balanced by another of him whipping a Russian bear to dance: "I'll teach you to send challenges. A few stripes *à la Nile* will soon bring you to a right understanding." Since then they had become increasingly explicit and lewd. There had been Emma posing naked for artists with the brief caption, "Lady H's Attitudes", and a decrepit Sir William as an antiquary examining classical curiosities that all too obviously symbolised senility, impotence and cuckoldry. One caricature showed Nelson and Emma smoking together (he puffing an enormous, phallic pipe) with her saying, "Pha! The old man's pipe is always out but yours burns with full vigour", and him replying, "Yes, yes – I'll give you such a smoke. I'll pour a whole broadside into you."

In contrast were the splendid portraits by the finest painters available, several of which now decorated the walls of Merton. He had been painted as a young captain by John Rigaud and as a war-worn rear-admiral by Lemuel Abbott, whose portrait of him remained Fanny's principal reminder of her lost love. Since his return from the Baltic he had sat for two more fashionable artists, Sir William Beechey and John Hoppner. Whereas the first portraits had shown him as a private man, nursing his ambitions, these displayed him as a public figure: more mature, confident and radiating the attraction of his vivid, brave yet sensitive personality. Nelson enjoyed the company of artists whose talk tended to range widely and be less bound by convention and Beechey, who had once painted his father and whose wife came from Norfolk, became a particular friend.

At a dinner table, he again met the President of the Royal Academy, Benjamin West, who had painted one of his favourite pictures. Nelson, who regretted his lack of education in the appreciation of art, which had been started by William Locker and expanded by Sir William, then said: "But there is one picture whose power I *do* feel. I never pass a print-shop, where your *Death of Wolfe* is in the window, without being stopped by it." He then asked why West had not painted more with such themes. "Because, my lord, there are no more subjects." "Dammit, I didn't think of that," said Nelson. "My lord," continued West, "I fear that your intrepidity may yet furnish me with another such scene and, if I should, I shall certainly avail myself of it." "Will you?" replied Nelson, offering him a glass of champagne. "*Will* you, Mr. West? Then I hope I shall die in the next battle!"[1]

Unlike Wolfe, Nelson had become a national hero in his lifetime. Never before had an Englishman seized the imagination of his country-men with such intensity and in such fine focus. The Royal Navy was the embodiment and implementation of the national will and by far the nation's largest and most efficient military or industrial organisation, but hitherto its commanders had been little more than names printed in capital letters by newspaper editors and balladeers; their likenesses in print or pottery were usually stylised and sometimes interchangeable. Now Nelson emerged not only as the hero who won victories, fought alongside his men and had the wounds to prove it, but was, above all, instantly recognisable. Even the clumsiest engraver of popular prints could make sure of this by giving his blue coat an empty sleeve and its breast an array of stars and medals. Other naval heroes were admired or feared; if they were seen by the British public at all, it would be a glimpse of a man walking between a carriage and a doorway, or a distant figure in blue, white and gold at some state occasion. Nelson was different: he was always out and about; the state of his health apparent. His feats of arms might seem superhuman but his personal qualities were human and humane. In the pantheon of national heroes, Nelson was unique.

He himself had basked in this admiration ever since it had begun after his boarding and capture of two enemy ships at St. Vincent. But, so far, this had been confined to the ports where he had come ashore, his native Norfolk and, of course, London. Bath society had thrown admiring glances over its fluttering fans but he had yet to present himself to the mass of the British people, who lived away from the sea and outside London. That June he had been the most admired guest at a fund-raising dinner given for a naval orphanage at the London Tavern on Ludgate Hill, although accompanied by his former commanding officer, Sir Hyde Parker, and the histrionic Captain Sir Sidney Smith, who had failed to burn all the French ships in Toulon but had fought brilliantly against the French in the Levant. In the speeches after dinner the latter's display of

[1] Benjamin West painted a companion-picture, *The Death of Nelson*, in 1806.

emotion was more than Nelson had allowed himself in public; speaking of the orphaned children of friends killed in action, it was reported in the *Naval Chronicle*: "his head sunk – the big tear rolled down the hero's cheek. A solemn silence prevailed for several minutes until Sir Sidney was roused by the thunder of applause which followed." Nelson's touch on the public imagination was more subtle.

London had taken him to its heart. When the Lord Mayor had invited him to ride in his carriage through the City in his inaugural procession, the crowds had again taken the horses from the traces and dragged the coach up Ludgate Hill. An ecstatic Charlotte watched and wrote to her mother: "I wish you could have seen all the people jumping up to the carriage to see my uncle and thousands of people round him looking at him.... All the ladies had their handkerchiefs out of the windows when my uncle passed, they and the people calling out, 'Nelson for ever'."[1]

But most of Britain knew him only from newspaper reports, prints and ballads. This was about to change. Both he and the Hamiltons wanted a holiday and there were two motives for a tour to the west: Sir William and he were to receive honorary degrees in law from Oxford University and the former was also anxious to visit his estates in Wales. This could be combined with visits to friends and sight-seeing and in July they left Merton for Oxford, where they were to be joined by Nelson's brother William and his family and the Matchams.

The tour began with the expected flourish. Nelson was made a freeman of the city at the town hall; there was a tour of the colleges and the prison and the usual crowds to cheer them outside The Star inn, where they had been staying. On 22nd July, Nelson and Sir William had their honorary degrees conferred upon them with full academic ceremonial. Once again, the newspapers reacted with a mixture of admiration and mockery: the *Morning Post* joked that Nelson should have become a Doctor of Divinity "because of his knowledge of *cannon* laws" and the *Morning Herald* that Sir William had also received a degree "but whether that of L.L.D. or A.S.S. the records of the University do not say". William Nelson was given a Doctorate of Divinity to match one accorded by his own university, Cambridge, in honour to his brother;

---

[1] Nelson was well aware of his heroic standing and it is possible that, consciously or unconsciously, he tried to model himself on Sir Francis Drake. Peter Kemp has pointed out that he would sometimes use the same form of words. For example, he wrote to Addington in the summer of 1801: "Should Mr. Bonaparte put himself in our way, I believe he will wish himself even in Corsica." In 1588, Drake had written to Walsyngham: "I doubt it not that ere it be long, so to handle the matter with the Duke of Sidonia as he shall wish himself at St. Mary Port among his orange trees."

then the party set out for Blenheim to inspect the more tangible rewards bestowed by a grateful nation upon the hero of an earlier war.

Emma had joked that Blenheim Park would have looked like a kitchen-garden compared with the estate that Nelson should already have been given but, waiting outside the vast palace for admission, a stinging rebuff was delivered. The Duke of Marlborough was in residence, they knew, but the functionary to whom they had announced their arrival returned from within without an invitation to meet His Grace, or even to enter, but with the offer of refreshments to be served to the visitors in their carriage or at some vantage-point in the grounds. The offer was coldly refused and the coachman ordered to whip up his horses and head for the gates bound for Woodstock and a welcoming inn. Emma was furious, declaring: "The splendid reward of Marlborough's services was because a woman reigned and women have great souls." Sir William looked surprised and hurt, while Nelson bitterly reflected that this was what he must expect from "the great". Next day they continued to Gloucester, where there was a hearty welcome from crowds and the cathedral's bells and another tour of a city, including the gaol. Here the Matchams left the party to head for Bath, while "Lord Nelson's tourists", as a newspaper had described them, took the road for the Welsh border and a welcome untainted by snobbery and gossip.

West of Gloucester, the road ran through the wooded hills of the Forest of Dean and Nelson's professional instincts quickened, for here grew the raw material of shipbuilding and here, as wherever he encountered such forestry, he sought "the conversation of gentlemen in the oak countries". So he learned that the forest was suffering from neglect, the lack of new planting and the destruction of self-sown trees by sheep, pigs and deer. He made notes and in the evenings, when they were staying at inns, drafted a memorandum for the Prime Minister, beginning: "The Forest of Dean contains 23,000 acres of the finest land in the Kingdom, which, I am informed, if in a high state of cultivation of oak, will produce about 9,200 loads of timber, fit for building ships of the line every year ... The state of the Forest at this moment is deplorable; for, if my information is true, there is not 3,500 load of timber in the whole Forest fit for building ... " He continued to give details of the practical and economic problems of timber-growing and suggested means of overcoming them.

The party's next stop was to be at Ross-on-Wye, from where they were to travel down the river through picturesque scenery to Monmouth. Embarking in a large boat with a table and chairs set beneath an awning, they were rowed through the Wye Valley, past the red stone walls of Goodrich Castle, the crags and hanging woods of Symonds Yat along what Nelson described as "a little gut of a river". As it flowed from the hills into the open country around Monmouth, the crowds on the banks thickened, a band played *See the Conquering Hero Comes!* and puffs of smoke followed by distant reports of a saluting gun began on the summit of a steep hill called the Kymin above the town. There, he was told, a naval war memorial had just been erected and his hosts were eager that he should see it. There was no time for the excursion as they had promised to be at Sir William's estate for the fourth anniversary of the Battle of the Nile and a celebration dinner in Milford, but they accepted an invitation to break their journey again at Monmouth on their return.

The road ran through Brecon and more cheering crowds and knots of villagers along the way to Milford, where they stayed at the New Inn. Here they were met by Charles Greville, who managed his uncle's estate and were made welcome by the Earl of Cawdor, whose splendour might not equal the Duke of Marlborough's but who signified the approval of his guests by fashionable society hereabouts. The anniversary of the battle on 1st August was commemorated with a dinner at the inn and Nelson cheered his listeners with his forecast that Milford Haven was as fine a harbour as Portsmouth; indeed, it reminded him of the great anchorage at Trincomalee in Ceylon. The party attended a regatta and a cattle show and Sir William laid the foundation-stone of a new church. After a pleasant week, they departed for more civic receptions at Haverfordwest, Swansea, Carmarthen, Merthy Tydfil and so back to Monmouth on 18th August to stay in the modern and comfortable Beaufort Arms.

During the two days and nights spent at Monmouth, Nelson at last felt fully at ease with the British public, which had hitherto been so unpredictable in its response. The stay began well when, next morning, the party embarked in coaches each drawn by four horses for the steep ascent of the Kymin. At the summit they were entertained to breakfast at the Pavilion, a circular belvedere built by local gentry belonging to the Kymin Club for summer entertaining. Nelson admired the tremendous view towards the mountains of Wales and then was led across the grass to the Naval Temple, the war memorial: a stone gazebo surmounted by a statue of Britannia, enscribed with the names of contemporary naval heroes – including himself – and decorated with a mural of the Battle of the Nile. "To the boast of Monmouth, this Temple is the only monument of the kind erected to the English Navy in the whole range of the Kingdom," he told his delighted hosts. Others had been planned but never built: "Money has been collected to erect such a structure without accomplishing its purpose. This at the Kymin is enough, for which the admirals, whose services are here recorded, are very much obliged to you." Then, to establish the intimacy he now felt for those responsible, Nelson decided that the party would walk back to Monmouth down a steep, winding footpath through the trees and bramble-bushes to the river Monnow and into the town, where a banquet awaited.

The worthies of Monmouth had gathered in the handsome assembly-rooms of the Beaufort Arms to dine on venison from the Duke of Beaufort's estate at Badminton and be addressed by the guest of honour. Nelson, a small, dramatic figure; blue, white and gold uniform glittering with decorations and stars rose to give one of his rousing speeches, passionate if platitudinous. But now he was more in tune with his audience and he did not proclaim the virtues of King and Country only in impersonal rhetoric. This time he spoke directly to the people of the Welsh borders:

> If ever war was again to take place, I would send every ship, every regular soldier out of the Kingdom and leave the nation to be protected entirely by the courage of her sons at home. Suppose the French were to land in England, they might plunder and destroy a village, they might burn Monmouth, but I will engage for it they never would advance as far as Hereford for they would always find Britons ready to receive them.

When he sat down to claps and cheers, Emma rose to sing *Rule Britannia* and, as an encore, a patriotic song that was particularly popular in the West Country and included the lines:

> Come hither all ye youths of Bath,
> Whose bosoms pant for glory. . . .

After dinner the party walked through the town, past the statue of King Henry V, who had been born in the castle there, for coffee with the town clerk in a summerhouse in his garden. Next morning, they toured the town, inspected the church and the schools and Nelson walked into the bookshop and doffed his hat to the startled bookseller and printer, Charles Heath. "Monarchs have taken off their hats to your Lordship," he protested. "Permit me to replace yours on your head." He then asked permission to print the text of the speech Nelson had made the night before. "I am an old man and may not live long," replied Nelson, who was due to celebrate his forty-fourth birthday a month later. "It is my wish that posterity should know my sentiments; therefore do it."

From Monmouth, the tour continued through Ross to Hereford, where the Duke of Norfolk presented Nelson with the freedom of the city in an applewood box as a reminder of the cider industry and the newspaper report of the occasion made a good-natured joke: "The branch of an apple tree in full bearing being presented to Lord Nelson at Hereford, his Lordship, with all the gallantry of Paris, presented the *apple* to Lady Hamilton, thereby acknowledging her Ladyship a perfect VENUS." From there they travelled to Ludlow, and Worcester, where Nelson ordered a large service of armorial porcelain from the china factory. Stopping at villages and country houses along the way, he left his mark by giving his name to taverns and prize produce. "There is no man so busily employed in England as Lord Nelson," quipped the *Morning Post.* "In one place we meet him as a *gooseberry*, in another as a *carnation* – sometimes we find him a *racehorse* and sometimes a prize *ram.*"

On the last day of August they arrived in Birmingham to inspect the factories, mostly engaged in metal-working and including Boulton's, the medal-makers, some of whose products Nelson was already wearing. "It is a singular fact," reported the *Morning Post*, "that more *éclat* attends Lord Nelson in his provincial rambles than attends the King." This was demonstrated during two visits to the theatre. While watching *The Merry Wives of Windsor*, the actor playing Falstaff spoke the words, "Before the best lord in the land I swear it", and waved a hand towards Nelson's box to the cheers of the audience. The other visit was remembered by a nine-year-old boy, Charles Macready,[1] the son of the theatre's manager, who recalled the occasion:

The news of his arrival spread like wildfire and when his intention of going to the theatre got wind, all who had heard of it ... flocked there to behold him and do him honour ... The box-office-was literally besieged ... and every place soon taken. At the hour of commencement my father was waiting with candles to conduct the far-famed hero through the lobby ... to his box. The shouts outside announced the approach of the carriage: the throng was great but, being close to my father's side, I had not only a perfect view of the hero's pale and interesting face, but listened with such eager attention to every word he uttered ... Nothing, of course, passed unnoticed by my boyish enthusiasm: the right-arm empty sleeve attached to his breast, the orders upon it ... but the melancholy expression of his countenance and the extremely mild and gentle tones of his voice impressed me most sensibly...

When with Lady Hamilton and Dr. Nelson, he entered his box, the uproar of the house was deafening and seemed as if it would know no end. The play was at length suffered to proceed, after which was a sort

---

[1] Charles Macready (1793–1873) became a celebrated actor-manager in London; managed the Covent Garden and Drury Lane theatres and was renowned for his performance as King Lear.

of divertissement in honour of the illustrious visitor, from one song of which I can ... recollect one couplet:

> We'll shake hands; if they won't, why, what then?
> We'll send our brave Nelson to thrash 'em again!
> Derry down derry, etc.

The crowded house was frantic in its applause at this sublime effusion. Lady Hamilton laughing loud and without stint, clapped with uplifted hands and all her heart and kicked her heels against the footboard of the seat, while Nelson placidly and with his mournful look (perhaps in pity for the poet) bowed repeatedly to the oft-repeated cheers. Next day, my father called at the hotel to thank his Lordship ... In the hall of the hotel were several sailors waiting to see him, to each of whom the great admiral spoke in a most affable manner, inquiringly and kindly, as he passed through to his carriage, and left them, I believe, some tokens of his remembrance.

They travelled on to Warwick for more celebrations and then a quiet interlude at Althorp to visit his friend Lord Spencer, who had resigned as First Lord of the Admiralty when Pitt's administration had ended the year before. The tour was over and on 5th September the party arrived back to Merton with Nelson ruminating that "although some of the higher powers may wish to keep me down, yet the reward of the general approbation and gratitude for my services is ample reward for all I have done, but it makes a comparison fly up to my mind not much to the credit of some in the higher offices of the state".

Rewarded and refreshed, Nelson looked about for fresh activity but most of his friends were away at their country houses and he wrote to Davison at his home in Northumberland that "London seems absolutely deserted and so hot and stinking that it is truly detestable". He missed this well-informed friend and told him: "I own myself selfish enough to wish you in St. James's Square, for at your breakfast I heard all that was going on in the great world and it was a central place where anyone could meet me." As it was, he complained: "I am really so very little in the world that I know little, if anything, beyond what newspaper reports say respecting our conduct on the affairs of the Continent. It is true I have seen Mr. Addington and Lord St. Vincent several times. ..."

He had made the most of these meetings and the Prime Minister had discussed possible threats to peace now that Bonaparte had made himself First Consul for life and so was confirmed as the dictator of France. He responded with his own opinions and expertise: sending a memorandum to Addington suggesting that the British should continue to occupy

Malta, despite the agreement to evacuate under the Treaty of Amiens, unless it could become the responsibility of the Kingdom of the Two Sicilies supported by a Russian guarantee. To St. Vincent he sent another about recruiting for the Navy, suggesting that seamen should be given some security and status by being registered and that, whether employed or not, should, after five years' war service, be paid two guineas a year, and after eight years, four guineas. "It may appear, at first sight, for the State to pay, an enormous sum," he added, "but when it is considered that the average life of a seaman is, from *old* age, finished at forty-five years, he cannot many years enjoy the annuity."

He also wrote to Addington about his own finances, which had become worrying since the expense of the tour, and his cause for complaint that other admirals – notably St. Vincent and Duncan – had been rewarded with larger pensions for lesser victories than his. He enclosed an account of his income and property showing that, after paying Fanny her annual allowance of £1,800, a pension of £200 to Maurice's "poor Blindy" and £150 towards his nephew's education, his own annual income was only £768. His capital, tied up in his property at Merton, amounted – when the mortgage and loans were deducted – to £10,000. Brooding upon this, the old resentments came to the surface again and he wrote: "I presume to make only one remark: was it, or not, the intention of his Majesty's Government to place my rewards lower than Lord St. Vincent or Lord Duncan?"

There was a deeper discontent in Sir William Hamilton, for whom the triumphant tour had been exhausting and, even for a man of his sophisticated acquiescence, a continual humiliation from the knowing looks and titters that the *Tria Juncta in Uno* inspired. His neglect by his wife had been accentuated during the preparations for Nelson's birthday. This was celebrated by a dinner party and a musical evening at Merton, attended by William Nelson and his family and their neighbours, the Goldsmids and the Perrys. After dinner the Miss Goldsmids played the piano, several Italian opera-singers performed and the climax came, as usual, when Emma sang a new song:

> Then live, ever live, to our gratitude dear,
> The hope of our Navy! May Fortune endeavour
> His days and his friends to increase ev'ry year,
> And NELSON and glory be coupled for ever!

In reporting the event in the *Morning Chronicle*, James Perry wrote of his hostess: "There is no voice in England, which combines such uncommon volume and quality of tone with such richness of cultivation; and which receives from expression, gesture and articulation such force of truth and feeling ... Lady Hamilton displayed the wonders of her talent ... "

But Sir William was unable to speak to Emma with the benevolent authority he had once commanded and instead wrote a letter to her:

I have passed the last forty years of my life in the hurry and bustle that must necessarily be attendant on a public character. I am arrived at an old age when some repose is really necessary and I promised myself a quiet home and altho' I was sensible, and said so when I married, that I should be superannuated when my wife would be in her full beauty and vigour of youth. That time is arrived and we must make the best of it for the comfort of both parties.

Unfortunately our tastes as to the manner of living are very different. I by no means wish to live in solitary retreat, but to have seldom less than twelve to fourteen at table, and those varying continually, is coming back to what was so irksome to me in Italy during the latter years of my residence in that country ... I have no complaint to make, but I feel that the whole attention of my wife is given to Lord N. and his interest at Merton. I well know the purity of Lord N.'s friendship for Emma and me, and I know how very uncomfortable it would make his Lordship, our best friend, if a separation should take place, and am therefore determined to do all in my power to prevent such an extremity, which would be essentially detrimental to all parties, but would be more sensibly felt by our dear friend than by us.

Provided that our expenses in housekeeping do not increase beyond all measure (of which I own I see some danger), I am willing to go upon our present footing; but as I cannot expect to live many years, every moment to me is precious, and I hope I may be allowed sometimes to be my own master and pass my time according to my own inclination, either by going on my fishing parties on the Thames, or by going to London to attend the Museum, the R. Society, the Tuesday Club and auctions of pictures. This is my plan and we might go on very well, but I am fully determined not to have more of the very silly altercations that happen too often between us and embitter the present moments exceedingly.... There is no time for nonsense or trifling. I know and admire your talents and many excellent qualities but I am not blind to your defects and confess having many myself; therefore let us bear and forebear for God's sake.

This cleared the air, at least, and Sir William enjoyed another fishing expedition on the Thames. He stayed in London to take the chair at a meeting of the Royal Society, when his friend Sir Joseph Banks, the botanist, was taken ill, and invited Nelson to accompany him to a gathering of the Literary Society. Emma's hospitality would overwhelm Merton at Christmas, of course, but meanwhile he was able to pass a few placid weeks.

Nelson was enjoying his own public and private lives. As he had expected, unemployed naval officers, hoping for help, wrote him or called at the house. Despite occasional irritation, he was always helpful. When Lieutenant Fellows, who had been purser of the *Agamemnon*, wrote from a debtors' prison, Nelson sent him £25 with the assurance that "although I am not in a situation to lend money, you shall not want for my assistance".

Another was young George Parsons, who had been a midshipman in the *Foudroyant* and subsequently served under Lord Keith during the landings in Egypt. He had qualified as a lieutenant but his commission had not been signed when the war had ended and no more officers were now needed. In the hope of Nelson's help, he called at Merton and was recognised by the admiral's servant Tom Allen, who agreed to show him into the study "although under some apprehension of the nature of our reception", as Parsons recalled:

> The voice of Lord Nelson, denoting vexation, reprimanded my friend and declared most truly that he was pestered to death by young gentlemen, his former shipmates. Tom pushed me into the room and went in search of able auxiliary, who entered the study in the most pleasing shape – that of a lovely and graceful woman; and, with her usual fascinating and playful manner, declared, 'His Lordship must serve me.' His countenance, which until now had been a thunder-cloud, brightened; and Lady Hamilton was the sun that lightened our hemisphere. She, with that ready wit possessed by the fair sex alone, set aside his scruples of asking a favour of the first Admiralty Lord, by dictating a strong certificate, which, under her direction, he wrote. 'Now, my young friend,' said her ladyship with that irresistible smile, which gave such expression of sweetness to her lovely countenance, 'obey my directions minutely; send this to Lord St. Vincent at Brentwood, so as to reach him on Sunday morning.' My commision as an officer was dated the same as the aforesaid certificate . . .

Most of his naval friends were ashore and at home and several of his old friends in the West Indies had returned to spend their fortunes. Amongst these were Hercules Ross, who wrote regularly and warmly from Scotland, where he was busy building "a new mansion in the ancient castle style, new church to correspond, public roads and bridges". The two met in London and were joined by a third: Dr. Benjamin Moseley, who was now senior physician at the Royal Hospital in Chelsea, which cared for Army pensioners as Greenwich provided for the Navy's. Nelson found him stimulating company and consulted him about his eyesight, which seemed to be failing: the eye damaged in Corsica was no worse but the left eye was now showing signs of strain. Experienced and amusing as Moseley was, another friend doubted his ability to help; Richard Bulkeley, who had served with the Liverpool Blues in Nicaragua and had returned to Shropshire, writing anxiously: "Do, my good Lord, tell me who you consulted besides Moseley, who, although an *excellent physician*, is not, I apprehend, a professional occulist."

It was easy to visit Dr. Moseley because if Nelson travelled between Merton and London by the new Battersea Bridge rather than Westminster, both the Royal Hospital and his niece Charlotte's school were on the road. At the former was another reminder of the past: the wife of a Colonel Matthews, a newly-appointed staff officer there, proved to be the former Mary Simpson, the sixteen-year-old he had loved in Quebec, now aged thirty-six. Another reminder of lost love was his spasmodic correspondence with Mary Moutray, who was living with her married daughter in Ireland. Any lingering regrets had long been extinguished by Emma and Nelson's occasional letters to her were friendly but brief, leaving to Collingwood the pleasures of an affectionate friendship maintained by correspondence.

In November, 1802, Nelson was preparing to spend more time in London to attend the House of Lords because the new Parliamentary session was due to be opened by the King on the 23rd of that month. There was restlessness in the air: Bonaparte was belligerent again and was active in Italy, annexing Piedmont; there was political unrest at home and rumours of plots and even insurrection. On the evening of Tuesday, 16th November, ripples of alarm ran through London, radiating from a commotion in some mean streets to the south of the Thames in Lambeth. It was not until later in the week that sensational newspaper reports began to appear and Nelson again became aware of the name Despard.

Under the heading "CONSPIRACY" the *St. James's Chronicle* reported on its front page:

It is with much regret that we have to state that Colonel Despard and associates have been apprehended for a conspiracy of the most atrocious and shocking description. Colonel Despard appears to have been at the head of the plot ... One of the Bow Street officers at the head of a strong party of the London, Surrey and Kent patrols ... proceeded on Tuesday night, about a quarter after nine, to the Oakley Arms in Oakley Street, Lambeth, where they found Colonel Despard and 32 labouring men and soldiers, English, Irish and Scotch; the whole of whom they took into custody ... The leading feature of the conspiracy is of so shocking a description that we cannot mention it without pain and horror. The life of our beloved Sovereign, it appears, was to be attempted on Tuesday next by a division of the conspirators, while the remainder were to attack the Tower and other public places ... Folly and wickedness must have combined in the devising of so foul and extraordinary a proceeding.

Could this be the Despard he had known so well in Nicaragua? He had heard nothing of him for twenty years and he had had brothers in the Army, so it was not until Nelson travelled to London for the opening of Parliament that he knew that the conspirator was indeed his old friend, once the dashing young captain of the Liverpool Blues who, with himself, had brought the expedition to Nicaragua within sight of success. The story that he heard was bizarre. Despard, too, had survived the disaster on the Rio San Juan and had begun a successful career as a colonial administrator in those regions. Inevitably, he had become entangled in disputes between rival factions among the settlers and this finally led to his recall to London in 1790 for an official enquiry. He had returned with his black mistress and begun an interminable wait for the case to begin. But to the Colonial Office the bickering that brought him back was so irrelevant that it was shelved; indeed, had Despard been more of a realist he would have known it would never be resolved. Instead, he waited impatiently in London coffee houses and taverns and fell into conversation with fellow-Irishmen and with members of the radical "corresponding societies". His frustration found relief in subversive talk and, finally, action. Because of his military experience he had found himself leading a small revolutionary group of working-men and disaffected soldiers and this had led to the hatching of a plot.

Colonel Despard's conspiracy aimed high: to assassinate the King and overthrow the administration. Single-handed he recruited scores of supporters, walking from tavern to tavern – a gaunt, upright figure, recognisable by the green umbrella he habitually carried – making speeches in smokey back rooms and then wild plans.

The *coup d'état* that was being discussed at the Oakley Arms that Tuesday night was to be launched on the day the King opened Parliament. Indeed, the signal would be his assassination: as he returned to St. James's Palace from Westminster and was crossing the Horse Guards Parade, he would be blown to pieces by the great Turkish cannon brought back from the victorious campaign in Egypt, which would have been secretly loaded with four cannon-balls and chainshot during the previous night. At once, a battalion of the Guards at the Tower was to mutiny and seize the Bank of England and the Houses of Parliament. The capital's communications would be cut by stopping the mail-coaches and smashing the Admiralty's semaphore towers. This would be the signal for the Guards to mutiny at Windsor Castle and for insurrections at Manchester, Leeds, Sheffield and Birmingham. That, at least, was Despard's plan.

An informer had betrayed the plot and, on 23rd November, the King opened Parliament without incident. On that day, Nelson made a speech in the House of Lords, calling upon the government to prepare for renewed war and his friend James Perry published in the *Morning Chronicle* the report that he had said "no man was more for peace than he was, it was to obtain it he fought, and the enjoyment of it constituted the chief part of his happiness; but he deprecated having it on dishonourable terms." While he was in London attending the House, he was told that Colonel Despard, who had been arraigned for trial early in the coming year, had asked if he would appear in court as a witness for the defence. This was the first case concerning treason that had involved him since he had reacted so ruthlessly at Naples three years before but this time he agreed to speak on behalf of the accused.

The trial was arranged for February and meanwhile there was much to occupy Nelson. He spoke successfully in the House of Lords in support of Lord St. Vincent's proposed commission of enquiry into the chicanery of prize-agents, who, he said, cheated sailors "from the highest admiral in the service to the poorest cabin-boy that walks the street" of their rewards. Paradoxically, his own long litigation against St. Vincent over prize-money came to a head when judgement was given in favour of the latter and Nelson's lawyer at once lodged an appeal. Christmas at Merton was as hectic as expected and Emma described it in a letter to Kitty Matcham, who had been unable to bring her family to join the party: "Here we are as happy as kings and much more so ... " She gloried in his new political career, asking, "Don't you think he speaks like an angel in the House of Lords?", adding her own view: "I love him, adore him, his virtues, his heart, mind, soul, courage, all merit to be adored and everything that concerns his honour glory and happiness."

It was in strange contrast to such jollity that on 7th February, 1803, Nelson drove in his carriage through the streets of Lambeth and Southwark lined by new brick terraces to the Sessions House in Horsemonger Lane, Newington, for the trial of Colonel Edward Despard and twelve others on the charge of treason. Nelson was the first witness to be called by the defence and again saw his old friend – last seen in the camp at the edge of the Nicaraguan jungle before the walls of the Castillo de la Inmaculada Concepción on the Rio San Juan. Both men had changed: Nelson, now aged forty-four, erect and smart in well-cut civilian clothes, the familiar face marked by success and command; Despard, now in his early fifties, ravaged by worry and resentment, his hair cropped short, his clothes shabby.

"How long has your Lordship known Colonel Despard?" asked the counsel for the defence.

"It is twenty-three years since I saw him," replied Nelson. "I became acquainted with him in the year 1779 at Jamaica. He was, at that time, lieutenant in what were called the Liverpool Blues. From his abilities as an engineer, I know he was expected to be appointed."

"I am sorry to interrupt your Lordship," the judge broke in, "but we cannot hear, what I dare say your Lordship would give with great effect, the history of this gentleman's military life; but you will state what has been his general character."

"We went on the Spanish Main together," Nelson continued. "We slept many nights together in our clothes upon the ground; we have measured the height of the enemy's wall together. In all that period of time, no man could have shown more zealous attachment to his Sovereign and his country than Colonel Despard did. I formed the highest opinion of him at that time as a man and an officer ... Having lost sight of him for the last twenty years, if I had been asked my opinion of him, I should certainly have said, 'If he is alive, he is certainly one of the brightest ornaments of the British Army'."

Nelson was briefly cross-examined by the counsel for the prosecution to confirm that he had known nothing of the accused for two decades and then he withdrew. Two days later, Despard was found guilty and – although the jury recommended mercy in his case – he was, together with his associates, condemned to the dreadful fate of traitors: "That you ... be hanged by the neck, but not until you are dead, but that you be taken down again and, whilst you are yet alive, your bowels be taken out and burnt before your face; and that afterwards your head be severed from your body and your body divided into four quarters and your head and quarters be at the King's disposal. And may God Almighty have mercy on your soul."

Soon afterwards Nelson received a letter from Despard, enclosing a petition and he forwarded both to the Prime Minister, Henry Addington, without comment, although he did suggest a pension or grant for "Mrs. Despard". Later Nelson read the letter to Lord Minto who described it as "extremely well written and ... affecting from any other pen. It spoke in a high strain ... of his gratitude to Nelson, whose evidence, he says, produced the jury's recommendation. Whether his days were many or few, he said, he would have no other inscription on his tomb than the character given him by Nelson at the trial. Nelson merely sent the letter and petition ... to Mr. Addington, who told Nelson afterwards that he and his family had sat up after supper, weeping over the letter."

Mercy was forthcoming only in the commuting of the sentence to death by hanging with beheading to take place after death. The sentence was carried out on a scaffold before the prison in Horsemonger Lane on the morning of Monday, 21st February, 1803, before a crowd of twenty thousand. Colonel Despard behaved with composure and when another of the condemned remarked to him, "I am afraid, colonel, we have got into a bad situation," he replied, "There are many better and some worse." On the scaffold he delivered a dignified speech hoping that "the principles of liberty, justice and humanity will triumph over falsehood, despotism and delusion", and refused Christian comfort from the chaplain because he was an atheist. Then he adjusted the noose so that, with the knot tightened below his left ear, it would break his neck instantly; this it did. Colonel Despard was thereupon decapitated, his head shown to the crowd with the words, "This is the head of a traitor!" and, later that day, he was buried in an unmarked grave outside the north door of St. Paul's Cathedral in a burial ground as he was entitled by his residence in London. "We had a great deal of conversation about Despard," noted Minto after another evening with Nelson. "Lord Nelson seems to have ... behaved with a due mixture of generosity and private feeling with public propriety."

The winter holiday had ended with a dance given for the children by Emma, after which they had moved to the house in Piccadilly, which would be more convenient for the House of Lords and further entertaining. Sir William had been unwell but he had been able to attend the Queen's birthday reception, which Nelson declined, possibly because there was a risk that he might meet Fanny there. In February, Emma held a musical evening for a hundred guests at the house, when, reported one newspaper: "Her Ladyship sang several bravura songs and played very difficult concertos on the pianoforte with such rapidity of execution as not only astonished but electrified her auditors."

This was the grand finale of the *Tria Juncta in Uno* for, as they planned their return to Surrey, Sir William grew weaker. Sensing that his life was ending, he decided to stay at his London house rather than cast a shadow over Merton Place. Dr. Moseley was summoned from Chelsea but there was nothing he could do and Nelson decided, "He can't in my opinion get over it", while his secretary Francis Oliver simply said, "He is going off as an inch of candle".

Sir William faced the inevitable with stoicism, telling his nephew, Charles Greville: "I do not wish to see any friend who is wiser or better than I am and may be desirous to prepare me for death. You will not, I know, let them intrude or to disturb my tranquility." A few days later, Nelson wrote to Alexander Davison: "Wednesday, 11 o'clock, 6th April, 1803. Our dear Sir William died at 10 minutes past ten this morning in Lady Hamilton's and my arms without a sigh or a struggle. Poor Lady Hamilton is, as you may expect, desolate."

Next day, James Perry reported his death at length in his *Morning Chronicle*, loyally paying tribute to Emma's devotion: "Never was union productive of more perfect felicity." He did not mention the presence of Nelson, who had probably given him the news, describing how Sir William had "without a struggle or a sigh, breathed his last breath in her arms". Sir William's body began the long journey by hearse to the churchyard at Selbeck in Pembrokeshire where he was to lie beside his first wife, the adoring, demure Catherine. His heir, as expected, was Charles Greville, but he had arranged an annuity of £800 for Emma and the paying of her debts. To Nelson he left a favourite portrait of Emma – a flattering little enamel by Bone after a painting of her as a Bacchante by a French artist – with the dedication that it was "a small token of the great regard I have for his Lordship; the most virtuous, loyal and truly brave character I have ever met with."

Nelson, with his sense of public propriety, had at once moved out of the Hamiltons' house into lodgings over a saddler's shop in Piccadilly and there he stayed for a month, regularly visiting the Admiralty and reading the newspapers to keep abreast of the worsening relations with France. The renewal of war seemed more likely than ever: Bonaparte was active in Italy again and the particular issue of contention was his insistence that Britain relinquish Malta to the Tsar of Russia as its titular sovereign. Nelson had already been told by the Admiralty that he was to command in the Mediterranean and that was where the Navy would probably be most needed. The announcement of his appointment was made on 14th May and, two days later, Britain declared war on France.

Before leaving London, he accompanied Emma to a christening at Marylebone parish church, when no parentage was entered in the register, for the child was their daughter Horatia. She was now aged two, still boarded with the nurse, Mrs. Gibson, in Little Titchfield Street, and was known by the familiar, fictitious surname of Thompson and as Lord Nelson's god-daughter. This done, he took the road to Portsmouth, where his flagship awaited him. She was to be the *Victory*, the most powerful and handsome ship the Royal Navy could offer the admiral commanding in the Mediterranean, who, as St. Vincent had once said, should be "an officer of splendour".

He hoisted his flag on 18th May, eager to be away, writing to the First

Lord of the Admiralty next day: "If the Devil stands at the door, the *Victory* shall sail tomorrow forenoon." As the great ship was made ready for sea, he retired to his day-cabin, which occupied the width of the after end of the main deck, to compose a letter to Emma. "I feel from my soul," he wrote, "God is good and in His due wisdom will unite us ... When you look upon our dear child, call to your remembrance all you think that I would say ... and be assured that I am thinking of you and her every moment. My heart is full to bursting." Religious thoughts kept recurring. He had already written another letter to the Society for the Promotion of Christian Knowledge asking for a consignment of Bibles and Prayer Books for the use of his ship's company "consisting of 874 men". Brooding on mortality, he ended a letter " ... believe me, my dear Emma, your most faithful and affectionate friend till Death and, if possible, longer".

The *Victory* sailed accompanied by the frigate *Amphion*, commanded by Thomas Hardy, and the *Naval Chronicle* reported: "This morning, about 10 o'clock, his Lordship went off in a heavy shower and sailed with a northerly wind." Off Ushant, they were to meet a squadron under the command of Admiral Cornwallis – his old friend "Billy Blue" of Port Royal – charged with blockading the naval base of Brest. Should he be in urgent need of reinforcement, the Admiralty had ordered, the *Victory* was to be left with him and Nelson should continue his voyage in the frigate.

Two days after writing that first letter to Emma, he sat at the mahogany writing-table by the long row of windows with the expanse of heaving sea beyond, where he could see her portrait in pastels and a little crayon sketch of Horatia, and began another. "We are now in sight of Ushant and shall see Admiral Cornwallis in an hour," he wrote. "I am not in a little fret on the idea that he may keep the *Victory* and turn us all into the *Amphion*. It will make it truly uncomfortable." Then he looked to the future with tranquillity: "I assure you, my dear Emma, that I feel a thorough conviction that we shall meet again with honour, riches and health and remain together till a good old age." He thought of Horatia, too: "I look at your and my God Child's picture but, till I am sure of remaining here, I cannot bring myself to hang them up." Finally reverting to his subterfuge of writing to her as Mrs. Thompson, he added, "Be assured that my attachment and affectionate regard is unalterable; nothing can shake it! And pray say so to my dear Mrs. T. when you see her. Tell her that my love is unbounded to her and her dear sweet child and, if she should have more, it will extend to all of them." This was no flight of fancy, for he knew Emma to be pregnant again.

That day there was no sign of Cornwallis's ships, nor the next, for they had been blown off-station by a gale. Rather than delay longer, Nelson and his staff reluctantly transferred to the cramped quarters of the frigate and, leaving the *Victory* to await his friend, sailed on into the Bay of Biscay. It was as uncomfortable as he had expected but he was content, writing to Emma: "Our wind has been foul, blowing fresh and a nasty sea ... Your dear picture and Horatia's are hung up, it revives me even to look upon them. Your health is as regularly drunk as ever."

Passing Lisbon and calling for a day at Gibraltar, where he told the Governor that war was declared and heard the latest reports of French naval and diplomatic activity, he set course for Malta. Nelson did not waste the long, hot days of the voyage across the western Mediterranean, using the time to write letters and, in particular, began a long memorandum to the Prime Minister setting down his thoughts on Mediterranean strategy.

As he continued this on the next stage of the voyage to Naples, he had changed his view of the importance of Malta. No longer was the island as irrelevant as he had said in his speech to the House of Lords. "I now declare," he wrote, "that I consider Malta as a most important outwork to India that will ever give us great influence in the Levant and, indeed, all southern parts of Italy. In this view, I hope we shall never give it up." In his *tour d'horizon* he touched upon Sicily and here the sentimentality of his former views had been replaced by sharp realism: "The state of Sicily is almost as bad as a civilised country can be. There are no troops fit to be called such, with a scarcity of corn never known and, of course, bread so dear that the lower class of people are discontented. The nobles are oppressors and the middle rank wish for a change; and, although they would prefer us to the French, yet I believe they would receive the French rather than not change from the oppression of the nobles."

When the *Amphion* anchored of Messina to buy fresh fruit and vegetables "the lower class of boat-people" had come aboard and Nelson reported their behaviour to Addington: "Their expressions were strong and ought to be received with caution, yet ... you may gather sentiments to form a pretty accurate opinion. '*Vive il Re! Vive Inglese!* When will the English come back to Messina?' On asking them if they had any Jacobins in the city, 'Yes, the gentry who wear their hats so – on one side of the head' – *vide* Bond Street loungers."

On 25th June, the frigate passed the tip of the Sorrento peninsula and the magnificent, familiar view opened before Nelson. "Close to Capri," he wrote to Emma, "the view of Vesuvius calls so many circumstances to my mind that it almost overpowers my feelings." As he entered the bay, he mused about "*Dear Naples*, if it is what it was" but knew that it was not. The Kingdom of the Two Sicilies was neutral, although French troops had occupied the ports of Brindisi and Taranto and he thought it prudent to make contact with Sir John Acton in writing rather than provoke the French by going ashore. So he had sent a comforting letter to the chief minister assuring him that "a ship of war – and, generally, of the line – shall, on some pretence or other always be in the Bay of Naples to prevent that worst of all accidents, the loss of the Royal Family".

From the *Amphion*'s deck, Nelson could see the places he remembered so well: the Palazzo Reale, the Palazzo Sessa and even the little Villa Emma on the shore at Posillipo. There was to be another reminder of Neapolitan days soon after, when the frigate finally joined the British squadron blockading Toulon on 8th July. There were nine sail of the line and three frigates under Rear-Admiral Sir Richard Bickerton and, after the formalities of handing over command to Nelson, he reported recent incidents in the blockade, amongst which was the capture of a small French merchant ship. The usual practice would have been to send her with a prize-crew to a friendly port where she could be sold and the proceeds distributed as prize-money. But her cargo at once brought Sir William Hamilton to mind and, imagining what his reaction would have been, Nelson ordered her to England and himself wrote a letter to the Prime Minister, explaining:

> There has been taken in the *Arab*, French corvette, 26 cases of statues, busts, etc., etc., from Athens for the French Government. I have taken upon me to order them to be sent to England assigned to Sir Joseph Banks as President of the Royal Society for, if our Government choose to buy these articles of antiquity, I think it but proper that it should have the offer. They would sell well in this country. Lord Elgin, I am told, offered £6,000 for a part of them. Of course, the captors think them of great value, but the more valuable, the more desirable for our country to obtain.

Before the end of July, the *Victory*, released from duty off Brest, arrived in Toulon, bringing the strength of Nelson's fleet to ten sail of the line and three frigates. His immediate task was to watch a French fleet of similar strength within the port: "My first object must be to keep the French fleet in check and, if they out to sea, to have force enough to *annihilate* them." His wider aim was to prevent further invasion of the Kingdom of the Two Sicilies and to protect Malta and Gibraltar, the importance of which had been enhanced by France forcing Portugal to exclude the British from the Tagus anchorage. He could concentrate on these essentials because other threats had diminished: the Russians, neutral but unfriendly, had withdrawn most of their ships to the Black Sea and the perennial problem of the North African pirates attacking merchant shipping was being largely contained by an unexpected ally, the United States Navy.

The ultimate purpose of his presence off Toulon was by far the most important: the defence of England against invasion. The threat of this had long been at the forefront of British fears but, at last, the *Grande Armée*, more than 120,000 strong, was encamped in the Pas de Calais and in Belgium and Bonaparte himself was at Boulogne. Before the barges could sail, the French must command the Channel and that could only be attempted by concentrating all their squadrons. Those were now kept apart and in port by the Royal Navy under Lord Keith in the North Sea, Cornwallis off Ushant and Nelson off Toulon.

Adding a personal piquance and an immediacy to the threat was that the French fleet blockaded by Nelson was under the command of Admiral La Touche-Tréville, who had repulsed the attack on Boulogne two years before. "La Touche was sent for on purpose," Nelson was certain, "because as he beat me at Boulogne, to beat me again; but he seems very loath to try." In the hope that he would come out, Nelson kept most of his own ships beyond the horizon with only a weak squadron within sight of the French watch-towers. "My system is the very contrary of blockading," he explained. "Every opportunity has been offered the enemy to put to sea, for it is there we hope to realise the ... expectations of our country." To a friend of Abraham Goldsmid's, he repeated: "There seems an idea that I am blocking up the French fleet in Toulon. Nothing could be more untrue. I have never blockaded them a moment. All my wish and the anxious wish of this fleet is to have them out."

But while the enemy could lie snug in port, the British ships had to keep the sea in the Gulf of Lyons, whipped by storms and gales: the north-westerly mistral, the north-easterly greco and the familiar warm wind of the sirocco from Africa. The ships were sea-worn, short of supplies and in need of repair, kept on station and ready for action by the skill and resilience of their crews. They had been in this state when he arrived and then, as weeks became months, the task of keeping ships and men seaworthy and ready for action became in itself a challenge to equal any he had met.

As an advanced base, Nelson chose the bleak Maddalena Islands off the north coast of Sardinia but he sometimes cruised briefly off other coasts. It was essential to provide his men with fresh fruit and vegetables to prevent scurvy and maintain morale with a change of scene, however distant, across the heaving sea. He wrote to Dr. Moseley in Chelsea:

Situated as this fleet has been, without a friendly port where we could get things so necessary for us, yet I have, by changing the cruising ground, not allowed the sameness of prospect to satiate the mind – sometimes by looking at Toulon, Villefranche, Barcelona and Rosas;

then running round Minorca, Majorca, Sardinia and Corsica; and two or three times anchoring for a few days and sending a ship to the last place for *onions*, which I find the best thing that can be given to seamen; having always good mutton for the sick and cattle when we can get them and plenty of fresh water.

To one of his captains, Moubray of the *Active*, he wrote explaining how he would send a ship into port to "purchase 50 head of good sheep for the use of the sick on board the different ships ... and 30,000 good oranges for the fleet with onions and any other vegetables that will keep about eight to ten days ... to remove the taint of the scurvy".

When storms were blowing and the ships were battened down, running before the gale with sails furled, life for more than eight hundred men in each of the big ships was miserable on the dark, damp, cramped mess-decks. On fine days a Mediterranean cruise was enjoyable, particularly for the officers. One such day was described by Dr. Gillespie, a doctor on board the flagship:

At six o'clock my servant brings a light and informs me of the hour, wind, weather and course of the ship, when I immediately dress and generally repair to the deck. Breakfast is announced in the Admiral's cabin, where Lord Nelson, Rear-Admiral Murray (the Captain of the Fleet), Captain Hardy, Commander of the *Victory*, the chaplain, secretary, one or two officers of the ship and your humble servant assemble and breakfast on tea, hot rolls, toast, cold tongue, etc., which when finished we repair upon deck to enjoy the majestic sight of the rising sun (scarcely ever obscured in this fine climate) surmounting the smooth and placid waves of the Mediterranean, which supports the lofty and tremendous bulwarks of Britain, following in regular train their Admiral in the *Victory*.

Between the hours of seven and two, there is plenty of time for business, study, writing and exercise. At two o'clock a band of music plays till within a quarter of three, when the drum beats the tune called *The Roast Beef of Old England*, to announce the Admiral's dinner, which is served up exactly at three o'clock and which generally consists of three courses and a dessert of the choicest fruit, together with three or four of the best wines, champagne and claret not excepted. If a person does not feel himself perfectly at ease, it must be his fault, such is the urbanity and hospitality which reign here ...

Coffee and liqueurs close the dinner about half-past four or five o'clock, after which the company generally walk the deck, where the band of music plays for nearly an hour. At six o'clock, tea is announced, when the company again assemble in the Admiral's cabin, where tea is served up before seven o'clock and, as we are inclined, the party continue to converse with his Lordship, who at this time generally unbends himself, though he is at all times free from stiffness and pomp as a regard to proper dignity will admit, and is very communicative. At eight o'clock a rummer of punch with cake or biscuit is served up, soon after which we wish the Admiral a good night (who is generally in bed before nine o'clock). Such is the journal of a day at sea in fine, or at least moderate, weather, in which this floating castle goes through the water with the greatest imaginable steadiness.

Nelson himself rose even earlier than the doctor and described his own day thus:

> My routine goes on so regular that one day, except the motion of the ship, is the same as the other. We rise at five, walk the deck till near seven ... breakfast at seven precisely ... Dine at three, in fine weather always some of the captains; in general, twelve at table ... after coffee and tea, no more eating. At a quarter or half-past eight, give the necessary orders for the night, go to bed, sleep and dream of what is nearest my heart.

On Sunday he attended the service taken by his chaplain, Alexander Scott, and afterwards usually spoke to him "on the subject of the sermon, either telling him of its being a good one, or remarking that it was not so well adapted as normal to the crew – the admiral always being anxious that the discourse should be sufficiently plain for the men, and the chaplain, with the liability of a scholar, being sometimes tempted into a too learned disquisition". Scott was a linguist and so had become interpreter and, sometimes, intelligence officer for Nelson, who described him as "a very sober, unassuming man, very learned, very religious and very sickly. He reads, which is more I dare say, than any of our proud churchmen, the lessons of the days in German, Latin, Greek and English every day."

Nelson himself was abstemious, partly because doctors had advised a light diet with little wine and meat after attacks of gout. Dr. William Beatty, also serving in the *Victory*, noted that, " ... he ate very sparingly, the liver and wing of a fowl and a small plate of macaroni in general composing his meal, during which he occasionally took a glass of champagne. He never exceeded four glasses of wine after dinner, and seldom drank three; and even those were diluted with Bristol or common water." He took plenty of exercise, "generally walking on deck six or seven hours in the day" and took few precautions against the discomforts of wind and weather. The doctor noted:

He possessed such a wonderful activity of mind as even prevented him from taking ordinary repose seldom enjoying two hours of uninterrupted sleep; and, on several occasions, he did not quit the deck the whole night. At these times, he took no pains to protect himself from the wet, or night air, wearing only a thin great coat; and he has frequently, after having his clothes wet through with rain, refused to have them changed, saying that the leather waistcoat which he wore over his flannel one, would secure him from complaint. He seldom wore boots and was consequently very liable to have his feet wet. When this occurred he has often been known to go down to his cabin, throw off his clothes and walk on the carpet in his stockings for the purpose of drying the feet of them. He chose to adopt this uncomfortable expedient rather than give his servants the trouble of assisting him to put on fresh stockings, which, from his having only one hand, he could not himself conveniently effect.

Captain Hardy was a disciplinarian who never hesitated to order a flogging but the admiral set a relaxed tone, joking with the sailors and treating his officers with courtesy. One of them, Lieutenant Joseph Willcock remembered two examples of this. Once he was on the quarterdeck when Nelson came up from his cabin, went up to the quartermaster at the wheel and said, as he recalled, "Quartermaster, keep the ship's head so-and-so."

"She is, my Lord," replied the sailor.

"I say she is not."

"She is, my Lord."

"What, you mean to tell me I lie, do you?"

"Yes, my Lord."

At this, the admiral walked over to his flag captain with a laugh and said, "Look, Hardy, that man tells me I lie!"

Once Willcock recounted he had been in the ship's office near the top of the ladder leading up from Nelson's cabin and usually guarded by a marine sentry. On this occasion the sentry was absent, Willcock opened the door and nearly knocked Nelson to the deck.

"Mr. Willcock, can't you see what you are doing?" snapped the admiral and walked away. That evening the lieutenant was due to dine with Nelson and when he joined the other guests in the great cabin, the admiral came up to him and said, "Mr. Willcock, I hope I did not hurt you just now?" Willcock apologised again and hoped that Nelson had not been hurt. "No, no," he was told. "If I had, the sentinel alone was to blame."

According to Willcock, Nelson was "generally mild and calm in his temper" but became irritable in bad weather when he felt seasick, or the stump of his arm ached. He saw himself as keeping the degree of detachment necessary to a commander, telling Emma: "Although I am good friends with all yet I am intimate with none beyond the cheerful hours of meals."

Yet he was able to remain a good friend to those in trouble, however distant. When he heard that young Captain William Layman was to be court-martialled for losing his ship, a sloop, by shipwreck, he felt partly responsible as he had urged him to be lenient in blaming his officer of the watch when reporting to the Admiralty. So he wrote to the First Lord pleading Layman's case – to no avail, in the event – and concluded: "If I had been censured every time I have run my ship, or fleets under my command, into great danger, I should long ago have been *out* of the Service and never *in* the House of Peers."

The routine of a life to which he was attuned – even the regularity of the gales – amongst men who admired and, indeed, loved him restored Nelson to self-confidence and tranquillity. Even the separation from Emma was bearable and he was no longer tormented by jealousy and frustration. When she wrote suggesting that she join him – even embarking in the *Victory* in preference to staying at Naples or Gibraltar – he rejected the idea as firmly as he once had to Fanny, if with more affection. "Imagine what a cruise off Toulon is," he wrote to her. "Even in summer-time we have a hard gale every week and two days' heavy swell. It would kill you; and myself to see you ... " Instead, confident of her fidelity, he delighted in the bundles of vivid, scrawled letters that arrived when a boat pulled across to the *Victory* from a ship fresh from England. He himself wrote letters full of response to her gossip and messages for little Horatia who now that Sir William was gone, had been moved from her London lodgings to Merton and this was confirmed to her father when a letter from Emma enclosed a lock of her hair. "You have sent me in that lock of beautiful hair a far richer present than any monarch in Europe could if he were so inclined. Your description of the dear angel makes me happy. I have sent to Mr. Falconet to buy me a watch and told him if it does but tick and the chain *full* of trinkets, that is all which is wanted." He had remembered that "she was always fond of my watch I might have promised her one: indeed, I gave her one which cost sixpence!" So now he sent her another, with instructions: "I send you a watch which I give you permission to wear on Sundays and on very particular days when you are dressed and have behaved exceedingly well and obedient. I have kissed it ... "

When Emma told him how well Horatia could walk and he imagined her playing on the lawn, he suddenly remembered the ornamental canal and quickly wrote to Emma: "As my dear Horatia is to be at Merton ... a strong netting, about three feet high, may be placed round the Nile that the little thing may not tumble in; and then you may have ducks again in it. I forget at what place we saw the netting; and either Mr. Perry or Mr. Goldsmid told us where it was to be bought. I shall be very anxious until I know this is done." Yet, even now, the fiction of his guardianship of the child was maintained and he wrote to Charlotte, thanking her for her help at Merton with "the dear little orphan Horatia. Although her parents are lost, yet she is not without a fortune and I shall cherish her until the last moment of my life and *curse* them who curse her and Heaven *bless* them who bless her!" His delight in the child supported him when he eventually heard that early in 1804, Emma had given birth to another daughter, who was to be named after her at his request but died before she could be christened.

Dreams of home were a comfort during the stormy winter months – as was the news that he had finally won his appeal against Lord St. Vincent over prize-money – but professional duties were uppermost in Nelson's mind, particularly when spring brought signs of enemy activity in Toulon. Occasionally La Touche-Tréville had ships at the harbour mouth and a few put to sea, although briefly. "My friend sometimes plays bo-peep in and out of Toulon, like a mouse at the edge of her hole," laughed Nelson. Once, eight ships of the line and two frigates came out but were chased back into port next day. Hearing that the French admiral sent a very different account to Paris, he wrote angrily to his brother: "You will have seen Monsieur La Touche's letter of how he chased me and how I *ran*. I keep it and, by God, if I take him, he shall *eat* it!" There was to be no such opportunity for in August, La Touche-Tréville suddenly died and his opponent accorded him the wry obituary: "He has given me the slip. The French papers say he died of walking so often up to the signal-post to watch us: I always pronounced that would be his death." His successor was Admiral Pierre Villeneuve, whom Nelson remembered as captain of the *Guillaume Tell*, one of the two fugitives from Aboukir Bay.

Despite this spur to activity, Nelson's health was deteriorating and his sight was again causing anxiety. That summer there were bouts of illness. "I really believe that my shatter'd carcase is in the worst plight of the whole fleet," he wrote to Dr. Andrew Baird, who had tended young Parker at Deal. "I have had a sort of rheumatic fever they tell me but I have felt the blood quickening up the left side of my head and the moment it covers my brain I am fast asleep. I am now better of that and with violent pain in my side and night sweats with heat in the evening and quite flush'd. The pain in my heart and spasms I have not had for some time. Dr. Mcgrath ... now gives me camphor and opium ... " He told Emma:

> ... the constant anxiety I have experienced have shook my weak frame and my rings will hardly keep upon my fingers. What gives me more than all is that I can every month perceive a visible (if I may be allowed the expression) loss of sight. A few years must, as I have always predicted, render me blind. I have often heard that blind people are cheerful, but I think I shall take it to heart. However, if I am so fortunate as to gain a great victory over the enemy, the only favour I shall ask will be for permission to retire, and, if the contrary, I sincerely pray that I may never live to see it.

In December, he heard that the Admiralty had granted him leave but his joy was tempered on hearing that, because of his impending absence, the sea area west of Gibraltar was to be split from the Meditarrenean command and made the responsibility of Vice-Admiral Sir John Orde. This was a double blow for he disliked Orde and these waters were the most productive of prize-money. "You know I never was Fortune's golden favourite," he complained. "Mine is the Age of Iron. Sir John Orde's, that of gold."

Any hope of an early return was banished before the end of the year by the news that Bonaparte, who had just proclaimed himself Emperor Napoleon I, had forced Spain to declare war on Britain again. The strategic balance had changed dangerously. Hitherto, Nelson had never been seriously worried by the threat of invasion across the Channel since he knew the difficulties at first hand. "I do not believe that the French will," he had said, "for, although I hear of their blustering at Boulogne and of Bonaparte's being there parading, I can never believe that they can succeed beyond getting a few thousands on shore to be massacred. When he has tried and failed, I think we shall have peace."

Yet this became a possibility if the French, Spanish and Dutch squadrons in port at the Texel, Brest, Rochefort, Ferrol, Cadiz, Cartagena and Toulon could escape the British blockading squadrons and combine. Together with more than fifty sail of the line, they would outnumber any fleet that could be set against them and, in theory at least, they could command the Channel long enough for the *Grande Armée* to cross. This indeed was the strategy that Napoleon planned. His fleets and squadrons were to burst through the blockade, escape into the Atlantic and concentrate in the West Indies, then, in one enormous and invincible fleet, return to Europe and sweep the Royal Navy from the Channel. If all could not escape the blockade, some could, then unite as planned and free the others on their return. Then the invasion of England could begin.

On the first day of 1805, the French squadron in Rochefort broke through the British blockade and disappeared to westward. Then, on a stormy night two weeks later, Villeneuve escaped from Toulon, eluding Nelson's frigates in the dark. There was no clue to their destination: it might be Sardinia, Naples, Palermo, Malta or even Egypt for the only sighting report to reach the *Victory* was that they were steering south-east. Nelson at once followed in that direction with eleven sail of the line and two frigates, in as acute an agony of anticipation as in the summer of 1798: "I am in a fever! God send I may find them!" There was no sign of the enemy off Sardinia and his frigates saw none off Naples or Malta. He sailed through the Straits of Messina, again suspecting a landing in Egypt, and at the end of the first week in February was off Alexandria to find the port empty and torpid. Back at Malta on the 19th, he at last heard the truth: that the gales that had helped Villeneuve escape had driven him back into Toulon. Reporting this to the Admiralty, Nelson wrote, "I have consulted no men, therefore the whole blame of ignorance in forming my judgement must rest with me. I would allow no man to take from me an atom of my glory had I fallen in with the French fleet; nor do I desire any man to partake any of the responsibility. All is mine, right or wrong ... " There was also some professional satisfaction in the outcome, as he wrote to Collingwood: "Bonaparte has often made his boast that our fleet would be worn out by keeping the sea and that his would be kept in order ... by staying in port; but he now finds, I fancy, if Emperors hear truth, that his fleet suffers more in a night than ours in a year."

Napoleon's revised plan was for Villeneuve to escape again and collect the Spanish squadron, commanded by Admiral Gravina, from Cadiz, while Ganteaume broke out of Brest and released the ships in Ferrol. The two groups would then cross the Atlantic to a rendezvous at Martinique before sailing eastward to the Channel. No hint of this had reached Nelson, so when news reached him on 30th March, while he was lying off the coast of Majorca, that Villeneuve had escaped again and that the French ships had been loading muskets and saddles at Toulon, he again suspected an expedition within the Mediterranean. This time he took no precipitate decision but moved to the island of Ustica north of Palermo to await further news. It came on 18th April, when he heard that the French fleet had passed Gibraltar ten days before, heading west.

Contrary winds delayed his pursuit, and it was not until the beginning of May that he was able to sail out of the Mediterranean. His initial deduction was that Villeneuve was steering north for Brest and the Channel and he decided on the usual precautionary move of making for Ushant or Scilly to await further news. Leaving one ship of the line and a squadron of frigates in the Mediterranean, he sailed across the Gulf of

Cadiz from Cape Trafalgar towards Cape St. Vincent and met at sea the flagship of a Portuguese rear-admiral, a Scottish mercenary named Donald Campbell. From him he heard the news that Villeneuve was crossing the Atlantic. Immediately he set course for the Caribbean, undeterred by the odds against success: the French were a month ahead of him and at twice the strength of his own nine ships of the line.

"Although I am late," he considered, "yet chance may have given them a bad passage and me a good one." Speed was all-important but Nelson never lost the touch of inspired leadership, as he showed when one of his ships proved slower than the rest and he wrote to her captain, Richard Keats: "I am fearful that you think the *Superb* does not go as fast as I could wish. However that may be (for if we all went ten knots I should not think it fast enough), yet I would have you assured that I know and feel the *Superb* does all that which is possible for a ship to accomplish; and I desire that you will not fret upon the occasion." Despite this drag on their progress, the fleet managed to average five knots with all sails set and in twenty-four days arrived among the Windward Islands, which he had not sighted for eighteen years.

The enemy might be found in any Caribbean anchorage and if so Nelson planned to repeat the devastating tactics of Aboukir Bay and Copenhagen. If they met at sea, he told his captains: "Take you a Frenchman apiece and leave me the Spaniards. When I haul down my colours, I expect you to do the same; and not till then. We shall not part without a battle." At Barbados, General Brereton, who commanded the garrison at St. Lucia, reported that the enemy fleet had sailed south towards Tobago and Trinidad. Nelson had thought they were more likely to have headed north towards the French island of Martinique but acted on the information, expecting a climactic action. "I find myself within six days of the enemy," he wrote to Emma on 4th September, "and I have every reason to hope that the 6th of June will immortalize your own Nelson ... Pray for my success and my laurels I shall lay with pleasure at your feet and a sweet kiss will be ample reward for all your faithful Nelson's hard fag." But the beautiful bays of those islands, where he had expected to fight, were empty; the report had been wrong. He wrote to her again: "Ah, my Emma, June 6th would have been a great day for me ... I have ever found that if I was left and acted as my poor noddle told me was right I should seldom err."

He turned north to Grenada and found that Villeneuve had at least been there and captured a convoy of British sugar-ships off the coast. The Leeward Islands might also have been attacked, so he continued northward to find that the enemy had been there, too, but had gone. He stopped off Antigua, where Mary Moutray had once enchanted him, and sighted the cone of Mount Nevis and the green slopes where he had courted Fanny. Where had the enemy gone? To attack Jamaica, or to replenish at Martinique? Brooding on the possibilities, he concluded that as Villeneuve had not pressed home his attacks and was constantly on the wing, he might have achieved his aim of drawing the British away from Europe in pursuit and now be on his way back across the Atlantic. So, having to act upon speculation, he himself set course for the Azores and Gibraltar. The closest he came to sighting his quarry was on 21st June at midnight when he noted: "Saw three planks, which I think came from the French fleet. Very miserable, which is very foolish."

The enemy were not at the Azores either, and, on 20th July, the pursuing British anchored off Gibraltar and Nelson at last went ashore. "Employ'd completing the Fleet with provisions and stores," he recorded. "Went on shore for the first time since June 16th, 1803, and from having my foot out of the *Victory*, two years wanting ten days."

"It has almost broke my heart," he wrote to Lord Barham, who had just been appointed First Lord of the Admiralty, and he put the blame for his failure to fight and destroy the enemy squarely on the inaccurate report by General Brereton in Barbados. To Emma, he wrote: "After two years hard fag it has been mortifying, not being able to get at the enemy ... John Bull may be angry but he never had an officer who has served him more faithfully."

The long pursuit had been no more successful for the French and Spanish. Although Villeneuve and Gravina had reached the rendezvous across the Atlantic, Ganteaume had been unable to break out of Brest. They had awaited him, then, hearing that Nelson was following, Villeneuve disregarded Napoleon's orders and fled back to Europe. Off Finisterre, he was intercepted by a British squadron under Admiral Calder. The wind was light, the weather hazy and, although two Spanish ships were taken, nightfall stopped the fighting and Calder failed to press home his advantage next morning. Villeneuve led his fleet into Vigo on 28th July and two days later – on the seventh anniversary of his escape from Aboukir Bay – got into Ferrol. The French and Spanish fleets were back in port but the ports opened on to the Atlantic so that the risk remained: the enemy could again try to concentrate and challenge the British in the Channel.

Nelson returned home for leave that was long overdue and, despite his disappointment, found himself more popular than ever. Not only was he the admiral who grappled so ferociously with the enemy in combat but who would chase that enemy half way round the world. Had he, and not Calder, caught the combined fleets off Finisterre the result, it was agreed, would have been very different. Nelson would have none of that and wrote to Fremantle: "I should have fought the enemy; so did my friend Calder; but who can say that he will be more successful than another? I only wish to stand upon my own merits and not be comparison, one way or the other, upon the conduct of a brother officer." To his brother William he wrote: "We must not talk of Sir Robert Calder's battle: I might not have done so much . . ."

His achievement that summer was encapsulated by Hugh Elliot, Lord Minto's brother, who was now British ambassador at Naples, in a letter to him. "Either the distances between the distant quarters of the globe are diminished, or you have extended the powers of human action," he wrote. "After an unremitting cruise of two long years in the stormy Gulf of Lyons, to have proceeded, without going into port, to Alexandria, from Alexandria to the West Indies, from the West Indies back again to Gibraltar; to have kept your ships afloat, your rigging standing and your crews in health and spirits, is an effort such as never was realised in former times nor, I doubt, will ever again be repeated by any other admiral. You have protected us for two long years and you saved the West Indies by only a few days." He had become the champion of the nation. "You have put us out of conceit with all other admirals," wrote Richard Bulkeley, his friend from Nicaraguan days: "Look into your own acts and read the public papers for the last four months, then judge if John Bull will consent to give up his *sheet anchor.*"

Above and beyond such achievement was the inspiration of the nation's imagination. It touched every individual and each responded much as did Hercules Ross who, from the comfort of his sumptuous new home at Rossie Castle in Scotland, wrote to him: "I have both by night and day accompanied your Lordship across the Atlantic and as far to the westward as the scene of our earlier days, and imagination has often carried me aloft to look for the flying enemy. Though disappointed, thank God, my noble friend has returned in health. But there still remains some great action to be achieved by him worthy of his fame."

CHAPTER XII

Trafalgar
(1805)

"When I came to explain to them the *Nelson touch*, it was like an electric shock. Some shed tears, all approved – 'It was new – it was singular – it was simple!' "
— Vice-Admiral Viscount Nelson to Lady Hamilton from
H.M.S. *Victory*, 1st October, 1805

"What a day of rejoicing was yesterday at Merton," wrote Emma Hamilton to Kitty Matcham on 21st August, 1805. Nelson had left the *Victory* at Spithead the day before, landed at the sally-port on Portsmouth Point, paid his respects to the Commander-in-Chief then gone straight to The George coaching inn and ordered a post-chaise to take him home. He sat drinking tea in the parlour while he waited and rain splattered the windows but, undeterred by either, was on the road by nine and travelled through the night. At six o'clock next morning he drove through the gates of Merton before the household was awake.

"How happy he is to see us all!" declared Emma. He was entranced with Horatia, now a vivacious child of four and a half and already learning to play the piano and speak a little French and Italian from the exuberant and motherly woman she knew as her guardian. Merton Place had changed, too; for Emma had been busy in his absence. The drawing-room, dining-room and library, hung with his and her portraits, gleamed with new glass and gilding. Upstairs, the five principal double bedrooms each had its own dressing-room and a new design of water-closet. Outside, the grounds had been enlarged to about seventy acres and extended on the far side of the road, beneath which a brick-walled tunnel had been constructed. A new walk leading to a white summer-house in the Classical taste had already been named "the poop" in his honour.

The house was visited and described on this day by a chance visitor, a Danish historian, J. A. Andersen, who had come to present the admiral's household with a copy of his account of the Battle of Copenhagen. He recorded:

Merton Place is not large, but a very elegant structure. In the balconies I observed a number of ladies, who I understood to be Lord Nelson's relations. Entering the house, I passed through a lobby, which contained amongst a variety of paintings and other *objets d'art*, an excellent marble bust of the illustrious admiral. Here I met the Rev. Dr. Nelson ... I was then ushered into a magnificent appartment, where Lady Hamilton sat on a window. I at first scarcely observed his Lordship, he having placed himself immediately at the entrance. The admiral wore a uniform emblazoned with the different Orders of Knighthood. He received me with the utmost condescension.

Andersen noticed that the lines on his face were deep and hard "but the penetration of his eye threw a light upon his countenance, which tempered its severity and rendered his harsh features in some measure agreeable ... Lord Nelson had not the least pride of rank; he combined with that degree of dignity, which a man of quality should have, the most engaging address in his air and appearance."

The morning after his arrival, Nelson and Emma set out for London together: he to call on Lord Barham at the Admiralty; she to await the arrival of two of his Bolton nieces from Norfolk at 11 Clarges Street, off Piccadilly, which she had rented to replace the house where Sir William had died. There Nelson collected them in his carriage at four, after a busy day of buying presents for Horatia and official appointments, the last of which had been a call on Mr. Pitt, who was again Prime Minister. The Government wanted Nelson's assessment of the strategic contingencies, the most dangerous of which was the combining of the French and Spanish fleets still believed to be scattered in squadrons in the Atlantic ports. British squadrons under Collingwood, Cornwallis, Calder and Bickerton watched them, but if the enemy could mass their ships, Napoleon's plan to command the Channel could be realised and the *Grande Armée* was still encamped along its southern shore. Early that year the old alliance of Russia, Prussia and Austria had been re-assembled to support Britain but even their massed manpower seemed unlikely to achieve much against the vigour of the French and the military genius of the Emperor.

During the coming month there were to be many meetings with ministers and senior officers in Whitehall and, before one with Lord Castlereagh, the Secretary of State for War and the Colonies, a chance meeting and the conversation which followed illustrated Nelson's response to recognition. He found himself in an ante-room of the Colonial Office in Downing Street and sharing it with a major-general of authoritative and aristocratic manner, more than ten years his junior. The soldier was to recall how he had met there:

... a gentleman, whom from his likeness to his pictures and the loss of an arm, I immediately recognised as Lord Nelson. He could not know who I was, but he entered at once into conversation with me, if I can call it conversation, for it was almost all on his side and all about himself and, in reality, a style so vain and so silly as to surprise and almost disgust me.

I suppose something that I happened to say may have made him guess that I was *somebody* and he went out of the room for a moment, I have no doubt to ask the office-keeper who I was, for when he came back he was altogether a different man, both in manner and matter.

Nelson had been told that his companion was Major-General Sir Arthur Wellesley the future Duke of Wellington just returned from a succession of brilliant campaigns in India. Wellesley continued:

All that I had thought a charlatan style had vanished and he talked of the state of the country and of the aspect and probabilities of affairs on the Continent with a good sense and a knowledge of subjects both at home and abroad that surprised me equally and more agreeably than the first part of our interview had done; in fact, he talked like an officer and a statesman.

The Secretary of State kept us long waiting and, certainly, for the last half or three-quarters of an hour, I don't know that I ever had a conversation that interested me more. Now, if the Secretary of State had been punctual and admitted Lord Nelson in the first quarter of an hour, I should have had the same impression of a light and trivial character that other people have had, but luckily I saw enough to be satisfied that he was really a very superior man; but certainly a more sudden or complete metamorphosis I never saw.

But contrasts, springing from insecurity and vulnerability, were part of his appeal for Nelson was a hero with whom everybody could identify. Here was a legendary hero who was also human and subject to ordinary worries and weaknesses. This was the one man who had been able to halt the once-invincible Napoleon; made familiar through all the media of communication, but who could also fail, suffer wounds and illness. Here was a man who could inspire the highest ideals and show the most sublime courage yet succumb to sexual temptation and be seen publicly to abandon his morally blameless wife for a loose, but generous-hearted woman of the people. He owed no allegiance to any social class, as his family background showed: his brother and sisters had worked as shop assistants even though his cousins were landowners. Indeed he was cold-shouldered by the court and courtly society and his friends ashore were unfashionable: a worldly diplomatist, an eccentric doctor, a Jewish financier, a newspaper editor, an artist, several colonials, unconventional Army officers and, of course, many naval officers; all of them interesting people.

Everybody knew how he would greet old shipmates, whatever their rank or lack of it, when met ashore and how he would help those fallen on hard times. Many knew, too, how he had spoken in defence of one of his men in court on a murder charge and spoken so highly of the past character and achievement of an old friend charged not only with conspiracy and treason but attempted regicide. This disregard for the barriers of social class and this loyalty to friends brought a deep and emotional response from those accustomed to patriotic platitudes. Nelson was not the figurehead of the nation, he was its embodiment, inspiring loyalty – indeed, love – that commanded not only the people's patriotism but their hopes for social change. He, more than the threat from France, far more than the monarch or his ministers, and more than anyone in living or inherited memory had united the British.

"I met Nelson today in a mob in Piccadilly and got hold of his arm, so that I was mobbed, too," wrote Lord Minto on 26th August. "It is really quite affecting to see the wonder and admiration and love and respect of the whole world; and the genuine expression of all these sentiments at once, from gentle and simple, the moment he is seen. It is beyond anything represented in a play or a poem of fame." On the same day, an American visitor, Benjamin Silliman, a newly appointed professor at Yale College, in London to buy books and laboratory equipment, saw him in the Strand and wrote in his journal:

> He was walking in company with his chaplain and, as usual, followed by a crowd ... Lord Nelson cannot appear in the streets without immediately collecting a retinue, which augments as he proceeds, and when he enters a shop the door is thronged till he comes out, when the air rings with huzzas and the dark cloud of the populace again moves on and hangs upon his skirts. He is a great favourite with all descriptions of people ... My view of him was in profile. His features are sharp and his skin is now very much burnt from his having been long at sea; he has the balancing gait of a sailor; his person is spare and of about middle height, or rather more and mutilated by the loss of an arm and an eye, besides many other injuries of lesser magnitude.

When in London, Nelson stayed at Gordon's Hotel in Albemarle Street for propriety's sake, rather than share Emma's new house in Clarges Street nearby, without Mrs. Cadogan there as chaperone. While he was the focus of attention, Emma was thinking of a future when he could continue the career she was planning for him in politics, using his popularity to become as much a man of power in peace as in war.

But politics had proved more complicated than expected, involving more than patriotic oratory and private persuasion. He admired the Prime Minister and had written to Emma from the *Victory* a year before to say that: "If Pitt is attentive to me, he shall have my vote." On the other hand he had come to know and like his former rival, Henry Addington, who had now resigned and been created Viscount Sidmouth. He had seen friends who had dabbled in politics get into difficulties: from Norfolk he had heard that the father of young Captain Hoste, the Reverend Dixon Hoste, was deep in debt over the financing of election campaigns; his own agent, Davison, had been convicted of bribery at election-time and imprisoned for a short spell. "He would only consult Lord Moira and such clever folks," Nelson had remarked, "but an ignoramus like me could only warn him not to touch the boroughs." The problem was that, on Davison's advice, he had allocated his proxy vote, during his own absence at sea, to this same Lord Moira.

He had met and been attracted to General the Earl of Moira at the House of Lords during the months of peace. Although noted as a disciplinarian on his campaigns in America and on the Continent, the peer had expressed surprisingly liberal views in the House – on such unfashionable subjects as the domination of Ireland and the treatment of debtors – and this had appealed to Nelson. But having chosen him to vote by proxy on his behalf, he had realised that Lord Moira was inconsistent and liable to dabble in party-politics. So, on his return from sea, he told his lawyer, William Haslewood: "I wish I had never given a proxy to Lord Moira; not that I can complain of his having used it improperly. He is a distinguished officer, an enlightened statesman and a man of too much honour to abuse so sacred a confidence. But I might have to consider that partiality might cloud the judgement and that Lord Moira might become attached to a party."

During the previous year, Nelson had assumed that initially his proxy vote was "entrusted to support Mr. Addington" but he "not having done anything for me or my friends", he decided that "I should not have given my vote against Mr. Pitt". Then there was always the future possibility of office – perhaps as First Lord of the Admiralty – so he had concluded a worried letter to Emma about his politics: "I am no party man as a tool; if I am to be part of Administration it alters the case." So he had finally withdrawn his proxy vote and told Davison that he had decided not to allocate it again. Now, determined to set matters straight before he returned to sea he confided in the Prime Minister, and told Haslewood what was said:

I was so full of the subject we were speaking of yesterday as to continue it in my interview with Mr. Pitt. I gave some specimen of a sailor's politics by frankly telling him that, not having been bred in courts, I could not pretend to a nice discrimination between the use and abuse of parties; and therefore must not be expected to range myself under the political banners of any man in or out of place. That England's welfare was the sole object of my pursuit; and where the tendency of any measure to promote a defeat that object seemed clear, I should vote accordingly without regard to other circumstances. That in matters where my judgement wavered, or to the full extent of which I might feel unequal, I should be silent as I could not reconcile to my mind the giving of a vote without full consideration of its propriety.

This was, in effect, the abdication of the political career upon which Emma had lavished such hopes. "Mr. Pitt listened to me with patience and good humour; indeed paid me some compliments," he told Haslewood, "and observed that he wished every officer in the service would entertain similar sentiments." To have admitted to the Prime Minister and to himself that he was no politician was a relief and he added that he "felt his mind at ease and expressed himself highly pleased with the liberal conduct and language of the Minister".

He was content to remain the popular hero, owing only simple, patriotic allegiances. Every print-shop displayed his portrait and, even amid the bustle of preparation, he was happy to pose for more artists, although two of them – a miniaturist and a modeller of wax medallions, Catherine Andras – had to share a sitting and draw opposite profiles. As they worked Nelson joked that he was not accustomed to being attacked from port and starboard at the same time.

He returned to the happy simplicities of his home. "What a Paradise he must think Merton," his sister Susannah Bolton told Emma archly, "to say nothing of the Eve it contains." As many relations as possible had been gathered to meet him – even including his brother Maurice's "poor Blindy" – and when Lord Minto called one Saturday afternoon he wrote:

> ... found Nelson just sitting down to dinner, surrounded by a family party of his brother the Dean,[1] Mrs. Nelson, their children and the children of a sister. Lady Hamilton at the head of the table and Mother Cadogan at the bottom. I had a hearty welcome. He looks remarkably well and full of spirits. His conversation is a cordial in these low times ... Lady Hamilton has improved and added to the house and the place

[1] This was either a mistake on Lord Minto's part or a courtesy title as William Nelson was a Prebendary of Canterbury and a Doctor of Divinity but not a dean.

extremely well without his knowing she was about it. He found it ready done. She is a clever being after all: the passion is as hot as ever.

This was home life as Nelson had long dreamed it should be with Emma as the loved and loving hostess, presiding over a house-party of his own family: his brother and sister, nephews and nieces and, above all, little Horatia. When he had changed out of his uniform on returning from meetings in London, he would play the part of a sober country gentleman, dressed in black coat for formal occasions and, for outings, sometimes in "a pair of drab green breeches and high black gaiters, a yellow waistcoat and a plain blue coat with a cocked hat, quite square, a large green shade over the eye and a gold-headed stick in his hand". Occasionally there were distinguished visitors to entertain as when the Duke of Clarence came over from Bushey Park for a talk. In such company Nelson felt no need to strike attitudes: his nephew, young George Matcham, remembered that his uncle "delighted in quiet conversation, through which occasionally ran an undercurrent of pleasantry not unmixed with caustic wit. At his table he was the least heard among the company and, so far from being the hero of his own tale, I never heard him allude voluntarily to any of the great actions of his life."

Even greater action was constantly on his mind for there was the prospect of the enemy fleets breaking out from their blockaded ports and concentrating, and their defeat would be his responsibility. If they could combine, he had told Pitt, "they will then have collected sixty or seventy sail of the line and there will be difficulty in overcoming them". Only a combination of all the available British squadrons could face this force and the Prime Minister had asked, "Now, who is to take command?" "You cannot have a better man than the present one," replied Nelson, "Collingwood." "No," said Pitt. "That won't do. You must take the command." He then asked if he could be ready, if necessary, in three days time and Nelson replied, "I am ready now."

He had already decided upon the tactics he would use if a fleet under his command met the enemy in the strength that was to be expected. When Captain Keats, late of the *Superb*, called on him at Merton, the two men walked in the garden while the admiral outlined his plan. "No day can be long enough to arrange a couple of fleets and fight a battle according to the old system," he began. He would divide his fleet into three divisions: one, composed of his fastest ships would be held in reserve; with the other two, he said. "I would go at them at once, if I can, about one-third of their line from their leading ship. What do you think of it? I'll tell you what I think of it. I think it will surprise and confound the enemy. They won't know what I am about. It will bring forward a pell-mell battle and that is what I want." In essence it would be the same tactics that had brought victory before: concentrating his ships with their high rate of fire to overwhelm more than half the enemy fleet before the head of their line could turn and come to its aid. He described his plan to Lord Sidmouth – the former Henry Addington – explaining that it would be effective even if the enemy line numbered a hundred sail of the line. When asked what he expected his own strength might be, he replied, "Oh, I do not count our ships."

This flouted the canons of the Fighting Instructions which had dictated the Navy's tactics throughout most of the eighteenth century. At the Battle of the Saints in the West Indies two decades before something of the sort had been tried: "Rodney broke the enemy's line in one place,"[1] explained Nelson, "I will break it in two." The advantage would be that the odds in the enemy's favour would be overcome; the British could cut off whatever number of enemy ships that would change the odds to their own favour. When the remainder of the enemy were able to join the action, they, too, would be outnumbered.

The awaited call came at five o'clock on the morning of 2nd September. The early morning peace of the garden at Merton was suddenly disturbed by hoof-beats and the grinding of iron-rimmed wheels on the gravel drive. A travel-stained post-chaise stopped at the door and a young man in the uniform of a captain of the Royal Navy alighted. He was Henry Blackwood of the frigate *Euryalus*, carrying dispatches for Admiral Collingwood to the Admiralty, and he had turned off the Portsmouth road to warn Lord Nelson of their content. There was no need for him to speak; Nelson was awake and as soon as he saw the young officer he told him: "I am sure that you bring me news of the French and Spanish fleets and that I shall have to beat them yet."

The news he brought was that Villeneuve had left Ferrol and joined with another fourteen sail of the line from Corunna. But, instead of attempting to release the French squadrons in Rochefort and Brest, he had steered south and taken refuge in Cadiz. He lay in the great anchorage with more than thirty French and Spanish ships of the line, watched by Collingwood, who was being reinforced by squadrons under Bickerton and Calder making his strength up to twenty-five. This could only mean that plans to dominate the Channel and invade England had been abandoned for the time being. But if Villeneuve could join forces with the other squadrons a whole new range of threats became possible.

Having told all he knew, Blackwood hurried on towards London, followed soon afterwards by Nelson. At once a series of conferences

---

[1] Nelson was wrong: Rodney broke the French line at three points.

began and it was decided that Nelson should leave for Cadiz in the *Victory* as soon as possible, his command to include the Atlantic approaches to the Straits of Gibraltar as well as the Mediterranean itself. But he was disturbed by the politicians' talk of blockading Cadiz and speculation over the number of ships that would be needed for this. "It is, as Mr. Pitt knows, annihilation that the country wants – not merely a splendid victory ... honourable to the parties concerned but absolutely useless in the extended scale." He would therefore need every ship of the line that could be ordered to join him.

While plans were being made in Whitehall, the house-party at Merton was breaking up; the Boltons departed for Norfolk, the youngsters returned to school and "poor Blindy", after her brief exposure to excitement, was, as Emma put it, "gone sad and alone to her nut-shell". Emma herself rose to the occasion. "I am again broken-hearted as our dear Nelson is immediately going," she told the wife of his nephew Tom Bolton,[1] "I have had a fortnight's dream and am awoke to all the misery of this cruel separation. But what can I do?" With him she was brave and supportive and when she made no attempt to hold him at Merton, he said: "Brave Emma! Good Emma! If there were more Emmas, there would be more Nelsons."

One of their last guests was Lord Minto, who was invited to dine at Merton on Thursday, 12th September. Dinner was arranged for half-past three but Nelson and Emma were delayed in London: he summoned for a farewell audience with the Prince of Wales – the once-feared seducer – at Carlton House, while she awaited his return at Clarges Street. They were two hours late and Minto passed the time with two other guests, who appeared to be neighbours but were not introduced until Nelson finally arrived, although the two men had met briefly in the past. At last the circumstances were remembered and Minto wrote to his wife: "I had a curious meeting ... with Mr. Perry, editor of the *Morning Chronicle*, whom I formerly sent to the King's Bench, or Newgate, I think for six months, for a libel on the House of Lords. I told Mr. Perry I was glad to have the opportunity of shaking hands on our old warfare."

This potential embarrassment briefly diverted attention from the mood of impending doom: Nelson was due to leave for Portsmouth the following night. Minto observed the scene with some detachment, although he again stressed his friendship for Nelson in the letter to his wife. "Lady Hamilton was in tears all yesterday," he wrote, "could not eat and hardly drink and near swooning, all at table." Even now he found their love difficult to understand. "It is a strange picture," he continued.

[1] Tom Bolton became the second Earl Nelson in 1835 on the death of his uncle William, whose heir had died in 1808.

"She tells me nothing can be more pure and ardent than this flame." Finally, he put it down to the odd contradictions in Nelson's character. "He is in many points a great man," he concluded, "in others a baby."

Before leaving home, Nelson was determined to seal the relationship with some religious ceremony. They exchanged wedding rings and were blessed, side by side, at a celebration of Holy Communion after which, while facing the priest, he took her hand and told her: "Emma, I have taken the Sacrament with you this day to prove to the world that our friendship is most pure and innocent and of this I call God to witness."

The last day was spent supervising the packing of luggage and in touring the grounds; Nelson careful not to spread the sombre premonitions that had always assailed him at such times. It was natural that a captain or an admiral should expect wounds or death before going into action, for he would be exposed on his quarterdeck throughout. This time there was the nagging memory of a West Indian fortune-teller, who when forecasting his future had said, on reaching the year 1805: "I can see no further." While the Matchams had been staying at Merton, he had recalled this when alone with his sister, sighing, "Ah, Katty! Katty, that gipsy." Amongst his officers he might speak of attaining victory or Westminster Abbey, but this time he appeared optimistic.

The final farewells after dinner that night were painful and he knelt to pray at the bedside of the sleeping Horatia, returning to look at her four times before walking through the front door and down the stone steps to the waiting chaise. One of his stable boys was holding open the door for him and he paused, as he climbed in, to say, "Be a good boy till I come back again." With that the coachman flicked his whip, the wheels ground on the gravel for the last time and he was away, the lights of the carriage-lamps flickering briefly among the trees until they disappeared.

As the chaise rocked and rattled down the road towards Portsmouth he composed a prayer that had been forming in his mind during the past days and when the journey was broken at a coaching-inn to change horses he copied it into his diary:

Friday night at half-past ten, drove from dear, dear Merton, where I left all which I hold dear in this world, to go to serve my King and Country. May the great God, whom I adore, enable me to fulfil the expectations of my country; and if it is His good pleasure that I should return, my thanks will never cease being offered up to the throne of His mercy. If it is His good Providence to cut short my days upon earth, I bow with the greatest submission, relying that He will protect those dear to me that I may leave behind. His will be done. Amen, amen, amen.

After the usual uncomfortable, sleepless night on the road with stops for tea and changing horses, the post-chaise bowled down the southern flanks of the chalk bluffs of the Hampshire coast, crossed the flat fields of Portsea Island towards the thickets of masts beyond the huddled red roofs of Portsmouth. A minute or two after passing through the white stone arch of the fortifications it stopped outside The George. The vicar of Merton was there, too, having brought his fourteen-year-old son to begin his naval career with Nelson in the *Victory* and he offered to take a letter back to Emma. So he wrote quickly: "6 o'clock, George Inn. My dearest and most beloved of women, Nelson's Emma, I arrived here this moment and Mr. Lancaster takes it. His coach is at the door and only waits for my line. *Victory* is at St. Helen's and, if possible, I shall be at sea this day. God protect you and my dear Horatia prays ever your most faithful Nelson and Bronte."

There was an official call to be made on the Commissioners of the Dockyard and then he was ready to embark. Two guests were coming out to dine in his flagship, George Canning, the Treasurer of the Navy, and George Rose, the Vice-President of the Board of Trade, but there would be difficulty in getting them aboard for the High Street between the inn and the sally-port was choked with crowds waiting to see him leave. So arrangements were changed and orders given for his barge to avoid Portsmouth Point and come ashore on the shingle at Southsea where the wheeled bathing-machines were parked. He and his retinue left The George by the back door walking through the fortifications and across Southsea Common to the beach. Word spread amongst the crowds and they rushed through the narrow streets to see him go. Some tried to grasp his hand, others knelt and prayed, many wept and soldiers of the Portsmouth garrison had to clear a way to the waiting boat. Amongst the crowd was Benjamin Silliman, the American who had seen him in the Strand three weeks before, who recorded that "by the time he had arrived on the beach some hundreds of people had collected in his train, pressing all around and pushing to get a little before him to obtain a sight of his face. I stood on one of the batteries near which he passed and had a full view of his person. He was elegantly dressed and his blue coat splendidly illuminated with stars and ribbons. As the barge in which he embarked pushed away from the shore, the people gave him three cheers, which his Lordship returned by waving his hat." Once they were away and headed for Spithead and St. Helen's anchorage, he took his place beside his flag-captain, Thomas Hardy. "I had their huzzas before," he said, "I have their hearts now."

On the morning of Sunday, 15th September, 1805, the *Victory* sailed before a light breeze; at sunset she was off Christchurch to the west of the

49 Climax at Trafalgar. Even James Gillray, who had often lampooned Nelson, was both moved and restrained by news of his death; however he could not resist caricaturing Emma Hamilton as Britannia, King George III as Captain Hardy and the Duke of Clarence as a sailor.

50 *Above left*: The defeated survivor. The Emperor Napoleon – painted in 1805 by Joseph Dorffmeister – turns his back on the English Channel and points towards his globe and alternative ambitions on the Continent after hearing the news of Trafalgar.

51 *Above right*: The fallen victor. After Nelson was buried at St. Paul's Cathedral, a wax effigy was commissioned for display at Westminster Abbey to attract paying visitors. Made by Catherine Andras, for whom Nelson had sat, it was so life-like that Emma Hamilton wanted to kiss its lips.

52 *Below*: The sense of occasion was captured by Turner in his epic painting of the Battle of Trafalgar, which was to give Britain maritime supremacy and global predominance for more than a century.

53 The anguish of grief at Nelson's death overwhelmed the triumph of his victory. The entire nation was stricken by the news – as is expressed in this contemporary caricature of a sailor and his girl at Portsmouth – whether they had been his friends, had seen him on his travels or just knew him as the embodiment of their aspirations and a hero with whom most could identify.

54 *Above*: Living memories of Nelson were shared by these veterans of Trafalgar illustrated in *The Graphic* of 1879. All senior retired officers, they had fought as midshipmen or probationary 1st class volunteers, like Admiral Percival Johnson (third from left), who had been on board the *Victory*.

55 *Below*: "The Immortal Memory" kept alive at Burnham Thorpe when, in 1985, the Rev. Cecil Isaacson, the ninth rector since Edmund Nelson – his church in the background – welcomed visitors from Bronte in Sicily and Nelson still attracted the attention of the news-media.

Needles and at nightfall fog came down. Next day, she was off Weymouth and Nelson was relieved that there was no need to shelter in the bay because the King was staying there and he had no wish to pay respects to the monarch who had made his disapproval of his private conduct so obvious. Writing to tell Emma of this, he assured her: "I love and adore you to the very excess of the passion but with God's blessing we shall soon meet again. Kiss dear Horatia a thousand times for me." Off Plymouth, the day after, he sent orders for two ships of the line, the *Ajax* and *Thunderer*, to join him as soon as possible. Out in the Atlantic, three days later, they encountered a frigate bringing the sick Admiral Bickerton home, and learned that the enemy were still in Cadiz. Off Lisbon, they heard the same. On the 26th, Nelson sent the *Euryalus* ahead with orders to Collingwood to put himself under his command, adding that, when the *Victory* joined the fleet, no salutes were to be fired so as not to alert the enemy in Cadiz of his arrival.

He arrived off Cadiz the next day, the eve of his forty-seventh birthday, and at last sighted the masts and yards of the enemy he had hunted so long: thirty-three French and Spanish sail of the line at anchor beyond the long spit of land on which the city lay. Within three miles of the harbour mouth the five British ships of the inshore squadron tacked to and fro, while Collingwood with seventeen sail of the line waited farther out to sea. In contrast to the fleet that Nelson had recently commanded, this one was not happy, for Collingwood was unable to present the kindly, humorous side of his character that his wife and daughters and Mary Moutray knew, to those he led. To them, he was known as "an old bear", a disciplinarian to equal St. Vincent but apparently without his underlying kindliness. There was no lively conversation at his dinner-table, for as young Captain Hoste, commanding the frigate *Eurydice* in his fleet, remarked, "Old Collingwood likes *quiet people*".

Officers and men in the ships off Cadiz longed for Nelson to arrive, although only a minority had served under him. "For charity's sake," Captain Codrington of the *Orion* had just written, "send us Lord Nelson, ye men of power!" His appeal was both personal and professional. One of the original "Band of Brothers" who had fought at the Nile, Sir Alexander Ball, now Governor of Malta, encapsulated his qualities:

Lord Nelson was an admiral, every inch of him. He looked at everything, not merely in its possible relation to the naval service in general but in its immediate bearings on his own squadron; to his officers, his men, to the particular ships themselves, his affections were as steady and ardent as those of a lover. Hence, though his temper was constitutionally irritable and uneven, yet never was a commander so enthusiastically loved by men of all ranks from the captain of the fleet to the youngest ship-boy.

After the happy meeting with the friend he called "dear Coll", there was a sad and embarrassing task to perform. One reason for low morale in Collingwood's fleet had been that its second-in-command was Sir Robert Calder, who had failed so miserably to strike more than a bruising blow at Villeneuve off Finisterre in August. Blithely unaware of the savage criticism and contempt he had aroused in England, he believed he had won a victory, albeit indecisive. "He has an ordeal to pass through, which I fear he little expects," Nelson told Collingwood, for it was his duty to tell Calder that he was required to return home and face a court martial for his failure.[1] He did what he could to soften the blow, first suggesting that he delay his departure until the enemy came out to fight, as he was confident that they would. Calder decided to leave immediately, taking passage in his own ship the *Prince of Wales*, a three-deck ship of the line mounting ninety guns. Nelson had expected him to sail in a small ship so as not to deprive the fleet of one that might be needed in battle, just as he himself had returned from the Baltic in a brig. But Calder was adamant and Nelson had not the heart to refuse him, only insisting that he wait until another ship of the line, the *Royal Sovereign* had arrived to become Collingwood's flagship as second-in-command. "He is in adversity," said Nelson by way of explanation.

The mood of the fleet changed as its seventeen thousand men realised that Nelson was amongst them. His own joy matched theirs. "The reception I met with on joining the fleet caused the sweetest sensation in my life," he wrote to a naval friend. "The officers who came on board to welcome my return forgot my rank as Commander-in-Chief in the enthusiasm with which they greeted me. As soon as these emotions were past, I laid before them the plan I had previously arranged for attacking the enemy." Their reaction to this he described in a letter to Emma: "When I came to explain to them the *Nelson touch* it was like an electric shock. Some shed tears, all approved – 'It was new – it was singular – it was simple!' and, from the admirals downwards, it was repeated – 'It must succeed, if ever they will allow us to get at them! You are, my Lord, surrounded by friends, whom you inspire with confidence.' "

He responded accordingly and his old friend Thomas Fremantle, now commanding the *Neptune*, said: "He has obligingly desired me to come to him without ceremony whenever I choose and to dine with him as often as I found it convenient. He looks better than ever I saw him and is grown

---

[1] Vice-Admiral Sir Robert Calder was acquitted of cowardice by the court martial but severely reprimanded for his failure to renew his action with Villeneuve.

fatter." Within three days of his arrival all his captains had dined with him in the *Victory* – fifteen of them on his forty-seventh birthday – and, across the polished silver and gleaming mahogany, he had enlarged upon plans and contingencies. He also speculated, as before, upon his own fate, but this time he was more specific. Before the Battle of the Nile, he had talked of attaining the glory of a victory or Westminster Abbey. Now he announced that, as he had been told that the Abbey was built upon marshy ground and might one day sink and disappear, he would prefer to be buried in St. Paul's Cathedral.

He was confident that Villeneuve would take his fleets to sea either in obedience to Napoleon's orders, or being forced out by lack of provisions in Cadiz. Look-outs perched in the tops of his frigates patrolling close inshore could count the number of enemy ships and the number of gun-ports in each and see which ensign they flew. Thus he knew that Villeneuve commanded eighteen French ships of the line (four of them mounting eighty guns; the rest, seventy-four); under his subordinate Spanish admiral, Gravina, were another fifteen sail of the line (four of them mounting 100 guns or more): thirty-three ships of the line in all. Of his own twenty-seven British ships, seven mounted ninety-eight or 100 guns, the others, mostly seventy-four and a few only sixty-four. Both sides had a few frigates and Nelson's need for more was desperate for he depended upon them for reconnaissance and communications. "I am most exceedingly anxious for more *eyes* and hope the Admiralty are hastening them to me," he complained. "The last fleet was lost to me for want of frigates; God forbid this should."

In the hope of enticing Villeneuve to sea, he repeated his tactics from the Toulon blockade, watching the harbour only with frigates and withdrawing the main fleet over the horizon. This was constantly changing for there were ships to be sent to Gibraltar for fresh water and provisions while others arrived from England, amongst them one of the original "Band of Brothers", Captain Berry now commanding Nelson's old ship the *Agamemnon*. "Here comes that damned fool Berry!" Nelson laughed. "*Now* we shall have a battle!"

Each day, he wrote letters as punctiliously as he had at Merton, once complaining that he had been seven hours at his desk. He wrote to his superiors in London, to other admirals at sea, to friends, naval and civilian; no request for help was ignored. To his friend Captain Frank Southeron he wrote about a lieutenant of the *Hydra* who had deserted and was "adrift in Italy at Naples or Rome, we think, very probably in prison for debt. His father is anxious to save the lad. He ... ran away with an opera dancer from Malta." He even arranged for his debts to be paid: "Supposed to be some two or three hundred pounds – and if now a few more are necessary to liberate the youth, I will be answerable. All we want is to save him from perdition."

To Alexander Davison he confided his thoughts about the immediate future:

> Let the battle be when it may, it will never have been surpassed. My shattered frame, if I survive that day, will require rest and that is all I can ask for. If I fall on such a glorious occasion, it shall be my pride to take care that my friends shall not blush for me: these things are in the hands of a wise and just Providence and His will be done ... Do not think I am low-spirited on this account, or fancy anything is to happen to me; quite the contrary. My mind is calm and I have only to think of destroying the inveterate foe.

On 14th October, the frigates reported that the enemy's fleet had moved closer to the harbour mouth, so he was convinced that they would come out. They might sail north to release Admiral Ganteaume from Brest; or they could sail south-east, making a run for the Straits of Gibraltar, the Mediterranean and refuge in Toulon; or they might come out to fight. It was time to make the final dispositions.

One of these was a special mission for his young friend William Hoste. As he had expected, the parson's son from Norfolk had commanded his frigate with dash and, not content with patrolling off Cadiz, had taken a Spanish privateer. On the 13th Hoste had been rewarded with the command of the finest frigate available, the *Amphion*, in which Nelson had once flown his flag as Commander-in-Chief. "I need not mention the kindness I have received from Lord Nelson," he wrote to his family: "His present appointment speaks for itself." Yet next day, the Admiral wrote in his diary: "Sent *Amphion* to Gibraltar and Algiers. Enemy at the harbour mouth." Her mission was to take a cargo of bullion to the former and a diplomatic letter to the latter.

It had long been necessary to avoid direct conflict with the pirate-states of North Africa – that could be left to the Americans – and to maintain trade and the use of their ports by British warships in need of replenishment. Nelson had his own ideas about dealing with the Dey of Algiers and, some months before, had written to Emma that he had been "so insolent that nothing but a good flogging will put him in order". But now he had to exercise the diplomacy he had displayed to such effect in the Baltic. He wrote to him: "I rely that nothing will ever be permitted to happen which can interrupt the most perfect harmony and good understanding which exists between your Highness ... and the British Nation. I am confident that your Highness will give orders for the most friendly reception of British ships in all the Ports of your Dominions ... " He was not entirely confident since the Dey's acquisitive eye and piratical instincts even suggested some risk to the courier's own ship, he added: "I shall be very anxious for the return of the frigate, that I may know the state of your Highness's health."[1]

In peacetime, this was the sort of mission for which the finest frigate in the fleet and its most promising young captain might have been chosen; and Emma Hamilton had said of William Hoste: "He will be a second Nelson." But Nelson was increasingly certain that the climactic action of the war at sea was imminent; he was desperately short of frigates to watch the enemy; if they did not come out of harbour, as he expected, he was planning to force them out with an attack by fire-ships and Colonel Congreve's new rockets and that would be the sort of action perfectly suited to young Hoste. Yet this most ardent of his fighting captains and his finest frigate he was sending away.

It is possible that the sight of Hoste had reminded him of other young men: particularly of Edward Parker, but also of John Weatherhead who had died off Tenerife, James Moutray, who had died in Corsica and several more. Although frigates were not supposed to fight in fleet actions, it would be impossible to keep the young man out of the most acute danger, for he would know himself to be under his patron's eye. So he was ordered away to safety, to survive whatever was to come as an embodiment of the "Nelson touch"; even as the son he would never have.

Such ideas would probably have been subconscious, for Nelson's affections were occupied with Emma and Horatia. With ships arriving from and departing for England, they maintained a correspondence. Emma had been staying with the William Nelsons at Canterbury and had seen their friends in London, while Horatia was again boarded with Mrs. Gibson in Little Titchfield Street. "My heart is broke away from her," she declared. "You will be even fonder of her when you return. She says, 'I love my dear, dear godpapa but Mrs. Gibson told me he kill'd all the people and I was afraid'. Dearest angel that she is! Oh Nelson, how I love her but how do I idolize you – the dearest husband of my heart, you are all in this world to your Emma. May God send you victory and home to your *Emma, Horatia and paradise Merton*, for when you are there it will be paradise."

These were dreamlike messages from another, distant world to the man reading them, alone in the cabin of his ship, heaving and creaking upon the Atlantic; conscious that upon his judgement, decisions and actions the future of his country – indeed, of Europe – might depend. On 18th October, more signals from the frigates off Cadiz, repeated by

[1] Nelson was unaware that the Dey had been assassinated in August.

other ships standing farther out to sea, finally reported to Nelson and he wrote another letter: "My dearest beloved Emma, the dear friend of my bosom, the signal has been made that the enemy's combined fleet are coming out of port. We have very little wind, so that I have no hopes of seeing them before tomorrow. May the God of Battles crown my endeavours with success. At all events I will take care that my name shall ever be dear to you and Horatia, both of whom I love as much as my own life; and, as my last writing before the battle will be to you, so I hope in God that I shall live to finish my letter after the battle. May heaven bless you, prays your Nelson and Bronte." Next day, he added another note to her, concluding: "May God Almighty give us success over these fellows and enable us to get a peace" and he wrote a postscript to Horatia, telling her to "love dear Lady Hamilton, who most dearly loves you. Give her a kiss for me".

As always before battle, Nelson had apprehensions of death or wounds. It would have been curious if he had not for he would be exposed on his quarterdeck until, after the first broadside, it was often hid by gunsmoke and even then roundshot, grapeshot and the chain and bar shot fired to cut rigging, would be flying. His aim was to assault the centre and rear of the enemy line, leaving the van to sail on or attempt to turn and fight while he destroyed the other two-thirds. With his own twenty-seven sail of the line attacking in two divisions – there were not enough ships to form a third in reserve – he would face the thirty-three enemy ships but with these tactics, the odds would be in his favour when the fighting began. Then courage, skill in ship-handling and gunnery would be decisive. His own ships' companies had been at sea continuously, sometimes for years, while the French and Spanish had spent most of that time in port. His guns' crews could fire at twice the rate of the enemy and had a technical advantage: the British guns were fired instantaneously by flintlock and lanyard, making aim and accuracy more effective; the French and Spanish still used the slow-match and power-train involving a delay before discharge which could throw the aim of gun-layers in a rolling ship. Finally, if it came to boarding and "service hand-to-hand", he had shown his men exactly what was expected of them by his own example. In the event of signals being invisible through the smoke, he told his captains in the written instructions he sent them: "No captain can do very wrong if he places his ship alongside that of an enemy."

On the morning of 20th October, Nelson's frigate's saw the last of the enemy ships of the line emerge from Cadiz. There were no means of telling what Villeneuve planned to do and no hint had reached the British of the events that had at last forced him to accept battle. Back in August, when Villeneuve had taken refuge in Ferrol, Napoleon had still expected that he would break out to join with Ganteaume's fleet from Brest and sail for the Channel to make his invasion possible. But the latter had been blockaded in port, while the former had run south to Cadiz; news of this reaching Napoleon soon after he had heard that Austria and Russia were to ally themselves with Britain against France. The invasion of England must therefore be postponed, he decided, and at the end of August the *Grande Armée* began to strike camp along the coast and begin the long march to Germany. Shortly before leaving Paris to lead his armies, Napoleon sent new instructions to Villeneuve: he was to sail into the Mediterranean with the combined French and Spanish fleets, land troops at Naples, to forestall any British attempt to reinforce the Austrians from the south; then make for Toulon. Villeneuve was relieved at what seemed an easier option than fighting his way to the Straits of Dover and that he was allowed to choose his date for departure. In the event this was forced upon him by the humiliating news that the more senior Admiral Rosily was on his way overland to Cadiz; not, as he had at first supposed, to offer support and advice but to supersede him. When he heard that he was already at Madrid but delayed there by a broken carriage-spring, he decided to leave for the Mediterranean while he was still in command. On the morning of 19th October, he had given the order for his fleet to sail. Twenty-four hours later, all thirty-three of them were clear of the harbour and steering south-west.

British frigates signalled each move to ships on the horizon and these repeated the news to the main fleet waiting some thirty miles from land. To avoid frightening Villeneuve back into port, Nelson ordered his fleet on to a parallel course to Villeneuve's, keeping about twenty miles to the westward. This he continued throughout the night of the 20th, then at four o'clock on the morning of the 21st October, he turned his fleet towards the north-east so that at dawn he would be about nine miles to windward of his enemy and in a commanding position from which to attack. By then, Villeneuve would be so far from Cadiz and from the Straits of Gibraltar sailing some thirty miles south-west of Cape Trafalgar; while Nelson hovered, ready to strike, with the wind in his sails. A battle would be inevitable.

The morning dawned clear with a light breeze but the ships were heaving over a slow Atlantic swell, which grew heavier, suggesting a gale approaching from the west. When it was light enough to signal by flags, Nelson ordered the fleet to take up battle formation: one division led by himself in the *Victory*; the other by Collingwood in the *Royal Sovereign*. It was a slow process since the great ships moved at no more than walking pace yet this did not lessen the certainty of a battle with the mass of enemy

ships that now were seen blocking the eastern horizon. "The French and
Spanish fleets were like a great wood on our lee bow," remembered Able
Seaman Brown, watching from Nelson's flagship, "which cheered the
hearts of any British tar in the *Victory* like lions anxious to be at it."

Nelson was pacing his quarterdeck, wearing his usual uniform coat
embroidered with the four stars of his principal honours, giving orders to
Hardy and the captains of his four frigates. This done, one of them,
Henry Blackwood, who had come to Merton with the news that had
brought them here, and Hardy were taken down to his cabin and asked to
witness a document. This was Nelson's new will in which he had written,
"I leave Emma Hamilton ... a legacy to my King and Country, that they
will give her ample provision to maintain her rank in life. I also leave to
the beneficience of my Country, my adopted daughter Horatia Nelson
Thompson; and I desire she will use in future the name of Nelson only.
These are the only favours I ask of my King and Country at this moment
when I am going to fight their battle ... "

At the moment of sighting the enemy it had been reckoned that action
could not be joined for about six hours, so that there was plenty of time to
prepare. All the ships had been cleared of partitions, furniture and
lumber, so that the decks were clear but for the long, parallel lines of
cannon along either side, run out of their open gun-ports. The scene was
majestic: the two columns of great ships, studding-sails spread wide to
catch the breeze, riding slowly over the long ocean swell; on the decks of
some, bands playing cheerful nautical tunes, particularly *Heart of Oak*;
every ship cleared and ready for action; some marines cleaning their
muskets again while sailors sharpened cutlasses and, here and there,
danced a hornpipe to pass the time. Nelson, talking with his officers in the
sunlight on the quarterdeck, recalled that it was both the anniversary of
his uncle Captain Maurice Suckling's action with the French in the West
Indies that had inspired his boyhood hero-worship, and also the day of
the autumn fair at Burnham Thorpe. He toured the ship with Hardy,
speaking to men at the guns and sometimes joking. One Irish sailor was
cutting a notch in a wooden gun-carriage, it was said; explaining that he
was adding it to the others he had carved to mark victories and doing so
now in case he was killed winning another. "You'll make notches enough
in the enemy's ships," laughed Nelson.

The long array of enemy ships, stretching some four miles across the
horizon, was slowly growing larger and it was possible to see the colours.
Some French ships were painted like the British, black with broad yellow
stripes running along each side so that, when their gun-ports were opened,
they looked chequered; others wore red or white stripes, or both, and
some were all black. The iron hoops around their masts were painted

black and Nelson had ordered that all his ships had theirs painted yellow so that they could be identified above the smoke of battle. At eleven o'clock, the *Victory* and *Royal Sovereign* were three miles from the enemy line; when they were one mile distant, they would come within range of the enemy's broadsides. Nelson went below to his cabin and there Lieutenant Pasco, the acting signals officer, following with a question about his duties, saw him on his knees writing and, as he said, "remained stationary and quiet until he rose".

All Nelson's religious instincts and beliefs had come together at this moment: his upbringing by his saintly father and his early memories of quiet Norfolk churches; his moment of spiritual inspiration and his vision of the "radiant orb" in the South Atlantic; his reliance upon Providence and prayer and the private relationship with the deity which, he felt, overrode the conventions of public morality. This expressed itself in his vigorous, easy prose. The prayer he composed that morning he wrote in his diary in the strong, crabbed hand that had become so familiar, under the date, "Monday, Octr. 21st, 1805". When Lieutenant Pasco saw him on his knees, he was writing:

> May the Great God, whom I worship, grant to my Country and for the benefit of Europe in general a great and glorious victory, and may no misconduct in anyone tarnish it, and may humanity after victory be the predominant feature in the British Fleet. For myself individually, I commit my life to Him who made me and may His blessing light upon my endeavours for serving my Country faithfully. To Him I resign myself and the just cause which is entrusted me to defend. Amen, amen, amen.

A few moments later, Nelson joined Pasco on deck and ordered him to make a signal. "I wish to say . . . 'England confides that every man will do his duty'," he told him. "You must be quick for I have one more to make, which is for close action." Pasco asked if he could substitute the word "expects", which was a single flag in the signal book, for "confides" which would involve a complicated hoist of alphabetical flags. "That will do," answered Nelson. "Make it directly." The flags flew up the halyards and the telescopes of the fleet were upon them. "What is Nelson signalling about?" growled Collingwood on the quarterdeck of the *Royal Sovereign.* "We all know what we have to do."

The British fleet was not sailing into action as Nelson had planned. The wind was so light that his two columns would not have time to form line abreast before meeting the enemy. Thus, as they approached, the enemy would be able to concentrate their fire on the leading ships, so being able to "cross the T" of their opponents; advantage that would usually prove decisive. Yet Nelson accepted the risk, realising that both the *Victory* and the *Royal Sovereign* might have to withstand the fire of broadsides concentrated on their bows nearly half-an-hour before they could bring their own to bear (see plan, page xvi).

The two leading ships were now a mile from the open gun-ports of the enemy line, and in the *Neptune*, sailing astern of the *Victory*, a midshipman saw what was imminent: "Their broadsides turned towards us, showing their iron teeth, and now and then trying the range of a shot ... that they might, the moment we came within point-blank, open their fire upon our van ships." At noon, the *Royal Sovereign* came under fire and the watching Nelson said: "See how that noble fellow Collingwood takes his ship into action! How I envy him!" And Collingwood, knowing what his friend would be thinking, turned to one of his officers as the round-shot flew and said: "What would Nelson give to be here!"

On the quarterdeck of the *Victory*, Nelson stood with Hardy and Blackwood while his secretary, John Scott, his chaplain, the Reverend Alexander Scott, and the surgeon Dr. William Beatty, talked nearby. The doctor worried that the four stars embroidered on the admiral's uniform would mark him as a target when they were within range of rifle-fire and that he should change into a plain coat.[1] "Take care, doctor, what you are about," warned the admiral's secretary. "I would not be the man to mention such a matter to him." Beatty tried and failed to do so, hovering near the admiral, awaiting a pause in his earnest talk with his officers. Blackwood was trying to persuade him to transfer to his frigate for safety and a clearer view of the action. When this was refused he and Hardy suggested that the ninety-eight gun ship sailing astern of the *Victory*, the *Téméraire* – so named after a famous ship once captured from the French – should lead the line and bear the brunt of the first broadsides. Nelson insisted that his flagship continue to lead but with the *Téméraire* and the *Neptune*, also of ninety-eight guns, in close support. In the event it was Hardy who raised the question of the coat, suggesting that the decorations might catch the eye of a sniper; he later said Nelson had replied that "he was aware it might be seen but it was now too late to be shifting a coat".

A shot, fired at extreme range, flew overhead and the admiral ordered Blackwood back to his ship. They shook hands and before the young captain climbed down the side to his boat, he said: "I trust, my Lord, that on my return to the *Victory* ... I shall find your Lordship well and in

[1] There is no evidence that Nelson courted death by wearing his decorations, although this has often been suggested. There is no doubt that he looked forward to his return, having written to Horatia two days earlier, "I shall be sure of your prayers for my safety, conquest and speedy return to dear Merton ..."

possession of twenty prizes." "God bless you, Blackwood," replied Nelson, "I shall never speak to you again." Another shot punched through the main topgallant sail. A moment later, another howled across the deck and split a man open; it was the admiral's secretary. "Is that poor Scott?" asked Nelson as seamen heaved the mangled body over the side.

The *Victory*, surging towards the enemy line, could not bring her own broadside to bear and was raked from bow to stern by their broadsides. One shot smashed the ship's wheel to splinters and she had to be steered by the forty seamen standing by the huge tiller on the lower gun-deck, helm-orders reaching them by messenger. Another shot cut through a file of marines standing along the rolled hammocks packed in netting along the bulwarks as a barricade and waiting to engage enemy snipers; eight were dead and Nelson ordered the survivors to be dispersed around the upper deck. Splinters of wood whirred across the quarter deck, one denting the silver buckle of Hardy's shoe; he caught the admiral's eye and Nelson said calmly: "This is too warm work to last long."

As a feint, the *Victory* had been steering for the enemy's van, but now Nelson ordered a turn that would swing the ship and those following her towards the twelfth in the line. He was looking for Villeneuve's flagship, hoping to fight her, ship to ship; but no admiral's flag could be seen except that of a Spanish rear-admiral flying from the colossal *Santissima Trinidad* of four decks and 140 guns, which he had hoped to capture at St. Vincent eight years before. Astern of her sailed one French ship of eighty guns and another of seventy-four: the *Bucentaure* and the *Redoubtable*, the former proving to be Villeneuve's flagship; the latter, the most efficient fighting ship in the combined fleets, whose captain, Lucas, had trained his men in boarding and sniping from the masts. At half-past twelve, Hardy asked the admiral which of these three ships, all firing into the *Victory*, they should challenge first. "It does not signify which we turn on board," replied Nelson. "Take your choice."

So the *Victory* turned towards the stern of the *Bucentaure* and, as she passed the array of elegant windows lighting the admiral's and captain's cabins, she unleashed her broadside: fifty guns loaded with two or three roundshot each, blew in her stern, dismounted twenty guns and killed or wounded half her crew. Then the *Victory* herself was raked by a broadside from the French eighty-four-gun ship *Neptune*, crossing her bows. Billowing smoke hid the collision of the fleets as Hardy ordered the helm over again to steer for the *Redoubtable*: the ships crashed together, their yards and rigging locking; their guns firing, muzzle to muzzle. Through the smoke, Lucas could be seen assembling boarders on deck to swarm across the bulwarks until a blast of grapeshot from the *Victory* cut them down. Astern of the British flagship the *Téméraire* followed through the gap she had forced, as the two British columns, ship by ship, joined battle. At the heart of it the two admirals and their heaviest ships fought in a vortex of smoke, flame and shattered ships.

"Engaging the French and Spanish admirals, one on each side," wrote Thomas Johns, an able seaman in the *Victory*, in a letter to his parents, "we was so involved in smoke and fire not to be seen by any of our frigates looking on for about half an hour and they thought we was blown up or sunk, having no less than five ships on us at the time, but we were bravely seconded by the *Téméraire* or we would have been sunk, it being their orders and intention to capture or sink Lord Nelson's ship."

An hour after the first shots, Nelson and Hardy still stood on the quarterdeck, pacing to and fro, stopping to give orders; mostly hidden by swirling smoke but sometimes revealed as it blew away. At about a quarter past one, Hardy turned to see Nelson on his knees. He was supporting himself with the fingers of his left hand on the bloodstained deck. Then he fell on to his left side. A sergeant-major of marines and two seamen lifted his shoulders and Hardy knelt beside him; he had been hit in the shoulder by a sniper's bullet from the *Redoubtable*. "They have done for me at last, Hardy," Nelson told him. "My backbone is shot through." The three men lifted him, on Hardy's orders, to carry him down the ladders to the surgeon on the orlop deck below the waterline. On reaching the middle deck, Nelson ordered them to stop and he gave orders to a midshipman for the adjustment of the tiller-ropes. Then he took a handkerchief from his pocket and spread it across his face in the hope that he would not be recognised by his men as he was carried below.

Down in the gloom of the lowest deck, lit by the faint glimmer of horn lanterns, Beatty, the surgeon, was busy with more than forty wounded and dying men until called: "Mr. Beatty, Lord Nelson is here. Mr. Beatty, the admiral is wounded." As he was lowered to the deck and the handkerchief fell from his face, he looked up at the surgeon and said, "Ah, Mr. Beatty! You can do nothing for me. I have but a short time to live; my back is shot through." While the doctor examined his wound and removed his blood-stained clothes, Nelson looked at his surroundings. Sailors carrying more wounded men down the ladder, stooped to clear the low beams, painted blood-red, to lay their loads in rows on the deck. In the gloom the figures of the surgeons and the surgeons' mates moved along the bodies, examining them or lifting them to a table covered with sailcloth to probe a wound, or conduct an amputation with knife and saw and with rum to deaden the pain. The scene was lit by the lanterns which dimmed or brightened as the concussion of broadsides from the decks above sucked the air from the orlop deck. The noise and vibration of the battle was thunderous, muffling the screams and moans of the injured men below.

Amongst those brought down was young midshipman Rivers, his leg shot away. As he saw Captain Hardy he muttered something about now being of no further use to him; Nelson heard and ordered, "Mind, Hardy, that youngster is not forgot." Dr. Scott, the chaplain, picked his way across the bodies to the admiral's side and his presence seemed to make Nelson aware of death. "Doctor, I told you," he said quickly, "Doctor, I am gone." Then, agitated and breathless, he added, "Remember me to Lady Hamilton. Remember me to Horatia. Remember me to all my friends. Doctor, remember me to Mr. Rose; tell him I have left a will and left Lady Hamilton and Horatia to my country."

The surgeon had completed his investigation of the wound. A musket ball, fired from above, had struck his left shoulder, penetrated deep into his chest and probably lodged in the spine but, he told Nelson, he would not put him to the pain of trying to probe the wound. He then asked him what sensations he felt and was told that his breathing was difficult, he had no feeling in the lower part of his body; he felt "a gush of blood every minute" within his chest. "I felt it break my back," he said. He was hot and thirsty and lemonade and watered wine was brought to him. "Fan, fan ... drink, drink," he kept whispering.

Among the explosions above, he heard a hoarse cheer and asked the reason. Lieutenant Pasco, also wounded, was lying nearby and raised himself on an elbow to explain that the gun-crews must have seen through their gun-port an enemy ship strike her colours. The admiral wanted news of the battle and called for Hardy: "Will no one bring Hardy to me? He must be killed." Then a midshipman came below to tell him that his flag-captain was engaged on deck but would come down as soon as possible. He asked the name of the midshipman and the purser, Mr. Burke, kneeling at his side, answered, "It is Mr. Bulkeley, my Lord." Turning his head towards the boy he said. "It is his voice. Remember me to your father." For a moment the memory returned of a brisk and friendly Army officer he had met in the jungle of Nicaragua. Then to the purser he said, "It is nonsense, Mr. Burke, to suppose I can live. My sufferings are great but they will soon be over."

During the hour since Nelson had been hit, the "pell-mell battle" that he had planned was fought. One after the other, the stately ships of the two British columns swung into action: Nelson's attacking the enemy's centre; Collingwood's, the rear. As Villeneuve's flagship had joined battle with the *Victory*, he had signalled to Rear-Admiral Dumanoir, who commanded the van, to turn back and support him. But the wind was so light that of the ten ships which managed to turn, only five joined the fighting. Meanwhile, the *Bucentaure* had been battered into a wreck by the *Victory*, and then by the *Conqueror*, until only one of her three masts still stood. At half-past one, Villeneuve, realising that Dumanoir could not lead his ships into action, himself had signal flags run up the halyards of his one remaining mast ordering the individual captains of the van to join him as best they could. Then that mast, too, crashed over the side and, at a quarter past two, Villeneuve surrendered his flagship to Captain Israel Pellew of the *Conqueror*. The action was now a succession of duels between ships, loosing broadsides into each other at point-blank range, half-hidden from each other by smoke. Only spasmodically did news reach the *Victory* of one French or Spanish ship after another striking their colours in surrender.

At about half-past two, Hardy came stooping beneath the beams to kneel by Nelson, shake his hand and report. "We have got twelve or fourteen of the enemy's ships in our possession," he said, "but five of their van have tacked and show an intention of bearing down on the *Victory*. I have therefore called two or three of our fresh ships around us and have no doubt of giving them a drubbing." "I hope none of our ships have struck?" asked Nelson. "No, my Lord," answered Hardy, "there is no fear of that." There was a pause; then Nelson said, "I am a dead man, Hardy. I am going fast. It will all be over with me soon. Come nearer to me. Pray let my dear Lady Hamilton have my hair and all the other things belonging to me." "Is your pain great?" he was asked. "Yes, but I shall live half an hour longer yet."

Hardy returned to the deck and Dr. Beatty came back to his side. "Ah, Mr. Beatty," he said, "all power and motion and feeling below my breast are gone. You very well *know* I can live but a short time. Ah, Beatty, I am too certain of it. You *know* I am gone." "My Lord," replied the surgeon, "unhappily for our country, nothing can be done for you" and he turned to stifle his sobs. "God be praised," whispered the dying man, "I have done my duty." Beatty asked about the pain and was told that it was so severe he wished he was dead, "yet one would like to live a little longer, too ... What would become of poor Lady Hamilton if she knew my situation?" His thoughts were interrupted by the jar and thunder of a broadside, the huge cannon bounding back in recoil on the deck above. "Oh, *Victory*! *Victory*! how you distract my poor brain!" His thoughts concentrated again. "How dear is life to all men."

Hardy returned fifty minutes after his first visit, and took his cold hand, congratulating him on "a brilliant victory". It was complete, he said, although he did not know how many enemy ships had surrendered, but he was certain of having taken fourteen or fifteen. "That is well," replied Nelson, "but I had bargained for twenty." Then with emphasis he gasped, "*Anchor*, Hardy, *anchor!*" He had felt the heave and lurch of the ship increase and knew that the gale he had forecast must be imminent. "I suppose, my Lord, Admiral Collingwood will now take upon himself the direction of affairs?" "Not while I live, I hope, Hardy. No, do *you* anchor, Hardy." "Shall we make the signal, sir?" "Yes, for if I live, I'll anchor."

There was another pause, then Nelson said, "Don't throw me overboard, Hardy." "Oh, no, certainly not." "Then you know what to do?" Nelson went on. "Take care of my dear Lady Hamilton, Hardy, take care of poor Lady Hamilton." Then he said faintly, "Kiss me, Hardy."[1] Hardy knelt and kissed his cheek. "Now I am satisfied," said Nelson. "Thank God I have done my duty." Captain Hardy stood, stooped and silent, for a moment, then knelt again and kissed Nelson's forehead. "Who is that?" he asked. "It is Hardy." "God bless you, Hardy."

Nelson now asked his steward, Chevalier, to turn him on to his right side. This may have eased the pain but it hastened the onset of death for the blood that had flooded the left lung, now began to drain into the right. "I wish I had not left the deck," he said, "for I shall soon be gone." His breathing became slow and shallow, his voice weaker and he whispered to his chaplain, "Doctor, I have not been a *great* sinner". Then, "Remember that I leave Lady Hamilton and my daughter Horatia as a legacy to my country . . . never forget Horatia." His distress increased with heat, thirst and pain which could be eased by Scott rubbing his chest. "Thank God I have done my duty," he was heard to mutter: "Drink, drink. Fan, fan. Rub, rub . . . " Then he became speechless. The chaplain and the purser were supporting his shoulders and his steward knelt at his side, none speaking. Then Chevalier called Dr. Beatty and the surgeon took Nelson's wrist: it was cold and he could feel no pulse. At this, Nelson opened his eyes, looked up and closed them again. The chaplain continued to rub his chest, while the purser held his shoulders until, at half-past four, the steward called the surgeon again. He confirmed what they already knew: Nelson was dead.

"Partial firing continued until 4.30 p.m.," Hardy entered in the *Victory*'s log, "when, a victory having been reported to the Right Hon. Lord Nelson, K.B., and Commander-in-Chief, he died of his wounds."

The great gale that Nelson had forecast now arose. The shattered ships, victors and vanquished, tossed and wallowed in heavy seas, filled

---

[1] There is a theory that Nelson had said, "Kismet, Hardy", using the Arabic word for fate. No contemporary evidence supports this, however, and the request reported by Dr. Beatty accords with the strong emotions that Nelson never shied from showing. Yet Dr. Beatty, who recorded what was said, noted, "From . . . the noise of the guns, the whole of his Lordship's expressions could not be . . . distinctly heard".

with exhausted, wounded and dying men. Collingwood, now commanding the British fleet, did not anchor as Nelson had ordered, and, as result,
only four of seventeen enemy ships they had captured survived the storm.
So it was not for several days that the extent of the victory and the loss
could be assessed. The British had lost no ships but nearly seventeen
hundred men had been killed or wounded. The combined French and
Spanish fleets had, however, lost eighteen ships captured or destroyed in
action, nearly six thousand men killed or wounded and twenty thousand
taken prisoner, including Admiral Villeneuve. Although it had not been
the total annihilation that Nelson had planned, it was a total victory: any
danger of invasion to Britain was averted; the Royal Navy had taken
command of the seas. Yet joy and satisfaction were drowned in sorrow at
the loss of Nelson.

When the storm had abated, the wounded put ashore at Gibraltar, the
ships made water-tight and the blood scrubbed from the decks, officers
and men wrote home to express these conflicting emotions. Amongst
them, Admiral Collingwood wrote to break the news of the death of their
friend to Mary Moutray, a widow aged fifty-four. "It was about the
middle of the action," he told her, "when an officer came from the *Victory*
to tell me he was wounded. He sent his love to me and desired me to
conduct the fleet. I asked the officer if the wound was dangerous and he,
by his look, told what he could not speak, nor I reflect upon now without
suffering again the anguish of that moment. You, my dear madam, who
know what our friendship was, can judge what I have felt. All the praise
and acclamations of joy for our victory only bring to my mind what it has
cost."

Alexander Scott, the chaplain who had tended the dying Nelson, wrote
from the *Victory* to a woman friend in England:

> You always mentioned Lord Nelson *con amore* and it is about him – I
> can neither think nor talk of anything else. Let the country mourn their
> hero; I grieve for the loss of the most fascinating companion I ever
> conversed with – the greatest and most simple of men – one of the
> nicest and most innocent – interesting beyond all, on shore, in public
> and even in private life. Men are not always themselves and put on
> their behaviour with their clothes, but if you live with a man on board a
> ship for years; if you are continually with him in his cabin, your mind
> will soon find out how to appreciate him. I could for ever tell you the
> qualities of this beloved man. I have not shed a tear for years before the
> 21st of October and since, whenever alone, I am quite like a child.

The ship's company of the *Victory* were as grief-stricken. "Great God!" a
seaman had exclaimed on hearing the news, "I would rather the shot had

taken off my head and spared his life." A boatswain's mate was unable to pipe the hands to quarters because of his tears. "Hang me, I can't do it!" he sobbed. "To lose him now! I wouldn't have cared if it had been my old father, brother or sisters if there were fifty more of them – but I can't think of parting with Nelson."

An uneducated seaman, James Bayley, wrote from the ship to his sister, telling his story of the battle and the death of Nelson: "It was his last words that it was his lot for me to go but I am going to Heaven, but never haul down your colours to France for your men will stick to you – them words was to Captn. Hardy and so we did – for we came off victorious and they have behaved well to us for they wanted to take Ld. Nelson from us, but we told Captn., as we brought him out we would bring him home, so it was so and he was put into a cask of spirits."

Nelson's body was preserved first in a cask of brandy – at Gibraltar, this was changed to spirits of wine – lashed to the mainmast and guarded day and night by a marine sentry as his cabin had been. The news was being carried to England by the schooner *Pickle*, her ensign flying at half-mast, in the form of the first despatch written by Collingwood on the day after the battle. This did not begin with news of the great victory which would change the course of history, but the death of one man. "Sir," he had begun writing to the Secretary of the Admiralty. "The ever to be lamented death of Vice-Admiral Lord Viscount Nelson, who, in the late conflict with the enemy, fell in the hour of victory, leaves me the duty of informing my Lords Commissioners of the Admiralty . . ."

EPILOGUE

"Let no funereal dirges rise
Around my Nelson's trophied bier,"
Cried Glory, bending from her skies,
"The Hero lives immortal here."

– *The Gentleman's Magazine*, February, 1806

At one o'clock on the cold and foggy morning of Wednesday, 6th November, 1805, the cobbled courtyard of the Admiralty in Whitehall suddenly rang with horses' hooves, harness and carriage-wheels. Windows were lighted, doors opened and two tired and travel-worn naval officers were admitted with urgent despatches from Admiral Collingwood. Old Lord Barham, the First Lord, was roused from sleep and at once sent messengers to the Prime Minister at 10 Downing Street and to the King at Windsor Castle.

Mr. Pitt, woken at three, was so stirred by the news that he dressed and waited for dawn by candlelight, alternately elated with triumph and distracted with grief. King George was told at seven and it was nearly five minutes before he could speak. Lord Barham was writing to Fanny, commiserating with her on the death of "your illustrious partner" and delegated the Controller of the Navy Board to inform Emma: he wrote a letter that was sent immediately to Clarges Street. The news was broken to London and the country by a hurriedly printed *Gazette Extraordinary*, followed by the newspapers and salutes of gunfire at the Tower and in Hyde Park.

Everybody seemed to remember where they were and what they did when they heard the news. "It was a sensation at once of patriotism, of pride and of gratitude," wrote James Perry in the *Morning Chronicle*. "Not a man who would not have given up his life to achieve such a victory. Not a man who would not have surrendered every part of the victory (except the honour of Britain) to save the life of Lord Nelson." Nor was the grief and joy confined to the British; the poet Coleridge heard the news in

Naples,[1] and there he found that despite the terrible year of 1799: "When Nelson died it seemed as if no man was a stranger to another: for all were made acquaintances in the rights of a common anguish." In the Mediterranean, Captain Hoste heard the news and declared, "I am as well as a man can be who has lost the best friend he ever possessed"; his grief intensified by having missed the great battle: "Not to have been in it is enough to make one mad; but to have lost such a friend besides is really sufficient to overwhelm me."

That Wednesday night, London was illuminated but, as the *Naval Chronicle* reported: "There was a damp upon the public spirit, which it was impossible to overcome. Even many of the devices and transparencies indicated that the loss of Lord Nelson was more lamented than the victory was rejoiced at." Abraham Goldsmid had set the tone by having just two rows of plain lamps lit on the façade of his town house in St. James's Square. The theatres presented commemorative tableaux; that at Covent Garden staging "a *coup d'oeil* that was both grand and affecting"; the stage was set with portraits of naval heroes while "the English fleet was riding triumphantly in the perspective and in front of the stage a group of naval officers and sailors were seen in attitudes of admiration. Suddenly a medallion descended representing a half-length of the Hero of the Nile surrounded with rays of glory and with these words at the bottom – 'HORATIO NELSON'. The effect was electrical and the house resounded with the loudest plaudits and acclamations." Then *Rule Britannia* was sung with an additional verse, ending,

> Rule, brave Britons, rule the main,
> Avenge the god-like Hero slain.

This was only the beginning. Every newspaper and periodical printed ballads, orations and hymns in Nelson's praise. There was, announced one orator, "a noble emulation among journalists, poets, historians and artists to enumerate the virtues of his mind, exhibit the heroic deeds of his life and render his memory the admiration of all succeeding generations". Amongst the "epic effusions" were those of enthusiastic amateurs including George Canning, the politician and Treasurer of the Navy, and even the Duchess of Devonshire, who began, "*Nelson, by valour led to deathless fame ...*" Sermons were devoted to Nelson at

---

[1] News of Trafalgar reached Naples on 3rd December by the brig *Alcion*. As Nelson had promised the Royal Family, a British ship of the line was to hand for protection. This was the *Excellent* and she fired a salute of twenty-one guns in honour of the victory followed by thirty minute-guns to mourn Nelson with "his Lordship's flag at half-mast and a white ensign in the same manner".

services of thanksgiving; the Rev. Weeden Butler wrote an anthem begining:

> Britons! you heard Trafalgar's story;
> You triumph in your Country's glory:
> Mourn o'er the relics pale and gory
> Of brave, immortal Nelson.
> To earth and war our hero's dead;
> To Heaven and peace his spirit sped;
> Twine your green laurels for the head
> Of brave, immortal Nelson.

The circumstances of his death were an echo of the Christian tradition: the sacrificed saviour of his people. Not only was the immortality of his spirit emphasised but there were familiar figures in the background: the twelve surviving members of "The Band of Brothers", his disciples; even a female figure striking allegorical attitudes: a Mary Magdalene as imagined by Romney, perhaps. An element of love was inherent in all the memories of him; sometimes from direct experience of friendship or loyalty; more often from his reputation for generosity and humanity. That he had offended against his own standards of conduct had surely been redeemed by his blood. Like his own spiritual experience as a young man, this, too, was in the secular context of patriotism with Britainnia the deity. One long elegy entitled *The Tears of Britain* concluded:

> "O art thou gone!" Grief checks her faltering tongue,
> High beats her heart with deeper anguish wrung –
> Her silent grief the mournful gloom pervades –
> Each hovering spirit of the midnight shades,
> In moody concert, joins BRITANNIA's moan,
> The trees weep dew, the hollow mountains groan
> With sighs impregnated; the flying gales
> Her dear departed Hero's loss bewails;
> While Echo babbles thro' the rocky shore,
> In doleful murmurs, NELSON IS NO MORE!
>
> But lo! what sudden blaze the scene illumes,
> Dispersing Night and her attendant glooms?
> And lo! what gleaming form, with radiant pride,
> Emerges glorious from the lucid tide?
> 'Tis NELSON's Shade! Immortal Vision! See!
> How beams his brow with heavenly majesty!
> And now his Spirit mounts on buoyant gales!
> And thus his voice the weeping Goddess hails!

"Britannia cease with tears to wash my shrine,
Ill-suited to a fate like mine!
Hark! that seraphic voice that bids me haste,
In climes celestial, heavenly bliss to taste..."

The iconography followed the versifying. Fashionable artists for whom he had never sat, now portrayed him from memory and other artists' impressions, Benjamin West, James Northcote and John Flaxman amongst them, followed by innumerable engravers, potters and manufacturers of commemorative trinkets. Statues and memorials were commissioned in towns throughout the country and there was immediate talk of building a temple in his honour; a gigantic version of the little naval shrine that he had admired on the Kymin above Monmouth, or even one in the form of a statue of Britannia four storeys high.

As a rival attraction to the tomb being prepared in St. Paul's Cathedral, Westminster Abbey commissioned the medallion-maker Catherine Andras, for whom Nelson had sat just before leaving London for the last time, to make a life-sized wax effigy of him wearing one of his own uniforms. This was a remarkable likeness and later when Emma took Horatia to see it soon after completion she declared that "the direction and form of the nose, mouth and chin and the general carriage of the body was exactly his". It was a trying experience for her and her escort recorded that "tears flowed down her lovely face". She asked to be allowed to re-arrange a lock of the artificial hair to the way he had worn it but, when the glass case was unlocked, her control almost gave way. "She would have kissed the lips," said her companion, "but the guide assured her the colour was not dry."

Tangible recognition was accorded to the living. William was given an earldom, a grant of £99,000 with which to buy a suitable estate and he and his heirs an annual pension of £5,000 in perpetuity. Both of Nelson's sisters were given £15,000 and Fanny an annual pension of £2,000. Emma Hamilton and Horatia were given nothing and, three days after the news of Nelson's death arrived, her mother wrote to George Rose at the Admiralty, "Lady Hamilton's most wretched state of mind prevents her imploring her dear, good Mr. Rose to solicit to Mr. Pitt to consider the family of our great and glorious Nelson ..." But Pitt was ill and the problem of the hero's mistress was set aside.

Once the shock of the news was past, some tried to put the death of Nelson into the context of his life. "Such a death is the finest close and the crown, as it were, of such a life," mused Lord Minto. "If his friends were angels and not men they would acknowledge it as the last favour Providence could bestow ... His glory is certainly at its summit ... but he

might have lived at least to enjoy it." Abraham Goldsmid[1] tried to help
Emma by being briskly realistic, writing to her: "His time was to die and,
if not by a shot, you might have lost him by sickness." A clergyman, the
Rev. Hugh Worthington, preaching on the official day of public thanksgiving for the victory, 5th December, made it seem divinely ordained:
"The Eternal Disposer of events and of nations most awfully proclaimed
the truth that He is able to save or to destroy. Interesting lesson! In the
very moment of victory, He has withdrawn the instrument by which He
wrought it ... O heavenly Father, we bow to Thy will!"

The day before this sermon was preached at the Salters' Hall in
London, the mortal remains of Horatio Nelson returned to Spithead.
The *Victory*, towed from Gibraltar by another ship of the line since most
of her masts had been shot away in the battle, was on passage up-
Channel to the Thames. During this last stage of her voyage Dr. Beatty
and his assistants began to perform an autopsy on Nelson's body. Taken
from its preserving spirits, it proved to be in surprisingly life-like
condition, except for a slight discolouration of the lips. First the surgeon
traced the course of the musket-ball. This, fired from the mizzen-top of
the *Redoubtable*'s mast at a range of about fifty feet, had penetrated his left
shoulder, cut obliquely through the left lobe of the lungs, severed a large
branch of the pulmonary artery, fractured his spine and lodged in the
muscle of his back. Death had been caused by the flooding of the lungs
with blood. Otherwise, Beatty discovered, the vital organs were healthy,
although small, and he might have lived to a great age although, his
sighted eye was, he maintained, deteriorating so that he would soon have
been blind.[2] So it seemed that Nelson's lifelong symptoms of ill-health
were due mostly to fevers, endemic complaints of life aboard ship and in
the tropics and stress, both physical and mental; and his wounds.

In counterpoint to the return home of his broken body was the effect
the distant sight of the *Victory* had upon the only man he is recorded to

---

[1] Abraham Goldsmid remained loyal to Emma and helped her financially. In 1809, his
elder brother Ascher bought Merton Place but sold it again six years later and it was
demolished in 1846. He himself faced a financial crisis in 1810 and committed suicide.

[2] Nelson's early ill-health was probably due to "ague" a low-intensity fever then common
in marshy areas of East Anglia. This was followed by repeated bouts of malaria which
began on his voyage to India in 1775 but there is no evidence that he suffered from
yellow fever on the expedition into Nicaragua, as has been suggested. He was affected
by scurvy when commanding the *Albemarle* in 1781. Fears of heart trouble and
tuberculosis were unfounded and Surgeon-Commander P.D. Gordon Pugh, the
author of *Nelson and his Surgeons* (London, 1968) believes his chest symptons may have
been due to effort syndrome or "soldier's heart". He disputes Beatty's diagnosis of
impending blindness, believing that Nelson suffered from bilateral pterygia and
symptoms induced by worry over the condition of his sighted eye.

have feared, the Prince of Wales, who had taken such a fancy to Emma. On 6th November, he had been "affected most extremely" by the news of Nelson's death, according to his mistress, Mrs. Fitzherbert and now, in a letter to the wife of the diarist Thomas Creevy, written from the Royal Pavilion at Brighton, she reported: "Before Prinny went off he took a seat by me to tell me all this bad news had made him bilious and that he was further overset yesterday by seeing the ship with Nelson's body on board."

After passing Brighton and Dover, the *Victory* arrived at the Nore, where Nelson had begun his life at sea. Here, preparations began for the journey up the Thames to Greenwich, where his body was to lie in state in the great Painted Hall of the Royal Hospital before being taken to London for the funeral at St. Paul's Cathedral. Already the new Earl Nelson was fussing about the protocol and seemliness of the proceedings and asked John Tyson, one of Nelson's former secretaries and a trustee, to make enquiries. "How is the body to be landed at Greenwich," Tyson asked William Haslewood, "in a cask of spirits and rolled into the Painted Chamber? Or decently carried there in his coffin? I am sure you would prefer the latter and so would the Earl." So Dr. Moseley was asked by the new Lord Nelson to go down the river and supervise "this painful ceremony", although Tyson himself thought this unnecessary and rather ridiculous: "I presume he has come into this plan in order that Moseley may have the *éclat* of placing him in a coffin. You know, sir, a physician is not wanted for the *dead* – all mere vanity this!"

In the event, the body was placed into the coffin made from the mainmast of *l'Orient* seven years before and which he had prized with such grim humour; appropriately, this was done on board the *Victory*. The coffin was then encased in another of lead and this, in turn, within one of wood and taken up the Thames to Greenwich, accompanied by Nelson's chaplain, Alexander Scott, and John Tyson. There it lay in state for three days in the Painted Hall before being escorted to a funeral barge by five hundred naval pensioners, many of whom had known Nelson when young. The boat itself was his own barge from the *Victory*, pulled by his own crew, and the accompanying mourners were led by two of his old commanding officers, Admiral of the Fleet Sir Peter Parker, who had recognised his talents in the West Indies a quarter of a century before, and Admiral Lord Hood, who had given him his head in the *Agamemnon* and who was now Governor of the Royal Hospital at Greenwich.

Nelson's body was taken to London in a procession of black-draped boats and barges between banks lined by thousands. It was no stately progress because this boat-service, like those in his life, was dogged by problems; on this occasion by a south-westerly gale. So, as the flotilla approached the Tower of London and the great dome of St. Paul's and the minute-guns began to boom, his arrival by boat was once again attended by the sound of wind and gunfire.

The coffin was landed at Whitehall stairs and taken to the Admiralty where it lay that night in the small, panelled room to the left of the entrance hall still attended by the chaplain. He was buried next day, Thursday, 9th January, 1806, with all the pomp at the nation's command. Now encased both in the wood of *l'Orient* and an outer coffin covered with black velvet and decorated with gilded emblematic and heraldic devices, he was borne through London on a funeral car designed to suggest a ship of the line. Nearly ten thousand soldiers marched in the procession that was so long that its head had reached the cathedral before the rear had left Whitehall. Sailors from the *Victory* walked ahead of their dead admiral carrying the white ensign that the ship had flown off Cape Trafalgar, sometimes opening the folds to show the shot-holes to the silent crowds. The body of Nelson was accompanied along the Strand and Fleet Street by friends who remembered him there, including Alexander Davison and William Haslewood. Thirty-one admirals and a hundred captains attended him, often meeting each other face to face after years of separation by the sea, having conversed only by signal-flags read through telescopes. Through the silent streets the procession wound to the slow beat of the Dead March played on pipes and muffled drums and, as the funeral car approached, a ruffling sound ran ahead of it as the men watching from pavement, windows and rooftops, bared their heads.

The funeral service lasted for four hours. Beneath the dome hung a chandelier of a hundred and thirty lamps; below the floor of the aisle an elevator had been built to lower the coffin into the crypt. All took place according to hopes and plans – the perfect, sunlit winter's day; the well-ordered procession and the immense, reverent crowds – until the last moment. Then the forty-eight seamen from the *Victory* were to fold the battle-ensign and lay it upon the coffin; but, when the time came, they rent a sheet of cloth from the flag and tore it into pieces: one for each man. It was an impulsive, emotional initiative worthy of Nelson himself.

When the coffin was at last lowered into the crypt it was laid in a black marble sarcophagus originally designed for Cardinal Wolsey three centuries before. He lay not only amongst the great; some seventy paces from his tomb, outside the north door of the cathedral and in an unmarked grave, rested the remains of one of the many friends he had remembered, however changed their fortunes: Edward Despard, the executed traitor.

The lives touched most directly by his own continued. Emma Hamilton, grief-stricken and compulsively re-reading the bundles of his letters she had kept, wrote upon the last, which had been brought to her by Captain Hardy, the words: "Oh miserable, wretched Emma. Oh glorious and happy Nelson." She had Horatia to comfort her and together they spent nine years of decline. All hope of a pension faded when, a fortnight after Nelson's funeral, William Pitt died. Other friends helped with money, or pleaded for a pension in recognition of her diplomatic services in Naples, but to no avail. Her income from her husband's legacy was adequate but her extravagance continued; she was confined for debt; finally she took Horatia to exile in Calais. There she sickened, embittered and irritable from heavy drinking, and she died on 15th January, 1815, at the age of fifty. Horatia was brought back to England to stay first with the Matchams and then with the Boltons in Norfolk; it was while staying with the latter in Burnham Market, that she was courted by the curate, the Rev. Philip Ward and they married in 1822. She lived until 1881 having brought up a large Victorian family, knowing herself to be the child of Lord Nelson but not knowing the identity of her mother.

Fanny lived in comfortable but sad retirement, attended by Josiah, who had proved as successful in commerce as he had been inadequate as a naval officer. She moved house frequently, finally settling in a prim, red-brick house overlooking the sea at Exmouth, where she and her husband had once spent a happy holiday. She died, ten months after her son, on 6th May, 1831, aged seventy-three.

Earl Nelson hugely enjoyed the splendour that he had done nothing to earn until 1808. Then, his son and heir Horatio, who had been teased about his name at Eton and had became Viscount Trafalgar, died of typhoid; the earldom was therefore inherited by his nephew, Susannah Bolton's son Tom in 1835. His daughter Charlotte, who had also shared the pleasures of Merton, married her childhood admirer Samuel Hood in 1810, became Baroness Bridport and inherited the dukedom of Bronte from her father.

At sea, Cuthbert Collingwood, raised to the peerage after Trafalgar, succeeded Nelson in command of the Mediterranean Fleet. He remained at sea for five more arduous years of war and died of cancer in 1810, when he joined his friend in the crypt of St. Paul's Cathedral. Nelson's young protégé, William Hoste, also the son of a Norfolk parson and whom Emma Hamilton had said would become a "second Nelson", fought a Trafalgar in miniature. In 1811, his squadron of frigates destroyed a stronger enemy squadron at the Battle of Lissa in the Adriatic. When leading his ships into action, Captain Hoste, conscious of his own inspiration and that he stood on the quarterdeck of the *Amphion*, which had once flown Lord Nelson's flag, inspired his ships' companies with the signal, "Remember Nelson".

Nelson was remembered; he has never been forgotten. He gave his country more than the century of unchallenged maritime supremacy when the British Empire was expanded and consolidated he gave the nation in general and the Royal Navy in particular the implacable self-confidence that remained a decisive factor when, in 1940, invasion was again threatened. He set new standards for a new class of naval officer: before Nelson officers had often been recruited from the social extremes of British society; he had established the breed of middle-class, professional naval officers, from whom exceptional standards of courage and initiative would now be expected. Not all the consequences were what he would have wished: the British also acquired a reputation for self-satisfaction and arrogance, both nationally and personally. The Navy became over-confident; his standards of training were allowed to deteriorate and it had to learn painful lessons in the first global conflict before it could recover its skills for the second.

Two examples from the extremes of the spectrum of those concerned with the defence of their country can illustrate his hold upon imagination. At about the time of Horatio's death a small boy,[1] leaving home to become a cadet in the training-ship *Britannia* at Dartmouth, was asked why he wanted to become a naval officer and replied: "To avenge my friend Nelson." A century later a foreigner, similarly inspired, Caspar Weinberger, Secretary of State for Defense of the United States, gave an address at a Trafalgar Day dinner and said: "Moral leadership, like Nelson's must begin with confidence in ourselves ... Yet self-confidence has not always been popular in recent years ... We still revere Lord Nelson, not in spite of his boldness and insubordination but because of it. In Admiral Lord Nelson – ardent, unruly, supremely self-confident – a nation and a principle found concrete form in a man."

From the year of his death, Nelson's memory was strengthened by the naming of ships, mountains, streets and even towns after him – not just flowers and vegetables as in his lifetime. The building of memorials continued – the most celebrated being his statue, set on its column standing 145 feet above London in Trafalgar Square, completed in 1843 – and reached a zenith with the centenary of his death. Then his father's church at Burnham Thorpe was restored and, two decades later, his flagship, the *Victory*, was also restored and docked at Portsmouth as a magnificent relic. The story of Nelson remained a national legend, retold in innumerable books and plays, then in films and on television;

---

[1] His name was Leslie Hammond and he rose to the rank of captain.

commemorated in paintings and even music. Each 21st October, Trafalgar Night dinners have been held and toasts drunk to "The Immortal Memory".

During the 180th anniversary year of Trafalgar piquant ceremonies and celebrations in Norfolk and Sicily associated Burnham Thorpe and Bronte as "twin villages". On a bright April day, when a sharp wind blew from the North Sea and stretched the white ensign flying from the tower of the church, a coach drew up outside the Lord Nelson inn – formerly The Plough, where Nelson had once entertained his neighbours – and a delegation of Sicilians alighted. Sallow Mediterranean faces, camel-hair coats and dark glasses mingled with apple-cheeks, tweeds and muddy boots in the parlour as toasts to "The Immortal Memory" were drunk in East Anglian ale and Marsala wine. In the forecourt of the inn, speeches were delivered by the chairman of the parish council, the landlord of the Lord Nelson and the mayor of Bronte. In conclusion, heads were bowed as the Rev. Cecil Isaacson, the ninth rector of Burnham Thorpe since Edmund Nelson, improvised a prayer. He gave thanks for the happy occasion, trusting that from such small beginnings greater goodwill might grow, and concluded, "And we thank Thee, O Lord, for the life of Horatio Nelson and for his services to – " He paused, as if unsure for which services it would still be appropriate to express gratitude: there had been two world wars since Trafalgar and the British Empire was gone. Then he said, " – to humanity."

At first this sounded odd in the recollection of his thundering broadsides and the scandal of Emma. But, on reflection, the allusion seemed more apt. It is the humanity of Horatio Nelson that has been remembered.

CHRONOLOGY

1758 29th September, Horatio Nelson born at Burnham Thorpe.
1767 26th December, Catherine Nelson, Horatio's mother, dies.
1770 27th November, Horatio Nelson entered as midshipman for the *Raisonnable*.
1771 March, Nelson joins the *Raisonnable*.
    August, transfers to the *Triumph* and sails for the West Indies in merchant ship.
1772 Returns to England and rejoins the *Triumph*.
1773 June to September, sails with the expedition in search of an Arctic route to the Pacific.
    Appointed midshipman in the frigate *Seahorse* and sails for East Indies.
1775 Invalided from his ship with malaria.
    War of American Independence begins.
1776 August, returns to England.
1777 9th April, passes examination for lieutenant.
    10th April, appointed to the frigate *Lowestoft*.
    19th July, arrives at Port Royal, Jamaica.
1778 France allied with American rebels against Britain.
    July, Captain Maurice Suckling dies.
    September, appointed first lieutenant in the *Bristol*.
    December, appointed commander of the *Badger*.
1779 June, promoted post-captain in command of the frigate *Hinchinbroke*.
    Spain allied with France against Britain.
1780 February to April, takes part in disastrous expedition into Nicaragua.
    April, appointed to command the frigate *Janus* but too ill.
    1st December, arrives at Portsmouth.
1781 August, appointed to command the frigate *Albemarle*.
    Autumn, escorting Baltic convoy.
    18th October, Cornwallis surrenders to Washington at Yorktown.

1782 April, crosses the Atlantic to Quebec.
November, joins Lord Hood's squadron off New York and returns to the West Indies.

1783 March, fails to take Turks Island.
June, returns to England.
War of American Independence ends.
October to January, 1784, at St. Omer in France.

1784 March, appointed to command the frigate *Boreas* and sails for the West Indies.
28th July, arrives at English Harbour, Antigua, and meets Mary Moutray.

1785 20th March, Mary Moutray and her family sail for England.
May, Nelson meets Fanny Nisbet.

1786 November to March, 1787, aide-de-camp to Prince William Henry.

1787 11th March, marries Frances Nisbet at Nevis.
July, sails for England.
17th December, trial of James Carse for murder in London.
Captain Nelson on half-pay.

1788 Unemployed in Norfolk.

1789 French Revolution begins.

1793 6th January, re-employed by the Admiralty.
21st January, execution of King Louis XVI of France.
26th January, appointed to command the *Agamemnon.*
7th February, joins the *Agamemnon.*
June, sails for the Mediterranean.
July and August, off Toulon.
27th August, occupation of Toulon.
September, visits Naples and meets the Hamiltons.
22nd October, action with French frigates.
19th December, Toulon recaptured by the French.

1794 January to August, campaign in Corsica.
12th July, right eye injured at Calvi.

1795 14th March, action with the *Ça Ira.*
December, Admiral Jervis succeeds Lord Hood as Commander-in-chief, Mediterranean.

1796 March, appointed commodore.
May, joins the *Captain.*

1797 13th February, leaves the Mediterranean.
14th February, plays decisive part in the Battle of Cape St. Vincent.
Promoted rear-admiral, created Knight of the Bath.

Hoists flag in the *Theseus*. Returns home.

April-May, mutinies in Royal Navy ships at Spithead and the Nore.

3rd to 5th July, boat actions off Cadiz.

24th July, failure of attack on Santa Cruz, Tenerife. Nelson loses right arm.

11th October, Admiral Duncan defeats Dutch at Camperdown.

1798 March and April, hoists flag in the *Vanguard* and joins Lord St. Vincent's fleet off Cadiz.

July, pursuing French fleet in the Mediterranean.

1st August, destroys the French fleet in Aboukir Bay.

22nd September, arrives at Naples.

Turkey and Russia declare war on France.

6th November, created Baron Nelson of the Nile.

26th November, King Ferdinand and Marshal Mack take Rome.

December, Ferdinand and Mack routed by the French.

23rd to 26th December, Nelson rescues Bourbons and Hamiltons from Naples and takes them to Palermo.

1799 23rd January, the French take Naples.

June, Lord Keith succeeds Lord St. Vincent as Commander-in-Chief, Mediterranean.

8th June, Nelson transfers to the *Foudroyant*.

24th June, returns to Naples and cancels truce with the rebels.

29th June, Admiral Caracciolo executed.

July, disobeys orders to sail for Minorca.

8th August, returns to Palermo.

August to December, commands in the Mediterranean during Lord Keith's absence. Created Duke of Bronte and given Sicilian estate.

23rd August, Bonaparte escapes from Egypt.

9th October, Bonaparte reaches France.

12th December, Bonaparte becomes First Consul.

1800 January, Lord Keith returns to the Mediterranean.

18th February, Nelson captures *Le Généréux*.

24th April, visits Maltese waters with the Hamiltons.

14th June, arrives in Leghorn with the Hamiltons on the way home.

13th July, strikes flag in the Mediterranean.

5th September, Malta finally falls to the British.

July to November, Nelson visits European cities on the journey home.

8th November, meets Lady Nelson in London. Spends Christmas at Fonthill with the Hamiltons.

1801 1st January, promoted vice-admiral.

13th January, hoists flag in the *San Josef*.

5th February, Horatia born to Emma Hamilton.

12th February, transfers to the *St. George*.

6th March, joins Admiral Parker at Yarmouth.

12th March, sails for the Baltic.

2nd April, the Battle of Copenhagen.

9th April, signs armistice with Denmark.

6th May, succeeds Parker as Commander-in-chief.

22nd May, created Viscount Nelson of the Nile and Burnham Thorpe.

19th June relieved by Admiral Pole.

1st July, lands at Yarmouth

27th July, takes command of the Squadron of a Particular Service for home defence.

15th August, failure of attack on Boulogne.

September, buys Merton Place.

1st October, Britain and France sign armistice.

22nd October, given leave and joins the Hamiltons at Merton.

29th October, takes his seat in the House of Lords.

1802 25th March, Treaty of Amiens formally ends war with France.

26th April, the Rev. Edmund Nelson dies.

1803 6th April, Sir William Hamilton dies.

16th May, Britain declares war on France and Nelson appointed Commander-in-Chief, Mediterranean.

18th May, hoists flag in the *Victory*.

6th July, joins the fleet off Toulon.

August, the French prepare to invade England.

1804 Nelson blockades the French Mediterranean ports.

14th December, Spain declares war on Britain.

1805 January–February, chases but fails to intercept Villeneuve's fleet.

4th April, hears that Villeneuve has again left Toulon.

8th April, Villeneuve breaks out into the Atlantic.

April to July, chases Villeneuve to the Caribbean and back across the Atlantic.

22nd July, Admiral Calder engages Villeneuve in indecisive action off Finisterre.

18th August, Nelson arrives at Portsmouth and returns to Merton.

20th August, the combined French and Spanish fleets reach Cadiz.

14th Sepbember, rejoins the *Victory*.

28th September, joins the British fleet off Cadiz: "The Nelson Touch."

21st October, Nelson destroys the combined French and Spanish fleets but is himself killed.

1806 9th January, Nelson's funeral at St. Paul's Cathedral, London.

BIBLIOGRAPHY

Bennett, Geoffrey, *Nelson the Commander* (1972)

Clarke, James, and John M'Arthur, *The Life and Services of Horatio Viscount Nelson* (1809)

Beatty, Sir William, *The Authentic Narrative of the Death of Lord Nelson* (1807)

Corbett, Sir Julian, *The Campaign of Trafalgar* (1910)

Drinkwater, Col. John, *A Narrative of the Battle of Cape St. Vincent* (1840)

Fothergill, Brian, *Sir William Hamilton* (1969)

Fraser, Flora, *Beloved Emma* (1986)

Fremantle, A. (ed.), *The Wynne Diaries* (1935–40)

Harrison, James, *The Life of the Rt. Hon. Horatio Viscount Nelson* (1806)

Gamlin, Hilda, *Nelson's Friendships* (1899)

Gérin, Winifred, *Horatia Nelson* (1970)

Giglioli, Constance, *Naples in 1799* (1903)

Gutteridge, H. C. (ed.), *Nelson and the Neapolitan Jacobins* (1903)

James, William, *The Naval History of Great Britain* (1826)

James, Admiral Sir William, *The Durable Monument: Horatio Nelson* (1948)

Keate, E. M., *Nelson's Wife* (1939)

Kennedy, Ludovic, *Nelson's Band of Brothers* (1951)

Knight, Cornelia, *The Autobiography of Miss Cornelia Knight* (1861)

Mahan, Admiral A. T., *The Life of Nelson* (1897)

Matcham, E. Eyre, *The Nelsons of Burnham Thorpe* (1911)

Minto, Countess of, (ed.), *The Life and Letters of Sir Gilbert Elliot, First Earl of Minto* (1874)

Moorhouse, E. Hallam, *Nelson in England* (1913)

Morrison, Alfred, (ed.), *The Hamilton and Nelson Papers* (1893–4)

Naish, George, P. B., (ed.), *Nelson's Letters to His Wife and Other Documents* (1958)

Nicolas, Sir Harris, *The Dispatches and Letters of Vice-Admiral Lord Viscount Nelson* (1844–46)

Oman, Carola, *Nelson* (1947)

Parsons, G. S., *Nelsonia Reminiscences* (1843)

Pettigrew, Thomas, *Memoirs of the Life of Vice-Admiral Lord Viscount Nelson* (1849)

Pocock, Tom, *Nelson and His World* (1968)

 Remember Nelson: The Life of Captain Sir William Hoste (1977)

The Young Nelson in the Americas (1980)
Pope, Dudley, *The Great Gamble* (1972)
Pugh, P. D. Gordon, *Nelson and His Surgeons* (1968)
Rathbone, Philip, *Paradise Merton* (1973)
Rawson, Geoffrey (ed.), *Nelson's Letters from the Leeward Islands* (1953)
Russell, Jack, *Nelson and the Hamiltons* (1969)
Sichel, Walter, *Emma, Lady Hamilton* (1905)
Southey, Robert, *The Life of Horatio Lord Nelson* (1813)
Tours, Hugh, *The Life and Letters of Emma Hamilton* (1963)
Warner, Oliver, *The Battle of the Nile* (1960)
A Portrait of Lord Nelson (1965)
The Life and Letters of Vice-Admiral Lord Collingwood (1969)

NOTES ON SOURCES

Printed sources

The foundation of the study of Nelson must be Sir Harris Nicolas's seven-volume work, *The Dispatches and Letters of Vice-Admiral Lord Viscount Nelson*, supported by the earlier *Letters of Lord Nelson to Lady Hamilton*, published anonymously in 1814, the later *Hamilton and Nelson Papers*, edited by Alfred Morrison, and George Naish's *Nelson's Letters to His Wife*. To these must be added a number of essential biographies, including those by Clarke and M'Arthur, who knew Nelson; James Harrison, who was instructed by Emma Hamilton; Robert Southey and James Pettigrew of the last century and Carola Oman and Oliver Warner of this one. Nuggets of Nelsoniana can, of course, be found in other biographies, although some must be treated with caution.

The background to his life can be seen reflected in the earlier volumes of his favourite periodical *The Naval Chronicle*, other magazines of the period and the files of contemporary newspapers in the British Library at Colindale and in the local history sections of the libraries at Norwich, Portsmouth and Bath. There is much to read about Nelson in *The Mariner's Mirror*, the journal of the Society for Nautical Research; the volumes published annually by the Navy Records Society; and the *Nelson Dispatch*, the journal of the Nelson Society.

Manuscript sources

The bulk of the surviving Nelson papers are to be found in London in the care of the National Maritime Museum at Greenwich, the Manuscripts Department of the British Library and the Public Record Office at Kew. Twelve collections have been brought together at the National Maritime Museum, including most of those from his own family; guides to them can be found in the *Personal Collections* volume of the *Guide to Manuscripts in the National Maritime Museum* (1977) and in an article by K. F. Lindsay-MacDougall in *The Mariner's Mirror*, Vol. 41, No. 3 (1955).

The British Library collection includes the Spencer and Egerton papers and much that is relevant to Sir William Hamilton. At the Public Record Office, the Admiralty and Colonial Office files yield much concerning Nelson's naval career and service in the Caribbean, while Sir William Hamilton's reports from Naples can be found in the Foreign Office files. Also there are the captains' logs and ships' muster-books to add detail to the scene at any given moment in that period.

The manuscripts in the Nelson Collection at the Monmouth Museum, Gwent, formed the basis of George Naish's *Nelson's Letters to His Wife*, but many documents remained unpublished. Other Nelson letters and relevant papers are in the possession of Lloyd's in London and at the Royal Naval Museum, Portsmouth, to which Mrs. Lily McCarthy presented much of her notable collection of Nelsoniana.

The papers of Nelson's friends and contemporaries at the National Maritime Museum include those of Admirals of the Fleet Lord St. Vincent (also at the British Library), Sir William Parker and Sir William Cornwallis; Admirals Lord Hood, Sir Thomas Fremantle (also at Buckinghamshire County Library, Aylesbury), Sir Thomas Foley and Sir Richard Keats; Rear-Admiral Sir Edward Berry; Lord Minto (also at the National Library of Scotland); and the Rev. Alexander Scott. The complete collection of letters and papers of Captain Sir William Hoste were sold at auction in 1975, bought by a dealer and dispersed but not before it had been recorded on microfilm at the National Maritime Museum.

In addition, many private collections, large and small, have been consulted. They have included those of Sir Nicholas Bonsor, Bt., M.P., Mr. Bryan Hall, Mr. Richard Hough, Mrs. June Jeffreys, Admiral Sir Horace Law, Mr. M. A. K. Murray, Mr. Michael Nash, Mr. Hercules Ross and others who wish to remain anonymous. In several cases it has not been possible to trace the present ownership of papers consulted over the past twenty years.

Notes on chapters

CHAPTER I

The principal source of information on Nelson's early life is Clarke and M'Arthur's biography. The Rev. Edmund Nelson's notes on his family at the National Maritime Museum and other family history can be found in *The Nelsons of Burnham Thorpe* by M. Eyre Matcham (1911). Sources for the background to life in Norfolk include files of the *Norfolk Chronicle*. Accounts of Nelson's voyage to the Arctic are given in his own autobiographical notes, *A Voyage Towards the North Pole* by Constantine Phipps (1774), the anonymous *Journal of the Voyage* (1772) and in the research on the expedition by Ann Savours published as the paper *The 1773 Phipps Expedition towards the North Pole* published in *Arctic* (1984).

CHAPTER II

Accounts of the campaign in Nicaragua are given in *A Brief History of the Late Expedition against Fort San Juan* by Dr. Thomas Dancer (1781) and in the *Treatise on Tropical Diseases* by Dr. Benjamin Moseley (1795 and 1804). Manuscript accounts are among the Colonial Office Papers at the Public Record Office (CO 137/74–79, 80–1, CO 5/236–7, 263 and CO 152/64; amongst Admiralty papers: ADM 1/242; and War Office papers: WO 1/683). More manuscript material is at the British Library: Add. MSS. 34903, 34913 and 34961. A full account of the campaign is given in *The Young Nelson in the Americas* by the present author (1980).

CHAPTER III

A small collection of papers relating to Captain and Mrs. Moutray is in the Nelson Collection at the Monmouth Museum and details of the career of Captain Moutray can be found in *Biographia Navalis* by John Charnock (1794–8). References to Mary Moutray in Nelson letters can be found in the Bridport Papers and the National Maritime Museum (BRP/6) and in others at Monmouth. At this period *Nelson's Letters to His Wife*, ed. George Naish (1958) becomes relevant.

CHAPTER IV

The affair of Lieutenant Schomberg is described in *The Naval Miscellany*, edited by Christopher Lloyd for the Navy Records Society (1952).

A full account of the trial for murder of James Carse can be found in *The Old Bailey Sessions Papers, 1788* and in the article *Horatio Nelson and the Murderous Cooper* by H. L. Cryer in *The Mariner's Mirror*, Vol. 60, No. 1. Many of Nelson's letters relating to this period are at Monmouth and in private collections. Printed sources include *The Nelsons of Burnham Thorpe* (see notes for Chapter I), *Coke of Norfolk and His Friends* by A. M. W. Stirling (1908) and *Nelson in England* by E. Hallam Moorhouse (1913).

CHAPTER V

Many of Nelson's letters from the Mediterranean at this period are at Monmouth, as is his journal of the campaign in Corsica. The letters from William Hoste to his family from the *Agamemnon* are in the Hoste Papers on microfilm (plus some original documents) at the National Maritime Museum. More Nelson correspondence from this time is at the Public Record Office (FO 79/1) and his letter to Adelaide Correglia is at the Huntington Library, California. Printed accounts of these years include *The Life and Letters of Sir Gilbert Elliot, First Earl of Minto*, ed. the Countess of Minto (1874) and *Sir William Hamilton* by Brian Fothergill (1969), both of which continue to be relevant.

CHAPTER VI

Manuscript accounts of the attack on Tenerife are in the Hoste Papers and in the Webley Journal now at the Mariners' Museum, Newport News, Virginia, U.S.A. An original Spanish account in the collection of Mr. Michael Nash was published by the Nelson Society as *Santa Cruz, 1797* (1984), and the journal of Don Bernardo Cadogan was published in the *Daily Telegraph* on 18th August, 1896. A good account of the attack is in the article *Nelson at Santa Cruz*, by J. D. Spinney published in *The Mariner's Mirror*, Vol. 45, No. 3. Another account is in *The Wynne Diaries*, ed. Anne Fremantle (1935–40).

CHAPTER VII

An eye-witness account of the Battle of the Nile is in the Webley Journal (see notes for Chapter VI) and more familiar descriptions were written by Captain Edward Berry in his *Authentic Narrative . . . of the Glorious Battle of the Nile* (1798) and by Captain Ralph Miller, published in *The Dispatches and Letters*, Vol. 7, ed. Sir Harris Nicolas (1844–46); a sailor's account is in *The Life and Adventures of*

John Nicol, Mariner (1822). Captain Hoste's description of taking the news to Naples is in the Hoste Papers and Emma Hamilton's account is in the British Library (Add. MSS. 34,389) and Mr Morrice Murray's collection. Sir William Hamilton's letters and reports to London are at the Public Record Office (FO 70/11–12); other manuscripts relevant are at Monmouth. Amongst printed accounts of the scene at Naples are those in Brian Fothergill's *Sir William Hamilton* (1969), Walter Sichel's *Emma, Lady Hamilton* (1905), Flora Fraser's *Beloved Emma* (1986) and Cornelia Knight's *Autobiography*. A Description of the Palazzo Sessa by Dr. Carlo Knight was published in *Napoli Nobilissima* (Vol. 24, No. 1–2, 1985) and of his other Neapolitan houses in Vol. 20,. No. 5–6. Lady Spencer's account of the arrival in London of the news from Aboukir Bay is in a letter belonging to Commander Richard Phillimore.

CHAPTER VIII
The fall of the Parthenopean Republic are described in *Nelson and the Neapolitan Jacobins*, ed. H.C. Gutteridge (1903), *Naples in 1799* by Constance Giglioli (1903) and, more light-heartedly, in *Nelsonian Reminiscences* by G.S. Parsons (1843). Many relevant letters were published in Sir Harris Nicolas's, Alfred Morrison's and George Naish's volumes of letters and in *The Keith Papers* (1927, 1950, 1955). The return across the Continent is described in *Lord Nelson's Journey Through Germany* by K.P. Keigwin in *The Mariner's Mirror*, Vol. 21, no. 2.

CHAPTER IX
An account of Nelson's homecoming, inspired by Emma Hamilton, is in James Harrison's biography of 1806 and the printed collections of letters are all essential sources. The visit to Fonthill is described in biographies of William Beckford, including *The Life of William Beckford* by M.W. Oliver (1932) and *The Caliph of Fonthill* by H.A.N. Brockman (1956); E. Hallam Moorhouse's *Nelson in England* (1913) is useful on this period. Manuscripts relating to Nelson's personal life are in the Newhouse Papers. The essential work on the Baltic campaign is Dudley Pope's *The Great Gamble* (1972) and the most celebrated eye-witness account of the Battle of Copenhagen was written by Lt. Col. William Stewart and published in Clarke and M'Arthur's biography.

Many of Nelson's letters of this period are in private collections and the prayer he composed on 10th February, 1801 is in Mr. Richard Hough's.

CHAPTER X
Letters relating to Nelson's personal life on his return from the Baltic are in the Newhouse Papers and Bonsor Papers; many others are in private collections. Others in the National Maritime Museum (notably in the Bridport Papers), the British Library and at Monmoth. French manuscript accounts of the attack on Boulogne are in the *Archives Nationales*, Paris (*Marine* BB4 153, Folios 1–68). The period is well represented in the principal British collections. Nelson's brief political career can be studied in the *Proceedings of the House of Lords* for the relevant dates, letters by Emma Hamilton in the Newhouse Papers, other private collections and the account of his last meeting with William Pitt is among the

Nelson Papers at Monmouth (Vol. 6, p. 29). Life at Merton is described by Charlotte Nelson in letters amongst the Bonsor Papers.

CHAPTER XI

Both the Bonsor and Newhouse collections cover the period of Merton and the tour to the West Country. Regional newspapers described Nelson's provincial visits and *Lord Nelson's Visits to Monmouth* by Horatia Durrant has been published in the *Memorials of Monmouth* series by the Monmouth Antiquarian Society. The young Charles Macready's account of Nelson and the Hamiltons in Birmingham is from *Macready's Reminiscences and Selections from his Diaries*, ed. Sir Frederick Pollock (1875). The verbatim report of the trial of Col. Despard is from the shorthand notes taken by the Gurney family, who published it in 1803 as *The Trial of Edward Marcus Despard Esq., for High Treason.*

Much of Edmund Nelson's final correspondence with Fanny Nelson is at Monmouth and letters about his death and funeral are at Newhouse. Nelson's letter about the antiquities captured at sea is in *The Life of Sir Joseph Banks* by Edward Smith (1911) and his letters written from the Mediterranean and during the chase across the Atlantic are mostly in the British Library, the National Maritime Museum and at Monmouth. Nelson's health is discussed in *Nelson and His Surgeons* by Surgeon Commander P. D. Gordon Pugh, R.N. (1968) and T. C. Barras's *Vice Admiral Lord Nelson's Lost Eye* in *Transactions of the Ophthalmological Societies of the United Kingdom* (1986).

CHAPTER XII

Nelson's final days in England are described in the memoirs of Lord Minto and by the American visitor Benjamin Silliman in *A Journal of Travels in England, Holland, Scotland and of Two Passages over the Atlantic* (New York, 1810). Nelson's letters written on board the *Victory* are in the principal collections and in private ownership. The Battle of Trafalgar has been the subject of many books, including Sir Jillian Corbett's *The Campaign of Trafalgar* and Oliver Warner's *Trafalgar*; Nelson's *Trafalgar Memorandum* was published by the Navy Records Society, Vol. 29. Detailed accounts of the action were published in *The Naval Chronicle*, Vols. 14, 15, 16 (1806–7). The doctor who attended the dying Nelson, Dr. William Beatty wrote *The Authentic Narrative of the Death of Lord Nelson* (1807).

NELSONIAN SITES

Places that Nelson knew, and that he would still recognise, abound and any pilgrimage in his footsteps – and his wake – must begin at Burnham Thorpe in Norfolk. It remains a quiet, rural village: the "dear Burnham" of "homesteads by the stream" he remembered when at sea.

The Parsonage he knew was demolished on his father's death in 1802 and its bow-fronted successor built to survive in the garden and grounds where he had worked "as it were for the purpose of being wearied" when unemployed. He wrote in his autobiographical sketch that he had been born there but local tradition suggests two alternative birthplaces: the Shooting Box and Ivy House Farm, both of which survive. His father's church of All Saints was heavily restored for the centenary of the Battle of Trafalgar in 1905; in his day it was dilapidated, a flat-roof having replaced its original beams and then lacking a south aisle. Now, without its box-pews, it looks bare but for the Nelson monuments – his parents are buried before the altar and his brother Maurice and sister Susannah and her family just outside in the churchyard. Perhaps the building most recognisable to him, inside and out, would be the inn, where he entertained his neighbours before taking command of the *Agamemnon* in 1793, which he knew as The Plough; it is now, of course, the Lord Nelson; its parlour still keeps its wooden settles and has no bar.

Nearby, the old houses around the green at Burnham Market can have changed very little and, of course, the tide still sweeps up the creek at Burnham Overy Staithe, where he first saw ships and the sea. The school buildings he knew – the 14th century Norwich School and what was then the new red-brick building at the Paston School, North Walsham – still stand. Three of the grander houses he visited are as he would remember them: Holkham Hall, where Thomas Coke's study, where he arranged the formalities of his half-pay when unemployed, is now the Coke family's dining-room; Wolterton Hall, where he and Fanny stayed with Lord and Lady Walpole; and Barton Hall, where his sister Kitty and her husband George Matcham lived in some style. In contrast, the village shop at North Elmham, which his brother Suckling managed so unsuccessfully, survives as "Nelson House."

Other Nelsonian sites in East Anglia include The Wrestlers inn at Great Yarmouth, where he and the Hamiltons stayed on their return from the Mediterranean in 1800 and most of which still stands. Roundwood, the house Fanny had prepared for him near Ipswich, was demolished in 1960.

In London, few of the buildings he knew now survive. The Admiralty itself, Admiralty House, where he and Fanny dined with the Spencers, and the former Navy Office in Somerset House remain, of course, but most of his lodgings have long gone. The survivors are 141 New Bond Street, where he recovered from the loss of his arm, and 5 Cavendish Square, the house rented by Fanny's uncle, John Herbert in 1787. In Bath, however, most of the houses where he lodged still stand: they include 2 Pierrepont Street, where he recuperated from the campaign in Nicaragua, and 17 New King Street, where he was re-united with Fanny on his return from Tenerife. The Pump Room, the Assembly Rooms and the various medicinal baths are much as he would have known them.

At Deal in Kent, which he made his headquarters when commanding the Squadron on a Particular Service in 1801, the original Three Kings inn, where the Hamiltons stayed, still stands on the edge of the beach; most of Middle Street survives, although there is more than one theory as to which is the house where Captain Parker died; the young man's tomb remains in the churchyard of St. George's, although it has been moved some yards from the grave. Nelson's travels with the Hamiltons have given traditions, and sometimes myths, to many houses and inns on their routes to Fonthill and later to Milford Haven. At Monmouth, for example, the Beaufort Arms building survives, as do several houses he visited there together with the Naval Temple and the Pavilion on the Kymin where the party breakfasted.

At Portsmouth, many Georgian buildings in the naval dockyard are those he would have known and, of course, the greatest Nelsonian site of them all is his flagship, the *Victory*, preserved there in dry-dock since 1925.

Of Merton Place, Nelson's home in Surrey, nothing remained after demolition following its final sale in 1846 and the building of streets and then council flats on the site. However, in the church of St. Mary the Virgin, the heraldic hatchments of Nelson and Sir William Hamilton, both presented by Emma Hamilton, survive and have recently been restored through the generosity of Mrs. Lily McCarthy. At Bronte, the Castello di Maniace, to which Nelson hoped to retire with Emma, is still furnished with the belongings of the descendants of Nelson's niece Charlotte. When the present Lord Bridport sold the house and estate to the municipality of Bronte a few years ago he was told that, under Italian law, his heirlooms, furniture and pictures were now part of the national heritage and could not be removed from Sicily.

Most Nelsonian sites abroad are in the Caribbean or the Mediterranean, but at the Indian port of Madras, Fort St. George looks much as it did when he was a midshipman, except that a high-rise office block now stands on the Grand Parade. In Jamaica, old buildings survive in the former capital, Spanish Town, including the shell of the King's House, where he met General Dalling, which was gutted by fire. Near Kingston, Fort Charles, which he commanded when French invasion threatened in 1779, is now part of a police establishment; Fort Augusta, across the harbour is a prison, and most of the other fortifications survive. Admiral's Mountain, the house on Cooper's Hill outside Kingston, where Nelson recuperated under the care of Lady Parker on his return from Nicaragua, has recently been restored.

At Antigua, the naval dockyard at English Harbour has been restored as the island's major tourist attraction since the first appeal to raise funds for its preservation was launched in 1953; it is now called Nelson's Dockyard. Most of the wooden buildings, including the Admiral's House, were built shortly after Nelson was based there and nothing remains of the Moutrays' house "Windsor" on the hill behind the dockyard. However, the basic structure of the dockyard and its berths are as he knew them; Clarence House was completed for Prince William Henry in 1787 just after Nelson left but he may have seen the work in its early stages and discussed the plans with his royal friend.

The island of Nevis is as beautiful today as it was when Nelson met Fanny Nisbet there in 1785. However, since the collapse of the sugar industry and its replacement by subsistence farming and tourism it is no longer an island of well-kept sugar plantations, busy sugar mills and handsome plantation houses. Some of the surviving houses have been converted into small hotels as have the factory buildings at Montpelier; the house itself, where Nelson and Fanny met, has long gone but has recently been rebuilt. Fig Tree Church survives as do many stone-built houses in the capital, Charlestown, although the original Court House, where the American captains' litigation against Nelson was initiated, was gutted by fire in 1873 and rebuilt.

The most obscure Nelsonian site of all must be the Castello de la Inmaculada Concepción on the Rio San Juan in Nicaragua. This, being on the border of Costa Rica, may have suffered during the civil war and subsequent insurgency but stood, when the author visited it in 1978, a sinister fortress, blackened by damp; its outer walls sloping slightly like the Aztec pyramids of Mexico. On the summit of a little green hill commanding the gates of the castle were traces of earthworks which might have been Nelson's battery. Then, as, presumably, now, it could only be reached by canoe.

The shores of the Mediterranean became intimately familiar to Nelson. The fortifications and natural defences of Toulon can still be found, as can those at Bastia and Calvi on Corsica. At the latter, the exact route by which he had his guns hauled to the siege batteries from the little bay of Porto Agro can be traced. Sadly the massive boulder, which bears the plaque announcing it to be the site of his wounding in the eye, has recently had a bungalow built upon it. In Genoa, the Palazzo Reale where he visited the Doge stands in the Via Balbi and all along the coast of Italy remain fortifications and harbours he knew. In Naples itself, the Palazzo Sessa, where the Hamiltons lived, survives in multi-occupation at the end of a narrow street above the Piazza dei Martiri, and their beach-house, the Villa Emma, still stands above the beach at Posillipo, although much altered and its rear cut away by the building of the coast road. In the city, most of the buildings that played a part in the tragedy of 1799 still stand, including the Palazzo Reale, the Castel Nuovo, the Castel dell'Ovo and the Castel Sant'Elmo and many palaces and churches. The most important Nelsonian site in the Mediterranean is the wide, sandy-shored Aboukir Bay, where the sea still curls over the shoal east of Nelson's Island on which the *Culloden* ran aground.

The scene of his second great victory at Copenhagen has changed beyond recognition with the extension of the harbour and dockyard into the shallow waters where the battle was fought. However, the earthworks of the Trekroner Battery are now a public park and the royal palace of Amalienborg, where Nelson negotiated the truce, remains. Of his last and greatest victory off Cape Trafalgar there is, of course, nothing to be seen from the rocky shore except the restless sea. The final Nelsonian site is in the crypt of St. Paul's Cathedral.

INDEX